SCHOLASTIC

ACTIVE™ Grammar for Classes 9 and 10

Anne Seaton   Rosalind Fergusson

Name ______________________________

Class ______________________________

First published as English Grammar for Students and English Grammar for Students with Exercises by Learners Publishing Private Limited

This edition 2012
Reprinted 2012, 2014 (fifth time), 2015, 2016 (twice), 2017, 2018, 2019 (thrice), 2020, 2021, 2025

ISBN 978-81-8477-745-1

Preface

Active Grammar for Classes 9 and 10 covers all the essentials of grammar. There are ten chapters, the first eight of which deal with individual word classes, phrases and clauses. Chapter 9 shows how these can be put together to form sentences and Chapter 10 shows how cohesive devices can be used to make sentences into paragraphs and texts. This arrangement leads the students step by step from grammar at word level, through grammar at sentence level, to grammar at text level.

Each chapter is divided into units dealing with different aspects of the main topic. For example, in Chapter 1 'Nouns', there are separate units for countable nouns, uncountable nouns, proper nouns, collective nouns, and so on. Each unit opens with a short passage showing how the item is used in context, in a section called 'What do they look like?' The following sections answer such questions as 'What are they?', 'How are they formed?' and 'How do you use them?' They contain simple, concise explanations, numbered for ease of use, with contextual examples that clearly illustrate the point being made. Complex issues (such as the changes involved in turning direct speech into indirect speech) are broken down into separate steps to make the information easier to assimilate.

Each unit ends with a 'Practice' section containing a variety of exercises to test what has been learnt. These are graded for difficulty, usually ending with a cloze passage or a similar contextual exercise. In Chapters 1 to 9, there is also a 'grammar for writing' exercise in which students are asked to produce a short passage of their own. The last nine units of Chapter 10 deal with the main text types: notes, procedures, explanations, information reports, factual recounts, personal recounts, expositions, narratives and poetry. Each of these units highlights the main grammatical features of the text type and contains a writing exercise.

 ISBN 978-81-8477-745-1

Contents

 ISBN 978-81-8477-745-1

CHAPTER 4 Verbs

CHAPTER 5 Tenses and aspects

CHAPTER 6 Adverbs

 ISBN 978-81-8477-745-1

CHAPTER 7 Prepositions

CHAPTER 8 Connectors and clauses

CHAPTER 9 Sentences

CHAPTER 10 Paragraphs and texts

 ISBN 978-81-8477-745-1

1 NOUNS

 ISBN 978-81-8477-745-1

UNIT 1

NOUNS

What do they look like?

Liverpool is a large **city** in **England**, on the west **coast** of the **country**. It became an important commercial **port** in the nineteenth **century**. It has **theatres**, **museums**, **art galleries** and many **shops**. **People** who have lived there all their **lives** speak with a characteristic **accent**.

What are they?

1 Nouns are naming words. They are words for people, animals or things:

brother | child | nurse | singer | dog | arm

paper | beauty | idea | parrot

2 There are two main types of nouns: **common nouns** and **proper nouns**.

- A **common noun** is a **word** for a person, animal, place or thing, for example:

  teenager | hyena | station | candle | enjoyment

- A **proper noun** is the **name** of a **particular** person, animal, place or thing. It always begins with a capital letter, for example:

  John | Lassie | Taipei | the Yangtze | September | Christmas

3 Common nouns can be divided into **countable nouns** and **uncountable nouns**.

- **Countable nouns** can be **singular** or **plural**. That is, they can refer to one item or more than one item:

  a girl | an elephant | my idea | girls | elephants | windows | ideas

 ISBN 978-81-8477-745-1

- **Uncountable nouns** are words for **masses** or **qualities**. They cannot be made plural:

milk | snow | anger | history

4. Countable nouns and uncountable nouns can be divided into **concrete nouns** and **abstract nouns**.

- **Concrete nouns** are things you can see and touch:

door | horse | cars | bread | water

- **Abstract nouns** are things you cannot see or touch:

rule | name | lessons | safety | health

How do you use them?

1. A **noun** can be the **subject** of a **verb**. The subject is the person or thing that performs the action of the verb:
   - *The **students** were reading quietly.*
   - ***Murder** is a very serious crime.*

2. A **noun** can be the **object** of a **verb**. The object is the person or thing that receives the action of the verb:
   - *I opened the **door**.*
   - *Read the **poem** aloud.*

3. A **noun** can be the **object** of a **preposition**. The object usually follows the preposition:
   - *I walked into the **room**.*
   - *We often run along the **footpath** for **exercise**.*
   - *Which **lecture** are you going to?*

4. A **noun** can be the **complement** of a **linking verb**. Linking verbs, such as *be* or *feel*, have a complement instead of an object:
   - *Are you a **doctor**?*
   - *I feel a **fool**.*

5. A **noun** can be used like **an adjective** before another noun. The **first noun** describes or defines the **second noun**:
   - ***Rain** clouds were approaching.*
   - *We are planning to review the **school** curriculum.*

 ISBN 978-81-8477-745-1

PRACTICE

Exercise 1

Underline all the nouns in the following passage, including those that occur more than once.

Most of the students have computers in their homes. They use them for both work and play. The Internet is particularly useful for research on a wide range of subjects. It gives students all the information they need to write their essays. They can also use the Internet to communicate with their friends by email. Many of them enjoy social networking on websites such as Facebook. They can load photographs from their mobile phones and digital cameras on to the site for everyone to see.

Exercise 2

At the end of each sentence, write CC if the noun in bold print is ***concrete and countable****, CU if it is a* ***concrete uncountable*** *noun, AC if it is an* ***abstract countable noun*** *and AU if it is an* ***abstract uncountable noun.***

1. Jack was drinking a **glass** of lemonade. __________
2. I do not have enough **time** to finish this work. __________
3. There was only one spelling **error** in the essay. __________
4. Please do not walk on the **grass**. __________
5. The elephant uses its **trunk** to lift things. __________
6. Someone has spilt **paint** on the floor. __________
7. Kate wrote her **address** on a piece of paper. __________
8. **Safety** is more important than speed. __________

Exercise 3

In each sentence, put a ring around the noun that is the object of a preposition. The first one has been done to help you.

1. Susan told us all about her (holidays).
2. Who painted that portrait of your mother?
3. I listened to the radio while I washed the dishes.
4. Which station will you be arriving at?
5. The flight to Beijing has been delayed.
6. Tom wiped his feet on the mat before he entered the house.

 ISBN 978-81-8477-745-1

UNIT 2

COUNTABLE NOUNS AND THEIR PLURALS

What do they look like?

There are several different **classes** of **animals**. **Foxes** and **mice** belong to the **class** called **mammals**. **Geese** and **sparrows** are **birds**. They have **feathers**, a **beak** and **wings**. **Salmon** and **sharks** are **fish**. They swim in **rivers** and **oceans**. **Mosquitoes** and **flies** are **insects**, and **snakes** and **lizards** are **reptiles**.

How do you use them?

1. You use a **singular countable noun** to talk about an item that can be counted:

   book | child | cherry | eye | mistake | idea | hour

2. A singular countable noun cannot stand alone. You often use ***a*** or ***an***, known as the **indefinite article**, before countable nouns:

   a book | **a** child | **a** cherry | **a** mistake

   an hour | **an** eye | **an** idea

3. You can also use ***the***, known as the **definite article**, with a countable noun. You use ***the*** instead of ***a*** or ***an*** when there is only one such item in existence, or only one that you could possibly mean:
   - *Look at **the** moon!*
   - *May I switch on **the** television?*

 ISBN 978-81-8477-745-1

4 Other determiners, such as ***my*** or ***this***, can be used instead of ***a***, ***an*** or ***the***:
- *Jane lent me **her** pen.*
- *Whose is **this** jacket?*

5 You use a **plural countable noun** to talk about more than one item:

book	children	cherries	eyes	mistakes	ideas	hours

6 Plural nouns can be used on their own in general statements:
- *I don't like **apples**.*
- ***Dolphins** are **mammals**.*

7 A plural noun can also be used with ***the*** or another determiner:
- *I don't like **the** apples that grow on **those** trees.*
- ***Most** mammals have **four** legs.*

8 You cannot use ***a*** or ***an*** with plural nouns. You use ***some*** instead:
- *Mum bought a cabbage and **some** carrots.*
- *There are **some** errors in this book.*

9 You use a **singular verb** when the subject is a **singular noun**:
- *This **soup** **tastes** delicious!*
- *Our **house** **was built** in 1980.*

10 You use a **plural verb** when the subject is a **plural noun**:
- *My **parents** **work** at the local hospital.*
- *Your clean **clothes** **are** in the drawer.*

How do you make singular nouns plural?

1 Many nouns are made plural simply by adding ***s***:

book	→	books	cliff	→	cliffs
idea	→	ideas	kangaroo	→	kangaroos
tray	→	trays	valley	→	valleys

2 Most nouns ending in ***ch***, ***sh***, ***s*** or ***x*** add ***es*** to form the plural:

arch	→	arches	fox	→	foxes
brush	→	brushes	class	→	classes

 ISBN 978-81-8477-745-1

3 Many nouns ending in single ***o*** just add ***s*** to form the plural:

cello	→	cello*s*	kilo	→	kilo*s*
kimono	→	kimono*s*	rhino	→	rhino*s*
studio	→	studio*s*	video	→	video*s*

But some well-known nouns ending in single ***o*** add ***es***:

cargo	→	cargo*es*	dingo	→	dingo*es*
echo	→	echo*es*	hero	→	hero*es*
potato	→	potato*es*	tomato	→	tomato*es*
tornado	→	tornado*es*	veto	→	veto*es*

And with some nouns both plural forms are acceptable:

halo	→	halo*s* or halo*es*	mango	→	mango*s* or mango*es*
mosquito	→	mosquito*s* or mosquito*es*	zero	→	zero*s* or zero*es*

4 Nouns that end in a consonant followed by ***y*** form their plural by changing the ***y*** to ***i*** and adding ***es***:

baby	→	bab*ies*	diary	→	diar*ies*
fly	→	fl*ies*	spy	→	sp*ies*

5 Some nouns that end in single ***f*** form their plural by changing the ***f*** to ***v*** and adding ***es***:

calf	→	cal*ves*	elf	→	el*ves*
half	→	hal*ves*	leaf	→	lea*ves*
loaf	→	loa*ves*	self	→	sel*ves*
sheaf	→	shea*ves*	shelf	→	shel*ves*
thief	→	thie*ves*	wolf	→	wol*ves*

But some nouns ending in single ***f*** just add ***s***:

belief	→	belief*s*	gulf	→	gulf*s*
chef	→	chef*s*	reef	→	reef*s*
chief	→	chief*s*	roof	→	roof*s*

6 These nouns ending in ***fe*** have the plural ***ves***:

knife	→	kni*ves*	life	→	li*ves*
wife	→	wi*ves*			

But other nouns ending in ***fe*** just add ***s***:

giraffe	→	giraffe*s*	safe	→	safe*s*

7 The plural of some nouns is the same as the singular. Many are names for animals and fish:

aircraft	→	*aircraft*	bison	→	*bison*
carp	→	*carp*	deer	→	*deer*

 ISBN 978-81-8477-745-1

salmon	→	*salmon*	sheep	→	*sheep*
species	→	*species*	trout	→	*trout*

8 Certain well-known nouns have an irregular plural form which does not end in ***s***:

child	→	*children*	foot	→	*feet*
goose	→	*geese*	louse	→	*lice*
man	→	*men*	mouse	→	*mice*
tooth	→	*teeth*	woman	→	*women*

9 Many words used in English come from other languages. Some of them keep the foreign form of plural. Here are a few examples:

antenna	→	*antennae*	bacterium	→	*bacteria*
cactus	→	*cacti*	criterion	→	*criteria*
fungus	→	*fungi*	oasis	→	*oases*

10 For **compound nouns** (nouns made up of two or more words), you usually make the final part plural:

classroom	→	*classrooms*	toothbrush	→	*toothbrushes*
grandchild	→	*grandchildren*	fire engine	→	*fire engines*
word processor	→	*word processors*	forget-me-not	→	*forget-me-nots*

However, if the first part of a hyphenated compound is a noun and the second part is not, you usually make the first word plural:

passer-by	→	*passers-by*	lily-of-the-valley	→	*lilies-of-the-valley*
runner-up	→	*runners-up*	son-in-law	→	*sons-in-law*

11 Some words are always plural. They do not have a singular form. Here are some examples:

binoculars | cattle | clothes | contents | goggles | police

pyjamas | scissors | shorts | trousers

PRACTICE

Exercise 1

*Fill in the blanks with the correct **plural** form of the noun provided.*

1. There are no ______________ left in the box. (***match***)
2. One of these ______________ must fit the lock. (***key***)
3. Tom cleaned his ______________ before going to bed. (***tooth***)
4. Two of the ______________ were injured. (***fireman***)

 ISBN 978-81-8477-745-1

5. The insects use their ______________ to feel things around them. (*antenna*)
6. We had ______________ and peas with the fish. (*potato*)
7. All the ______________ have fallen from the trees. (*leaf*)
8. Your sisters' husbands are your ______________. (*brother-in-law*)
9. Is it cruel to keep animals in ______________? (*zoo*)
10. The children told each other ghost ______________ before they went to sleep. (*story*)

Exercise 2

Choose the correct form of the verb to fill the blanks in the following sentences.

1. My father ______________ (*cycles/cycle*) to work every day.
2. The police ______________ (*thinks/think*) the murderer was a woman.
3. The cakes in the window ______________ (*looks/look*) delicious.
4. Bacteria ______________ (*is/are*) too small to see without a microscope.
5. One of these cups ______________ (*has/have*) a broken handle.
6. The mice ______________ (*was/were*) running around the room.
7. My trousers ______________ (*needs/need*) washing.
8. The geese ______________ (*has/have*) escaped from the field.
9. Salmon ______________ (*swims/swim*) up the river to lay their eggs.
10. The man wearing glasses ______________ (*is/are*) my uncle.

Exercise 3

Underline all the singular countable nouns in the following passage.

I sat down at my desk to write a letter to my grandparents. They had sent me a lovely necklace for my birthday, and I wanted to thank them. I took a piece of paper from one of the drawers of my desk and picked up a pen. On the second line, the pen ran out of ink, so I had to find another. I wrote several more lines, then read what I had written. There were at least three mistakes, so I screwed up the paper and threw it in the bin. I decided to phone my grandparents instead.

 ISBN 978-81-8477-745-1

UNIT 3

UNCOUNTABLE NOUNS

What do they look like?

Mum: Peter, can you do a bit of **shopping** on your way home from **work**?

Peter: OK, Mum. I should have enough **time**. But you'll have to give me a list and the **money** to pay for it.

Mum: We need some **meat** and vegetables, a kilo of **rice**, a loaf of **bread** and a packet of **coffee**.

What are they?

Uncountable nouns cannot be made plural and cannot be used with ***a*** or ***an***. They are divided into two main classes:

1. **Concrete uncountable nouns** represent types of **food** or **material**, which you can see and touch:

   butter | dust | hay | ice | ink | milk | paper | plastic | rice | sand | silver | water | wood

2. **Abstract uncountable nouns** represent **qualities** or **concepts**, which you cannot see or touch:

   advice | anger | darkness | education | fear | freedom | health | history | information | love | peace | speed

How do you use them?

1. You can use **uncountable nouns** on their own in general statements:
   - *I don't like **cheese**.*
   - *It's easier to give **advice** than to take it.*

 ISBN 978-81-8477-745-1

2. They can be used with ***some*** in a specific situation:
   - *There's **some cheese** in the fridge.*
   - *Let me give you **some advice**.*

3. They can be used with ***the*** when it is clear what you are referring to:
   - *Put **the cheese** back in the fridge.*
   - ***The advice** Jack gave me was very useful.*

4. They can also be used with other **determiners**:
   - ***That cheese** is quite delicious!*
   - *Sue was very grateful for **your advice**.*

5. You use a **singular verb** when the subject is an **uncountable noun**:
   - ***Ice is** frozen water.*
   - *Grandma's **health has improved** recently.*

6. Some **uncountable nouns** look like plural countable nouns because they end in ***s***. You must use a **singular verb** when one of these words is the subject:
   - *The **news is** not very good.*
   - ***Measles is** a serious illness.*
   - ***Mathematics is** my favourite subject.*

7. It is possible to use ***a piece of*** and other similar expressions before many **uncountable nouns**:

a drop of blood	**a slice of** bread	**a bar of** chocolate
a speck of dust	**a pane of** glass	**a grain of** sand

   You use such expressions in order to refer to a single unit of the mass represented by the uncountable noun:
   - *Add **a pinch of salt** to the pastry mixture.*
   - *That's **a** nice tuneful **piece of music**.*

   You can make the expressions plural and use numbers or other determiners with them:
   - *I watched her put **four lumps of sugar** in her coffee.*
   - *There were **a few drops of blood** on the carpet.*

8. Some **uncountable nouns** can also be used as **countable nouns**:
   - *The box is made of **metal**.* (uncountable)
   - *Gold is **a** precious **metal**. **Metals** such as iron and steel are used in industry.* (countable)
   - *I've made a pot of **coffee**.* (uncountable)
   - *Waiter, another **coffee** please! I ordered two **coffees** and a glass of cola.* (countable)

 ISBN 978-81-8477-745-1

- *There's some **melon** left. Would you like a piece of **melon**?* (uncountable)
- *I've bought **a melon**.* (countable)

- *Helen has lovely wavy **hair**.* (uncountable)
- *Mum pulled out **a** grey **hair**. Dad has lots of grey **hairs**.* (countable)

- *The sensor detects **movement** and sets off an alarm.* (uncountable)
- *Everyone admired the dancer's graceful **movements**.* (countable)

Forming nouns from adjectives and verbs

Most of the nouns in the examples below are **abstract uncountable nouns**, but some can also be used as **countable nouns** (e.g. *ability* and *action*) or as **concrete nouns** (e.g. *decoration* and *equipment*).

1. You can add the ending ***ness*** to many adjectives to form nouns that refer to a quality or state:

cold	→	cold*ness*	great	→	great*ness*
useful	→	useful*ness*	shy	→	shy*ness*

If the adjective ends in **y** and has more than one syllable, you change the **y** to ***i*** before adding ***ness***:

friendly	→	friendl*iness*	happy	→	happ*iness*
lonely	→	lonel*iness*	lazy	→	laz*iness*

2. You can add ***y***, ***ty*** or ***ity*** to some adjectives to form nouns that refer to a quality or state:

jealous	→	jealous*y*	loyal	→	loyal*ty*
equal	→	equal*ity*	honest	→	honest*y*

If the adjective ends in **y** or **e**, you remove this letter before adding ***ity***:

jolly	→	joll*ity*	mature	→	matur*ity*
active	→	activ*ity*	severe	→	sever*ity*

If the adjective ends in ***ble***, you change this to ***bility*** to form the noun:

able	→	a*bility*	noble	→	no*bility*
likeable	→	likea*bility*	legible	→	legi*bility*

3. You can add ***y***, ***ry*** or ***ery*** to some adjectives to form nouns that refer to an activity:

deliver	→	deliver*y*	forge	→	forg*ery*
mock	→	mock*ery*	flatter	→	flatter*y*

 ISBN 978-81-8477-745-1

4. You can add the ending ***ment*** to some verbs to form nouns that refer to an activity or a state:

manage	→	manage*ment*	treat	→	treat*ment*
equip	→	equip*ment*	amaze	→	amaze*ment*
amuse	→	amuse*ment*	punish	→	punish*ment*

5. You can add ***ion*** or ***ation*** to some verbs to form nouns that refer to an activity:

reject	→	reject*ion*	discuss	→	discuss*ion*
act	→	act*ion*	form	→	form*ation*

If the verb ends in ***e***, you remove this letter before adding ***ion*** or ***ation***:

educate	→	educat*ion*	decorate	→	decorat*ion*
explore	→	explor*ation*	promote	→	promot*ion*

Sometimes other changes have to be made:

conclu*de*	→	conclu*sion*	perm*it*	→	perm*ission*
inten*d*	→	inten*tion*	expan*d*	→	expan*sion*

6. You can add ***ance*** or ***ence*** to some verbs to form nouns that refer to a state or process:

appear	→	appear*ance*	exist	→	exist*ence*
prefer	→	prefer*ence*	perform	→	perform*ance*

If the verb ends in ***e***, you remove this letter before adding ***ance***:

guide	→	guid*ance*	assure	→	assur*ance*

Some nouns ending in ***ance*** or ***ence*** are formed from adjectives, by changing final ***t*** to ***ce***:

brillian*t*	→	brillian*ce*	importan*t*	→	importan*ce*
patien*t*	→	patien*ce*	confiden*t*	→	confiden*ce*

7. You can add ***ing*** to many verbs to form nouns that refer to an activity or a state:

sing	→	sing*ing*	read	→	read*ing*
suffer	→	suffer*ing*	play	→	play*ing*

These nouns are called **gerunds**, and you will learn about them in Unit 37.

 ISBN 978-81-8477-745-1

PRACTICE

Exercise 1

*The following passage contains a number of uncountable nouns. Put **C** after the **concrete** nouns and **A** after the **abstract** nouns.*

Everyone should understand the importance ( ) of a healthy diet. You should eat plenty of fruit ( ) and vegetables, and not too much fat ( ) and sugar ( ). Regular exercise ( ) is also good for your health ( ). Try walking or cycling to school, or your place of work ( ), instead of going by car or bus. If this gives you a thirst ( ), then satisfy it with water ( ), not a sweet drink such as cola ( ).

Exercise 2

*Fill in the blanks with a **noun** formed from the adjective or verb provided.*

1. A good ____________ (***educate***) is very important.
2. The children jumped up and down in ____________ (***excite***).
3. I do not have enough ____________ (***patient***) to be a teacher.
4. Jane's ____________ (***happy***) turned to sorrow when she heard the bad news.
5. These changes will improve the ____________ (***usable***) of the computer.
6. The exercises are graded according to ____________ (***difficult***).
7. We had a ____________ (***discuss***) about what to do next.
8. The article made no ________ (***refer***) to the possible side-effects of the drug.

Exercise 3

*Underline all the **uncountable nouns** in the following passage. If any occur more than once, you need only underline the first occurrence.*

Scientists have developed a new kind of cream that can be used to treat baldness. Bald men can rub it on their head and then wait for their hair to grow back. I told my grandfather about this, but he said it sounded like nonsense. 'I have spent a lot of money on so-called cures for baldness over the years,' he said, 'and none of them have worked.' I looked at Grandpa's smooth, shiny head and knew that he was telling the truth. I asked him if he minded being bald. 'Not any more,' he replied. 'I've realized that it is something that comes naturally with old age, like poor eyesight and loss of memory.'

 ISBN 978-81-8477-745-1

UNIT 4

PROPER NOUNS

What do they look like?

I went to **Australia** with my parents to visit my cousin **Peter**. We left on **Monday** 16th **November** and returned two weeks later. While we were there we visited many famous sites. For **Mum**, the highlight of the trip was going to **Sydney Opera House** to see an opera by **Wagner**.

What are they?

Proper nouns always begin with a **capital letter**.

1. A proper noun can be the name of a **particular person**, real or make-believe:

David | May Ling | Dr Brown | Miss Lee | Granny | Uncle
Robert | Queen Elizabeth | Beethoven | Ali Baba

2. The **days** of the week and the **months** of the year are proper nouns:

Sunday | Monday | Tuesday | Wednesday
Thursday | Friday | Saturday

January | February | March | April | May | June | July
August | September | October | November | December

3. A proper noun can be the name of a particular place, such as a **country**, **city**, **ocean**, **river** or **mountain**:

Egypt | the United States of America | Beijing | New Delhi
the Atlantic Ocean | Lake Michigan | the Yangtze | Mount Fuji

4. The names of famous **buildings** and **monuments** are proper nouns:

the Great Wall of China | the Colosseum | Angkor Wat
Sydney Opera House

 ISBN 978-81-8477-745-1

5 **Nationalities, languages and beliefs** are proper nouns:

the British	an Australian	French	Japanese	Buddhism
Communism	Muslims	a Christian		

6 A proper noun can be the name of a **company, organization, or institution**:

Learners Publishing	the Red Cross	Nanyang Technological University

7 A proper noun can be the name of a **festival or special event**:

Ramadan	Christmas	Mother's Day	the Olympic Games

How do you use them?

1 Most **proper nouns** stand alone, without an article, and are used with a **singular verb**:

- ***Paris*** ***is*** *the capital of France.*
- ***Is*** ***Mandarin*** *a difficult language to learn?*

2 Some proper nouns are always used with ***the***, which does not have a capital *t*:

- *The ship sailed across* ***the*** ***Pacific Ocean***.
- *Did you visit* ***the*** ***Statue of Liberty***?

3 A few proper nouns are countable nouns, which can be used with ***a*** or ***an*** (or other determiners) and made plural:

- *Sally's brother is* ***a*** ***Buddhist***.
- ***Several*** ***Americans*** *and* ***an*** ***Australian*** *were killed in the crash.*

4 You can occasionally use other proper nouns like countable nouns:

- *The accident happened on* ***a*** ***Monday***.
- *There are* ***three*** ***Michaels*** *in my class at school.*

5 When you use words like ***Mum***, ***Dad***, ***Grandma*** and ***Grandpa*** alone as names, without a determiner, they are proper nouns and begin with a capital letter:

- *Can we stay up late tonight,* ***Mum***?
- *I bought a bunch of flowers for* ***Grandma***.

However, when you use them with words like ***my***, ***his***, ***their*** or ***a***, they are common nouns and do not begin with a capital letter:

- *The twins asked* ***their*** ***mum*** *if they could stay up late.*
- *Tom hasn't got* ***a*** ***grandma***.

 ISBN 978-81-8477-745-1

6. Similarly, you use ***Aunt*** and ***Uncle*** with names and ***aunt*** and ***uncle*** with determiners:
   - *My favourite **aunt** is **Aunt** Julie, my mother's sister.*
   - *Sue has two **uncles: Uncle** Jim and **Uncle** Dick.*

7. The word ***God***, with a capital letter, is used by people who believe that there is only one supreme being. You use ***god***, without a capital letter, to talk about one of a number of gods in other religions:
   - *Christians worship **God** in a building called a church.*
   - *Ganesh is a Hindu **god**.*

PRACTICE

Exercise 1

The writer of this postcard has not used capital letters for proper nouns. Rewrite it correctly below.

Hi philip

We are spending new year in switzerland and are having a lovely time. On tuesday, jane and I went skiing with dad and on wednesday, we went to the cinema to see a film starring brad pitt. There's lots to do here and the weather is very good. We shall be back in singapore on 8th january. I'll see you at school on the first day of term. Don't forget that it's miss brown's birthday. I've bought her some swiss chocolates – I hope she likes them!

love

robert

 ISBN 978-81-8477-745-1

Exercise 2

Rewrite the following sentences correctly. Some of the words with capitals shouldn't have them, and some of the words without capitals should have them.

1. My Cousin has sailed across The Pacific ocean.

   ____

2. The date of the Wedding is friday 6th August.

   ____

3. sally's uncle taught Her how to use the computer.

   ____

4. Have You ever been to the great Wall Of china?

   ____

5. The Capital of malaysia is Kuala lumpur.

   ____

6. Our french teacher's Name is Mr green.

   ____

7. John and his Brother Paul are students at Oxford university in england.

   ____

8. She hopes to win a gold Medal at the Olympic games.

   ____

9. I went to the library with dad to find a Book about the Wildlife of Australia for my School project.

   ____

10. Jane worked at the local Bank for a few months and then got a job with a company called Acme financial solutions.

   ____

 ISBN 978-81-8477-745-1

UNIT
5

COLLECTIVE NOUNS

What do they look like?

This is what happens at the beginning of the school concert. The **orchestra** plays while the **choir** walks on to the stage. The **staff** take their seats at the side of the hall. The **audience** stand while the national anthem is sung, then they sit down again.

What are they?

Collective nouns are words for **groups** of people, animals or things:

army | audience | band | choir | class | club

committee | community | company | crew

crowd | family | flock | gang | government | group

herd | jury | navy | orchestra | staff | team

How do you use them?

1. Most **collective nouns** are countable nouns, which can be used with ***a*** or ***an*** (or other determiners) and made plural:
   - *Carol plays the drums in* ***a band****.*
   - ***Both teams*** *played well.*

2. However, you often use ***the*** before **collective nouns**:
   - ***The jury*** *entered the courtroom.*
   - *Some of* ***the staff*** *may lose their jobs.*

 ISBN 978-81-8477-745-1

3. You can use a singular or plural verb with a **singular collective noun**. You use a **singular verb** when you are thinking of the group as a **unit**:

- ***My family comes** from Hong Kong.*
- ***The committee is** too large.*

You use a **plural verb** when you are thinking of the group as **individuals**:

- ***My family were** pleased to see me again.*
- ***The committee are** considering further action.*

4. If you use a **singular verb**, you refer to the group with **singular pronouns** and **determiners** such as ***it*** and ***its***:

- *The community **has** grown and **it** needs **its** own recreation centre.*
- *The company **looks** after **its** employees and **itself**.*

If you use a **plural verb**, you refer to the group with **plural pronouns** and **determiners** such as ***they*** and ***their***:

- *The team **have** been practising hard, so **they** hope to win **their** next match.*
- *The gang **were** arguing among **themselves**.*

5. Some **collective nouns** can be used with ***of*** + **a plural noun**:

- *A **crowd of fans** had gathered outside the theatre.*
- *Jack painted a picture of **a flock of sheep** grazing in a field.*

You can use a **singular** or **plural verb** with phrases like these, depending on whether you are thinking of the group as a **unit** or as **individuals**:

- *The **swarm of bees was** clinging to a tree trunk.*
- *A **herd of cattle were** slowly crossing the road in front of us.*

PRACTICE

Exercise 1

*Fill in the blanks with the **collective nouns** in the box using each one only once.*

herd	gang	team	flock	crowd	group	swarm	panel

The coach stopped and a ________ of people got out. They were a ________ of artists who had come to the countryside to paint pictures for a competition. A ________ of judges would decide which was the best. They found a suitable spot, with a good view of the surrounding farmland. A ________ of sheep were grazing in a field nearby, and a ________ of cattle could be seen in the distance. Suddenly, they were attacked by a ________ of

 ISBN 978-81-8477-745-1

bees. They ran down to the road, where a ________ of workmen were digging a ditch. Some of the artists fell into the ditch and hurt themselves. The coach driver took them to hospital, and a ________ of doctors and nurses attended to their injuries.

Exercise 2

*Choose the correct form of the **verb** to fill the blanks in the following sentences.*

1. The club ________ (*was/were*) founded last year and it meets every month.
2. The jury ________ (*is/are*) still considering their verdict.
3. The band ________ (*consists/consist*) of two guitarists, a singer and a drummer.
4. A gang of robbers ________ (*has/have*) stolen the painting, but they won't be able to sell it.
5. The team ________ (*hopes/hope*) that its winning streak will continue.
6. The crew ________ (*wears/wear*) matching T-shirts and baseball caps.
7. The family ________ (*has/have*) been forced to leave their home.
8. The government ________ (*was/were*) criticized for the way it handled the crisis.
9. My class ________ (*contains/contain*) some of the brightest students in the school.
10. A flock of sheep ________ (*was/were*) blocking the road and we couldn't get past them.

Exercise 3

*Fill in the blanks by matching the words in the box with the **collective nouns** in the sentences.*

birds	children	directors	elephants
kittens	onlookers	scientists	trees

1. A herd of ________ appeared in the distance.
2. A team of ________ have been working on this problem.
3. We watched a flock of ________ fly past.
4. A crowd of ________ had gathered at the scene.
5. Sally looked after the cat and her litter of ________.
6. A group of ________ were standing at the bus stop.
7. There was a clump of ________ in the middle of the field.
8. The board of ________ will discuss the issue at their next meeting.

 ISBN 978-81-8477-745-1

UNIT 6

MASCULINE, FEMININE AND COMMON-GENDER NOUNS

What do they look like?

My **aunt** and **uncle** have three **children**: two **sons** and one **daughter**. Michael, the eldest, is at university studying to be a **doctor**. His younger **brother**, James, wants to be a **policeman**. Their **sister** would like to go into show business and become an **actress**.

Here are some pairs of **masculine** and **feminine** nouns:

MASCULINE	FEMININE	MASCULINE	FEMININE
husband	wife	tiger	tigress
uncle	aunt	fox	vixen
brother	sister	bull	cow
nephew	niece	gander	goose
prince	princess	drake	duck
actor	actress	peacock	peahen

Some of these nouns, such as ***actor***, ***fox*** or ***duck***, can be used as **common-gender** nouns for both males and females.

How do you use them?

1. **Masculine** nouns (or nouns belonging to the **masculine gender**) are words for men and boys, and male animals or birds:

   father | son | nephew | fireman | bull | drake

2. **Feminine** nouns (or nouns belonging to the **feminine gender**) are words for women and girls, and female animals or birds:

   mother | daughter | niece | waitress | cow | hen

3. You use **masculine pronouns** and **determiners**, such as ***he***, ***him*** and ***his***, to refer to **singular masculine nouns:**
   - *My **brother** thinks **he** will fail **his** driving test.*
   - *Alice saw a **policeman** and asked **him** to help.*

 ISBN 978-81-8477-745-1

4 You use **feminine pronouns** and **determiners**, such as ***she***, ***her*** and ***hers***, to refer to **singular feminine nouns**:

- *The **girl** said that the book was **hers**.*
- *The **lioness** will attack if **she** thinks **her** cubs are in danger.*

5 There is also a large class of **common-gender nouns**, which can refer to both males and females:

child | baby | relation | teacher | painter

architect | doctor | deer | chicken

6 Below are some more **masculine** and **feminine** nouns. In the third column are **common-gender** equivalents with the same meaning:

MASCULINE	FEMININE	COMMON-GENDER
boy	girl	child
man	woman	adult
father	mother	parent
son	daughter	child
king	queen	monarch
policeman	policewoman	police officer
spaceman	spacewoman	astronaut
stag	doe	deer
ram	ewe	sheep
stallion	mare	horse
cock	hen	chicken

7 In formal English, you refer to common-gender nouns for people with ***he*** or ***she***, ***his*** or ***her,*** etc. if the person's sex is not known or mentioned:

- *A good **teacher** knows how to deal with the disruptive pupils in **his** or **her** class.*
- *A **child** could hurt **himself** or **herself** on that broken glass.*

In informal English, you can use ***they***, ***their***, etc.:

- *A good **teacher** knows how to deal with the disruptive pupils in **their** class.*
- *A **child** could hurt **themselves** on that broken glass.*

Some people object to this use of plural pronouns and determiners (***they***, ***their***) to refer to a singular noun (***teacher***). In order to avoid the problem, you can sometimes rewrite the sentence with a **plural noun**:

- *Good **teachers** know how to deal with the disruptive pupils in **their** classes.*
- *Children could hurt **themselves** on that broken glass.*

 ISBN 978-81-8477-745-1

PRACTICE

Exercise 1

Read the following passage. Put M after the masculine nouns, F after the feminine nouns and C after the common-gender nouns.

The Jackson family went to look at a litter of puppies ( ). The children ( ) had been asking for a dog ( ) for a long time. Now that Tom was ten years old and his sister ( ) was eight, their parents ( ) thought they were old enough to have a pet. Their father ( ) was very enthusiastic about the idea, but his wife ( ) was not so keen. She was a writer ( ) and worked from home. This meant she would probably be the person ( ) responsible for looking after the dog. Mr Jackson was a policeman ( ). He sometimes worked a night shift, and he liked the idea of having a dog to guard the family while he was not there.

Exercise 2

Fill in the blanks with a suitable personal pronoun or determiner according to the gender.

1. A vixen attacked our chickens but ______________ didn't wound them seriously.
2. The emperor was highly respected by ______________ people.
3. A ewe had got caught in some barbed wire, but the farmer managed to free ______.
4. Mr Brown's niece has passed all ______________ exams.
5. The gander hissed at me and flapped ______________ wings.
6. The bull is dangerous: keep away from ______________!

Exercise 3

Rewrite these sentences in the plural.

1. A good parent treats all his or her children equally.

   ____

2. Each student must pay for his or her own books.

   ____

3. The monarch has a right to expect everyone to obey him or her.

   ____

4. A child should be able to dress himself or herself at this age.

   ____

5. An architect rarely has to live in the building he or she has designed.

   ____

6. Each guest helps himself or herself to food from the buffet.

   ____

 ISBN 978-81-8477-745-1

UNIT 7

NOUN PHRASES

What do they look like?

A taxi stopped outside **Jack's house** and **a smartly dressed young woman with a suitcase** got out. 'Do you know **that woman**?' Jack asked **his mother**, who was standing beside him at **the window**. 'Yes, it's **your cousin May from China**,' she replied. 'She has come to stay with us for **a few days**.'

What are they made up of?

1. A noun phrase can consist simply of an **article** or other **determiner** + **noun**:
   - *a storm*
   - *my relations*
   - *the postman*
   - *these fashions*
2. There may be more than one **determiner** before the **noun**:
   - *all my relations*
   - *both of the cars*
   - *some of these fashions*
   - *a few more hours*
3. There may be one or more **adjectives** before the **noun**:
   - *a violent storm*
   - *my new green jacket*
   - *some wonderful news*
   - *cool, clear, fresh water*
4. There may be a **present participle** or **past participle** before the **noun**:
   - *a broken chair*
   - *those screaming children*
   - *dazzling light*
   - *his mended bicycle*
5. These **adjectives** or **participles** may be modified by an **adverb**:
   - *some really wonderful news*
   - *slowly moving traffic*
   - *his newly mended bicycle*
   - *an utterly unsuitable outfit*
6. There may be a **possessive form** before the **noun**:
   - *Mary's computer*
   - *the boys' parents*
   - *yesterday's news*
   - *her horse's mane*
7. There may be another **noun used like an adjective** before the **main noun**:
   - *mountain scenery*
   - *our science teacher*
   - *the Singapore skyline*
   - *four cream cakes*

 ISBN 978-81-8477-745-1

8. A noun phrase can also have a **word**, **phrase** or **clause** after the **main noun**:
   - ***the house opposite***
   - ***the people invited***
   - ***a man with a beard***
   - ***a stool to sit on***
   - ***the road home***
   - ***children playing in the garden***
   - ***the reason for my journey***
   - ***the discovery that the earth moves round the sun***

9. The **main noun** is called the **head** of the noun phrase. However, a noun phrase can also have a **pronoun** as its head:
   - ***something strange***
   - ***those with their own computers***
   - ***anyone waiting***
   - ***everything in the drawer***

How do you use them?

1. You can use a noun phrase as the **subject** of a **verb**:
   - ***A strange-looking balloon was** circling overhead.*
   - ***The men repairing the road stopped** work.*

2. You can also use a noun phrase as the **object** of a **verb**:
   - *We **reached the summit** by late evening.*
   - *The bomb **damaged several houses nearby**.*

3. A noun phrase can be the **object** of a **preposition**:
   - *We reached the summit **by late evening**.*
   - *The bomb damaged several houses **in the surrounding area**.*

4. A noun phrase can also be the **complement** of a **linking verb**:
   - *The upturned bucket **made a satisfactory seat**.*
   - *I **felt a complete idiot**.*

Using noun phrases in apposition

Noun phrases are sometimes placed beside (or **in apposition to**) other nouns and noun phrases to add further information about them or identify them more exactly.

1. You can put a **noun phrase in apposition** before the name of someone or something:
   - ***My sister Jill** is a teacher.*
   - *Have you seen **the science-fiction film Star Wars**?*

2. Most often, a **noun phrase in apposition** comes after the **word or phrase** it explains. In this case, you must put commas around the phrase in apposition:
   - ***Mike's new car, a Honda**, uses less fuel than his old one.*
   - ***The bird of peace, the dove**, can be seen in the corner of the picture.*
   - ***Mr Lal, our football coach**, is retiring next year.*
   - *They moved to **Penang, an island off the coast of Malaysia**.*

 ISBN 978-81-8477-745-1

PRACTICE

Exercise 1

Fill in the blanks with any words of your choice to expand the nouns into noun phrases.

1. The girl was wearing ______ ______ ______ jacket.
2. There were ______ ______ ______ apples in the greengrocer's window.
3. A man ______ ______ ______ ______ asked me where I was going.
4. ______ ______ ______ woman sat down for a rest.
5. The sun shone brightly in ______ ______ ______ sky.
6. Mum gave everyone a bowl of ______ ______ soup.

Exercise 2

Put a ring around the noun phrases in the following passage.

My parents gave me a smart new bike for my twelfth birthday. I cycled to the post office after lunch and left my bike outside. When I came out, it had gone! A woman standing nearby said she had seen a tall boy with glasses take the bike and ride it away. She described the boy's clothes, but she didn't know the colour of his hair because he was wearing a hooded jacket. From the description, I recognized the boy immediately. It was my elder brother. He had 'stolen' my bicycle to teach me to take better care of it in future.

Exercise 3

In each of the following sentences, say whether the noun phrase in bold print is the subject, object or complement by writing S, O or C in the brackets.

1. I heard **a loud noise** ( ) and ran to investigate.
2. **The building on the corner** ( ) used to be a prison.
3. Does **your sister** ( ) know how to swim?
4. Miss Black is **our English teacher** ( ).
5. Don't forget to lock **the front door** ( ) when you leave the house.
6. This clearing seems **a good place for a picnic** ( ).

 ISBN 978-81-8477-745-1

Exercise 4

Insert the missing commas in the following sentences to show the noun phrases in apposition.

1. Our school the oldest building in the village is to be demolished.
2. Sally has a holiday job at Kwiksave the supermarket where her mother works.
3. Jack asked Mr Lee his next-door neighbour to help him lift the crate.
4. The eagle a large bird of prey lives in a nest called an eyrie.
5. I wore my usual wedding outfit a red skirt and a white blouse.
6. How could they sack Peter the hardest-working person in the company?

Exercise 5: grammar for writing

Write a short passage, about 100 words long, using at least ten of the following nouns in noun phrases.

bank	bridge	day	friends	men	people	river
sister	sunshine	walk	water	way	weather	words

 ISBN 978-81-8477-745-1

2 PRONOUNS & DETERMINERS

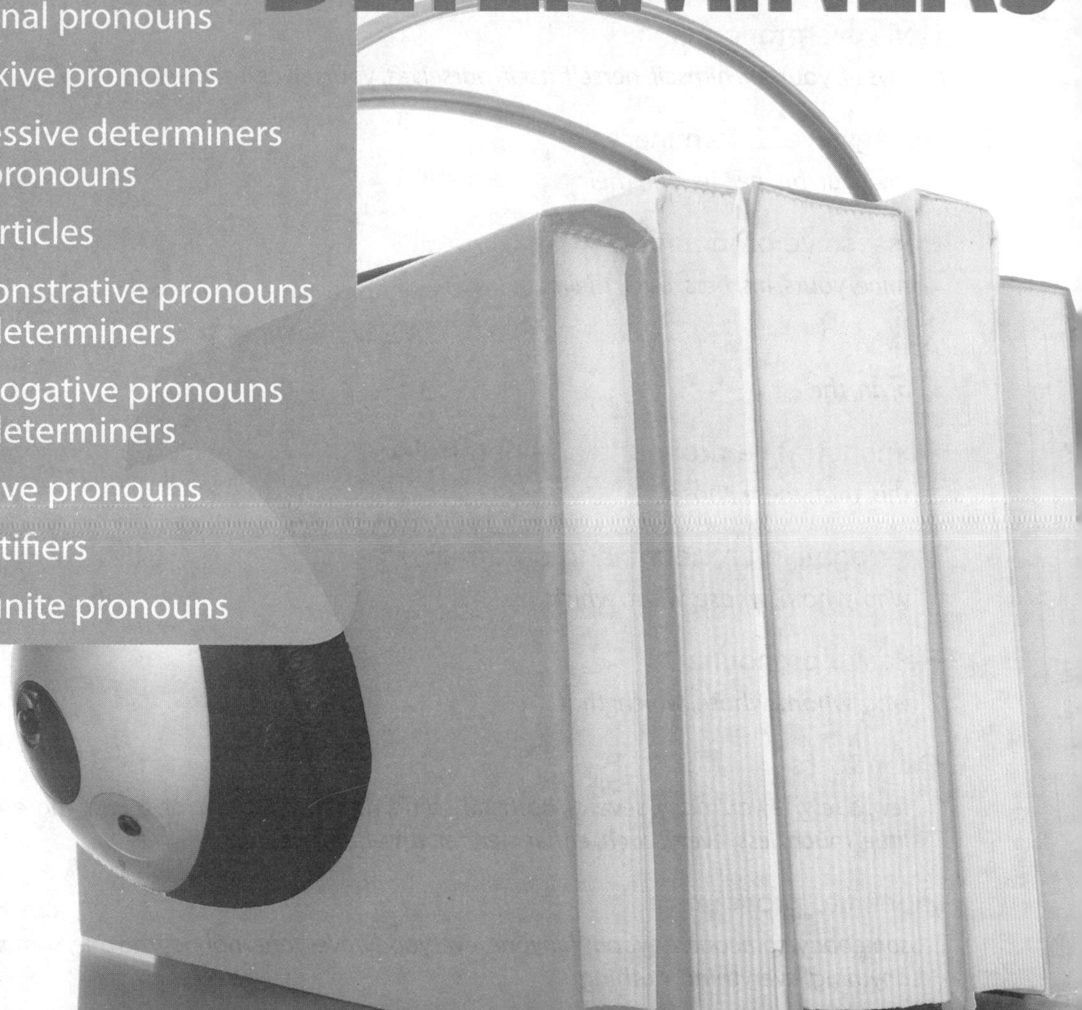

 ISBN 978-81-8477-745-1

UNIT 8

PRONOUNS AND DETERMINERS

What do they look like?

Sue: **Whose** is **this** jacket? Does **it** belong to **you**?

Kate: No, **mine** has **a** zip up **the** front.

Sue: Perhaps **it** is Carol's.

Kate: Yes, **it** could be. **She** told **me** that **she** had lost **her** jacket, **which** had **a lot of** money in **the** pocket. **She** was afraid **someone** might have stolen **it**.

Personal pronouns

I, me, you, he, him, she, her, it, we, us, they, them

Reflexive pronouns

myself, yourself, himself, herself, itself, ourselves, yourselves, themselves

Possessive determiners

my, your, his, her, its, our, their

Possessive pronouns

mine, yours, his, hers, ours, theirs

Articles

a, an, the

Demonstrative pronouns and determiners

this, that, these, those

Interrogative pronouns and determiners

who, whom, whose, what, which

Relative pronouns

who, whom, whose, which, that

Quantifiers

few, a few, fewer, many, several, both, all, some, none, enough, a lot, lots of, more, most, little, much, less, every, each, either, neither, any, half, no, etc.

Indefinite pronouns

somebody/someone, anybody/anyone, everybody/everyone, nobody/no one, something, anything, everything, nothing

 ISBN 978-81-8477-745-1

What are they?

1. Pronouns **stand alone.** They do the job of nouns and noun phrases by standing in place of them. Pronouns usually **refer back** to a noun or noun phrase already mentioned. This helps to give a text cohesion, which you will learn more about in Unit 74. Here are some examples:
   - *My sister* (noun phrase) *has been clearing out our house.* ***She*** (pronoun) *called me yesterday.*
   - *I've just found **a lot of books*** (noun phrase) *in the basement. What shall I do with **them*** (pronoun)*?*

2. Pronouns are **shortcuts.** They allow you to avoid repeating nouns and noun phrases, for example:
   - *Aunt Mary gave me **this necklace.** I only wear **it*** (= the necklace) *on special occasions.*
   - *There were **two cups** on the shelf. **Both*** (= the two cups) *had broken handles.*

3. Determiners are like **adjectives.** They always come before a noun. Some identify the people or things you mean, for example:
   - ***My** sister has been clearing out **the** basement of **our** house.*
   - ***Those** books look quite valuable.*

4. Some determiners refer to **quantity**, for example:
   - *There is **some** milk in the fridge.*
   - *Alan has **many** friends.*

How do you use them?

Pronouns

1. Pronouns **stand alone**:
   - ***She** called **me** yesterday.*
   - ***What** shall **I** do with **these**?*
   - *Jack wanted some chocolate cake, but there was **none** left.*

2. A pronoun can be the **subject** of a verb, for example:
   - ***They** don't understand.*
   - ***Few** are chosen.*
   - ***That** sounded like thunder.*

3. A pronoun can be the **object** of a verb, for example:
   - *Jane made **it**.*
   - *The witch changed **herself** into a frog.*
   - ***Which** do you prefer?*

 ISBN 978-81-8477-745-1

4 A pronoun can be the **object** of a **preposition**, for example:

- *Would you like to come* ***with me****?*
- *There are enough seats* ***for everyone****.*
- ***To whom*** *is the letter addressed?*

5 A pronoun can be the **complement** of a **linking verb**:

- *There's only one hotel in the town, and this* ***is it****.*
- *I saw someone, but I didn't realize it* ***was you****.*

Determiners

1 **Determiners** come at the beginning of a **noun phrase**:

- ***My bicycle*** *has been stolen from* ***the garden shed****.*
- ***Which shelf*** *shall I put* ***these valuable china ornaments*** *on?*
- *Jack wanted* ***some chocolate cake****, but there was none left.*

2 As a general rule, **singular countable nouns** need an **article** or a **determiner**:

a spoon	***the*** spoon	***any*** spoon
each spoon	***this*** spoon	***my*** spoon

3 But **plural nouns** and **uncountable nouns** can be used with or without an **article** or a **determiner**:

- *We need eggs, flour and sugar.*
- *Can you see* ***those*** *boats on* ***the*** *water?*
- ***The*** *students handed in* ***their*** *homework.*

PRACTICE

Exercise 1

In the following passage, underline all the ***determiners*** *and put a ring round all the* ***pronouns****.*

Kate felt hungry, so she went to the kitchen to make herself a sandwich. She cut two slices of bread and spread them with butter. Then she opened the fridge and looked inside, trying to decide what filling to put in her sandwich. There was some cheese, a packet of sliced ham and a few eggs. Which should she choose? At that moment, her brother Billy came into the kitchen. 'What are you doing?' asked Billy. 'Making a sandwich,' replied Kate. 'Shall I make you one too?' 'No thanks,' said Billy, 'I have just had lunch at my friend's house.'

 ISBN 978-81-8477-745-1

Exercise 2

Say whether the underlined pronouns and determiners in the following sentences are possessive (P), demonstrative (D) or interrogative (I).

1. Do you know <u>whose</u> mobile phone is ringing? ( )
2. Tom didn't tell <u>his</u> mother where he was going. ( )
3. <u>That</u> is the strangest thing I have ever heard! ( )
4. Please wipe <u>your</u> feet on the mat before you come in. ( )
5. Why are you wearing <u>those</u> old jeans? ( )
6. I asked the teacher <u>what</u> I should do next. ( )
7. <u>Which</u> button should I press? ( )
8. The bicycle in the garage is <u>mine</u>. ( )
9. She wondered <u>who</u> the stranger was. ( )
10. <u>This</u> is the oldest building in the village. ( )

Exercise 3

Look at the pronouns in bold print and say whether they are the subject (S), object (O) or complement (C) of the verb.

1. We invited the twins but **they** ( ) could not come.
2. The old man spends **little** ( ) on food.
3. Is **it** ( ) raining?
4. I can't remember who told me **that** ( ).
5. Let **me** ( ) help **you** ( ) tidy the room.
6. The burglar must have been **someone** ( ) small enough to climb through the window.
7. **Which** ( ) do you prefer – the green one or the red one?
8. **Something** ( ) is wrong with Sally. She hasn't been **herself** ( ) all week.
9. Fifteen of the passengers were taken to hospital, but **most** ( ) were only slightly injured.
10. Tom said that the money was **his** ( ).

 ISBN 978-81-8477-745-1

UNIT 9

PERSONAL PRONOUNS

What do they look like?

It was a fine day, so **I** decided to go for a walk. **I** phoned Jenny and asked **her** if **she** would like to come with **me**. **We** met at the park gate. Two of our friends walked past. Jenny invited **them** to join **us**, but **they** were busy. 'See **you** at school tomorrow,' **I** said.

PERSON	SINGULAR		PLURAL	
	Subject	Object	Subject	Object
First	*I*	*me*	*we*	*us*
Second	*you*	*you*	*you*	*you*
Third	*he* *she* *it*	*him* *her* *it*	*they*	*them*

How do you use them?

1. **Personal pronouns** are used to represent the person or people speaking, the person or people they are addressing, and the people or things they are talking about:
   - *'I can't do my homework,' said Joe to his sister. 'Will **you** help **me** with **it**?'*
   - ***We** have some presents for **you**. Here **they** are.*

2. The **first person** pronouns are ***I, me***, ***we*** and ***us***. You use ***I*** (always with a capital letter) or ***me*** to refer to yourself. You use ***we*** or ***us*** to refer to any group in which you include yourself:
   - ***I** am taking my brother and sister to the park. Would you like to come with **us**?*
   - *Dad drove **me** to the airport. **We** arrived in plenty of time.*

3. The second **person pronoun** is ***you***, which has the same form for singular and plural. You use ***you*** to refer to the person or people you are talking to:
   - *'These flowers are for **you**, Grandma,' I said.*
   - *Be quiet, children! **You** are making far too much noise.*

 ISBN 978-81-8477-745-1

4 The **third person** pronouns are ***he***, ***him***, ***she***, ***her***, ***it***, ***they*** and ***them***. You use ***he*** or ***him*** to refer to **a man**, **boy** *or* **male animal**. You use ***she*** or ***her*** to refer to **a woman**, **girl** *or* **female animal**. You use ***it*** to refer to **a thing** (or to an animal or a baby whose sex you don't know). You use ***they*** or ***them*** to refer to several people or things:

- ***My dad*** *met* ***my mum*** *at a dance.* ***He*** *fell in love with* ***her*** *immediately.*
- *Slice* ***the potatoes*** *and put* ***them*** *in* ***a dish***. ***It*** *must be an ovenproof dish with a lid.*

5 The pronouns ***I***, ***he***, ***she***, ***we*** and ***they*** are **subject pronouns**. They are used as the **subject** of a **verb**, for example:

- ***I called*** *to the men but* ***they did not hear*** *me.*
- *Jenny had a lot of work to do.* ***She asked*** *her brother for help, but* ***he was*** *too busy.*
- ***We are going*** *to the cinema.*

6 The pronouns ***me, him, her, us*** and ***them*** are **object pronouns**. They are used as the **object** of a **verb** or **preposition**, for example:

- *The men* ***did not hear me*** *when I called* ***to them.***
- *Jenny phoned her brother and* ***asked him*** *to do some shopping* ***for her***.
- *Would you like to come to the cinema* ***with us***?

7 The pronouns ***you*** and ***it*** have the same form as subject and object:

- ***You should have asked*** *someone to go to the hospital* ***with you.***
- *I don't like your cat.* ***It scratched*** *me when I tried to* ***stroke it***.

8 Object pronouns are also used as the indirect object of a **verb**:

- *I ran to my mother and* ***gave her*** *a kiss.*
- *The children's father* ***read them*** *a story.*

9 After ***than***, you can use the subject pronoun or the object pronoun:

- *Tom is taller* ***than I***. (subject pronoun, short for ***than I am***)
- *Tom is taller* ***than me***. (object pronoun, used after preposition)

10 Take care to choose the right pronoun when it is part of a phrase such as ***Jane and I*** or ***my friend and me***:

- ***Sally and I have been invited*** *to Jack's party.* (the pronoun ***I*** is part of the subject, so ***Sally and me*** would be wrong)
- *Jack* ***has invited Sally and me*** *to his party.* (the pronoun ***me*** is part of the object, so ***Sally and I*** would be wrong)

 ISBN 978-81-8477-745-1

PRACTICE

Exercise 1

*Fill in the blanks with the correct **personal pronouns**.*

John went to the shopping mall to look for a birthday present for his sister. _____ did not know what to buy _____, but hoped to find something suitable in one of the department stores. '_____ wonder if _____ would like some perfume,' _____ thought. Her favourite brand was on sale, but _____ was far too expensive. John moved on to the handbag department. There _____ was relieved to see Sally and Kate, two girls from his class at school, who waved to _____. 'Can _____ help _____?' John asked _____. 'I want to buy a handbag for my sister. Which one do _____ think _____ would like?' Sally and Kate had a look around. _____ chose a nice leather bag at a reasonable price. '_____ think your sister would love this,' _____ said.

Exercise 2

*Fill in the correct **personal pronoun**, then say whether it is a **subject pronoun** or **object pronoun**, and which **person** it is. The first one has been done to help you.*

1. Excuse <u>me</u>: is this the train for London? — <u>*object, 1st person singular*</u>
2. Children, _____________ may go home now. — _______________
3. Passengers are reminded to keep their luggage with _______ at all times. — _______________
4. Barbara promised that _____________ would phone this evening. — _______________
5. 'Was the weather good?' 'Yes, ___________ was sunny and warm.' — _______________
6. The principal thanked _____________ all for our cooperation. — _______________
7. Where are Jane and Susan? ____________ are very late today. — _______________
8. Has anyone seen my keys? ____________ left them on the table. — _______________

 ISBN 978-81-8477-745-1

9. Tom and I wanted to go to the wedding, but ________ were not invited. ____________________

10. 'Can I help ____________?' the assistant asked me. ____________________

Exercise 3

Choose the correct **personal pronouns** *to fill in the blanks.*

1. Didn't you hear _____ (*she/her*) calling your name?
2. The girl picked up the puppies and gave _____ (*they/them*) a hug.
3. Mrs Brown said her husband and _____ (*she/her*) were going on holiday.
4. Will you take a photo of _____ (*we/us*) on my camera?
5. Michael's sister can run faster than _____ (*he/him*) can.
6. Mum, can you drive Carol and _____ (*I/me*) to the cinema?
7. Jack asked me to help _____ (*he/him*).
8. My friend and _____ (*I/me*) often go shopping together.
9. The policeman wanted to know where _____ (*we/us*) were going.
10. I am not as keen on football as _____ (*they/them*) are.

 ISBN 978-81-8477-745-1

UNIT 10

REFLEXIVE PRONOUNS

What do they look like?

It was a peaceful scene. The children were playing happily by **themselves**. Peter was cutting out a picture, taking care not to hurt **himself** with the scissors. Alice had dressed up in some old clothes of her mother's and was looking at **herself** in a mirror. The cat was sitting on the rug, washing **itself**.

PERSON	SINGULAR	PLURAL
First	*myself*	*ourselves*
Second	*yourself*	*yourselves*
Third	*himself* *herself* *itself*	*themselves*

How do you use them?

1. **Reflexive pronouns** refer back to the person or animal that is the subject of the verb:
   - *I made this cake **myself**.*
   - *Be careful with that knife. You could cut **yourself**.*
   - *The boy helped **himself** to a large slice of cake.*
   - *Jane felt very proud of **herself** for passing the exam.*
   - *The hedgehog rolled **itself** into a ball.*
   - *Tom and I washed **ourselves** in the stream.*
   - *You must behave **yourselves**, children, when you are at Grandma's house.*
   - *Baby birds are too young to look after **themselves**.*

2. You can use a reflexive pronoun as the **object** of a verb or preposition:
   - *I hurt **myself**.*
   - *The girl was sitting by **herself**.*

3. You must use a reflexive pronoun, not an object pronoun such as ***me*** or ***them***, when the subject and object of a verb are the same person or thing. Such verbs are called **reflexive verbs**:
   - *The **children** enjoyed **themselves** at the party.*
   - ***You** did not express **yourselves** clearly enough.*

 ISBN 978-81-8477-745-1

4. A reflexive pronoun can also be the **indirect object** of a verb:
   - *We found **ourselves** a couple of chairs.*
   - *You can make **yourself** a cup of tea while you're waiting.*

5. Reflexive pronouns are often used as **emphasizers**. They are added to draw attention to a noun or personal pronoun:
   - *I didn't see the accident **itself**, but I heard the crash.*
   - *She had trained the horse **herself**.*
   - *Joe **himself** is to blame for his problems.*

PRACTICE

Exercise 1

Fill in the blanks with the correct reflexive pronouns.

1. Jane and Tim helped ______________ to food and drink.
2. The princess looked at ______________ in the mirror.
3. My sister and I made ______________ some sandwiches.
4. The house ______________ is at least four hundred years old.
5. I wouldn't have done it that way ______________.
6. You and Billy could teach ______________ Japanese.
7. I didn't speak to the president ______________, just his secretary.
8. 'Did you paint that picture ______________?' the teacher asked me.
9. Aunt Julie told us to behave ______________.
10. The birds had made a cosy nest for ______________.

Exercise 2

*Say if the **reflexive pronoun** in bold print is the object (O) of a verb, the indirect object (IO) of a verb, the object of a preposition (OP) or an emphasizer (E). The first one has been done to help you.*

1. The castle **itself** (*E*) was closed, but we walked in the grounds.
2. Take a good look at **yourselves** ( ).

 ISBN 978-81-8477-745-1

3. I decided to give **myself** ( ) a treat.
4. James finds it difficult to express **himself** ( ) in writing.
5. Alice was pretty pleased with **herself** ( ).
6. Dave **himself** ( ) didn't want a big birthday party.
7. We found **ourselves** ( ) some accommodation in the centre of the town.
8. If you don't take **yourself** ( ) seriously, no one else will.
9. Such young children should not be left by **themselves** ( ).
10. My grandfather built this house **himself** ( ).

Exercise 3

Choose the correct pronoun to fill in the blanks in the passage.

'Jenny, wake your little brother and sister and tell ______________ (*them/themselves*) it's time to get up,' said Mrs Clark. 'Make sure they wash ______________ (*them/themselves*) properly before they get dressed. Billy can wash and dress ______________ (*him/himself*) but Katy is too young, so you'll have to help ______________ (*her/herself*).' Jenny was still fast asleep. Her mother went over to her bed. 'Did you hear what I said to ______________ (*you/yourself*), or was I talking to ______________ (*me/myself*)?' she asked. Jenny yawned and sat up in bed. 'Sorry,' she said, 'what do you want ______________ (*me/myself*) to do?' At that moment, Billy and Katy appeared in the doorway. 'We've washed and dressed ______________ (*us/ourselves*)!' they announced proudly.

 ISBN 978-81-8477-745-1

UNIT 11

POSSESSIVE DETERMINERS AND PRONOUNS

What do they look like?

Alan: Give me back **my** book!

Mary: This isn't **your** book. It's **mine**. I don't know where **yours** is. But Sue probably won't mind if you borrow **hers**.

Alan: I ought to ask **her** permission first. Some people don't like lending **their** things. Tom once hit me for using a pen of **his** to write a note!

	DETERMINERS		PRONOUNS	
PERSON	**Singular**	**Plural**	**Singular**	**Plural**
First	*my*	*our*	*mine*	*ours*
Second	*your*	*your*	*yours*	*yours*
Third	*his* *her* *its*	*their*	*his* *hers*	*theirs*

The possessive ***its*** is used only as a determiner, not as a pronoun.

How do you use them?

1. You use possessive determiners like adjectives before a **noun**. They say who **possesses** or has something:
   - *Jack is in **his** **bedroom**.*
   - *I've lost **my** favourite **CD**.*
   - *The cat carried **its** **kittens** into the garden.*
   - *Take off **your** dirty **boots** before you come in.*

2. Possessive pronouns **stand alone**. They often replace a phrase made up of a possessive determiner and a **noun**. This avoids the repetition of a noun that has already been mentioned:
   - *I've had my breakfast. Has Sally had **hers** (= her **breakfast**)?*
   - *Those drinks are **ours** (= our **drinks**).*
   - *Joe has finished his homework, but the twins are still doing **theirs** (= their **homework**).*
   - *You can borrow my mobile phone if you can't find **yours** (= your **mobile phone**).*

 ISBN 978-81-8477-745-1

PRACTICE

Exercise 1

Rewrite each sentence, changing the possessive determiner to a possessive pronoun. The first one has been done to help you.

1. Jane said it was her book. *Jane said the book was hers.*
2. That is my mobile phone. ______________________
3. Are these your football boots? ______________________
4. My brother thought it was his cap. ______________________
5. Those are our seats. ______________________
6. The men said it was their van. ______________________
7. Mum thought it was her bag. ______________________
8. This is your desk. ______________________
9. The lion and lioness knew it was their cub. ______________________
10. Is that his dog? ______________________

Exercise 2

Rewrite the sentences in the form This is + possessive determiner + noun. The first one has been done to help you.

1. Mr Brown owns all this land. *This is his land.*
2. This CD belongs to my sister. ______________________
3. Our cat is the mother of this kitten. ______________________
4. My sister and I share this bedroom. ______________________
5. Sally gave you this pen. ______________________
6. I bought this necklace. ______________________
7. This is the lid for that box. ______________________
8. I borrowed this book from Tom. ______________________
9. My grandparents live in this house. ______________________
10. Mum poured this drink for you. ______________________

 ISBN 978-81-8477-745-1

Exercise 3

Fill in the blanks with the correct possessive determiners and pronouns.

1. I phoned Susan but __________ number was engaged.
2. This must be __________ glass, David. I put __________ on the piano.
3. 'Can we help?' asked Sue and Kate. It's a trick of __________ to offer help when all the work is done.
4. Tell Charles that one of __________ friends called to see him while he was out.
5. You can borrow __________ calculator if you can't find __________.
6. My sister and I went to visit __________ mother in hospital.
7. The police apologized and said it was __________ fault.
8. Joe knew that the camera was __________, but he couldn't prove that he owned it.
9. The dog ran to greet us, wagging __________ tail.
10. 'Are these seats __________?' asked the twins before they sat down.

Exercise 4

Fill in the blanks in the following passage with the correct possessive determiners and pronouns.

At the end of term, all the lost property was laid out in the school hall. Students could come and take away anything that was __________. 'Those are __________ gloves,' cried Michael. 'I thought I'd left them on the bus. Jack let me borrow __________, but they didn't fit me very well.' 'That lunchbox is __________,' said Anne. __________ mother had been very cross when she lost it. 'Look, Peter,' said someone else, 'isn't that __________ football? Whoever brought it to lost property obviously didn't know it was __________.' 'It isn't, it's __________,' cried the twins, snatching __________ ball from Peter's hands. 'Look, it has __________ names on it!'

 ISBN 978-81-8477-745-1

UNIT 12

THE ARTICLES

What do they look like?

To make baked custard, you need milk, sugar and eggs. First, you break **the** eggs into **a** bowl and beat them, slowly mixing in **the** sugar. Then, you boil **the** milk in **a** pan and add it to **the** sugar and eggs. Finally, you put **the** mixture into **an** ovenproof dish and bake it for **an** hour.

What are they?

1. The articles are the words ***a, an*** and ***the***. They belong to the **determiner** word class. They always come before a **noun** or at the beginning of a **noun phrase**:
   - ***a document***
   - ***an insect***
   - ***the sky***
   - ***a cool, refreshing drink***
   - ***an unexpected happening***
   - ***the open front door***

2. The article ***a*** is called the **indefinite article**. It has the form ***an*** before a vowel sound:
   - ***a** dog*
   - ***an** hour*
   - ***a** helpful young woman*
   - ***an** intelligent child*

3. The article ***the*** is called the **definite article**. It always has the same form:
   - ***the** correct answer*
   - ***the** winners*
   - ***the** environment*
   - ***the** most delicious tomatoes*

How do you use them?

1. You use ***a*** or ***an*** with **singular countable nouns** only:
   - ***A person** lives in **a house**, but **a mouse** lives in **a hole**.*
   - ***An icon** like this is called **an hourglass**.*

2. You can also use ***the*** with **singular countable nouns**:
   - ***The mouse** ran out of its hole and across **the floor**.*
   - *Click on **the icon** at **the top** of **the screen**.*

3. You do not use ***a*** or ***an*** with **plural nouns** or **uncountable nouns**:
   - ***People** live in **houses**, but **mice** live in **holes**.*
   - ***Sugar** is sweet.*

 ISBN 978-81-8477-745-1

4. However, you can use ***the*** with **plural nouns** and **uncountable nouns**:
   - *Do you know **the people** who live in these houses?*
   - *Please pass me **the sugar**.*
5. Several **expressions of quantity** use the indefinite article:
   - *I've thought of **a few** good reasons.*
   - *You're wasting **a lot of** water.*
   - *There's **a little** rice left.*
6. You use ***the*** with **superlatives** and other words that make something or someone **unique**:
   - *Which of you is **the best runner**?*
   - *Maggie was **the only person** who got **the last question** right.*
7. ***The*** can be used before certain **adjectives**, to change them into **nouns** representing a whole class of people:
   - ***The French** have excellent taste in most things.*
   - *This new law will help **the unemployed**.*

You will learn more about these adjectives in Unit 18.

a or an?

1. You use ***a*** before a consonant sound (including some vowels when they sound like 'y' or 'w'):
   - ***a** car*
   - ***a** uniform*
   - ***a** fine day*
   - ***a** European city*
   - ***a** house*
   - ***a** one-man band*
2. You use ***an*** before a vowel sound (including silent 'h'):
   - ***an** apple*
   - ***an** honest man*
   - ***an** old man*
   - ***an** MP*
   - ***an** hour*
   - ***an** SOS*

a/an or the?

1. You use ***a*** or ***an*** when you are not referring to any particular person or thing from a number of possible ones:
   - *You ought to speak to **a doctor**.*
   - *I took **an umbrella** with me.*
   - *The sun has gone behind **a cloud**.*
2. In contrast, you use ***the*** with a singular uncountable noun when you are referring to a particular person or thing, or when there is only one:
   - *You ought to speak to **the doctor** who gave you this medicine.*
   - *I took **the umbrella** you gave me for my birthday.*
   - ***The sun** has gone behind a cloud.*
   - *Please close **the door**.*

 ISBN 978-81-8477-745-1

3. Similarly, you use ***the*** (instead of no article) with **uncountable nouns** and **plural nouns** to refer to a particular thing or group of things:
   - ***Apples*** *are good for you, and* ***the apples*** *that grow on this tree are delicious.*
   - *I looked for* ***information*** *on the Internet, but* ***the information*** *I found was inaccurate.*

4. You use ***a*** or ***an*** the first time you mention **a thing or person**, and ***the*** when you refer to them again:
   - *Take* ***an apple*** *and* ***a knife****, then use* ***the knife*** *to peel* ***the apple****.*
   - ***A girl*** *and* ***a boy*** *were playing nearby.* ***The girl*** *looked much younger than* ***the boy****.*

When is an article not needed?

1. **Plural nouns** and **uncountable nouns** can be used **without** an article to talk about things or people in general:
   - ***Bees*** *are* ***insects****.*
   - ***Bridges*** *are built by* ***engineers****.*

2. However, you use ***the*** before **plural nouns** and **uncountable nouns** referring to specific things or people:
   - ***The bees*** *left their hive to search for nectar.*
   - ***The bridges*** *across this river are hundreds of years old.*

3. Most **proper nouns** do not need an article:
   - *I saw* ***Jack Lee*** *in the shopping mall.*
   - *Have you ever been to* ***Japan****?*

4. However, you use ***the*** before the names of rivers, seas, mountain ranges, islands, deserts, buildings and monuments:

   the *River Kwai,* ***the*** *Atlantic Ocean,* ***the*** *Alps,* ***the*** *Aleutian Islands,* ***the*** *Sahara,* ***the*** *Taj Mahal,* ***the*** *Great Wall of China*

5. You do not use an article before the name of a **game**:
   - *My father taught me how to play* ***chess****.*
   - ***Cricket*** *is more popular than* ***football*** *in our school.*

6. However, you use ***the*** before the name of a **musical instrument** that you play:
   - *My father taught me how to play* ***the guitar****.*
   - *Alice is beating a rhythm on* ***the drum****.*

7. A number of **singular countable nouns** are used without articles in certain situations, often after **prepositions**:
   - *What did you learn* ***at school*** *today?*
   - *You would get there quicker* ***by plane****.*
   - *Let's talk about this* ***after lunch****.*
   - *He'll end up* ***in prison****!*
   - *The children have gone* ***to bed****.*
   - *They left* ***before breakfast****.*

 ISBN 978-81-8477-745-1

PRACTICE

Exercise 1

Fill in the blanks with a or an.

1. The man was carrying ______ briefcase and ______ umbrella.
2. Chop up ______ large onion and add it to the mixture.
3. You will need ______ pencil, ______ eraser and ______ ruler.
4. It is ______ honour to be asked to present the prizes.
5. Is there ______ university in this town?
6. Don't forget that there is ______ 'n' at the end of the word 'solemn'.
7. My aunt has ______ oak tree and ______ eucalyptus tree in her garden.
8. We had ______ unexpected visit from the inspector.
9. I gave David ______ CD for his birthday.
10. The man was wearing ______ orange T-shirt.

Exercise 2

Rewrite the following sentences, adding the where it is required.

1. Sun was shining, so we went for a walk in park.

   ____

2. There's a telephone in every room at hotel.

   ____

3. Children who live next door go to school by bus.

   ____

4. I've put book you lent me on table.

   ____

5. We went into library to shelter from rain.

   ____

6. This is oldest house in village.

   ____

7. I saw Jenny doing exercises in gymnasium.

   ____

8. Let's go to cinema after lunch.

   ____

 ISBN 978-81-8477-745-1

9. I asked policeman if he could tell me way to station.

____

10. There is a ramp at main door for people in wheelchairs.

____

Exercise 3

Each of the following sentences contains two errors. Sometimes the wrong article has been used, sometimes an article is missing and sometimes an article has been used where it is not needed. Rewrite the sentences correctly.

1. There was lot of traffic in a town centre.

____

2. We watched boys playing the basketball.

____

3. I saw the strange light in sky last night.

____

4. Tom waited at a bus stop for a hour, but no bus came.

____

5. My sister goes to the different school from one I go to.

____

6. They sailed across an Atlantic Ocean to the America.

____

Exercise 4

Fill in the blanks in the following passage with the correct ***articles.***

'Your father has just rung to say that he's asked some people to dinner,' said Mrs Morris to her daughter Lucy. Lucy wasn't surprised. It was quite ____________ usual occurrence for her father to invite business guests home at short notice. 'Fortunately, I've got ____________ leg of lamb in ____________ fridge,' continued Mrs Morris. 'We can have ____________ apple pie I made yesterday for dessert, but we need ____________ starter.' 'Why don't you do ____________ avocado salad, Mum?' suggested Lucy. 'It's ____________ easy starter to make, it's ____________ one I like best and it's ____________ huge favourite with everyone.' 'That's ____________ excellent idea,' replied her mother. 'You can go to ____________ greengrocer's and get some avocados while I prepare ____________ lamb.'

 ISBN 978-81-8477-745-1

UNIT 13

DEMONSTRATIVE PRONOUNS AND DETERMINERS

What do they look like?

David: Do you know all **these** people?

Carol: Yes, **this** is Jack, my next-door neighbour. **That** girl over there is his daughter.

David: And who are the elderly couple looking at the picture on the wall?

Carol: **Those** are my grandparents. **This** house used to belong to them, and **that** is a photo of them on their wedding day.

SINGULAR	PLURAL
this	*these*
that	*those*

How do you use them?

1. You use demonstrative determiners like adjectives before a **noun** to show which thing or person you mean:
   - *Could you tell me the price of **that** **handbag** in the shop window?*
   - *Look at **these** **strange little insects** on my sleeve.*

2. Demonstrative pronouns **stand alone.** They sometimes replace a phrase made up of a demonstrative determiner and a **noun**:
   - *Whose boots are **those** (= those **boots**)?*
   - ***This** (= this **girl**) is my sister Tina.*

3. You use ***this*** and ***that*** before (or in place of) **singular nouns**:
   - ***This** **plate** is cracked.*
   - ***That** is the hospital where I was born.*

4. You use ***these*** and ***those*** before (or in place of) **plural nouns**:
   - ***Those** **bananas** are not ripe enough to eat.*
   - ***These** are the only keys I could find.*

 ISBN 978-81-8477-745-1

5. You use ***this*** and ***these*** to talk about things or people **near** to you:
   - *Please read* ***this*** *booklet thoroughly before operating the machine.*
   - *Those boots belong to my brother.* ***These*** *are mine.*

6. You use ***that*** and ***those*** when you talk about things or people **further away**:
   - *Do you see* ***those*** *odd-looking clouds?*
   - ***That*** *is my brother James over there.*

7. You use ***this*** and ***these*** to refer to the **present situation**, or to what is about to happen:
   - *Listen carefully.* ***These*** *instructions are important.*
   - *We're going to New Zealand for our holidays* ***this*** *year.*
   - *Look,* ***this*** *is how you do it.*
   - ***These*** *are worrying times.*

8. You use ***that*** and ***those*** to refer to **the past** and **the more distant future**:
   - *What was* ***that*** *noise?*
   - ***Those*** *points will be dealt with later.*
   - *'We're going to America next year.' '****That*** *will be exciting.'*
   - ***Those*** *were the days!*

PRACTICE

Exercise 1

In the following passage, underline all the demonstrative determiners and put a ring round all the demonstrative pronouns.

'This is the house that is for sale,' said Dad as he stopped the car. 'What do you think of it?' Mum looked at the house. 'I don't like the shape of those upstairs windows,' she said, 'but it looks OK apart from that.' We walked up the path and rang the doorbell. The owner, Mrs Green, was expecting us. 'Come this way,' she said, leading us into a large room at the front of the house. 'We use this room as our lounge,' she said, 'and that is our dining room across the hall.' Mum walked over to the window. 'I like these curtains. Will you be selling them with the house?' she asked. 'No,' replied Mrs Green, 'I'm afraid those are not for sale!'

 ISBN 978-81-8477-745-1

Exercise 2

Say whether the words in bold print are pronouns (P) or determiners (D).

1. **Those** ( ) storms must have been very frightening.
2. I'll get my revenge for **this** ( ) one day.
3. 'Hello, is **that** ( ) Susan?' said the caller.
4. **These** ( ) are the main points.
5. **That** ( ) dog has just bitten my ankle!
6. **These** ( ) socks are OK but **those** ( ) need mending.
7. **That** ( ) must be the key that opens **this** ( ) lock.
8. I know you've told me **this** ( ) many times before, but I keep forgetting.
9. My father took **that** ( ) photo of me on my first birthday.
10. **Those** ( ) are the most expensive shoes in the shop.

Exercise 3

Choose the correct demonstrative pronoun or determiner to fill in the blanks.

1. Look at ______________ (*this/that*) man at the top of the telegraph pole!
2. Few married women went out to work in ______________ (*these/those*) days.
3. I fell down the steps, and ______________ (*this/that*) is how I broke my ankle.
4. Would you like to borrow ______________ (*this/that*) book when I've finished reading it?
5. ______________ (*This/That*) is the best party I've ever been to.
6. ______________ (*These/Those*) shoes are so comfortable, I don't want to take them off!
7. Whose is ______________ (*this/that*) bicycle outside?
8. I have had ______________ (*this/that*) rash on my arm for several days.
9. ______________ (*These/Those*) are Sam's boots over there.
10. The main problem is ______________ (*this/that*): we do not have enough money.

 ISBN 978-81-8477-745-1

UNIT 14

INTERROGATIVE PRONOUNS AND DETERMINERS

What do they look like?

Mum: **Whose** hat is this? And **whose** is this briefcase?

Anna: They belong to a man who called earlier. He wanted to know **what** my name was and **which** school I went to.

Mum: **What** time did he come, and **who** was he?

Anna: About an hour ago. He said his name was Mr Black, or Mr Brown – I can't remember **which**.

DETERMINERS	PRONOUNS
what	*what*
which	*which*
whose	*whose*
	who
	whom

How do you use them?

1 **Interrogative determiners** and **pronouns** are mainly used in questions:

- ***Which*** *bus goes to the station?*
- ***Who*** *is your favourite actor?*

2 You use interrogative determiners like adjectives before a **noun** to ask for people and things to be identified:

- ***What tools*** *do you have?*
- ***Which students*** *are coming on the tour?*
- *Do you know* ***whose car*** *this is?*

 ISBN 978-81-8477-745-1

3 Interrogative pronouns **stand alone**. They sometimes refer to what follows, or to what has gone before:

- ***Whose** are these boots?*
- *There are two men in the photograph. **Which** is your father?*
- ***What** are you reading?*
- *I don't know **who** broke the window.*

4 ***What*** asks for a choice from the **whole range** of things. ***Which*** asks for a choice from a **particular group** of things:

- *'**What time** shall I come?' 'I can make you an appointment for 9.15, 10.30 or 11.45. **Which time** suits you best?'*
- *'**What drinks** do they sell?' 'They have lemonade and cola. **Which** do you prefer?'*

5 Because ***which*** asks for a choice from a group, it is often followed by ***of*** + a **pronoun** or a **noun phrase**:

- ***Which of you** saw what happened?*
- *The judges could not decide **which of the contestants** deserved the prize.*

6 ***Whose*** means 'of which person':

- ***Whose hair** is longer, Jane's or mine?*
- ***Whose** are these sunglasses?*

7 ***Who*** and ***whom*** are used only as pronouns, not as determiners. They refer only to people, not to things:

- ***Who** is your best friend?*
- *To **whom** should I send the letter?*

8 ***Who*** can be used as the **subject** or **object** of a **verb**. ***Whom*** is used only as the **object**:

- ***Who broke** the window?*
- ***Who** (or **whom**) **are** you **inviting** to your party?*

9 ***Whom*** is used as the object of a **preposition** when the preposition comes immediately before the pronoun. You can use ***who*** instead if the preposition is separated from its object:

- ***To whom** should I send the letter?*
- ***For whom** are you knitting that sweater?*
- ***Whom** (or **who**) should I send the letter **to**?*
- ***Who** (or **whom**) are you knitting that sweater **for**?*

 ISBN 978-81-8477-745-1

PRACTICE

Exercise 1

*Say whether the **interrogatives** are determiners (D) or pronouns (P). If you think they are determiners, say which noun they qualify. The first one has been done to help you.*

1. What facilities are available at the leisure centre? *D, facilities*
2. Which are your favourite subjects at school? ______
3. What is that awful smell? ______
4. I don't know which way to go. ______
5. Whose desk is this? ______
6. Who should I give the money to? ______
7. What lies have your friends been telling you about me? ______
8. With whom did you spend the afternoon? ______
9. Whose are those dirty socks? ______
10. Do you know which key opens this door? ______

Exercise 2

Choose the correct interrogative determiner or pronoun to fill in the blanks.

1. Do you know ______ (*who/whom*) wrote this book?
2. ______ (*Which/What*) do you prefer: tea or coffee?
3. I couldn't decide ______ (*what/which*) present to open first.
4. Tell me ______ (*what/which*) you want me to do.
5. To ______ (*who/whom*) was the letter addressed?
6. ______ (*What/Which*) opportunities are available for a physics graduate in this company?
7. Find out ______ (*which/whose*) dog this is and take it back to its owner.
8. ______ (*Who/Whom*) came first in the cycle race?
9. ______ (*Who/Which*) is taller: Sam or Joe?
10. The judges will decide ______ (*what/whose*) essay is the best.

 ISBN 978-81-8477-745-1

Exercise 3

Fill in the blanks in the following dialogue with the correct interrogative determiners and pronouns.

Mr Lee: Today, we're going to have a science quiz, and here's the first question. ______________ of these animals is not a fish: the shark, the dolphin, the trout or the sea horse?

Tom: The dolphin.

Mr Lee: Correct. Next question. ______________ 19th-century invention is still sometimes used to send messages, and ______________ was it?

Kate: Samuel Morse; it was the Morse code.

Mr Lee: Very good. Next question. ______________ colour is next to red in the spectrum?

Joe: Yellow.

Mr Lee: No, that's wrong. ______________ knows the right answer?

Anna: Orange.

Mr Lee: Correct. ______________ is that noise I can hear? This is not a quiz question; I can hear a mobile phone ringing. ______________ is it?

Kate: Sorry, sir, it's mine. I forgot to switch it off.

Mr Lee: OK, last question. With ______________ did James Watson work on the structure of DNA? Does anyone know the answer? No? Then go back and find out!

UNIT
15

RELATIVE PRONOUNS

What do they look like?

Robbers broke into a delivery van **whose** driver had gone for a lunch break. The goods **that** they stole, **which** are worth thousands of dollars, were computers and other electronic devices. The police would like to speak to anyone **who** saw the incident, or to **whom** the goods may have been offered for sale.

	PEOPLE	THINGS
subject	*who* or *that*	*which* or *that*
object	*who, whom* or *that*	*which* or *that*
possessive	*whose*	*whose*

How do you use them?

1 The relative pronouns ***who, whom, whose*** and ***which*** look the same as interrogative pronouns. However, instead of asking questions, they introduce an extra piece of information called a **relative clause**. The purpose of this clause is to identify or tell you more about the people or things that have just been mentioned:

- *Where is the waiter* ***who served us****?*
- *The cousins with* ***whom I spent my holidays*** *taught me how to swim.*
- *I have a friend* ***whose mother drives a taxi****.*
- *Suitcases* ***which you can wheel along*** *are the easiest to use.*
- *I'll find out the address to* ***which you must send your application****.*

2 You can use the relative pronoun ***who*** as the **subject** or **object** of a **verb**. ***Whom*** is used only as the **object**:

- *The police want the woman* ***who telephoned*** *them last night to contact them again.*
- *Is there anyone here* ***who*** *(or* ***whom****) you* ***haven't met*** *before?*

 ISBN 978-81-8477-745-1

3. The relative pronouns ***who*** and ***whom*** can also be the **object** of a **preposition**. But if the preposition comes **before** the pronoun, you must use ***whom***:
   - *I don't know the girl* ***who*** *(or* ***whom****) you were dancing* ***with****.*
   - *I don't know the girl* ***with whom*** *you were dancing.*

4. You use ***who*** and ***whom*** to refer to a **person** or **people**:
   - ***Students who*** *pass all their exams will receive a prize.*
   - *There was* ***nobody*** *to* ***whom*** *she could turn for help.*

5. You use ***which*** to refer to a **thing** or **things**. It can be the subject or object of a verb or the object of a preposition:
   - *You have to attend to* ***the problems which*** *need solving most urgently.*
   - *Here is* ***the book which*** *Michael lent me.*
   - *This was* ***something*** *for* ***which*** *I was not prepared.*

6. You can use the relative pronoun ***that*** instead of ***who, whom*** and ***which*** in many contexts, but not after a **preposition**:
   - *Is there anyone here* ***that*** *you haven't met before?*
   - *Here is the book* ***that*** *Michael lent me.*
   - *There was nobody* ***to whom*** *she could turn for help.* (not *There was nobody to* ***that*** *...*)
   - *This was something* ***for which*** *I was not prepared.* (not *This was something for* ***that*** *...*)

7. The relative pronoun ***whose*** can refer to a **person, people, thing** or **things**:
   - *In the next room was a man* ***whose*** *voice was very loud.*
   - *Parents* ***whose*** *children misbehave should be punished.*
   - *She sold me a teapot* ***whose*** *handle was broken.*
   - *Outside my bedroom are two trees* ***whose*** *branches touch my window.*

8. However, some people disapprove of using ***whose*** to refer to a thing or things. They prefer to use a phrase containing ***of which*** instead:
   - *She sold me a teapot the handle* ***of which*** *was broken.*
   - *Outside my bedroom are two trees the branches* ***of which*** *touch my window.*

You will learn more about relative pronouns and relative clauses in Unit 64.

PRACTICE

Exercise 1

Fill in the blanks with suitable ***relative pronouns****. If two or three correct answers are possible, choose one and write the others at the end of the sentence.*

1. I spotted the girl beside ____________ I'd been sitting on the train. ____________
2. Children __________ parents read to them get a good start in education. __________
3. Did you ever find the brooch ____________ you lost at the wedding? ____________
4. Here is someone ________________ you simply must meet. ________________

 ISBN 978-81-8477-745-1

5. This is the drawer in __________ all the keys are kept. __________
6. The police have removed the car __________ was blocking the entrance. __________
7. The boy __________ I'd been talking to walked away. __________
8. The teacher to __________ leaving present we contributed has written us a lovely letter. __________
9. The film __________ I was watching was rather scary. __________
10. The people __________ we travelled with were very friendly. __________

Exercise 2

Say whether the words in bold print are relative pronouns (R) or interrogative pronouns (I) in this context.

1. This is the CD **which** ( ) Alice gave me.
2. **Who** ( ) should I invite to my party?
3. Nobody knows **whose** ( ) bicycle this is.
4. Is this the girl with **whom** ( ) you were travelling?
5. I went to buy a new phone, and the assistant asked me **which** ( ) I wanted.
6. Have you spoken to the man **whose** ( ) window you broke?
7. I don't know the number of the house in **which** ( ) they live.
8. She asked him **who** ( ) he was and what he was doing there.

Exercise 3

Fill in the blanks in the following passage with suitable relative pronouns. There may be two or three correct answers, but you need only give one.

Jenny has decided to apply for a job __________ was advertised in the local newspaper. The job __________ she's applying for is a post as nanny to the children of a couple __________ spend a lot of time abroad. The address to __________ she has to write is in Bermuda. The advertisement asks for a character reference, so Jenny has to contact someone __________ can supply one for her. The couple __________ children Jenny would be looking after obviously have a jet-setting lifestyle. That is something __________ Jenny isn't used to, but she's not going to miss the chance of a job __________ offers plenty of opportunity for travel.

 ISBN 978-81-8477-745-1

UNIT 16

QUANTIFIERS

What do they look like?

Bobby cut the cake into **ten** slices and gave a slice to **each** of his guests. There was **none** left for him, but he didn't mind. He had already had **enough** to eat. **Most** of the party food had gone – there were just **a few** sandwiches left on **one** of the plates.

What are they?

1 **Quantifiers** are **quantifying determiners** and **pronouns**. They express amount, quantity or number:

- *You've made **several** mistakes.*
- *Have you had **enough** to eat?*
- ***Most** students cycle to school, but **some** come by car.*
- *'Is there **any** milk in the fridge?' 'No, there is **none** left.'*
- *I phoned Sally **three** times and got through at the **third** attempt.*

2 Some **quantifiers** consist of more than one word:

- *I have **a few** letters to write.*
- *'Would you like cream in your coffee?' 'Just **a little**, please.'*
- *Tom has **a lot of** friends.*
- *Peter couldn't finish his dinner because he had had **too much***

How do you use them?

1 You can use the following **quantifiers** before or in place of plural nouns:

all, any, both, enough, few, a few, fewer, half, a lot (of), many, more, most, not enough, not many, several, some, too many

- ***All** birds have wings, but **a few** cannot fly.*
- *Sue bought **some** sweets and gave **half** to her brother.*
- *'Do we need **more** chairs?' 'No, we have **enough**.'*
- *I dropped **several** plates, but I don't think **any** are broken.*

 ISBN 978-81-8477-745-1

2. You can use the following **quantifiers** before or in place of **uncountable nouns**:

all, any, enough, half, less, little, a little, a lot (of), more, most, much, not enough, not much, some, too much

- *There was **a lot of** work to be done, and I promised to do **half**.*
- *You must spend **more** time studying and **less** watching television.*
- *There's **not much** paint left, but I only need **a little**.*

3. You can use the following **quantifiers** before or in place of **singular countable nouns**:

another, any, each, either, half, neither, one

- ***Each** child received a gift but only **one** said thank you.*
- *If **neither** jacket fits you, I'll try to find **another**.*

4. You can also use ***every*** as a **determiner** before a **singular uncountable noun**, but you cannot use it as a **pronoun**:

- *I have read **every** book on this shelf.*

5. You can use ***no*** as a **determiner** before a **singular**, **plural** or **uncountable noun**, but you cannot use it as a **pronoun**:

- ***No** child of mine will ever go hungry!*
- *There are **no** spoons in the drawer.*
- *I had **no** difficulty learning the language.*

6. However, you can use ***none*** as a **pronoun** instead:

- *There are no spoons on the table and **none** in the drawer.*
- *Tom asked his mother for some money because he had **none**.*

7. Note that you must use ***few***, ***a few*** and ***fewer*** to talk about a small number of things (in other words, with a **plural noun**). If you want to talk about a small amount of something (in other words, with an **uncountable noun**), you must use ***little***, ***a little*** or ***less***:

- *There was **little** traffic on the road – just a **few** cars.*
- *Alice should eat **fewer** sweets and drink **less** cola.*

8. Similarly, you must use ***many*** to talk about a large number of things (in other words, with a **plural noun**) and ***much*** to talk about a large amount of something (in other words, with an **uncountable noun**):

- *Your work shows **much** improvement, but there are still **many** mistakes.*
- *Alice eats **too many** sweets and drinks **too much** cola.*

9. If you put a **quantifier** before another **determiner** (such as ***the***, ***this***, or ***my***), you usually need to separate them with ***of***:

- *I've informed **most of my** friends.*
- *We don't have **enough of those** vegetables.*

10. However, you can use ***all***, ***both*** and ***half*** before another **determiner** with or without ***of***:

- *Have you contacted **all your** clients (or **all of your** clients)?*
- ***Half these** documents (or **Half of these** documents) could be thrown away.*

 ISBN 978-81-8477-745-1

Agreement

1. When you use a quantifier as a **pronoun**, the **verb** agrees with the 'missing' noun:
   - *I dropped two eggs but **neither** (= neither egg) **was** broken.*
   - *I dropped two eggs and **both** (= both eggs) **were** broken.*

2. The pronouns ***each***, ***either*** and ***neither***, for example, are only used in place of **singular nouns**, so the verb is always **singular**:
   - *The children have no boots, but **each** (= each child) **has** a waterproof jacket.*
   - *You can borrow this skirt or that one, if **either** (= either skirt) **fits** you.*

3. The pronouns ***a few***, ***many*** and ***several***, for example, are only used in place of **plural nouns**, so the verb is always **plural**:
   - *The shelf is full of books, but only **a few** (= a few books) **belong** to me.*
   - *We have invited twenty people and **several** (= several people) **have** already said they can come.*

4. The pronouns ***all***, ***some*** and ***any***, for example, can be used with a **singular** or **plural verb**, depending on the context:
   - *I knocked over a jug of milk and **some** (= some milk) **was** spilt.*
   - *I dropped the eggs and **some** (= some eggs) **were** broken.*

You will learn more about agreement in Unit 35.

Numbers

1. You can use numbers as **determiners** or **pronouns** before or in place of **countable nouns**:
   - *I have **one** **brother** and **two** **sisters**.*
   - *There are **thirty** **apartments** in the block, **five** on each floor.*

2. The words ***one***, ***two***, ***three***, etc. are called **cardinal numbers**. Most of them are used with **plural nouns**, but you use ***one*** with a **singular countable noun**:
   - *Most cars have **four** **wheels**, but a bicycle has only **two**.*
   - *Mr Brown picked **five** **apples** from the tree and gave **one** **apple** to each child.*

3. The words ***first***, ***second***, ***third***, etc. are called **ordinal numbers**. They are typically used with **singular countable nouns** because they refer to individual things or people and the **order** in which they come:
   - *Mrs Lee lives on the **fourth** **floor** and her brother lives on the **seventh**.*
   - *You're the **fifth** **person** who has asked me that question!*

 ISBN 978-81-8477-745-1

Reciprocal pronouns

1. The phrases ***each other*** and ***one another*** are called reciprocal pronouns. They refer to a situation in which each member of a group does the same thing to all the others:
   - *The dogs chased* ***each other*** *round and round the tree.*
   - *We send* ***one another*** *cards at Christmas.*

2. Some people prefer to use ***each other*** to talk about a group of two, and ***one another*** for larger groups:
   - *Tom and Kate are very fond of* ***each other****.*
   - *If the apples touch* ***one another*** *in the box, they will rot more quickly.*

3. However, it is not incorrect to use the pronouns the other way round:
   - *Tom and Kate are very fond of* ***one another****.*
   - *If the apples touch* ***each other*** *in the box, they will rot more quickly.*

4. Notice the difference between a **reciprocal pronoun** and a **reflexive pronoun**:
   - *The child's parents blamed* ***each other****.* (= The mother blamed the father and the father blamed the mother.)
   - *The child's parents blamed* ***themselves****.* (= The mother and the father thought they were both to blame.)

PRACTICE

Exercise 1

Use the quantifiers in the box to replace the words and phrases in ***bold print*** *without changing the meaning of the sentence. Use each quantifier once only, and write it in the brackets after the word or phrase it replaces.*

every	few	little	much	several	some

1. Many people try, but **not many** (____________) succeed.
2. I laugh **each** (____________) time I read this story.
3. There were **a few** (____________) tickets left.
4. Put **a little** (____________) oil in the pan.
5. Uncle Jack spends **a lot** (____________) of his leisure time in the garden.
6. There is **not much** (____________) difference between these two colours.

 ISBN 978-81-8477-745-1

Exercise 2

Choose suitable quantifiers to fill in the blanks. Do not use the same word or phrase more than once, and do not use any numbers apart from one.

1. Joe can speak Japanese, but ______________ of his parents can.
2. I dropped ______________ of my earrings in the street; I doubt if I'll find another to match.
3. ______________ the twins ride, but I don't think ______________ owns a horse.
4. Don't eat too ______________ ice cream.
5. I couldn't find ______________ scissors, so I used a knife instead.
6. This car uses ______________ petrol than our old one, so it is cheaper to run.
7. "Did I make ______________ mistakes?" "No, just ______________."
8. There are ______________ students in our class, so we don't need so many desks.

Exercise 3

Use the quantifiers in the box to fill the blanks in the following passage.

a few	all	any	both	each	either	first
little	most	neither	no	second	some	two

Tom was near the end of his final year at university. Like ______________ his fellow-students, he was applying for jobs, and had ______________ interviews for jobs in publishing. ______________ were of interest to him, and he intended to accept ______________ post if it was offered to him. ______________ had its own advantages, though ______________ was well paid. When he went for the ______________ interview, he looked at the other applicants and thought that ______________ seemed better qualified for the job than he was. In fact, ______________ seemed over-qualified. Tom had ______________ experience of the publishing industry, and ______________ experience of ______________ kind of paid work, apart from ______________ holiday jobs. However, to his surprise and delight, he was offered the post. He didn't need to go to the ______________ interview!

Exercise 4: grammar for writing

Write a short passage called 'Protecting the Planet', about 100 words long, using twelve different quantifiers. When you have finished, underline the words and phrases that are quantifiers.

____

____

 ISBN 978-81-8477-745-1

UNIT 17

INDEFINITE PRONOUNS

What do they look like?

The audience was waiting for the show to begin. **Nobody** realized that there was **anything** wrong. Then **someone** said they could smell smoke. **Something** was on fire. Flames appeared, and **everybody** rushed for the exit. There was **nothing** that **anyone** could do to stop the blaze. **Everything** was burnt – the building and all its contents.

THINGS	PEOPLE
something	*someone* or *somebody*
anything	*anyone* or *anybody*
everything	*everyone* or *everybody*
nothing	*no one* or *nobody*

How do you use them?

1. You use an **indefinite pronoun** when you are not referring to any particular person or thing:
   - *There's **something** stuck to the bottom of my shoe.*
   - *Are there enough seats for **everybody**?*
   - *Can I do **anything** to help?*
   - ***No one** can beat James at chess.*

2. The pronouns ***anything*** and ***anyone/anybody*** are often used in place of ***something*** and ***someone/somebody*** in **questions** and **negative sentences**:
   - *I thought I heard **someone** call my name. Is **anyone** there?*
   - *I need **something** to wear to Jane's wedding. I don't have **anything** smart enough.*

3. You can put an **adjective** after an **indefinite pronoun**:
   - *Did you meet **anybody** **interesting** at the party?*
   - ***Nothing** **definite** has been decided.*

 ISBN 978-81-8477-745-1

4. The indefinite pronouns are **singular**. You use them with a singular verb, for example:
   - ***Is anybody** going to meet you at the station?*
   - ***No one makes** better curry than you do.*

5. However, you may use the plural pronouns ***they them*** and ***themselves***, and the plural determiner ***their*** to refer to ***someone/somebody, anyone/anybody, everyone/everybody*** and ***no one/nobody***:
   - ***Somebody** has left **their** coat behind.*
   - *Can **everyone** see **themselves** in the mirror?*

6. Some people prefer to use ***he or she***, ***him or her***, ***himself or herself*** and ***his or her*** to refer to these indefinite pronouns:
   - ***Somebody** has left **his or her** coat behind.*
   - *Can **everyone** see **himself or herself** in the mirror?*

PRACTICE

Exercise 1

Fill in the gaps with suitable indefinite pronouns.

1. 'Would you like something to eat?' 'Yes, please, I haven't eaten ______________ all day!'
2. 'Is there anything you haven't told me?' 'No, I've told you ______________.'
3. 'Did anybody phone while I was out?' 'Yes, ______________ phoned half an hour ago. They said they'd call back later.'
4. 'Was there anyone else in the room?' 'No, there was ______________ there but me.'
5. 'Is everything all right?' 'No, there's ______________ wrong with my computer.'
6. 'Has everything been done?' 'Yes, there's ______________ left to do.'
7. 'Is anyone missing?' 'No, ______________ is here.'
8. 'Can somebody help you with this problem?' 'No, I don't think ______________ can help.'
9. 'Is everyone telling the truth?' 'No, I think ______________ is lying.'
10. 'Can you see anything?' 'Yes, I can see ______________ small and dark in the corner.'

 ISBN 978-81-8477-745-1

Exercise 2

*Rewrite the following sentences, replacing **they**, **their**, etc. with **he or she**, **his or her**, etc.*

1. If anyone needs help, they must ask the instructor.

   ____

2. Nobody likes to hear their work being criticized.

   ____

3. Everyone helped themselves to food.

   ____

4. Someone must have taken the key home with them.

   ____

5. Everybody thinks theirs is the most urgent problem.

   ____

6. Did anybody park their car on the drive?

   ____

7. No one can lift a heavy weight like this by themselves.

   ____

8. When somebody asks you a question, you should answer them politely.

   ____

Exercise 3

*Fill in the gaps in the following passage with suitable **indefinite pronouns**. (Use **someone**, **anyone**, etc. rather than **somebody**, **anybody**, etc.)*

'Has ____________ seen my engagement ring?' asked Lucy. 'I'm sure I was wearing it when I came to work this morning, but I may have left it in the ladies' room when I washed my hands. I hope ____________ hasn't stolen it from there.' 'I don't think ____________ here would steal it,' said Diane, 'and ____________ from outside has been in the office today. Think about ____________ you have done since you came to work. You might remember ____________ useful. And if you ask ____________ in the office, ____________ might have seen what happened to it.' Lucy sent an email to all her colleagues, but she had heard ____________ from ____________ by lunchtime. She was beginning to get rather worried. 'Is ____________ wrong?' asked her boss, who had not received Lucy's email. Just then, one of the cleaners came into the office. 'Does this belong to ____________ here?' she asked, holding up the missing ring. 'I found it when I was sweeping the ladies' room. It nearly ended up in the bin!'

 ISBN 978-81-8477-745-1

3 ADJECTIVES

 ISBN 978-81-8477-745-1

UNIT 18

ADJECTIVES

What do they look like?

It was a **bright**, **sunny** day. A **young** boy was walking through the woods. He was looking for something **unusual** to take to school the **following** day. Suddenly, he spotted a **large brown** nut on the ground. It was **round** and **shiny**. This was just what he needed – his teacher would be very **impressed**.

What are they?

1. An **adjective** is a **describing word.** It describes **people** or **things**. Words for people and things are nouns. So **adjectives** describe **nouns**.

2. Adjectives tell you such things as the **size**, **shape**, **colour**, **material** or **quality** of a person or thing:

   a **tiny** insect | a **round** mat | a **purple** dress
   plastic spoons | **sticky** rice | a **boring** film

3. You can use adjectives in **recounts** and **narratives** to give vivid descriptions of the setting or the people and things involved. You can also use them in **procedures** to make it clear exactly what is needed, and in **information reports** to give precise details of people, animals, places or things.

Where do you put them?

Adjectives can come in **three positions** in a sentence: **attributive**, **predicative** and **postpositive.**

1. You can put an adjective **before** the noun that it describes (or 'qualifies'). This is the **attributive** position:
   - *My **wealthy** cousins rent a **spacious** apartment.*
   - *There was a **nationwide** search for the **missing** children.*

   Nouns used as adjectives are always in the attributive position:
   - *You must obey the **school** rules.*
   - *Put the tray on the **coffee** table.*
   - *The house has a **swimming** pool and a **tennis** court.*
   - *Our **hotel** room was very small.*

 ISBN 978-81-8477-745-1

2. You can put an adjective **after** a **linking verb,** such as ***be***, ***become***, ***feel***, or ***get***. This is the **predicative** position. The adjective is the **complement** of the linking verb:
   - *The box* ***is*** ***empty***.
   - *It* ***was getting*** ***dark***.
   - *I* ***feel*** ***sick***.
   - *Ben* ***seemed*** *rather* ***upset***.

   Some adjectives can **only** be used in the **predicative** position. They include:

   afraid | alike | alive | alone | asleep
   awake | glad | ready | unwell

   You can say, for example:
   - *The baby is* ***asleep***.
   - *The man felt* ***unwell***.

   but you **cannot** say 'the asleep baby' or 'the unwell man'.

3. You can put an adjective **directly after** a **noun** (or **pronoun**). This is called the **postpositive** position:
   - *We cannot complete the job in the* ***time*** ***available***.
   - *Are you doing* ***anything*** ***interesting*** *this evening?*
   - ***Nobody*** ***suitable*** *applied for the post.*
   - ***Those*** ***present*** *gave their full support to the scheme.*

   There are certain **fixed noun phrases** in which the **adjective** is postpositive:
   - *He was tried by* ***court*** ***martial***.
   - *The gang threatened to kidnap the* ***heir*** ***apparent***.

How do you use them?

1. You can use **two or more adjectives** in a string:
   - *The girl had* ***long black*** *hair.*
   - *The day was* ***calm***, ***sunny*** *and* ***warm***.

2. If there is also a **determiner**, it comes **before** any **attributive adjectives**:
   - ***My*** ***clumsy*** *sister broke* ***a*** ***valuable*** *ornament*
   - *What shall I do with* ***these*** ***dirty woollen*** *socks?*

3. Many **adjectives** can be used in phrases such as ***more … than***, ***as … as*** and ***so … that***:
   - *Geography is* ***more*** ***interesting*** ***than*** *history.*
   - *The film was* ***less*** ***scary*** ***than*** *I had expected it to be.*
   - *Sally's face went* ***as*** ***white*** ***as*** *a sheet.*
   - *Joe felt* ***so*** ***excited*** ***that*** *he could not sleep.*

 ISBN 978-81-8477-745-1

4. Some **adjectives** are frequently followed by a particular **preposition**:
   - *The basement is **full of** water.*
   - *Mum is **keen on** jazz music.*

   You will learn more about these in Unit 59.

5. Some **adjectives** can introduce a ***to*-infinitive**:
   - *Frank is always **eager to please**.*
   - *I was **afraid to mention** it.*
   - *The soup was too **hot to eat**.*
   - *It is **unfair** of you **to blame** Jenny.*

   You will learn more about these in Unit 38.

Adjectives that can become nouns

1. You can put ***the*** before certain **adjectives** to make them into nouns referring to a **class of people within the community**:

the blind	***the*** deaf	***the*** disabled	***the*** poor
the rich	***the*** innocent	***the*** sick	***the*** injured
the homeless	***the*** unemployed	***the*** old	***the*** young

   - *The government was accused of neglecting **the sick** and **the homeless**.*
   - *There are no facilities for **the disabled** at the leisure centre.*

2. You can also put ***the*** before certain **adjectives of nationality** to make them into nouns referring to the people of a country:

the British	***the*** Chinese	***the*** French	***the*** Japanese	***the*** Spanish

   - *Do **the Chinese** use the same alphabet as **the Japanese**?*
   - ***The Spanish** beat **the British** in yesterday's game.*

3. Since these nouns of class or nationality refer to **groups of people**, they are **plural nouns** used with a **plural verb**:
   - ***The young** (= young people) **have** a duty to help **the old** (= old people).*
   - ***The English** (= English people) **were** at war with **the French** (= French people) at this time.*

4. ***The*** can sometimes be placed before an **adjective** to make it into a **noun** referring to **an individual person**, especially in legal language. You use a **singular verb** with these nouns:
   - ***The deceased** (= the dead person) **was** a woman of considerable wealth.*
   - ***The accused** (= the accused person) **has** already admitted that he was at the scene of the crime.*

 ISBN 978-81-8477-745-1

5 ***The*** can be placed before many other adjectives to create **uncountable nouns** referring to **a general type of thing**:

- ***The supernatural has*** *always fascinated me.*
- *He's very skilful, but he cannot do* ***the impossible****.*

6 However, some adjectives are used as **uncountable nouns** without ***the***:

- *Even small children know the difference between* ***right*** *and* ***wrong****.*
- ***Red is*** *my favourite colour.*

PRACTICE

Exercise 1

Underline the adjectives in the following sentences. Say whether they are in the attributive (A), predicative (P) or postpositive (PP) position.

1. Do you like my new camera? ( )
2. Miss Williams is our English teacher. ( )
3. If you can't say something sensible, don't say anything at all! ( )
4. The fruit tasted bitter so I did not eat it. ( )
5. The police want to question the people involved. ( )
6. I wish I was good at sport! ( )
7. The books were in a cardboard box. ( )
8. Are all the eggs broken? ( )
9. There was nobody interesting at the party. ( )
10. Jack felt nervous before his interview. ( )

Exercise 2

Fill in the blanks with an adjective from box A and a noun from box B.

A: careless dark deep favourite heavy hot interesting loud silver tight

B: book cry hole meal mistake necklace rain shoes shower stain

1. I need an ______________ ______________ to read on the train.
2. Joe made a ______________ ______________ in the maths test.

 ISBN 978-81-8477-745-1

3. The spilt wine had left a ____________ ____________ on the carpet.
4. The weather forecast said there would be ____________ ____________ this afternoon.
5. It's bad for your feet to wear ____________ ____________.
6. Lunch is my ____________ ____________.
7. Dad likes to have a ____________ ____________ when he gets home from work.
8. The silence was broken by a ____________ ____________.
9. The woman was wearing a ____________ ____________.
10. The children had dug a ____________ ____________ in the sand.

Exercise 3

In the following passage, underline any nouns used as adjectives and put a ring round any adjectives used as nouns.

There was a council meeting in the town hall last Monday. The main subject of discussion was helping those in need. 'We must provide cheaper housing for the homeless,' said Mr Green. 'Several new apartment blocks have been built, but only the rich can afford to live there.' 'We must also give some thought to the young,' said Mrs Black. 'There is not enough for them to do in their leisure time – we need more sports facilities, such as a new athletics stadium.' 'Perhaps we should take a look at what other countries do,' suggested Mr Brown. 'How do the Japanese, for example, deal with these problems?' 'I hope you're not hoping to have a free holiday to Japan at our expense,' said Mrs White. Everyone laughed.

Exercise 4: grammar for writing

Write a short passage, about 100 words long, describing a person you know. Use a mixture of attributive and predicative adjectives in your description.

____

____

____

____

 ISBN 978-81-8477-745-1

UNIT 19

ADJECTIVES FORMED FROM OTHER WORDS

What do they look like?

Jane's father is a **successful** businessman. As a result, the family is very **wealthy**. They live in an **expensive** house in one of the most **desirable residential** areas of the city. The house is full of **luxurious** furnishings and **priceless** ornaments. Jane's mother wears **stylish** clothes and travels a lot. Everyone envies her **exciting** lifestyle.

Many common adjectives do not have a distinctive adjectival ending, for example:

good bad kind fat thin tall

small wide narrow fast slow

But a lot of adjectives do have a recognizable **adjectival ending**, which is added to a **noun**, a **verb** or another **adjective**, for example:

*wash**able*** *nation**al*** *legend**ary*** *concern**ed*** *depend**ent***

*thought**ful*** *hero**ic*** *interest**ing*** *green**ish*** *attract**ive***

*hope**less*** *friend**ly*** *danger**ous*** *health**y***

Some adjectives with these endings are not formed from other words, for example:

punctual instant ordinary magic English

positive previous strenuous silly

How do you form them?

1. You can add the endings ***ful, ous*** and ***y*** to **nouns**. They form adjectives that mean 'having this quality or thing':

help → help***ful*** danger → danger***ous*** sleep → sleep***y***

- *a **useful** tool*
- *this **mountainous** region*
- *her **dirty** hands*

 ISBN 978-81-8477-745-1

If the noun ends in a consonant followed by *y*, you change the *y* to *i* before adding ***ful*** or ***ous***:

beauty → beaut*iful*   fury → fur*ious*

If the noun ends in ***e***, you usually remove this letter before adding ***ous*** or ***y***, but not before adding ***ful***:

fame → fam*ous*   noise → nois*y*   grace → grace*ful*

If the noun ends in ***our***, you change this to ***or*** before adding ***ous***:

hum*our* → hum*orous*   rig*our* → rig*orous*

If the noun ends in a single vowel followed by a **consonant** other than ***w***, and has only one syllable, you **double the final consonant** before adding ***y***:

fu*n* → fu*nny*   mu*d* → mu*ddy*   BUT   sleep → sleep*y*   snow → snow*y*

2 You can add the ending ***less*** to **nouns**. It forms adjectives that mean 'not having this quality or thing':

care → care*less*   child → child*less*

- ***flightless*** *birds*
- *a* ***meaningless*** *word*

If the noun ends in a consonant followed by *y*, you change the *y* to *i* before adding ***less***:

pit*y* → pit*iless*   merc*y* → merc*iless*

3 You can add the endings ***al*** and ***ary*** to **nouns**. They form adjectives that mean 'of or being this thing':

option → option*al*   revolution → revolution*ary*

- ***vocational*** *training*
- *a* ***legendary*** *creature*

If the noun ends in ***e***, you usually remove this letter before adding ***al***:

nature → natur*al*   globe → glob*al*

If the noun ends in ***ce***, you change this to ***ti*** or ***ci*** before adding ***al***:

residen*ce* → residen*tial*   spa*ce* → spa*tial*   ra*ce* → ra*cial*

4 You can add the ending ***ic*** to **nouns**. It forms adjectives that mean 'of or like this thing':

hero → hero*ic*   patriot → patriot*ic*

- *her* ***artistic*** *ability*
- *the* ***scenic*** *route*

 ISBN 978-81-8477-745-1

If the noun ends in a **vowel** or ***y***, you remove this letter before adding ***ic***:

scene → scen***ic***	volcano → volcan***ic***
majesty → majest***ic***	geometry → geometr***ic***

5 You can add the ending ***ish*** to **nouns**. It forms adjectives that mean 'like or typical of this person or thing':

boy → boy***ish***	fool → fool***ish***

- *this **childish** behaviour*
- *a **girlish** smile*

You can also add the ending ***ish*** to **adjectives**. It forms adjectives that mean 'rather or a bit like this':

green → green***ish***	small → small***ish***

- *a **youngish** man*
- *the **yellowish** liquid*

If the noun or adjective ends in ***e***, you usually remove this letter before adding ***ish***:

style → styl***ish***	blue → blu***ish***

If the noun or adjective ends in a single vowel followed by a consonant other than ***w***, and has only one syllable, you double the final consonant before adding ***ish***:

sno***b*** → sno***bbish***	re***d*** → re***ddish***

6 You can add the ending ***ly*** to **nouns**. It forms adjectives that mean 'having this quality', 'being like this person' or 'happening once in this period of time':

cost → cost***ly***	mother → mother***ly***	week → week***ly***

- *an **orderly** queue*
- *the **friendly** policeman*
- *my **monthly** visit to Grandma*

You can also add the ending ***ly*** to **adjectives**. It forms adjectives that mean 'like this':

sick → sick***ly***	dead → dead***ly***

- *a **kindly** man*
- ***lonely** children*

7 You can add the ending ***some*** to **nouns**, **adjectives** and **verbs**. It forms adjectives that mean 'causing this thing, quality or action':

fear → fear***some***	lone → lone***some***	quarrel → quarrel***some***

- *an **awesome** achievement*
- ***wholesome** food*
- *that **meddlesome** woman*

8 You can add the endings ***ant,*** and ***ent*** and ***ive*** to **verbs**. They form adjectives describing a person or thing that is the **subject** of the **verb**:

repent → repent***ant*** differ → differ***ent*** construct → construct***ive***

- *An **expectant crowd expects** something to happen.*
- ***Dependent relatives depend** on someone else.*
- *An **attractive personality attracts** people.*

If the verb ends in ***e***, you remove this letter before adding ***ant***, ***ent*** or ***ive***:

please → pleas***ant*** observe → observ***ant*** relate → relat***ive***

If the verb ends in ***d*** or ***de***, you usually change this to **s** before adding ***ive*** (but not before adding ***ant*** or ***ent***):

defen***d*** → defen***sive*** deci***de*** → deci***sive***

9 You can add the ending ***able*** to **verbs**. It forms adjectives describing a person or thing that can be the **object** of the **verb**:

enjoy → enjoy***able*** read → read***able***

- *You can **wash** a **washable fabric.***
- *You can **depend** on **dependable people.***

You can also add the ending ***able*** to **nouns**. It forms adjectives that mean 'having this quality':

peace → peace***able*** fashion → fashion***able***

If the verb or noun ends in a consonant followed by ***y***, you change the ***y*** to ***i*** before adding ***able***:

rel***y*** → rel***iable*** den***y*** → den***iable***

If the verb or noun ends in ***e***, you often remove this letter before adding ***able***, but not always:

cure → cur***able*** forgive → forgiv***able***

BUT

manage → manage***able*** knowledge → knowledge***able***

If the verb or noun ends in a single vowel followed by a **consonant**, you usually **double the final consonant** before adding ***able***:

hu***g*** → hu***ggable*** regre***t*** → regre***ttable***

Note that some adjectives have the ending ***ible*** instead of ***able***, for example:

flex***ible*** contempt***ible*** sens***ible*** collaps***ible*** revers***ible***

horr***ible*** cred***ible*** poss***ible*** leg***ible*** ed***ible***

 ISBN 978-81-8477-745-1

10 You can add the ending ***ing*** to **verbs**. It forms a **present participle** used as an adjective. This adjective describes the **subject** of the verb:

flash → flash***ing***	interest → interest***ing***

- *A **frightening story** frightens people.*
- ***Shocking news** shocks people.*

You will learn more about present participles and their spelling rules in Unit 24.

11 You can add the ending ***ed*** to **verbs**. It forms a **past participle** used as an adjective. This adjective describes the **object** of the verb:

abandon → abandon***ed***	frighten → frighten***ed***

- *A ghost haunts the **house**. It is a **haunted house**.*
- *Medical matters interest many of our **students**. These **interested students** may go on to become doctors.*

You will learn more about past participles and their spelling rules in Unit 24.

You can also add the ending ***ed*** to **nouns**. It forms adjectives that mean 'having this thing':

beard → beard***ed***	talent → talent***ed***

PRACTICE

Exercise 1

Form adjectives by combining the given word with the ending. Remember that some words need to be changed before the ending is added.

1. life + less	=	______	2. geography + ic	=	______
3. fog + y	=	______	4. mercy + ful	=	______
5. slave + ish	=	______	6. compliment + ary	=	______
7. essence + al	=	______	8. glamour + ous	=	______
9. dance + ing	=	______	10. poet + ic	=	______
11. pit + ed	=	______	12. bead + y	=	______

 ISBN 978-81-8477-745-1

Exercise 2

Fill in the blanks with adjectives formed from the words in brackets, using two of the three endings given for each sentence.

1. It was a ______________ (*beauty*) day with a completely ______________ (*cloud*) sky. (*ary, ful, less*)
2. Sophie had a ______________ (*fever*) cold with a ______________ (*trouble*) cough. (*ish, ly, some*)
3. Our ______________ (*charm*) hosts made our stay most ______________ (*enjoy*). (*able, ed, ing*)
4. We took a ______________ (*leisure*) evening walk under the ______________ (*star*) sky. (*ful, ly, y*)
5. My teacher was quite ______________ (*compliment*) about my ______________ (*artist*) efforts. (*al, ary, ic*)
6. Paul has an ______________ (*attract*) smile and a ______________ (*please*) personality. (*ant, ish, ive*)
7. ______________ (*Education*) toys are a ______________ (*use*) way of helping young children learn. (*al, ant, ful*)
8. There are ______________ (*danger*) currents in the deep ______________ (*mud*) water. (*ary, ous, y*)
9. We made slow progress through the ______________ (*wind*) lanes and ______________ (*crowd*) streets. (*ed, ful, ing*)
10. The ______________ (*sleep*) boy lay down on the ______________ (*comfort*) bed. (*able, ive, y*)

Exercise 3

Fill in the blanks with adjectives by combining each word in brackets with one of the endings from the box. Use each ending only once.

able	al	ed	ful	ic	ing	ive	less	ly	y

There has been an ______________ (*alarm*) increase in the number of deaths among ______________ (*elder*) people in recent months. ______________ (*worry*) doctors have expressed their concern about these statistics. A major factor in the ______________ (*substance*) increase in deaths was the very cold winter. Older people are less ______________ (*act*) than others, and often live in ______________ (*draught*) homes, so they suffer far more from the ______________ (*harm*) effects of cold. There is also an ______________ (*economy*) factor. For some old people, having the central heating on all day is not an ______________ (*afford*) option. They spend many ______________ (*sleep*) nights worrying how they will pay their bills.

 ISBN 978-81-8477-745-1

UNIT 20

TYPES OF ADJECTIVES AND THEIR ORDER

What do they look like?

The man was wearing a **thick woollen** jacket and **faded blue** jeans. He had **short**, **dark**, **greasy** hair and an **ugly**, **unshaven**, **round** face. He said he worked for an **American financial** company, but I didn't believe him. I didn't like the look in his **shifty grey** eyes.

What are the different types?

There are several **types of adjectives**. They describe or express the following things:

- **size**: *large, small, tall, high, wide, long, deep, thin, thick, fat*
- **opinion**: *nice, nasty, horrible, beautiful, ugly*
- **quality**: *colourful, difficult, happy, easy, strong, strange*
- **age**: *young, old, new, elder*
- **temperature**: *hot, warm, cool, cold*
- **shape**: *round, flat, circular, square, pointed*
- **colour**: *blue, red, green, yellow, purple*
- **origin** or **nationality**: *English, French, Indian, Japanese, Australian*
- **material**: *cotton, leather, paper, plastic, steel, wooden, woollen*
- **type** or **class**: *electronic, automatic, medical, political, weekly, yearly*

What is the correct order?

You can use **two** or **more adjectives** before a noun, but the various kinds of adjectives have to be used **in the right order:**

size, opinion, quality, age, temperature, shape, colour, origin/nationality, material, type/class

- *a **long boring** story* [size, quality]
- *an **ugly grey** building* [opinion, colour]
- *a **little old** man* [size, age]
- *an **efficient new female** manager* [opinion, age, type]
- *a **large cool** drink* [size, temperature]
- *a **big square** mat* [size, shape]
- *a **thick green** book* [size, colour]

 ISBN 978-81-8477-745-1

- a ***small round red*** *badge* [size, shape, colour]
- ***warm woollen*** *clothing* [temperature, material]
- ***expensive Italian leather*** *shoes* [quality, origin, material]
- *the* ***Taiwanese political*** *system* [origin, type]

Nouns used as adjectives belong to the **type** or **class** group of adjectives. They come last in a **string of adjectives**:

- ***fluffy pink*** *bedroom slippers*
- ***ugly square brick*** *office buildings*

Using commas between adjectives

1. When you use a string of adjectives that are of **different kinds**, you don't need to put commas between them:
   - *a* ***high grey stone*** *wall* [size, colour, material]
   - *a* ***lengthy detailed chemical*** *analysis* [size, quality, type]

2. When you use a string of **quality** or **opinion** adjectives, you usually put commas between them, for example:
   - ***confident, ambitious, successful*** *people*
   - *a* ***nasty, mean, dishonest*** *trick*

3. Two **size** adjectives don't need a comma between them, but you can add a comma if you want to emphasize each adjective separately:
   - ***short fat*** *people*
   - *a* ***tall, thin*** *man*

4. If you use two or more **type** or **class** adjectives together, you should not put commas between them:
   - *my* ***weekly piano*** *lesson*
   - ***online academic reference*** *works*

5. If you use two adjectives together to describe something that has two different **colours** or is made of two different **materials** or involves two different **types** of things, you must put ***and*** between the adjectives:
   - *a* ***black and yellow*** *insect*
   - *a* ***steel and canvas*** *chair*
   - *an* ***apple and blackberry*** *pie*

6. If you use two adjectives after a **linking verb** (that is, in the **predicative position**), you put ***and*** between them. If you use more than two adjectives, you put **and** between the last two, and commas between the others:
   - *Her hair was* ***long and straight****.*
   - *Her hair was* ***long, straight, black and greasy****.*

 ISBN 978-81-8477-745-1

PRACTICE

Exercise 1

Put the adjectives in the box under the correct headings below.

annoying	awful	beautiful	bright	cardboard	huge	daily
digital	gentle	disgusting	glass	concrete	legal	low
manual	massive	photographic	metal	pleasant	silk	simple
slim	tiny	uncommon	weak			

SIZE	OPINION	QUALITY	MATERIAL	TYPE

Exercise 2

Rewrite the following sentences, putting the adjectives in bold print in the ***correct order.***

1. Whose are those **satin ballet lovely** shoes?

   ____

2. I've just been reading a **medical fascinating Swedish** report.

   ____

3. I put a **heavy English big** dictionary on top of the papers to stop them blowing away.

   ____

4. The park was full of **oak large beautiful** trees.

   ____

5. Do you like my **leather new black** jacket?

   ____

6. The man was driving a **sports shiny red** car.

   ____

 ISBN 978-81-8477-745-1

7. The town hall is a **big brick ugly** building.

____

8. There was a **marble Italian white** fireplace in the dining room.

____

9. We had to listen to a **political long boring** debate.

____

10. I need a **square picture small** frame to put this photo in.

____

Exercise 3

*Use the **adjectives** in brackets, in the **correct order**, to fill in the blanks. In some places, the order does not matter, but you may need to add a **comma** or the word 'and'.*

My grandfather lived in an __________ (*old ugly*) house at the end of a __________ (*long winding*) drive. It was surrounded by __________ (*coniferous tall*) trees which made it __________ (*dark gloomy*) inside. However, my grandfather was a __________ (*successful wealthy*) man and the house contained many treasures. In the centre of the dining room was a __________ (*huge mahogany*) table, which stood on a __________ (*Chinese colourful*) rug. There were __________ (*oil valuable*) paintings on the walls of this and other rooms. The lounge was __________ (*grand spacious*). It had a __________ (*large uncomfortable*) sofa upholstered in __________ (*grey pink*) fabric, with two matching chairs. An __________ (*ornate oval*) mirror hung over the __________ (*carved marble*) fireplace. All in all, the house had an __________ (*unfriendly unwelcoming*) atmosphere. Although I loved my grandfather, I did not enjoy visiting his home.

Exercise 4: grammar for writing

Write a short passage, about 100 words long, describing an outdoor place such as a town centre or a country scene. Your description should contain at least ten strings of two or three adjectives, in the right order.

____

____

____

 ISBN 978-81-8477-745-1

UNIT 21

COMPARATIVE AND SUPERLATIVE ADJECTIVES

What do they look like?

Henry is the **youngest** student in his class, and also one of the **tallest**. Most of the **older** boys and girls are **smaller** than him. Tom is the **cleverest** student, but his handwriting is the **most untidy**. Henry's handwriting is not perfect, but it is **better** and **more readable** than Tom's.

Adjectives have three forms or 'degrees': the **positive**, the **comparative** and the **superlative**. The normal base form of the adjective is the **positive**. The **comparative** and **superlative** forms are used in comparisons.

POSITIVE	COMPARATIVE	SUPERLATIVE
neat	*neater*	*neatest*
happy	*happier*	*happiest*
precious	*more precious*	*most precious*
difficult	*more difficult*	*most difficult*
good	*better*	*best*

How do you form them?

1. Adjectives with one syllable, and some **two-syllable** ones, have a **comparative** form ending in ***er*** and a **superlative** form ending in ***est***:

clean	*clean**er***	*clean**est***
narrow	*narrow**er***	*narrow**est***

2. If the adjective ends in ***e***, you remove this letter before adding ***er*** or ***est***:

close	*clos**er***	*clos**est***
gentle	*gentl**er***	*gentl**est***

3. If the adjective ends in a single vowel followed by a consonant other than *w*, and has only one syllable, you double the final consonant before adding ***er*** or ***est***:

hot	*hott**er***	*hott**est***
slim	*slimm**er***	*slimm**est***

 ISBN 978-81-8477-745-1

4 If a two-syllable adjective ends in a consonant followed by ***y***, you change the ***y*** to ***i*** before adding ***er*** and ***est***:

lonely	*lonel**ier***	*lonel**iest***
friendly	*friendl**ier***	*friendl**iest***

5 For most adjectives of **two or more syllables,** you use ***more*** to form the **comparative** and ***most*** to form the **superlative.** These words come before the adjective:

splendid	***more** splendid*	***most** splendid*
reasonable	***more** reasonable*	***most** reasonable*

6 Some adjectives have **irregular** comparative and superlative forms:

good	***better***	***best***
bad	***worse***	***worst***

far, ***farther*** or ***further***, ***farthest*** or ***furthest*** [***farther*** and ***farthest*** are used only to talk about distance]
old, ***older*** or ***elder***, ***oldest*** or ***eldest*** [***elder*** and ***eldest*** are used only to talk about members of a family]

7 Some **quantifiers** and **adverbs** have comparative and superlative forms:

few	***fewer***	***fewest***
little	***less***	***least***
many	***more***	***most***
much	***more***	***most***

You have already learnt about these **quantifiers** in Unit 16. You will learn about **comparative** and **superlative adverbs** in Unit 53.

8 Some adjectives, such as ***complete*** and ***unique***, cannot be used in comparative or superlative forms. One thing cannot be 'more complete' than another – it is either complete or not. Such adjectives are called **non-gradable adjectives**, and here are some more examples:
dead, equal, excellent, faultless, final, flawless, perfect, superb

How do you use them?

1 You use the **comparative** form when comparing **two** people or things, to express the idea that one deserves the adjective more than the other:

- *Mr Green has two daughters. His **younger** daughter is called Anna.*
- *These earrings are **more expensive** than those.*

 ISBN 978-81-8477-745-1

2 You use the **superlative** form when comparing **three** or **more** people or things, to express the idea that one deserves the adjective more than both or all the others:

- *Mrs Black has three sons. Her **youngest** son is called Tom.*
- *I bought the **most expensive** necklace in the shop.*

3 You can also form **comparatives** with *less* and **superlatives** with *least* to express the idea of one person or thing having less of a quality than the other or others:

- *This is a **less common** spelling of the word.*
- *Sally is the **least popular** girl in the class.*

4 You use the **positive** form of the adjective in comparisons with *as*:

- *The child's hands felt **as cold as** ice.*
- *This box is not **as heavy as** that one.*

5 You use the **comparative** form of the adjective in comparisons with *than*:

- *That box is **heavier than** this one.*
- *Tom wears **more elegant** clothes **than** his brother does.*
- *Choose any number **greater than** one.*

6 You can use **comparative adjectives** in pairs with *and* to express the idea of a situation intensifying:

- *My headache was getting **worse and worse**.*
- *The sky grew **lighter and lighter** in the east.*

7 You can use **comparative adjectives** in pairs with *the* to express the idea of one change causing another:

- ***The richer** she grew, **the more miserly** she became.*
- ***The clearer** the air is, **the brighter** the sun will be.*

8 You usually put *the* in front of a **superlative adjective**, but a possessive determiner or possessive noun is also possible:

- *There'll be a prize for **the finest** sandcastle.*
- *We wear **our oldest** clothes for gardening.*
- *Maths is **Hilary's best** subject.*

9 You can use a **superlative adjective** with *the* on its own as a **pronoun**, if the noun that it describes has already been mentioned:

- *There are over five hundred students in the school, and **the cleverest** go on to university.*
- *There are several routes – **the most scenic** takes you along the coast.*

10 You can use the **comparative** and **superlative** forms in the following construction: ***the*** + **comparative/superlative** + ***of*** + the people or things being compared:

- ***The taller of** the two buildings is an office block.*
- *On the football field, Joe was **the more talented of** the twins.*
- *Jennifer was **the most suitable of** several candidates.*
- *'Hamlet' is **the finest of** all Shakespeare's plays.*

 ISBN 978-81-8477-745-1

PRACTICE

Exercise 1

*Fill in the missing **positive**, **comparative** and **superlative adjectives** in the table.*

POSITIVE	COMPARATIVE	SUPERLATIVE
________	larger	________
________	________	furthest
enjoyable	________	________
________	________	ugliest
bad	________	________
________	simpler	________
new	________	________
________	________	wettest

Exercise 2

*Fill in the blanks with the correct form (**positive**, **comparative** or **superlative**) of the adjectives in brackets.*

1. Jenny's hair is ________ (***short***) than Carol's.
2. Which is the ________ (***expensive***) of the two houses?
3. This essay is not as ________ (***good***) as the last one you wrote.
4. Bill works on the top floor of the ________ (***tall***) building in the city.
5. The ________ (***soft***) the butter is, the ________ (***easy***) it will be to spread.
6. Your idea is ________ (***practical***) than mine; in fact, it's the ________ (***silly***) thing I've ever heard!
7. This is the ________ (***difficult***) exercise in the book.
8. The weather is much ________ (***hot***) in the summer.
9. I can't understand why the judges gave the prize to the ________ (***attractive***) painting!
10. Tom's exam results were ________ (***bad***) than everyone else's.

 ISBN 978-81-8477-745-1

Exercise 3

Each of the following sentences contains an error in the use of positive, comparative and superlative adjectives. Rewrite the sentences correctly.

1. This is the biggest of the two bowls.

____

2. Sally is more better at painting than Anne is.

____

3. My grandparents live in the most old house in the village.

____

4. Who is the younger: Jack, Tom or Bill?

____

5. The weather was not as worse as it was the week before.

____

6. My work is importanter than yours.

____

Exercise 4

Fill in the blanks in the following passage with the comparative or superlative form of the adjectives in brackets.

Uncle Jack paid a visit to the village where he lived with his parents and his _____ (*young*) brother when he was a boy. The changes he found there were _____ (*great*) than he had expected. Of course, the village was much _____ (*big*) than it had been. The _____ (*old*) building in the village, the school, was still standing. However, many others had been destroyed to make way for _____ (*modern*) buildings. The _____ (*remarkable*) difference was not a change at all. The area around the village seemed _____ (*flat*) than Uncle Jack remembered. His _____ (*happy*) childhood memories were of climbing the nearby hills with his _____ (*good*) friend, but the slopes seemed a lot _____ (*steep*) in those days!

 ISBN 978-81-8477-745-1

UNIT 22

ADJECTIVAL PHRASES

What do they look like?

The bus was **very late**, and the people **waiting at the bus stop** were becoming **extremely impatient**. A **red-haired** girl **in a leather jacket** asked the man **next to her** how long he had been waiting. He did not answer, but a **rather anxious-looking** woman **with a briefcase** said she had been there for nearly an hour.

What are they made up of?

1. An adjectival phrase can consist simply of an adverb + **adjective**:
   - *I have a very **useful** device for opening jars with tight lids.*
   - *Sue felt rather **sad** when she heard the news.*
   - *The operation was quite **painless**.*

2. It can also consist of an adverb + **participle**:
   - *He sent the manager a carefully **worded** letter.*
   - *We were stuck in a queue of slow-**moving** traffic.*

   If the adverb does not end in *ly*, it is joined to the adjective with a **hyphen**.

3. An adjectival phrase can be some other hyphenated set of words, such as a number + **noun**, a noun + **adjective**, an adjective + **participle** or a noun + **participle**:
   - *Mum works in a ten-**storey** building.*
   - *The water was crystal-**clear**.*
   - *He had baked us a delicious-**looking** cake.*
   - *These leather-**bound** books are valuable.*

4. It may be a **possessive expression**:
   - *That is **my father's** briefcase.*
   - *I can't wait for **next week's** episode!*

 ISBN 978-81-8477-745-1

5. **Adjectival phrases that follow the noun** can begin with a **preposition**, **adjective**, **participle** or **adverb**:
   - *The man* ***at the door*** *would not let us in.*
   - *People* ***allergic to nuts*** *have to be very careful of what they eat.*
   - *We sat on chairs* ***made of recycled plastic.***
   - *Jack was talking to a girl* ***wearing a red dress.***
   - *The* ***weather down here*** *is much better than it is at home.*

How do you use them?

1. You can put an adjectival phrase **before** the **noun** that it describes:
   - *This is a* ***really boring film.***
   - *The woman was wearing* ***blood-red lipstick.***

2. You can put an adjectival phrase **directly after** a **noun** (or **pronoun**):
   - *The* ***brick used to break the window*** *was found inside the room.*
   - ***Anyone willing to help*** *should give their name to Miss Lee.*

3. You can use an adjectival phrase as the **complement** of a **linking verb**:
   - *My voice* ***sounded strangely loud.***
   - *Such behaviour* ***is typical of teenagers.***

PRACTICE

Exercise 1

Underline the *adjectival phrases* *in the following sentences.*

1. That is a very interesting idea.
2. We are looking for someone with initiative for this highly challenging job.
3. The flowers in this vase are completely dead.
4. Jack has a well-paid job with a finance company.
5. The girl standing by the door looked strangely familiar.
6. The shop mainly sells electronic goods made in Japan.
7. I borrowed my brother's camera to take some photos of my new bike.
8. Motorcyclists wearing helmets are not allowed to enter the supermarket.
9. The words carved on the tombstone were hard to read.
10. Jane took her five-year-old sister to a park near their house.

 ISBN 978-81-8477-745-1

Exercise 2

Fill in the blanks in the following passage with adverbs from the box to form adjectival phrases. Use each adverb only once, and add hyphens if required.

absolutely	completely	extremely	highly	less
rather	really	surprisingly	very	well

Anna was not a __________ confident girl, and she felt __________ nervous before the concert. She had to play a __________ long violin solo with an __________ difficult passage in the middle. However, she need not have worried. As soon as she picked up her violin, she felt __________ calm. She gave an __________ flawless performance, and the audience applauded enthusiastically. Anna left the stage feeling __________ anxious, but __________ exhausted. 'I'm __________ glad that's over,' she said to her music teacher, Mr Brown. 'Now I'm going home for a __________ earned rest!'

Exercise 3: grammar for writing

Write a short passage of approximately 100 words about an animal or animals. Your passage must contain at least ten adjectival phrases of various types. It can be a narrative, a recount or an information report. When you have finished, underline each adjectival phrase and put a ring round the noun or pronoun it describes.

____

____

____

____

____

____

____

____

 ISBN 978-81-8477-745-1

4 VERBS

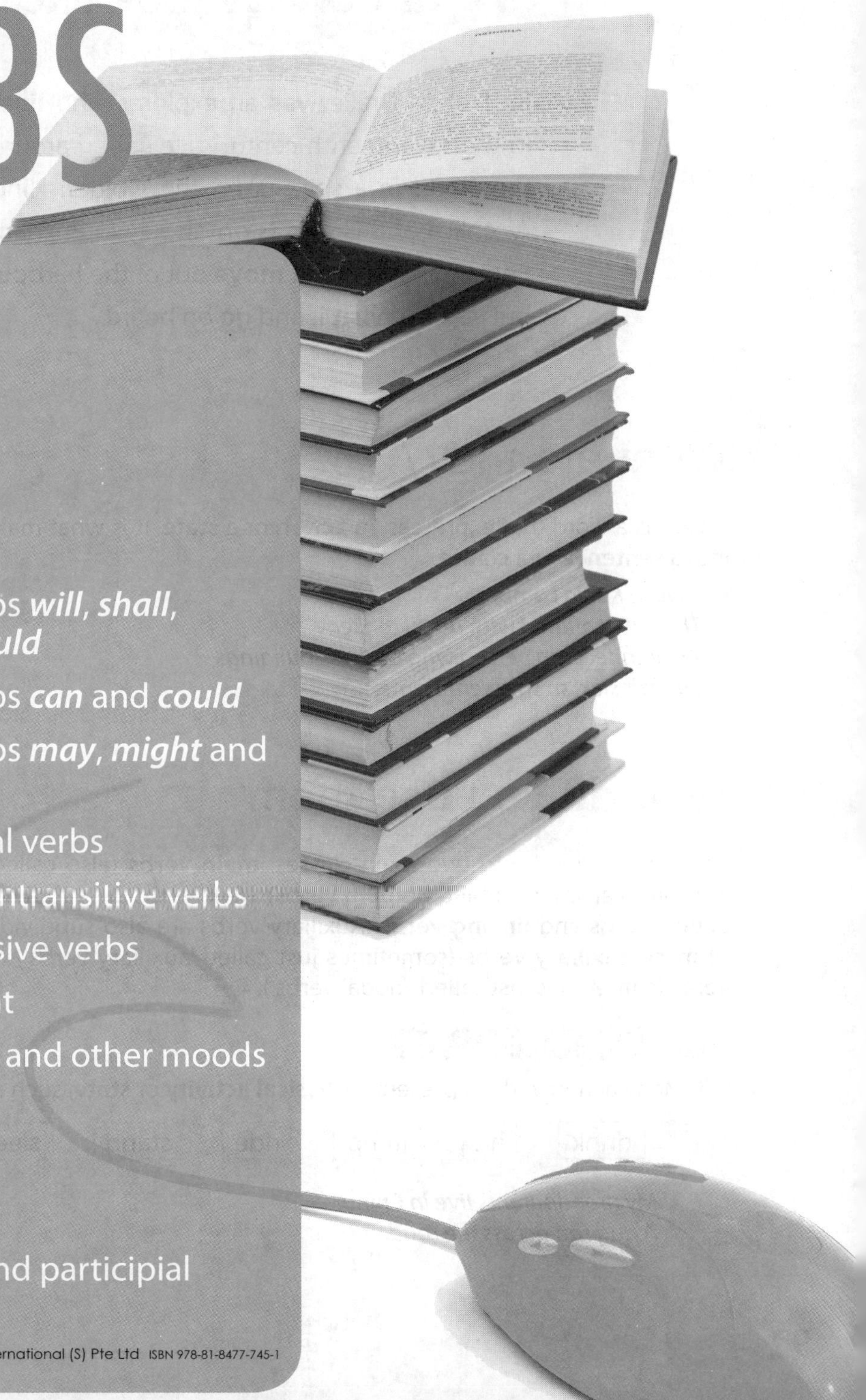

 ISBN 978-81-8477-745-1

UNIT 23

VERBS

What do they look like?

Sir Francis Drake **was** an explorer who **lived** in the seventeenth century. He **sailed** around the world in a ship called the 'Golden Hind'. A replica of this ship **is** on display in Brixham, England. It **does** not **move** out of the harbour, but you **can visit** it and **go** on board.

What are they?

A **verb** is a word that expresses an **action** or a **state**. It is what makes a group of words into a **sentence** or a **clause**:

- *I **live** in Kuala Lumpur.*
- *The ferry **collided** with an oil tanker.*
- *An architect **is** a person who **designs** buildings.*
- *Sue **felt** sick, so she **went** home.*

How do you use them?

Verbs are divided into two main classes, **main verbs** (also called **lexical verbs**) and **auxiliary verbs** (also called **helping verbs**). Main verbs are subdivided into two groups, **action verbs** and **linking verbs**. Auxiliary verbs are also subdivided into two groups, **primary auxiliary verbs** (sometimes just called 'auxiliary verbs') and **modal auxiliary verbs** (sometimes just called 'modal verbs').

Main verbs: action verbs

1 Many action verbs represent a **physical activity** or **state**, such as:

drink | hit | jump | ride | stand | sleep

- *My grandparents **live** in China.*
- *A dog **ran** across the road.*

 ISBN 978-81-8477-745-1

2. Other action verbs represent **mental activities or states**, such as:

think, know, remember ('thinking' verbs)
hear, see, smell ('sensing' verbs)
love, hate, suspect ('feeling' verbs)
own, possess, have ('possessing' verbs)

- *Jack **forgot** his brother's birthday.*
- *I **smelt** something burning.*
- *Everybody **likes** this music.*
- *Our next-door neighbour **keeps** bees.*

3. The person or thing that performs the action of a **verb** is the **subject**:

- ***The ball** **broke** the window.*
- ***Alice** **likes** cats.*

4. The person or thing that receives the action of a **verb** is the **object**:

- *The ball **broke** **the window**.*
- *Alice **likes** **cats**.*

Main verbs: linking verbs

1. A linking verb introduces a **fact** about a person or thing. This person or thing is the **subject** of the verb:

- ***The walls** **are** green.*
- ***Tom** **is** a doctor.*

2. A linking verb **links** the subject with a **complement**, which is often an **adjective** or **noun**:

- *The walls **are** **green**.*
- *Tom **is** **a doctor**.*

3. Sometimes, the complement is a **prepositional phrase** (a phrase beginning with a preposition) or an **adverb**:

- *Their house **was** **near the supermarket**.*
- *The taxi **is** **outside**.*

4. The example sentences above are formed with the most important **linking verb**, the verb ***be*** (***am***, ***is***, ***are***, ***was***, ***were***). Other **linking verbs** include ***appear***, ***become***, ***feel***, ***get***, ***go***, ***grow***, ***look***, ***seem***, ***smell***, ***sound***, ***taste***, ***turn***:

- *Luke **became** **an artist**.*
- *It **grew** **dark**.*
- *I **feel** **a fool**.*
- *The idea **sounded** **promising**.*

Primary auxiliary verbs

1. The examples above are positive statements containing verbs in the present or past tense. However, verbs are also used in **negative statements** and **questions**, and sometimes express **continuous** or **completed** action. For these purposes, they must be 'helped' by **primary auxiliary verbs**, which are ***be***, ***have*** and ***do***.

 ISBN 978-81-8477-745-1

2. The verb ***be*** is used with the ***ing* form** (the **present participle**) of a verb to express **continuous** action:
   - *Sally* ***is*** *working as a hairdresser.*
   - *My friends* ***were*** *looking for accommodation.*

3. The verb ***have*** is used with the ***ed* form** (the **past participle**) of a verb to express **completed** action:
   - *Somebody* ***has*** *moved the remote control.*
   - *A month later, the bruising* ***had*** *disappeared.*

4. The verb ***do*** is used with the **base form** (the **bare infinitive**) of a verb to form **negative statements** (with ***not***) and **questions**:
   - *I* ***do not*** *tell lies.*
   - *We* ***did not*** *realize it was a secret.*
   - ***Does*** *your dad play golf?*
   - ***Did*** *you see the shooting star?*

You will learn more about primary auxiliary verbs and their uses in Units 25, 26 and 27.

Modal auxiliary verbs

1. **Modal auxiliary verbs** are used to 'help' verbs express such things as **possibility** and **necessity**. They are followed by the **base form** (the **bare infinitive**) of a verb. Some important modal verbs are ***will***, ***would***, ***shall***, ***should***, ***can***, ***could***, ***may***, ***might***, ***must***:
   - *I* ***would*** *prefer to go to the cinema.*
   - ***Can*** *you swim?*

2. Some modal verbs express the **future**:
   - *We* ***shall*** *discuss this tomorrow.*
   - ***Will*** *the patient recover?*

3. Some modal verbs express **possibility**:
   - ***Could*** *this be the missing necklace?*
   - *The patient* ***might*** *not recover.*

4. Some modal verbs express **permission**:
   - *The children* ***may*** *have one cake each.*
   - ***Can*** *I go now?*

5. Some modal verbs express **necessity**:
   - *You* ***must*** *not touch this wire.*
   - *Unfit people* ***should*** *take more exercise.*

You will learn more about modal auxiliary verbs and their uses in Units 28 to 32.

 ISBN 978-81-8477-745-1

PRACTICE

Exercise 1

Say whether the verbs in bold print are being used as main verbs (MV), primary auxiliary verbs (PA) or modal auxiliary verbs (MA).

1. The helicopter **landed** (   ) in the middle of a field.
2. I **might** (   ) need some help.
3. Tom **says** (   ) he **can** (   ) speak French.
4. You **must** (   ) close all the windows before you **leave** (   ) the house.
5. The sun **was** (   ) shining and the sky **was** (   ) blue.
6. The label **had** (   ) come off the tin, so I **did** (   ) not know what it **contained** (   ).
7. She **could** (   ) not reach the apples that **were** (   ) hanging from the higher branches.
8. James **has** (   ) an elder brother who **is** (   ) in the army.
9. If you **annoy** (   ) the cat, it **will** (   ) scratch you.
10. **Does** (   ) anyone know what **happened** (   )?

Exercise 2

Fill in each blank with an appropriate linking verb from the box. Use each of the given words once only.

am	are	became	felt	grew	go
grow	is	look	looked	looks	seemed
smells	smelt	sounds	taste	turned	turns
was	were				

1. My grandfather ______________ a lawyer before he ______________ a teacher.
2. Sally ______________ a fool in her fancy-dress costume, but her mother thought she ______________ terrific.
3. The soup ______________ of cabbage, so I expected it to ______________ disgusting.
4. The litmus paper will ______________ blue if the liquid ______________ an alkali.

 ISBN 978-81-8477-745-1

5. It _______________ darker and the air _______________ colder.

6. The children _______________ actually more excited than they _______________.

7. The flower _______________ very attractive and _______________ lovely, too.

8. Most people's hair _______________ grey as they _______________ old.

9. The rocks _______________ not as heavy as they _______________.

10. I _______________ anxious because the exam _______________ really difficult.

Exercise 3

In the following passage, underline all the action verbs and put a ring round all the linking verbs.

Julia is a very talented musician. She plays several different instruments. Her father gave her piano lessons before she started school. She learnt the violin while she was at primary school and became a member of the school orchestra. When she went to secondary school, she took cello lessons. She still prefers the cello to the violin — she thinks it sounds more pleasant, though the instrument itself is much heavier to carry around! Like her friends, Julia also took an interest in pop music when she was a teenager. She decided to learn how to play the drums. This was not as easy as it looked, but Julia finally became a proficient drummer.

 ISBN 978-81-8477-745-1

UNIT
24

VERB FORMS

What do they look like?

My baby brother cannot **talk** yet. He **listens** when we are **talking**, as if he **understands** what we are **saying**. My mother **says** that I first **talked** when I was two years old, but she can't **remember** what I **said**. According to my father, I have **talked** continuously ever since, but I have never **said** anything interesting!

All verbs except ***be*** have up to five different forms, for example:

BASE FORM	THIRD PERSON SINGULAR, SIMPLE PRESENT	PRESENT PARTICIPLE	SIMPLE PAST	PAST PARTICIPLE
walk	*walks*	*walking*	*walked*	*walked*
carry	*carries*	*carrying*	*carried*	*carried*
put	*puts*	*putting*	*put*	*put*
break	*breaks*	*breaking*	*broke*	*broken*

What are they?

1. The **base form** is the verb without any endings added. It has the same form as the **bare infinitive**:
   - *I **attend** the same school as Jack.*
   - *Can you **carry** that heavy box?*

2. The **third person singular, simple present** ends in *s*:
   - *Jack **attends** the same school as me.*
   - *A ferry **carries** passengers across the river.*
   - *This box **is** very heavy.*
   - *A tricycle **has** four wheels.*

 ISBN 978-81-8477-745-1

3. The **present participle** (sometimes called the ***-ing*** **participle**) ends in ***ing***:
   - *We were **waiting** for the bus.*
   - *The boy **sitting** beside me is my brother.*

4. The **simple past** often ends in ***ed***:
   - *We **waited** over an hour for the bus.*
   - *A mouse **scurried** across the floor.*

5. The **past participle** (sometimes called the ***-ed/-en*** **participle**) often ends in ***ed*** or ***en***:
   - *We have **waited** long enough!*
   - *A valuable painting had been **stolen**.*

How do you use them?

Base form

1. You use the **base form** for the **simple present** of most verbs (except ***be***) in all persons except the third person singular:
   - *I **like** chocolate.*
   - *You **like** chocolate.*
   - *We **like** chocolate.*
   - *They **like** chocolate.*

   The simple present is a **tense** used to talk about present actions and states. You will learn more about it in Unit 42.

2. You use the **base form** for all persons of **modal verbs:**
   - *You **must** apologize.*
   - *She **must** help.*

3. You use the **base form** as a **bare infinitive** for the verb that is 'helped' by a **modal verb** or by ***do***:
   - *You **must apologize**.*
   - *She **did** not **help**.*

4. You use the **base form** as an **infinitive** (sometimes with ***to*** before it) for many other purposes:
   - *Joe made his sister **cry**.*
   - *They persuaded me **to leave**.*

   You will learn more about the infinitive and its uses in Unit 38.

5. You use the **base form** as the **imperative**, to give orders and instructions:
   - ***Walk** faster.*
   - ***Pull** the handle towards you.*

   You will learn more about the imperative in Unit 36.

 ISBN 978-81-8477-745-1

Third person singular, simple present

1. You use this form of the **verb** to talk about present actions and states when the subject is one of the pronouns ***he***, ***she*** or ***it***:
   - *He* ***wants*** *a drink.*
   - *She* ***tries*** *very hard.*
   - *It often* ***rains*** *at this time of year.*

2. You also use this form of the **verb** with other singular pronouns:
   - *This* ***requires*** *a lot of skill.*
   - *I don't know whose these books are — neither* ***belongs*** *to me.*

3. You also use this form of the **verb** with a singular noun or an uncountable noun:
   - *The car* ***has*** *a flat tyre.*
   - *Joe* ***watches*** *too much television.*
   - *Ice* ***melts*** *in warm weather.*

   Using the right form of the simple present is called **agreement**. You will learn more about this in Unit 35.

Present participle

1. You use a **present participle** with the auxiliary verb ***be*** to form the **continuous** tenses. These talk about actions that are still going on, or that went on for some time in the past:
   - *It is* ***raining.*** (present continuous)
   - *The cows were* ***grazing*** *in the field.* (past continuous)
   - *We have been* ***waiting*** *for nearly an hour.* (present perfect continuous)
   - *She had been* ***using*** *the wrong paint.* (past perfect continuous)

   You will learn more about the continuous tenses in Units 42, 43, 44 and 45.

2. You can also use a **present participle** as an adjective, or as part of an adjectival phrase:
   - *Dad has fixed the* ***leaking*** *tap.*
   - *A man* ***wearing*** *a motorcycle helmet entered the shop.*

   Adjectival phrases beginning with a present participle are also called **participial phrases**. You will learn more about these in Unit 40.

3. The *ing* form of a verb can also be used as a **noun**. In this case, it is called a **gerund** (or a **verbal noun**), not a present participle:
   - ***Cycling*** *is a good form of exercise.*
   - *Jane doesn't like* ***wearing*** *skirts or dresses.*

   You will learn more about gerunds in Unit 37.

 ISBN 978-81-8477-745-1

Simple past

1. You use the **simple past** to talk about past actions or states:
   - *I **opened** the window.*
   - *The grapes **tasted** sour.*

2. The **simple past** has the same form for all persons:
   - *I **searched** the garden.*
   - *You **searched** the garden.*
   - *She **searched** the garden.*
   - *We **searched** the garden.*
   - *They **searched** the garden.*

You will learn more about the simple past in Unit 44.

Past participle

1. You use a **past participle** with the auxiliary verb ***have*** to form the **perfect** tenses. These talk about completed actions:
   - *Someone **has locked** the door.* (present perfect)
   - *The prisoners **had escaped**.* (past perfect)

   You will learn more about the perfect tenses in Units 43 and 45.

2. You use a **past participle** with the auxiliary verb ***be*** to form the **passive** voice. This is a form of the verb in which the subject receives the action:
   - *The door **is locked** by the caretaker at eight o'clock every evening.*
   - *The prisoners **were released** from jail.*

   You will learn more about the passive voice in Unit 34.

3. You can also use a **past participle** as an adjective, or as part of an adjectival phrase:
   - *The **injured** man was taken to hospital.*
   - *A car **covered** with mud stopped outside our house.*

   Adjectival phrases beginning with a past participle are also called **participial phrases**. You will learn more about these in Unit 40.

How do you form them?

Third person singular, simple present

1. You usually form the **third person singular, present tense** of a verb by adding ***s*** to the **base form**:

jump	→	*jumps*	*run*	→	*runs*	*play*	→	*plays*
moo	→	*moos*	*sit*	→	*sits*	*close*	→	*closes*

 ISBN 978-81-8477-745-1

2. If the base form ends in a single ***o***, or in ***ch***, ***sh***, ***s***, ***x*** or ***z***, you add ***es***:

echo → ***echoes***	*go* → ***goes***	*wish* → ***wishes***	*gas* → ***gases***
kiss → ***kisses***	*mix* → ***mixes***	*fizz* → ***fizzes***	

3. If the base form ends in a consonant followed by ***y***, you change the ***y*** to ***i*** and add ***es***:

fly → ***flies***	*carry* → ***carries***

Present participle

1. You usually form the **present participle** of a verb by adding ***ing*** to the **base form**:

jump → ***jumping***	*play* → ***playing***	*carry* → ***carrying***
go → ***going***	*throw* → ***throwing***	*wish* → ***wishing***

2. If the base form ends in a consonant followed by ***e***, you remove this letter before adding ***ing***:

ride → ***riding***	*educate* → ***educating***

3. If the base form ends in a single vowel followed by a **consonant** other than ***w***, and has **only one syllable**, you **double the final consonant** before adding ***ing***:

run → ***running***	*set* → ***setting***	*gas* → ***gassing***	*rob* → ***robbing***

If a base form with this ending has **two syllables**, you usually **double the final consonant** before adding ***ing*** if the **second syllable is stressed**:

refer → ***referring***	*begin* → ***beginning***
control → ***controlling***	*kidnap* → ***kidnapping***

If the second syllable is unstressed, you usually just add ***ing***:

offer → ***offering***	*harden* → ***hardening***	*edit* → ***editing***	*gallop* → ***galloping***

Simple past and past participle

1. You often form the **simple past** and **present participle** of a verb by adding ***ed*** to the **base form**:

jump → ***jumped***	*play* → ***played***	*wish* → ***wished***	*offer* → ***offered***

2. If the base form already ends in ***e***, you just add ***d***:

educate → ***educated***	*tie* → ***tied***	*agree* → ***agreed***	*glue* → ***glued***

3. If the base form ends in a consonant followed by ***y***, **you** change the ***y*** to ***i*** before adding ***ed***:

carry → ***carried***	*bury* → ***buried***

 ISBN 978-81-8477-745-1

4 If the base form ends in a single vowel followed by a consonant other than *w*, and has **only one syllable**, you double the final consonant before adding *ed*:

clip → *clipped* *drag* → *dragged* *gas* → *gassed* *rob* → *robbed*

If a base form with this ending has **two syllables**, you usually double the final consonant before adding *ed* if the **second syllable is stressed**:

refer → *referred*	*control* → *controlled*
program → *programmed*	*kidnap* → *kidnapped*

5 The rules above apply to **regular verbs**. However, the simple past and past participle of many common verbs do not end in *ed*. They are **irregular verbs**, and you will learn about them in the following section.

Irregular verbs

1 Some irregular verbs use the **same form** for the simple past and past participle, but it is often quite different from the base form. Here are a few examples:

BASE FORM	SIMPLE PAST	PAST PARTICIPLE
dig	*dug*	*dug*
say	*said*	*said*
bring	*brought*	*brought*
teach	*taught*	*taught*

2 Some irregular verbs use **different forms** for the simple past and past participle:

BASE FORM	SIMPLE PAST	PAST PARTICIPLE
give	*gave*	*given*
see	*saw*	*seen*
eat	*ate*	*eaten*
do	*did*	*done*

3 Sometimes, one or both of the **irregular forms look the same as the base form** (though they may have a different pronunciation):

BASE FORM	SIMPLE PAST	PAST PARTICIPLE
come	*came*	*come*
let	*let*	*let*
put	*put*	*put*
read	*read*	*read*

4 Occasionally, the **simple past is regular** and only the **past participle is irregular**:

BASE FORM	SIMPLE PAST	PAST PARTICIPLE
show	*showed*	*shown*
sew	*sewed*	*sewn*

 ISBN 978-81-8477-745-1

5 There are no rules for the formation of irregular verbs – you just have to learn them. However, here are a couple of hints that might help you.

Firstly, a number of past participles end in ***n***, but no simple past forms do (unless the base form itself ends in ***n***):

BASE FORM	SIMPLE PAST	PAST PARTICIPLE
drive	*drove*	*driven*
break	*broke*	*broken*
lie	*lay*	*lain*
grow	*grew*	*grown*

Secondly, a number of verbs have ***i*** in the middle of the base form, ***a*** in the simple past and ***u*** in the past participle:

BASE FORM	SIMPLE PAST	PAST PARTICIPLE
sink	*sank*	*sunk*
drink	*drank*	*drunk*
ring	*rang*	*rung*
swim	*swam*	*swum*

PRACTICE

Exercise 1

*Fill in the blanks in the following table with the correct **verb forms**.*

BASE FORM	THIRD PERSON SINGULAR, SIMPLE PRESENT	PRESENT PARTICIPLE	SIMPLE PAST	PAST PARTICIPLE
________	**hurries**	________	________	________
write	________	________	________	________
________	________	**hearing**	________	________
________	________	________	________	**said**
________	________	________	**hopped**	________
forget	________	________	________	________
________	________	________	**existed**	________
________	________	**watching**	________	________
________	**plays**	________	________	________
________	________	________	________	**broken**

 ISBN 978-81-8477-745-1

Exercise 2

*Say whether the **verbs** in bold print are being used in the simple past (SP) or as a past participle (PP).*

1. Sally **said** ( ) she had **lost** ( ) her camera.
2. This building was **designed** ( ) by a man **called** ( ) Arthur Grimes.
3. The boy **laughed** ( ) and **ran** ( ) away.
4. Have you **read** ( ) the book I **lent** ( ) you?
5. I **cut** ( ) my finger on the **broken** ( ) glass.
6. The car has not **worked** ( ) properly since it was **serviced** ( ) last week.
7. Jane **slipped** ( ) on the **polished** ( ) floor.
8. The dog has not **drunk** ( ) the water you **put** ( ) in its bowl.

Exercise 3

Fill in the blanks with the correct form of the verb in brackets.

The shop where Carol ____________ (*work*) was ____________ (*rob*) yesterday afternoon. Two men ____________ (*run*) in and ____________ (*tell*) all the customers to ____________ (*lie*) face down on the floor. Everyone ____________ (*obey*) immediately because they ____________ (*think*) the robbers were ____________ (*carry*) guns. One of the men ____________ (*go*) to the counter and ____________ (*ask*) the shopkeeper to ____________ (*give*) him all the money in the till. Carol was ____________ (*load*) shelves at the back of the shop at the time. She ____________ (*see*) the robbers, but they did not ____________ (*see*) her. ____________ (*move*) as quietly as possible, she ____________ (*slip*) out through the back door and ____________ (*phone*) the police. Unfortunately, by the time the police ____________ (*arrive*), the robbers had ____________ (*go*). However, the shopkeeper has ____________ (*give*) the police a good description of the men. The police ____________ (*think*) they ____________ (*know*) who the robbers are, and they ____________ (*hope*) to ____________ (*arrest*) them very soon.

 ISBN 978-81-8477-745-1

UNIT 25

THE VERB *BE*

What does it look like?

Tomorrow **is** Sports Day, and the school grounds **are being** prepared for the event. I **am** taking part in five races. A famous athlete has **been** invited to present the prizes. I hope the weather will **be** fine. Last year, it **was** wet, and by the end of the day, we **were** all very muddy.

BASE FORM *be*				
	PRESENT TENSE		SIMPLE PAST TENSE	
	SINGULAR	PLURAL	SINGULAR	PLURAL
1st person	*I am*	*we are*	*I was*	*we were*
2nd person	*you are*	*you are*	*you were*	*you were*
3rd person	*he is* *she is* *it is*	*they are*	*he was* *she was* *it was*	*they were*
	PRESENT PARTICIPLE *being*		PAST PARTICIPLE *been*	

How do you use it?

The verb ***be*** is both a **main verb** and an **auxiliary verb**.

The main verb *be*

The **main** verb ***be*** is a **linking** verb. It **links** a subject with a **complement**.

1. The complement may be an **adjective** or **adjectival phrase**:
   - *I was sleepy.*
   - *Jennifer is good at swimming.*

 ISBN 978-81-8477-745-1

2 The complement may be a **noun** or **noun phrase**:

- *Those birds **are** geese.*
- *Einstein **was** a famous scientist of the 20th century.*

3 The complement may be **a prepositional phrase**:

- *The dishes **were** in the dishwasher.*
- *Jean **is** on the committee.*

4 The complement may be an **adverb** or **adverbial phrase**:

- *Mum and Dad **were** upstairs.*
- *The sports equipment **is** down in the basement.*

5 You can make ***be*** negative by putting ***not*** after it:

- *You **were** not careful enough.*
- *This **is** not my jacket.*

6 You can form questions with ***be*** by putting the **subject** after the **verb**. This reversed position of subject and verb is called **inversion**:

- ***Are** we late?*
- ***Was** the holiday a success?*
- *Where **is** my notebook?*

7 However, ***wh***-words always come at the beginning of the question, whether they are the subject or complement:

- ***What** was that noise?*
- ***Who** is afraid of spiders?*

The auxiliary verb *be*

The **auxiliary** verb ***be*** is a **primary auxiliary** verb.

1 You use the auxiliary verb ***be*** with the **present participle** of a verb to form the **continuous tenses**:

- *Jane **is** trying to do her homework.* (present continuous)
- *The boys **were** listening to the radio.* (past continuous)

You will learn more about the continuous tenses in Units 42, 43, 44 and 45.

2 You use the auxiliary verb ***be*** with the **past participle** of a verb to form the **passive voice**:

- *These plants **are** grown for food.* (passive simple present)
- *This book **was** written by Jane Austen.* (passive simple past)
- *A new housing estate **is being** built on the edge of the town.* (passive present continuous)
- *The zebra **was being** chased by a lion.* (passive past continuous)

You will learn more about the passive voice in Unit 34.

 ISBN 978-81-8477-745-1

3. When you make these sentences **negative**, you put ***not*** between ***be*** and the **participle** (or between ***be*** and ***being***):
   - *The boys **were not listening** to the radio.*
   - *These plants **are not grown** for food.*
   - *The zebra **was not being chased** by a lion.*

4. You can form questions by putting the **subject** between ***be*** and the **participle** (or between ***be*** and ***being***):
   - ***Were the boys listening** to the radio?*
   - ***Are these plants grown** for food?*
   - ***Was the zebra being chased** by the lion?*
   - *What **is Jane trying** to do?*
   - *When **was the book written**?*
   - *Where **is the new housing estate being built**?*

Contractions

1. You can shorten the verb ***be*** in the following ways:

*I **am***	→	*I'm*	*you **are***	→	*you're*	*he **is***	→	*he's*	*she **is***	→	*she's*
*it **is***	→	*it's*	*we **are***	→	*we're*	*they **are***	→	*they're*	*is **not***	→	*isn't*
*are **not***	→	*aren't*	*was **not***	→	*wasn't*	*were **not***	→	*weren't*			

   - *You**'re** my best friend.*
   - *It**'s** raining again.*
   - *Alice is**n't** here.*
   - *The students were**n't** listening to the teacher.*

2. You can also shorten ***is*** to ***'s*** also after most people's names, after most singular nouns, after certain other pronouns (***that, what, who***) and after certain adverbs (***where, how, here, there***):
   - ***Kate's** an artist.*
   - *The **weather's** lovely.*
   - ***That's** strange.*
   - ***Who's** in charge?*
   - ***Where's** the toilet?*
   - ***Here's** my bus.*

3. You usually use the contraction ***n't*** rather than ***not*** in negative questions:
   - ***Isn't** John coming with us?*
   - *Why **weren't** the shops open?*

4. In negative statements, you often have a choice between two contractions:
   - ***You're not** very observant.* or ***You aren't** very observant.*
   - ***Jack's not** coming with us.* or ***Jack isn't** coming with us.*

 ISBN 978-81-8477-745-1

PRACTICE

Exercise 1

*Rewrite these sentences in the **simple present** or **present continuous** tense.*

1. John was the captain of the basketball team.

____

2. The walls were made of mud and straw.

____

3. I was writing a letter to my cousin.

____

4. Some of the shops weren't open.

____

5. What were they trying to do?

____

6. You were pleased to hear the good news, weren't you?

____

7. My brother was frightened but I was not.

____

8. Everyone was being watched.

____

Exercise 2

*Rewrite these sentences, replacing full forms of **be** or **not** with contractions.*

1. I was not surprised about the result.

____

2. Today is the last day of term.

____

3. You are tired – take a rest.

____

 ISBN 978-81-8477-745-1

4. The keys were not on the table.

____

5. What is wrong with this computer?

____

6. I am trying to do my homework.

____

7. Oh, no! It is raining again!

____

8. Ask Tom and Paul if they are ready yet.

____

9. The television is not working.

____

10. There is a spare battery in the case.

____

Exercise 3

Fill in the blanks in the following passage with the correct full forms of the verb **be***.*

I ____________ looking forward to next weekend. On Saturday, my father and I ____________ going to visit Hareton House, which ____________ a big old house on the edge of the town. It used to ____________ the home of a man called Joseph Fox. He died in 1975, and the house has ____________ turned into a kind of museum. Joseph Fox ____________ a wealthy businessman who travelled all over the world. He bought interesting objects in each country he visited, and these ____________ now on display at the house. My mother and sister ____________ planning to come with us, but they have decided to visit my grandmother in hospital instead. She fell and broke her hip when she ____________ running for a bus last week. ____________ an active old woman, she feels very frustrated at having to lie in bed all day.

 ISBN 978-81-8477-745-1

UNIT 26

THE VERB *HAVE*

What does it look like?

A bicycle **has** two wheels. They **have** tyres that are filled with air. If a tyre **has** gone flat, you **have** to pump it up again. The earliest bicycles **had** wheels with solid tyres. Imagine **having** to ride along a bumpy road on one of those. It must **have** been very uncomfortable!

BASE FORM	THIRD PERSON SINGULAR, SIMPLE PRESENT	PRESENT PARTICIPLE	SIMPLE PAST	PAST PARTICIPLE
have	*has*	*having*	*had*	*had*

How do you use it?

The verb ***have*** is both a **main verb** and an **auxiliary verb**.

The main verb *have*

The **main** verb ***have*** is an **action** verb and is used in several ways.

1. It refers to **possession**:
   - *I **have** two mobile phones.*
   - *The stranger **had** a loud voice.*
2. It is used for **things that affect you**, such as illnesses, problems and tasks:
   - *I **have** a pain in my side.*
   - *We **had** an exam yesterday.*
3. It is used with a ***to-infinitive*** to express **obligation** or **necessity**:
   - *Everyone **has** **to carry** an identity card.*
   - *I **had** **to run** to the station because I was late.*

 ISBN 978-81-8477-745-1

4. It is used for **activities**:
   - *Dad **has** a shower every morning.*
   - *I **had** a run round the park.*

5. It refers to **eating** or **drinking**:
   - *I usually **have** my breakfast in the kitchen.*
   - *Joe **had** a drink of orange juice.*

The auxiliary verb *have*

The **auxiliary** verb ***have*** is a **primary auxiliary** verb.

1. You use the auxiliary verb ***have*** with the past participle of a verb to form the **perfect tenses**:
   - *Jane **has** passed her exam.* (present perfect)
   - *The mouse **had** died.* (past perfect)

   You will learn more about the perfect tenses in Units 43 and 45.

2. You use the auxiliary verb ***have*** with ***been*** (the **past participle** of ***be***) and the present participle of a verb to form the **perfect continuous tenses**:
   - *Timothy **has been** writing a book.* (present perfect continuous)
   - *The men **had been** working very hard.* (past perfect continuous)

   You will learn more about the perfect continuous tenses in Units 43 and 45.

3. You use the auxiliary verb ***have*** with ***been*** and the past participle of a verb to form the **passive voice** of the **perfect tenses**:
   - *The car **has been** repaired.* (passive present perfect)
   - *The house **had been** demolished.* (passive past perfect)

   You will learn more about the passive voice in Unit 34.

4. When you make these sentences negative, you put ***not*** between ***have*** and the **participle** (or between ***have*** and ***been***):
   - *The mouse **had** not **died**.*
   - *The men **had** not **been working** very hard.*
   - *The car **has** not **been** repaired.*

5. You can form questions by putting the subject between ***have*** and the **participle** (or between ***have*** and ***been***):
   - ***Has** Jane **passed** her exam?*
   - ***Had** the men **been working** hard?*
   - *What **have** you **done**?*
   - *Why **had** the house **been demolished**?*

 ISBN 978-81-8477-745-1

Contractions

1 You can shorten the auxiliary verb ***have*** in the following ways:

*I **have***	→	*I've*	*you **have***	→	*you've*	*he **has***	→	*he's*
*she **has***	→	*she's*	*it **has***	→	*it's*	*we **have***	→	*we've*
*they **have***	→	*they've*	*I **had***	→	*I'd*	*you **had***	→	*you'd*
*he **had***	→	*he'd*	*she **had***	→	*she'd*	*it **had***	→	*it'd*
*we **had***	→	*we'd*	*they **had***	→	*they'd*	*there **has***	→	*there's*
*there **had***	→	*there'd*	*have **not***	→	*haven't*	*has **not***	→	*hasn't*
*had **not***	→	*hadn't*						

- *I**'ve** lost my key.*
- *The mail has**n't** arrived yet.*
- *She**'d** broken her arm.*
- *The village had**n't** changed at all.*

2 You can also shorten ***has*** to ***'s*** after most people's names, after most singular nouns, after certain other pronouns (***that, what, who***) and after certain adverbs (***where, how, here, there***):

- ***Jack's** won a prize.*
- ***That's** ruined our chances!*
- *The **car's** broken down.*
- ***Where's** she gone?*

3 You usually use the contraction ***n't*** rather than ***not*** in negative questions:

- ***Haven't** you finished your homework yet?*
- *Why **hadn't** anyone called the police?*

4 It is best not to use contractions with ***have*** as a main verb, though they can be used in a few contexts:

- ***We'd** a good idea where they were hiding.*
- *I **haven't** any money.*

PRACTICE

Exercise 1

Fill in the blanks with the correct form of ***have***.

1. I love this book. I ______________ read it twice already.
2. ______________ Peter left for work yet?
3. I wish I ______________ visited Grandma again before she died.
4. Your apartment looks great. You ______________ made a lovely job of decorating it.
5. Jack ______________ mended my computer, so I can use it again.
6. Sue realized that she ______________ made a terrible mistake.

 ISBN 978-81-8477-745-1

7. I ________________ been waiting for nearly an hour, and I am not going to wait any longer!

8. ________________ you noticed that the picture was missing?

9. These boots ________________ been repaired several times.

10. Dad is feeling nervous because he ________________ to make a speech at the wedding.

Exercise 2

*Rewrite the following sentences as **questions**.*

1. The plane has arrived. ________________
2. All the windows had been broken. ________________
3. Jane hasn't sent her parents a postcard. ________________
4. I have told you this before. ________________
5. Tom has been sleeping in the guest room. Why ________________
6. The prisoners had escaped. How ________________
7. You haven't signed the letter. Why ________________
8. The children had been hiding. Where ________________
9. Someone had left the gate open. ________________
10. The car hasn't been repaired. ________________

Exercise 3

*In the following passage, underline all uses of **have** (in any of its forms) as a **main verb** and put a ring round all uses as an **auxiliary verb**.*

My mother has two brothers. I have never met either of them, but she has told me all about them. Uncle Jack used to be an airline steward. He had travelled many thousands of miles by the time he was thirty. Having had enough of flying, he then took a job in an insurance company. He has worked there ever since. His wife is employed by the same company and they have two children. Uncle Harry is a chef in a busy restaurant. He loves food and has a huge appetite, so this is the ideal job for him. Needless to say, he has put on rather a lot of weight over the years. His doctor says he will have to go on a diet, to avoid having health problems in later life.

 ISBN 978-81-8477-745-1

UNIT 27

THE VERB *DO*

What does it look like?

Joe: **Did** you see that wildlife documentary last night?

Kate: No, I **don't** often watch TV these days. After I've **done** the dishes and put the children to bed, there isn't time to **do** much else. My husband **does** what he can to help me, but he's often busy **doing** other things.

BASE FORM	THIRD PERSON SINGULAR, SIMPLE PRESENT	PRESENT PARTICIPLE	SIMPLE PAST	PAST PARTICIPLE
do	*does*	*doing*	*did*	*done*

How do you use it?

The verb ***do*** is both a **main verb** and an **auxiliary verb**.

The main verb *do*

The **main** verb ***do*** is an **action** verb and is used in several ways.

1. It expresses the general idea of **acting in any way**:
   - *What shall we **do** today?*
   - *You **did** the right thing in the circumstances.*
2. It expresses the idea of performing a **task** or **activity**:
   - *I'll **do** the cooking tonight.*
   - *The girls **did** a dance.*
   - *Dad usually **does*** (= washes and dries) *the dishes.*
3. It expresses the idea of **causing** a certain **result**:
   - *The storm **did** a lot of damage.*
   - *A walk in the fresh air will **do** you good.*

 ISBN 978-81-8477-745-1

4. You can use ***do*** with ***it, that, this*** or ***so*** to **refer back** to something that has just been mentioned:
   - *Jane twisted her hair round her finger — she often **did this** when she was nervous.*
   - *If you haven't signed the book, please **do so*** (= sign the book) *now.*

   This is a way of giving a text **cohesion**, which you will learn more about in Unit 74.

5. You can use ***do*** with an **adverb** to express **success** or **failure**:
   - *Joe **did well** in his exams.*
   - *Go on — you're **doing fine**!*

The auxiliary verb *do*

The auxiliary verb ***do*** is a **primary auxiliary** verb, chiefly used to form **negative sentences** and **questions.**

1. You use the auxiliary verb ***do*** with ***not*** to make most **main verbs** (except ***be***) **negative** in the **simple present** and **simple past**:
   - *I like apples but I **do not like** pears.* (simple present)
   - *Jane heard Tom's voice but she **did not hear** what he said.* (simple past)

2. You use the **base form** of the main verb after ***do not*** (or ***does not*** or ***did not***):
   - *Billy has two brothers but he **does not have** any sisters.*
   - *The children ate the chicken but they **did not eat** the rice.*

3. You can use the contractions ***don't***, ***doesn't*** and ***didn't*** (instead of ***do not***, ***does not*** and ***did not***) in informal contexts:
   - *I **don't like** pears.*
   - *Billy **doesn't have** any sisters.*
   - *The children **didn't eat** the rice.*

4. You also use ***do not*** or ***don't*** with the **base form** of any verb (including ***be***) in negative commands:
   - ***Don't be** so unkind to your little sister!*
   - *Please **do not touch** the exhibits.*

5. You also use the auxiliary verb ***do*** with most **main verbs** (except ***be***) to ask a **question** in the **simple present** and **simple past**:
   - ***Do** these books **belong** to anyone in this class?* (simple present)
   - *Where **did** you **put** the keys?* (simple past)

6. You use the **base form** of the main verb after ***do*** in questions:
   - ***Does** James **cycle** to school?*
   - *How **did** the police **catch** the thief?*

7. You put the **subject** between ***do*** and the **main verb** in questions:
   - ***Do you believe** in ghosts?*
   - *Why **did the plan fail**?*

 ISBN 978-81-8477-745-1

8 You usually use the contraction ***n't*** rather than ***not*** in **negative questions**:

- ***Doesn't** anyone know the right answer?*
- ***Don't** your parents like rock music?*
- *Why **didn't** the ice melt?*

9 You use the auxiliary verb ***do*** in **question tags** in the **simple past** and **simple present**. Question tags are short questions added at the end of a sentence, which refer back to other **verbs** in the main part of the sentence:

- *This door **needs** a fresh coat of paint, **doesn't it**?*
- *You didn't **tell** anyone else, **did you**?*

You will learn more about question tags in Unit 69.

10 You can also use the auxiliary verb ***do*** in various ways to **avoid repetition** and give a text **cohesion**:

- *'The soup smells delicious'. 'Yes, it **does**'.*
- *'I hate having to wear school uniform'. 'So **do** I'.*

You will learn more using ***do*** in these ways in Units 75 and 76.

PRACTICE

Exercise 1

*Rewrite each sentence first as a **question**, then as a **negative statement**.*

1. Alice wants to be a doctor.

____

2. The dog ran away.

____

3. Plants grow well in these conditions.

____

4. John had a party on his birthday.

____

5. This bus goes past the station.

____

6. The children put their toys away.

____

7. That car belongs to Mr Smith.

____

 ISBN 978-81-8477-745-1

8. The balloon burst.

____

9. I look silly in this hat.

____

10. Jane opened the box.

____

Exercise 2

*Fill in the blanks with the **present tense** of **do**, **have** or **be**.*

1. The television __________ not work properly.
2. Peter __________ wearing his best jeans.
3. __________ these shoes match this dress?
4. __________ you been waiting long?
5. This word __________ not used in formal English.
6. The idea sounds interesting, __________n't it?
7. Uncle Bill __________ come to stay for the weekend.
8. __________ you being treated well?

Exercise 3

Fill in the blanks in the following dialogue with the words from the box. You will have to use some of them more than once.

did	didn't	do	does	doesn't	doing	done	don't

Sam: What are you __________, Lucy?

Lucy: I'm making some sandwiches for your parents. You invited them to lunch today, __________ you?

Sam: Yes, I __________.

Lucy: I've __________ some smoked salmon sandwiches, but there won't be enough. __________ your parents like cold chicken?

Sam: My father __________, but I __________ think my mother is very fond of cold meat. __________ you buy any eggs?

Lucy: No, the supermarket __________ have any eggs.

Sam: Never mind. Mum __________ have a large appetite, so one or two smoked salmon sandwiches will be enough for her.

 ISBN 978-81-8477-745-1

UNIT 28

MODAL VERBS

What do they look like?

You **must** wear a helmet when you are cycling. Otherwise, you **could** suffer a serious head injury in an accident. Your helmet **might** even save your life. You **should** also wear something bright, so that car drivers **can** see you clearly. If you wear dark clothing, they **may** not notice you until it is too late.

The **modal verbs** are:

shall	should	will	would	can	could	may	might	must

There are also some **semi-modal verbs**, notably ***ought, need*** and ***used to.*** You will learn about these in Unit 32.

How do you use them?

1. **Modal verbs**, also called **modal auxiliary verbs**, are used with the **base form** (the **bare infinitive**) of a main verb:
   - *David* ***may phone*** *this evening.*
   - *You* ***must stop*** *writing now.*

2. You can use a modal verb to 'help' the main verb say that the action is **planned, certain, possible, likely, necessary, compulsory, allowed** or **advisable**:
   - *I* ***shall contact*** *you tomorrow.* (planned)
   - *You* ***will like*** *this book.* (certain)
   - *It* ***may rain*** *tomorrow.* (possible)
   - *The children* ***must be*** *hungry after their long walk.* (likely)
   - *You* ***can leave*** *at any time.* (allowed)
   - *Everyone* ***must sign*** *the document.* (compulsory)
   - *You* ***should wear*** *a sunhat.* (advisable)

   Some modal verbs have other uses, which you will learn about in the following units.

 ISBN 978-81-8477-745-1

3. You do not add *s* to a modal verb to form the **third person singular**:
   - *I **can** swim.*
   - *Jack **can** swim.*

4. Modal verbs do not have an ***ing*** form or a past participle. However, some use a different modal verb as a **past tense**:

PRESENT	PAST	PRESENT	PAST
can	*could*	*shall*	*should*
may	*might*	*will*	*would*

   - *I **can** swim quite well now, but last year I **could** not swim at all.*
   - *'**Will** David join us?' 'He said he **would**.'*

5. You can also use modal verbs with ***have*** or ***be*** and a **participle** to form **perfect** or **continuous tenses**:
   - *They **should** have told the police.*
   - *She **might** be waiting for us.*

6. You can form **negative sentences** by putting ***not*** after the modal verb:
   - *You **must** not **lose** this key.*
   - *He **could** not **have forgotten** my birthday.*

7. You can form **questions** by putting the **subject** after the modal verb:
   - ***Can** anyone else **hear** the owl?*
   - *Why **should** we **listen** to you?*

Contractions

1. Most modal verbs have **shortened negative forms** ending with ***n't***:

*should **not***	→ *should**n't***	*would **not***	→ *would**n't***	*could **not***	→ *could**n't***
*might **not***	→ *might**n't***	*must **not***	→ *must**n't***	*shall **not***	→ *sha**n't***
*will **not***	→ *wo**n't***	*can **not***	→ *ca**n't***		

You can also write ***can not*** as one word, ***cannot***.

2. You use these contractions in **negative questions** and **question tags**:
   - ***Can't** you wait a little longer?*
   - *Why **mustn't** we touch the wire?*
   - *Uncle John **will** get better, **won't** he?*

3. You can shorten ***shall*** or ***will*** to ***'ll*** after **personal pronouns**:
   - *We**'ll** take a taxi to the station.*
   - *Do you think it**'ll** rain tomorrow?*

Note that the usual shortened form of ***I shall not***, ***she will not***, etc. is ***I shan't***, ***she won't***, etc. (rather than ***I'll not***, ***she'll not***, etc.).

 ISBN 978-81-8477-745-1

4. You can also shorten ***would*** to ***'d*** after **personal pronouns**:
   - *Mary said **she'd** help us.*
   - *I asked the twins if **they'd** like to come too.*

Note that the usual shortened form of ***I would not***, ***she would not***, etc. is ***I wouldn't***, ***she wouldn't***, etc. (rather than ***I'd not***, ***she'd not***, etc.).

PRACTICE

Exercise 1

Rewrite the following sentences, replacing full forms with contractions.

1. I shall not be surprised if Jack wins.

   ____

2. Sue said she would phone us if she could not come.

   ____

3. You must not forget to shut the gate.

   ____

4. We cannot possibly eat all this food!

   ____

5. I shall try to persuade him, but it will not be easy.

   ____

6. You might not win the contest.

   ____

7. We will never sell our boat.

   ____

8. I thought it would be easier than this.

   ____

9. You should not have said that.

   ____

10. They promised they would help us.

   ____

 ISBN 978-81-8477-745-1

Exercise 2

Fill in the blanks with the correct form of the main verb in bold print. The first one has been done to help you.

1. Some of the class **left** early, and Mr Brown said the rest of us could ***leave*** whenever we liked.
2. I might ______________ the dress I **wore** for Joe and Kate's wedding.
3. It should ______________ warmer tomorrow than it **was** today.
4. Look at these pictures. Can you ______________ the man you **saw** outside the bank on the day of the robbery?
5. Sally **ate** half of the cake and Billy will probably ______________ the other half.
6. We shan't ______________ to the same restaurant we **went** to last week.
7. Dad **drove** us to the end of the road, but he wouldn't ______________ us any further.
8. It may ______________ longer to get down the mountain than it **took** to climb up it!
9. I **found** a suitable jar but I couldn't ______________ its lid.
10. The choir will ______________ the song they **sang** at last year's concert.

Exercise 3

*Underline all the **modal auxiliary verbs** in the following dialogue.*

Lisa: Are you and John going to Alice's party next Friday? She has invited a lot of guests, so it should be great fun.

Lucy: We may go, but I'm not sure yet. John might have to go away on business next week. If he does, he will not be back in time. Are you and Mike going?

Lisa: Mike would like to go, but he may have to work a late shift at the hospital that night. He will swap shifts with a colleague if he can. If not, I shall go to the party on my own.

Lucy: You can come with John and me, if you like. In fact, you and I could go together, without our boyfriends. We must not miss this party!

 ISBN 978-81-8477-745-1

UNIT
29

THE MODAL VERBS *WILL, SHALL, WOULD* AND *SHOULD*

What do they look like?

Bill: If I fail the exam tomorrow, I'**ll** have to take it again, **shan't** I?

Mum: Yes, you **will**. It **would** be a good idea to do some more studying tonight. **Shall** I help you?

Bill: No, our teacher said we **shouldn't** stay up late. She said we **should** go to bed early, so that we **won't** be too tired when we sit the exam.

How do you use them?

will and *shall*

1. You use *will* to talk about the **future.** It is used in **predictions** or to express **plans** and **intentions**:
   - *I **will** miss you when you go.* (prediction)
   - *If anyone hears us, they'**ll** answer.* (prediction)
   - *The Prime Minister **will** speak at tomorrow's debate.* (plan)
   - *We **will** leave at the end of the week.* (intention)

   In such contexts, you can use *shall* instead of *will* in the first person:
   - *I **shall** miss you when you go.* (prediction)
   - *We **shall** leave at the end of the week.* (intention)

2. You also use *will* or *shall* to express **insistence** or **determination**:
   - *You **will** tidy your room!* (insistence)
   - *No student **shall** borrow more than four books at a time from the library.* (insistence)
   - *I **will** never give up.* (determination)
   - *They **shan't** defeat us again!* (determination)

3. You can use *will* in **questions** to make a **request** or as a **polite invitation**:
   - ***Will** you be quiet?* (request)
   - ***Won't** you sit down?* (invitation)

 ISBN 978-81-8477-745-1

4. You can use ***shall*** in **questions** to make an **offer** or a **suggestion**:
   - ***Shall*** *I post this letter for you?* (offer)
   - ***Shall*** *we try a different method?* (suggestion)

would

1. The modal verb ***would*** can be used as the past tense of ***will*** or ***shall***, especially in **indirect speech** and **conditional clauses**:
   - *Jane said she* ***would*** *miss me.* (indirect speech)
   - *We vowed that they* ***would*** *not defeat us again.* (indirect speech)
   - *I* ***would*** *write to her if I knew her address.* (conditional clause)
   - *If anyone had heard us, they* ***would*** *have answered.* (conditional clause)

   You will learn about indirect speech in Unit 71 and conditional clauses in Unit 47.

2. You can also use ***would*** for **typical** or **habitual** actions or events in the past:
   - *My parents* ***would*** *often invite people to the house.* (typical)
   - *The dog* ***would*** *bark whenever it saw the postman.* (habitual)

3. You use ***would*** in the present (often with ***like*** or ***rather***) to make a **polite offer** or **request**, or to express a **desire** or **preference**:
   - ***Would*** *you* ***like*** *a cup of tea?*
   - ***Would*** *you close the door, please?*
   - *I* ***would like*** *to make a phone call.*
   - *Aunt Jean* ***would like*** *to visit New Zealand.*
   - *Many boys* ***would rather*** *play a game than read a book.*

should

1. The modal verb ***should*** is occasionally used as the past tense of ***shall*** in formal contexts:
   - *I knew I* ***should*** *soon be well again.*
   - *We vowed that they* ***should*** *not defeat us again.*

2. You use ***should*** to give (or ask for) **advice** and say what is the **right** or **sensible** thing to do:
   - *Everyone* ***should*** *eat plenty of fruit.*
   - ***Should*** *I have my hair cut short?*
   - *Alice* ***should*** *take more exercise.*
   - *I know I* ***should*** *have apologized.*
   - *You* ***should*** *always tell the truth.*
   - *The girls* ***should*** *not stay out so late at night.*

3. You can also use ***should*** to say what is **normally the case**, or what is **tentatively expected**:
   - *The door* ***should*** *open when the buzzer is pressed.*
   - *The figures in the two columns* ***should*** *add up to the same amount.*
   - *This question* ***should*** *be easier than the last one.*
   - *The results* ***should*** *come back from the laboratory on Wednesday.*

 ISBN 978-81-8477-745-1

4. You use ***should*** in **questions** to make a **tentative offer** or **suggestion**:
   - ***Should*** *I open the window?*
   - ***Should*** *we phone the police?*

PRACTICE

Exercise 1

Choose the correct word from the brackets to fill in the blanks.

1. This ______________ (*shall/should*) be the correct answer.
2. Tom ______________ (*will/would*) like to learn to drive.
3. ______________ (*Shall/Will*) I show you what to do?
4. It ______________ (*shan't/won't*) be easy to find a replacement.
5. Do you think I ______________ (*should/would*) apply for this job?
6. They promised they ______________ (*shouldn't/wouldn't*) leave without us.
7. I hoped it ______________ (*will/would*) stay fine for our picnic.
8. The computer ______________ (*won't/wouldn't*) work if you don't switch it on!
9. ______________ (*Shall/Should*) I have brought my swimsuit?
10. The boys ______________ (*shall/will*) be hungry when they get home.

Exercise 2

*Rewrite the following sentences in the **negative**, using **contractions**.*

1. You should go that way.

   ____

2. The ice will melt.

   ____

3. I shall ask Tony for help.

   ____

 ISBN 978-81-8477-745-1

4. The book should be on that shelf.

____

5. We will arrive in time.

____

6. I would like to be a stuntman.

____

7. He should have parked his car on the drive.

____

8. We shall need a lot of money.

____

9. I would have painted the door red.

____

10. Mum will be angry.

____

Exercise 3

Fill in the blanks with the words in the box, using each one only once.

'll	shall	shan't	should	shouldn't	will	won't	would	wouldn't

Sue: It's rather warm in here. ________ I open the window?

Jack: No, I don't think you ________. The wind ________ blow all my papers around. I've spent a long time putting them in order, and I ________ hate to have to start all over again!

Sue: OK, I ________ open the window, I ________ just open the door instead. That ________ cause too much of a draught. What are you writing?

Jack: It's a novel. I've been writing it for several years. My parents ________ believe me when I tell them I've finished it. They thought I ________ have the patience to write a whole book!

UNIT 30

THE MODAL VERBS *CAN* AND *COULD*

What do they look like?

Tony: **Can** you see that bird? It **couldn't** be that rare songbird we saw on TV last night, **could** it?

Mary: Possibly – I **can't** see it clearly enough to be sure.

Tony: I'll ask Dad if I **can** borrow his binoculars. Last time I asked him, he said I **could**, as long as I was careful with them.

How do you use them?

can

1. You use ***can*** to talk about **ability**:
   - *Philip **can** speak Russian.*
   - ***Can** you reach that shelf?*
   - *Some birds **cannot** fly.*
   - *We **can't** afford a new car.*

2. You also use ***can*** to say what is **possible**:
   - *In the desert, it **can** get very cold at night.*
   - *You **can't** be lucky all the time.*

3. ***Can*** is used informally to ask for, give or refuse **permission**:
   - ***Can** I come with you?*
   - *Jenny **can** sit next to me.*
   - *You **can't** watch television till you've done your homework.*

could

1. The modal verb ***could*** is sometimes used as the past tense of ***can***:
   - *Mozart **could** play the piano when he was only four years old.*
   - *We thought we **couldn't** afford a new car.*
   - *I wish I **could** speak Japanese!*

2. You can use ***could*** to make a **tentative offer** or **suggestion**:
   - *You **could** share my book, if you want.*
   - *Perhaps I **could** become a nurse.*
   - *We **could** eat in that new restaurant this evening.*
   - ***Could** this be the missing necklace?*

 ISBN 978-81-8477-745-1

3 You can also use ***could*** to make a **polite request**:

- ***Could*** *I borrow your pen?*
- ***Could*** *you make a bit less noise, please?*

PRACTICE

Exercise 1

Rewrite the following sentences using can, can't, could *or* couldn't. *The first one has been done to help you.*

1. My little brother is able to walk now.

   My little brother can walk now.

2. We are unable to come to your party.

3. Does Jane know how to play the piano?

4. They were not able to rescue the dog.

5. No one was able to find the missing keys.

6. Few of the villagers knew how to read.

7. Are you unable to run any faster?

8. Dad didn't know how to fix the car.

9. Are all birds able to fly?

10. I wish I knew how to swim.

 ISBN 978-81-8477-745-1

Exercise 2

Choose the correct word from the brackets to fill in the blanks.

1. Sally ______________ (*can/could*) already read and write when she started school.
2. I'm afraid I ______________ (*can/can't*) lend you any money.
3. I knew you ______________ (*can/could*) do it if you tried.
4. We listened, but we ______________ (*could/couldn't*) hear any birds singing.
5. ______________ (*Can/Could*) you guess what I'm holding in my hand?
6. I ______________ (*could/couldn't*) decide which to choose, so I took both.
7. Jack asked his boss if he ______________ (*can/could*) leave early.
8. Alice ______________ (*can/can't*) come with us if she doesn't want to go alone.
9. There ______________ (*can't/couldn't*) be much in the box because it's not very heavy.
10. The police searched the house but they ______________ (*could/couldn't*) find the murder weapon.

Exercise 3

Fill in the blanks with can, can't, could *or* couldn't.

I thought I ______________ swim well, but now I know that I ______________. Last week, I was at the beach with my friend Anna, when I heard someone shout 'Help!' I looked around, but I ______________ see anyone. Then I heard the voice again. 'I ______________ hear someone calling for help,' I said to Anna, 'but I ______________ see where they are.' Anna looked out to sea, and said she ______________ see a boy waving and shouting. 'One of us ______________ swim out and save him,' I said. 'Do you think I should try?' 'Yes,' said Anna. 'You ______________ swim better than I ______________.' So I ran into the water and swam out to the boy. I tried to pull him back to the shore, but I ______________ swim against the strong current. Fortunately, some men on the beach saw that we were struggling, and came to our rescue.

 ISBN 978-81-8477-745-1

UNIT 31

THE MODAL VERBS *MAY*, *MIGHT* AND *MUST*

What do they look like?

Jack: We **may** need to work late this evening. Otherwise, the project **might** not be finished on time. We **mustn't** miss our deadline.

Anne: OK, but I **must** call my parents and tell them. **May** I use your phone? I should be going to karate this evening, but the instructor said I **might** miss a class occasionally.

How do you use them?

may

1. ***May*** is used to express **possibility**:
   - *Take an umbrella – it* ***may*** *rain.*
   - *We* ***may*** *be going to Greece in May.*
   - *Some people* ***may*** *not agree with your idea.*
   - *I think I* ***may*** *have seen this film before.*

2. You can use ***may*** to ask for, give or refuse **permission**. It is more formal or polite than ***can***:
   - ***May*** *I sit here?*
   - *You* ***may*** *leave whenever you like.*
   - *Students* ***may*** *not use calculators during the exam.*

3. You also use ***may*** to make a **polite request**:
   - *Please* ***may*** *I have another cup of tea?*
   - ***May*** *I borrow your dictionary?*

might

1. The modal verb ***might*** can be used as the past tense of ***may***:
   - *They said I* ***might*** *leave whenever I liked.*
   - *Sally asked if she* ***might*** *have another cup of tea.*
   - *Grandpa* ***might*** *hear better if he wore his hearing aid.*

 ISBN 978-81-8477-745-1

2. ***Might*** can be used instead of ***may*** to express **possibility**:
   - *Take an umbrella — it **might** rain.*
   - *We **might** be going to Greece in May.*
   - *Some people **might** not agree with your idea.*
   - *I think I **might** have seen this film before.*

3. You can also use ***might*** to ask a **question** about **possibility**. You do not use ***may*** in this way:
   - ***Might** we need more milk?*
   - ***Mightn't** she be wrong?*
   - ***Might** he have missed the train?*
   - *Where **might** they have hidden the money?*

4. You can use ***might*** to make a **tentative** or **polite suggestion**:
   - *You **might** like to read this article.*
   - ***Mightn't** it be better to wait?*

must

1. ***Must*** is used to express **obligation**:
   - *Candidates **must** speak at least two languages fluently.*
   - *You **must not** drive without insurance.*
   - ***Must** I wear a safety helmet?*

2. ***Must*** is also used to express **necessity**:
   - *I **must** leave at once — I **mustn't** miss the 5.30 train.*
   - *Jenny **must** work harder at school.*
   - ***Must** you play that music so loud?*

3. In Unit 26, you learnt that you can use ***have*** with a **to-infinitive** to express **obligation** or **necessity**:
   - *Everyone **has to carry** an identity card.*
   - *I **had to run** to the station because I was late.*

   Because ***must*** does not have a past tense, you sometimes use ***had to*** instead of ***must*** in the past:
   - *I thought we **had to** wear safety helmets.*
   - *Sue lost her watch, so she **had to** buy a new one.*

4. ***Must*** can also express **certainty** or **strong probability**:
   - *The roof **must** be leaking — there's a puddle on the floor.*
   - *I **must** have forgotten to shut the gate.*

 ISBN 978-81-8477-745-1

PRACTICE

Exercise 1

Fill in the blanks with may *or* might.

1. What ______________ be wrong with the computer?
2. Please ______________ I leave the table?
3. You ______________ have passed the exam if you had worked harder.
4. This is my bicycle, and no-one else ______________ ride it.
5. Where ______________ the children hang their coats?
6. ______________ we find the information we need on the Internet?

Exercise 2

Fill in the blanks with an appropriate question tag. *(Remember that a positive question is followed by a negative question tag, and vice versa.)*

1. They might need some help, _____ _____?
2. We mustn't forget to invite Paul, _____ _____?
3. Joe may not have another cake, _____ _____?
4. I must lose some weight, _____ _____?
5. Your parents might not approve, _____ _____?
6. The weather might get worse, _____ _____?

Exercise 3

Choose the correct word from the brackets to fill in the blanks.

Any student wishing to go on the school trip to the National Theatre _____ (*may/must*) notify Mr Clark by Monday at the latest. There _____ (*might/must*) not be enough tickets for everyone. The cost per student is twenty dollars and this _____ (*might/must*) be paid in full at the time of booking. After booking, students _____ (*may/might*) not cancel unless they can find another student to take their place. The bus to the theatre will leave at midday, and all students _____ (*may/must*) bring a packed lunch to be consumed on the journey. You _____ (*may/might*) also bring something to eat or drink in the interval of the play. Students _____ (*might/must*) be well-behaved at all times, and do nothing that _____ (*may/might*) spoil the enjoyment of other members of the audience. After the play is over, everyone _____ (*may/must*) return on the transport provided. No student _____ (*may/might*) stay on in the city centre, even with their parents' permission.

 ISBN 978-81-8477-745-1

UNIT 32

THE SEMI-MODAL VERBS

What do they look like?

Alice had a rash on her arm. Her mother said she **ought** to ask the doctor about it. He might have to do some tests. 'You **needn't** worry,' she said, 'it's probably nothing serious. Your father **used** to get a rash like that on his ankles. He discovered that he was allergic to the wool in his socks!'

How do you use them?

ought

1. Like modal verbs, the **semi-modal verb *ought*** does not have a different form for the **third person singular**:
   - *You **ought** to take more exercise.*
   - *Sally **ought** to take more exercise.*

2. Unlike modal verbs, the **semi-modal verb *ought*** is followed by a ***to*-infinitive**:
   - *We **ought** **to invite** Uncle Bill to the wedding.*

3. You can use ***ought*** instead of ***should*** to give **advice** and say what is the **right** or **sensible** thing to do:
   - *I think you **ought** to paint the walls red.*
   - *Children **ought** to show respect to older people.*
   - *The council **ought** to put a fence round the playground.*

4. The negative form of ***ought*** is ***ought not*** or ***oughtn't***. You put ***not*** between ***ought*** and ***to***:
   - *You **ought not to** miss this great opportunity!*
   - *The jockey **oughtn't to** hit his horse so hard.*

5. In questions, you put the **subject** between ***ought*** (or ***oughtn't***) and ***to***:
   - ***Ought** **we** **to** contact Kate's parents?*
   - ***Oughtn't** **this door** **to** be locked?*
   - *Which book **ought** **I** **to** read first?*

6. You use ***ought*** without ***to*** in **question tags**:
   - *The engine oughtn't to make a noise like that, **ought it**?*
   - *The children ought to be in bed by now, **oughtn't they**?*

 ISBN 978-81-8477-745-1

need

1. You can use ***need*** as a **main verb** or as a **semi-modal verb**:
   - *Jack **needs** some new shoes.* (main verb)
   - *No one **need** pay more than they can afford.* (semi-modal verb)

2. The **main verb *need*** has forms ending with ***s***, ***ed*** and ***ing*** like other main verbs:
   - *Jack **needs** some new shoes.*
   - *Jack **needed** some new shoes.*
   - *Jack will be **needing** some new shoes soon.*

3. The **main verb *need*** can be followed by a ***to*-infinitive** or an ***ing* form**:
   - *The climbers **needed** **to rest**.*
   - *The floor **needs** **cleaning**.*

4. The **semi-modal verb *need*** is used only in **questions** and **negative statements** (often shortened to ***needn't***). It is followed by the **base form** (the **bare infinitive**) of a verb:
   - ***Need** we **show** our tickets when we go in?*
   - *I **needn't** **remind** you how important this is.*

5. The **semi-modal verb *need*** does not have an ***s*** form, an ***ed*** form or an ***ing*** form:
   - ***Need** the bridegroom make a speech?*
   - *The president **need** not attend all the meetings.*
   - *Mary was told that she **need** not wait.*

used

1. The **semi-modal verb *used*** (pronounced to rhyme with 'roost') exists only in the **past tense**. It is always followed by a ***to*-infinitive**, so most people refer to it as ***used to***:
   - *My grandparents **used** **to live** on a boat.*
   - *This building **used** **to be** the village school.*

2. You use it to talk about **situations that existed in the past**:
   - *People **used** **to think** the world was flat.*
   - *I **used** **to like** pop music best, but now I prefer classical music.*

3. You also use it to talk about **regular actions in the past**:
   - *The bell **used** **to ring** at twelve o'clock every day.*
   - *Dad **used** **to cycle** to work, but now he goes by bus.*

4. The negative form of ***used to*** is ***used not to***:
   - *There **used** **not** **to be** so much litter in the streets.*
   - *Mary **used** **not** **to wear** glasses.*

5. ***Used to*** and ***used not to*** are sometimes used on their own, referring back to an earlier **verb**:
   - *Carol **takes** more exercise than she **used to**.*
   - *I **like** coffee now, but I **used not to**.*

 ISBN 978-81-8477-745-1

PRACTICE

Exercise 1

Rewrite these sentences, using **ought (to)** *instead of* **should.**

1. The council should mend this road. It's full of holes.

2. I should make more of an effort, shouldn't I?

3. Shouldn't we wait for the others to arrive?

4. You should not put so much sugar in your tea.

5. The repair shouldn't cost very much, should it?

6. Should this jar have a lid on it?

7. That book should be on the top shelf.

8. People should not expect to be paid for doing nothing.

9. Do you think I should sell this big house and buy a smaller one?

10. The meat should be cooked by now, shouldn't it?

 ISBN 978-81-8477-745-1

Exercise 2

*Say whether **need** is used as a main verb (MV) or semi-modal verb (SM) in these sentences.*

1. These socks **need** ( ) mending.
2. I **need** ( ) to find a good dentist.
3. They **need** ( ) never know who gave them the money.
4. We **need** ( ) a hammer and some nails.
5. The doctor said that I **need** ( ) not worry.
6. If you **need** ( ) to make a phone call, you can borrow my phone.
7. **Need** ( ) all the children be vaccinated?
8. Does anyone **need** ( ) any help?
9. You **needn't** ( ) eat all the soup if you don't like it.
10. **Need** ( ) I write my name at the top of each page?

Exercise 3

Rewrite this passage replacing the verbs in bold print with a form containing used to.

This is the road where I **lived** when I was a boy. It **lay** on the edge of the town. Those houses **were not** there. That land **was** covered with fields, where farmers **grew** wheat, barley and other crops. I **helped** with the harvest sometimes. My younger sister Betty and I **walked** down this road to school. Betty **did not like** walking home alone in the evening. She **was** afraid of the dark, but she's much braver now! Betty and I **had** a dog called Max. We **took** him for long walks in the countryside. He **liked** chasing rabbits.

 ISBN 978-81-8477-745-1

UNIT 33

TRANSITIVE AND INTRANSITIVE VERBS

What do they look like?

Tom **works** at the grocer's shop. Sometimes he **serves** behind the counter; sometimes he **drives** the delivery van. When he **is serving** customers, he is always polite and **gives** everyone a friendly smile. When he is out in the van, he never **drives** too fast. His boss **considers** him a model employee!

What are they?

1. A **transitive verb** has an object:
   - *I **opened** the door.*
   - *Mum **woke** me.*

2. An **intransitive verb** has no object or complement:
   - *The audience **laughed**.*
   - *Dad **left** early this morning.*

3. Some verbs can have **two objects**, a direct object and an indirect object. They are called **ditransitive verbs**:
   - *He **asked** me the way.*
   - *Mum **read** the children a story.*

4. Some verbs can have an object and a complement. They are called **complex transitive verbs**:
   - *The judges **declared** Frank the winner.*
   - *I **painted** the door orange.*

 ISBN 978-81-8477-745-1

How do you use them?

1 The object of a **transitive verb** can be a **noun**, **pronoun**, **noun phrase** or **noun clause**:

- *The boys* ***were drinking*** ***lemonade****.*
- *Jane* ***thanked*** ***me****.*
- *An earthquake* ***has destroyed*** ***many of the buildings****.*
- *The president* ***announced*** ***that the war was over****.*

You will learn about noun clauses in Unit 65.

2 An **intransitive verb** does not have an object or complement. However, it may be followed by an **adverb** or a **prepositional phrase**:

- *The bomb* ***exploded****.*
- *Time* ***passed*** ***quickly****.*
- *We* ***went*** ***for a long walk****.*

3 You can use some **verbs** transitively (with an **object**) or intransitively:

- *I* ***opened*** ***the door****.* (transitive)
- *Mum* ***woke*** ***me****.* (transitive)
- *The door* ***opened****.* (intransitive)
- *I* ***woke*** *at six o'clock.* (intransitive)

Ditransitive verbs

1 **Ditransitive verbs** have **two objects**. The **direct object** is the thing you give or do for someone. The **indirect object** is the person who receives the thing:

- *Joe* ***cooked*** ***his parents an excellent meal****.*
- *Shall I* ***get*** ***you a drink****?*

2 You put the **indirect object** before the **direct object**:

- *Miss Lee* ***handed*** ***John his test paper****.*
- *The bank* ***lent*** ***us some money****.*

3 Many sentences with **ditransitive verbs** can be rewritten in the form **transitive verb** + (direct) **object** + **preposition** + (indirect) **object**:

- *Joe* ***cooked*** ***an excellent meal*** ***for*** ***his parents****.*
- *The bank* ***lent*** ***some money*** ***to*** ***us****.*

4 The **indirect object** of a **ditransitive verb** is usually a person, but it can also be an **animal** or a **thing**:

- *They* ***found*** ***the dog a good home****.*
- *I* ***must buy*** ***my car some new tyres****.*

5 If the **indirect object** is the same as the **subject**, you must use a **reflexive pronoun**:

- ***George*** *poured* ***himself*** *a glass of fruit juice.*
- ***The cat*** *gave* ***itself*** *a good wash.*

 ISBN 978-81-8477-745-1

Complex transitive verbs

1. **Complex transitive verbs** have an object and a complement. The complement is a noun or adjective that says something about the object.
   - *The team **elected** Jenny captain.*
   - *That noise **is driving** me mad.*

2. You put the complement after the object:
   - *I **consider** Michael my best friend.*
   - *You **call** these nouns uncountable.*

3. The **complement** can be a longer noun phrase or adjectival phrase:
   - *The judges **declared** Sally the most talented young dancer in the competition.*
   - *We **consider** this exercise too difficult for our students.*

PRACTICE

Exercise 1

Say whether the verb in bold print is transitive (T), intransitive (I), ditransitive (D) or complex transitive (C).

1. We **are waiting** for the bus. ( )
2. Tom **called** his brother a fool. ( )
3. The umpire **blew** his whistle. ( )
4. The children **ran** upstairs. ( )
5. Please **show** me your passport. ( )
6. I **passed** Sally a note. ( )
7. Mr Brown **drove** his car into the garage. ( )
8. The wizard's magic potion **made** him invisible. ( )
9. The teacher **gave** prizes to the students with the highest marks. ( )
10. The house **stands** on an island in the middle of the lake. ( )

 ISBN 978-81-8477-745-1

Exercise 2

Rewrite the following sentences using ditransitive verbs. The first one has been done to help you.

1. Dad bought a bike for James. *Dad bought James a bike.*
2. I'm sending an email to my cousin. ______
3. Alice played some music for her guests. ______
4. The boy would not tell his name to anyone. ______
5. Shall I fetch your slippers for you, Grandpa? ______
6. Please bring that book to me. ______
7. We'll keep a place for you at our table. ______
8. The children gave some food to the birds in the cage. ______
9. Kate sold her old computer to her friend. ______
10. Tom cut a large slice of cake for himself. ______

Exercise 3

In the following passage, underline all the transitive verbs and put a ring round all the intransitive verbs.(Ignore any linking verbs which are neither transitive nor intransitive.)

The aid workers arrived by helicopter. They landed in a field and unloaded boxes of food and medical supplies from the helicopter. The people of the village waited nearby. They looked tired and hungry. The aid workers gave a food parcel to each of them. It was not much, but the people were very grateful. They returned to their homes and fed their families. Then, the aid workers went to the hospital with the medical supplies. The doctors welcomed them and eagerly took the boxes of drugs and dressings. Now, they could treat their sick patients and bandage their wounds.

 ISBN 978-81-8477-745-1

UNIT 34

ACTIVE AND PASSIVE VERBS

What do they look like?

Typewriters **are used** very rarely in modern times. Most people **use** computers and printers instead. Old technology **has been replaced** by new technology (for example, DVDs and CDs **have replaced** videos and records) and machines now **do** work that **was done** by human beings in the past.

	ACTIVE	PASSIVE
Simple present	*use*	*is/are used*
Simple past	*used*	*was/were used*
Future	*will/shall use*	*will/shall be used*
Present continuous	*is/are using*	*is/are being used*
Present perfect	*has/have used*	*has/have been used*
Past continuous	*was/were using*	*was/were being used*
Past perfect	*had used*	*had been used*

What are they?

The **active** and **passive** forms of verbs are referred to as the **active voice** and the **passive voice.**

Active voice

1. When the subject of a **verb** is doing the action, you say the verb is **active**:
   - *The dog* ***barked.***
   - *Jane* ***won*** *the race.*

2. **Active verbs** that are **transitive** have a subject that performs the action, and an object that receives the action:
   - *Peter* ***drew*** *this picture.*
   - *Clouds* ***hid*** *the sun.*
   - *The hunter* ***shot*** *the bear.*
   - *Commuters* ***crowded*** *the platform.*

 ISBN 978-81-8477-745-1

Passive voice

1. When a sentence is changed so that the **object** of a **transitive verb** becomes its subject, you say the verb is **passive**:
   - *This picture* ***was drawn*** *by Peter.*
   - *The sun* ***was hidden*** *by clouds.*

2. A **passive verb** is often followed by a **preposition** and the **original subject** of the active verb:
   - *The bear* ***was shot by*** *the hunter.*
   - *The platform* ***was crowded with*** *commuters.*

3. Many sentences in the **passive voice** do not tell you who does the action:
   - *Our classroom* ***was painted*** *last week.*
   - *Breakfast* ***is served*** *between 7.00 and 9.00.*

4. Some verbs are always (or nearly always) used in the **passive**:
   - *My mother* ***was born*** *in 1970.*
   - *The school* ***is situated*** *in the centre of the village.*

How do you form passive verbs?

1. For the **passive** of the SIMPLE PRESENT TENSE, you use ***am***, ***is*** or ***are*** + past participle:
   - *Mrs Brown* ***teaches*** *physics and chemistry.* (active)
   - *Physics and chemistry* ***are taught*** *by Mrs Brown.* (passive)

2. For the **passive** of the SIMPLE PAST TENSE, you use ***was*** or ***were*** + past participle:
   - *The army* ***built*** *this bridge.* (active)
   - *This bridge* ***was built*** *by the army.* (passive)

3. For the **passive** of the PRESENT CONTINUOUS, you use ***am, is*** or ***are*** + ***being*** + past participle:
   - *Mr Thomas* ***is training*** *the players.* (active)
   - *The players* ***are being trained*** *by Mr Thomas.* (passive)

   Notice in the example above that the first part of the verb changes from ***is*** to ***are*** when the subject changes from singular (***Mr Thomas***) to plural (***The players***).

4. For the **passive** of the PAST CONTINUOUS, you use ***was*** or ***were*** + ***being*** + past participle:
   - *The kitchen staff* ***were preparing*** *the buffet.* (active)
   - *The buffet* ***was being prepared*** *by the kitchen staff.* (passive)

 ISBN 978-81-8477-745-1

5 For the **passive** of the PRESENT PERFECT, you use ***have*** or ***has*** + ***been*** + **past participle**:

- *The earthquake* ***has destroyed*** *many buildings.* (active)
- *Many buildings* ***have been*** ***destroyed*** *by the earthquake.* (passive)

6 For the **passive** of the PAST PERFECT, you use ***had*** + ***been*** + **past participle**:

- *A masked man* ***had robbed*** *the bank.* (active)
- *The bank* ***had been*** ***robbed*** *by a masked man.* (passive)

7 For the **passive** of the FUTURE, you use ***will*** or ***shall*** + ***be*** + **past participle**:

- *His family* ***will miss*** *him.* (active)
- *He* ***will be*** ***missed*** *by his family.* (passive)

Notice that if the object of the active sentence is a personal pronoun, you must change this to a subject pronoun (***him*** to ***he*** in the example above) when you make the sentence passive.

8 You cannot change **intransitive verbs** or **linking verbs** from active to passive, because they do not have an object:

- *I* ***stood*** *at the back of the queue.* (intransitive verb)
- *The* ***weather*** *turned colder.* (linking verb)

9 When **ditransitive verbs** are changed from active to passive, the **indirect object** usually becomes the **subject** of the **passive verb** and the **direct object follows the verb**:

- *The government* ***has told*** *the people* ***a lot of lies****.* (active)
- *The people* ***have been told*** ***a lot of lies*** *by the government.* (passive)

10 When **complex transitive verbs** are changed from active to passive, the **object** becomes the **subject** of the **passive verb** and the **complement follows the verb**:

- *Everyone* ***considers*** ***Tom*** *the better player.* (active)
- ***Tom*** ***is considered*** *the better player by everyone.* (passive)

When do you use the passive voice?

1 You can use the **passive voice** if the person or thing that receives the action is more important than the **agent** (the person or thing that performs the action):

- *Some priceless manuscripts* ***were destroyed*** *by the fire.*
- *The drowning child* ***was rescued*** *by a lifeguard.*

2 You can use the passive voice if **the agent is not known**:

- *My bicycle* ***has been stolen****.*
- *This box* ***was left*** *on my doorstep.*

 ISBN 978-81-8477-745-1

3. You can use the passive voice if it is **not necessary to name the agent**:
   - *Trespassers **will be prosecuted**.*
   - *The offices **are cleaned** every night.*

4. You can use the passive voice to **make a general statement**:
   - *Rice **is grown** in China.*
   - *Red wine **is** usually **drunk** at room temperature.*

5. You can use a **passive verb** followed by a *to*-infinitive to say **what everyone believes to be true**:
   - *He **was said** to have twenty children.*
   - *The president **is rumoured** to have resigned.*
   - *This **is thought** to be the tallest building in the country.*

   You can also use ***It*** as the subject of such sentences, changing the *to*-infinitive to a *that*-clause:
   - ***It was said** that he had twenty children.*
   - ***It is rumoured** that the president has resigned.*
   - ***It is thought** that this is the tallest building in the country.*

6. You can use the verbs ***have*** and ***get*** with an **object** and a **past participle** to express the idea of arranging for a job to be done:
   - *We're **having** our apartment **painted** next week.*
   - *You should **get** your hair **cut**.*

   You can also use ***get*** with or without an **object** to express the idea of being involved in a particular situation:
   - *I don't want this book to **get damaged**.*
   - *The dog **got** its tail **caught** in the door.*

   In Unit 72, you will learn more about using a mixture of active and passive verbs to add variety to your writing.

PRACTICE

Exercise 1

Change the following sentences from the passive voice to the active voice.

1. St Paul's Cathedral was designed by Sir Christopher Wren.

   ____

2. This vase was broken by my clumsy sister.

   ____

3. The house had been bought by a newly married couple.

____

4. The part of the mad scientist will be played by Jack Horner.

____

5. The seeds are carried by the wind.

____

6. The floor was covered with muddy footprints.

____

7. The problem has been made worse by pollution.

____

8. The soldier was awarded a medal by the president.

____

9. Lifejackets are worn by all the members of the crew.

____

10. Was the plan approved by the committee?

____

Exercise 2

*Change the following sentences from the **active voice** to the **passive voice**. You do not need to mention the subject of the active verb in the passive sentences.*

1. Someone had spilt ink on the rug.

____

2. Our teachers give us too much homework.

____

3. Everyone considered the woman a genius.

____

4. The council will hold a meeting in the town hall this evening.

____

5. People use this path as a shortcut to the station.

____

 ISBN 978-81-8477-745-1

6. They did not tell me the truth.

7. The men are repairing the car.

8. The band was playing a lively dance tune.

9. Nobody wears uniform at our school.

10. The girl said that some of the other students had bullied her.

Exercise 3

In the following passage, underline all the active verbs and put a ring round all the passive verbs. You can ignore any linking verbs.

The museum stands on the south bank of the river. It was built in the eighteenth century and houses a valuable collection of Chinese paintings that are believed to be more than a thousand years old. Historians have studied these paintings with interest. They show some ancient traditions that were discontinued long ago. In the basement of the museum, you will find some unusual stone objects. It is thought that some of these were used in religious ceremonies by early inhabitants of this region. Others were possibly weapons, but no one knows whether the people killed animals or enemies with them.

Excroisc 4: grammar for writing

Write a news report, about 100 words long, about an incident at a shopping mall, such as a fire or a robbery. Your passage should contain a mixture of active and passive verbs, including at least ten verbs in the passive voice. When you have finished, underline the passive verbs.

 ISBN 978-81-8477-745-1

UNIT 35

VERB AGREEMENT

What does it look like?

The match begins in half an hour, and **the spectators are** taking their seats in the stadium. There **is not enough room** for everyone. **A crowd has** gathered outside, where the match will be shown on a large video screen. **The home team are** hoping for a win, but **the other team has** not yet been beaten this season.

What is it?

Verb agreement is making a **verb** match its **subject**. For example, you have to use a **singular verb** with a **singular subject**, and a **plural verb** with a **plural subject**:

- *A spider* ***has*** *eight legs.*
- *Spiders* ***have*** *eight legs.*
- *I* ***am*** *in the football team.*
- *We* ***are*** *in the football team.*

How do you make the verb agree?

1. Difficulties mainly arise in the **simple present** when you have a **third-person subject** (such as a **noun** or one of the pronouns *he*, *she*, *it* or *they*). You have to decide whether it is **singular** or **plural**:
   - *My cousin* ***works*** *on a farm.* (singular)
   - *My cousins* ***work*** *on a farm.* (plural)

2. If the **subject is singular**, you need a **singular verb**. That is, you add ***s*** to a verb in the present tense (or use a form such as ***is, was, has, does***):
   - *The mouse* ***lives*** *in this cage.*
   - *He* ***does*** *not like cola.*
   - *This* ***is*** *my sister.*

   But remember that **modal auxiliary verbs** do not have a different third-person form ending in ***s***:

   - *The heating* ***should*** *come on automatically.*
   - *She* ***can*** *sit beside me.*

 ISBN 978-81-8477-745-1

3. If the **subject is plural**, you need a **plural verb**. That is, you use the **base form** in the present tense (or ***are*** or ***were*** for the verb ***be***):
   - *The mice **live** in this cage.*
   - *They **do** not like cola.*
   - *These **are** my sisters.*

4. There is no problem with most verbs in the **simple past** (except ***be***) because they have the same form in all persons, singular and plural:
   - *My cousin **worked** on a farm.* (singular)
   - *My cousins **worked** on a farm.* (plural)

5. Nor is there any problem with the **first and second persons** of most verbs in the **simple present** (except ***be***) because their singular and plural forms are the same:
   - *I **have** two dogs.* (singular)
   - *We **have** two dogs.* (plural)
   - *Do **you** need a rest, Tom?* (singular)
   - *Do **you** need a rest, children?* (plural)

6. However, remember that the verb ***be*** has ***I am*** in the **simple present**, and ***was*** for the **first and third persons singular** in the **simple past**:
   - *I **am** afraid.* (singular)
   - *We **are** afraid.* (plural)
   - *She **was** afraid.* (singular)
   - *They **were** afraid.* (plural)

How do you decide if the subject is singular or plural?

Nouns

1. You learnt about singular and plural nouns in Chapter 1. **Singular countable nouns** and **uncountable nouns** are used with a **singular verb**:
   - *This house **has** a flat roof.*
   - *The water **was** very cold.*

2. **Plural countable nouns** are used with a **plural verb**. However, you must remember that **some plural nouns do not end in *s***:
   - *These houses **have** flat roofs.*
   - *The children **want** to play outside.*
   - *Some sheep **were** grazing in the field.*
   - *The police **do** not know why the man was murdered.*
   - *Fungi **flourish** in warm damp conditions.*

 ISBN 978-81-8477-745-1

3. You must also remember that some **uncountable nouns** and **proper nouns** have the plural ending *s*, but they take a **singular verb**:
   - ***Good news*** ***is*** *always welcome.*
   - ***Measles*** ***is*** *a serious illness.*
   - ***Athletics*** ***is*** *my favourite sport.*
   - ***The United States*** ***is*** *a large county in North America.*

4. And you must not forget that nouns such as ***luggage, baggage, furniture, equipment*** and ***traffic*** take a **singular verb**, even though they refer to several items:
   - ***All our luggage*** ***has*** *been stolen.*
   - ***The furniture*** ***was*** *stored in a large warehouse.*

5. **Gerunds** (verbal nouns that end with *ing*) are always used with a **singular verb**:
   - ***Eating*** *too many sweets* ***is*** *bad for your health.*
   - ***Is*** ***cycling*** *allowed on the promenade?*

6. In Unit 5, you learnt that **collective nouns** can be used with a **singular or plural verb**. You use a **singular verb** when you are thinking of the group as a **unit**. You use a **plural verb** when you are thinking of the group as **individuals**:
   - ***My family*** ***comes*** *from Hong Kong.*
   - ***My family*** ***were*** *pleased to see me again.*

7. **Amounts**, **weights** and **distances** take a **singular verb**:
   - ***Eighty dollars*** ***is*** *too much to pay for those trainers.*
   - ***Two kilometres*** ***is*** *not very far.*

8. If the subject is a long **noun phrase** containing more than one noun, you must look for the **main noun** and make the **verb** agree with that:
   - ***The children playing in the garden*** ***are*** *my cousins.*
   - ***The advice that Jack's parents gave him before he set off on his travels*** ***has*** *been very useful.*

Pronouns

1. You use the **personal pronouns** ***he***, ***she*** and ***it*** with a **singular verb** and **all other personal pronouns** with a **plural verb** (except *be*):
   - ***He*** ***wants*** *to go home.*
   - ***We*** ***want*** *to go home.*

2. You use the **demonstrative pronouns** ***this*** and ***that*** with a **singular verb** and ***these*** and ***those*** with a **plural verb**:
   - ***That*** ***is*** *a good idea.*
   - ***These*** ***are*** *my best jeans.*

 ISBN 978-81-8477-745-1

3 You can use **possessive pronouns** (such as ***mine*** or ***yours***) and **interrogative pronouns** (such as ***whose*** or ***which***) with a **singular** or **plural verb**. You have to decide whether the pronoun refers to a singular noun or a plural noun:

- *These must be your boots — **mine are** black.* (*mine* = *my boots*)
- ***Whose is** that car?* (*Whose* = *Whose car*)

4 You use the **indefinite pronouns** (such as ***everyone*** or ***something***) with a **singular verb**, even if they refer to many people or things:

- ***Everyone likes** to be praised.*
- ***Does anything** in this box belong to you?*

See Unit 17 for information about using plural pronouns and determiners with indefinite pronouns.

5 You typically use the **quantifiers *either*** and ***neither*** with a **singular verb**:

- *You can sit in this seat or that one — **neither is** occupied.*
- ***Does either** of the twins play the piano?*

For the rules concerning ***either … or*** and ***neither … nor***, see the section **Nouns and pronouns linked by *or*** below.

6 You also use the **quantifiers *each***, ***one***, ***another***, ***little***, ***a little***, ***less*** and ***much*** with a **singular verb**:

- *There are many plants in the garden, and **each has** a different name.*
- ***Little remains** to be done.*
- ***Less was** known about the disease in those days.*

7 You use the **quantifiers *both***, ***few***, ***a few***, ***fewer***, ***several*** and ***many*** with a **plural verb**:

- *Sally dropped the plates, and **a few were** broken.*
- ***Both** of the twins **play** the piano.*

8 You can use most other **quantifiers** (including ***all, some, none, any, a lot*** and ***lots***) with a **singular** or **plural verb**. You have to decide whether the pronoun refers to a singular noun or a plural noun:

- ***Some** of the work **is** finished, but **lots** still **needs** to be done.* (singular verb to agree with 'work', even though 'lots' looks plural)
- ***Some** of the students **walk** to school, but **a lot come** by car.* (plural verb to agree with 'students', even though 'a lot' looks singular)
- *Sally dropped the plates, but **none were** broken.* (plural verb because more than one might have been broken)
- *There were four women outside, but **none was** my mother.* (singular verb because only one is likely to be the mother)

 ISBN 978-81-8477-745-1

Nouns and pronouns linked by *and*

1. You use a **plural verb** with two or more **nouns** (or **pronouns**) linked by ***and***, even if they are both (or all) singular:
   - *Vegetables and fruit **are** good for the body.*
   - *Blue and red **are** my favourite colours.*
   - *He and I **have** become close friends.*
   - *Brazil, Peru and Argentina **are** in South America.*

2. However, in a few cases, a pair of nouns joined by ***and*** represents a **single thing or idea** and takes a **singular verb**:
   - *Law and order **is** the government's main concern.*
   - *Steak and chips **is** my favourite dish.*
   - *'Pride and Prejudice' **is** a novel by Jane Austen.*
   - *The Stars and Stripes **is** the national flag of the USA.*

3. If a **singular noun** is linked to another noun by a phrase such as ***together with***, ***as well as*** or ***in addition to***, you must use a **singular verb**:
   - *Aunt Mary, **together with** three of her friends, **is** coming for lunch.*
   - *Basketball, **in addition to** the games already taught, **has** become part of the curriculum.*

Nouns and pronouns linked by *or*

1. When **nouns** or **pronouns** are linked by ***or***, the **verb** usually agrees with the **noun or pronoun closest to it**:
   - *Susan or James **has** the information you need.*
   - *The letter or letters **are** delivered by hand.*
   - ***Have** you or Richard been telling tales about me?*

2. The same rule applies to ***either … or*** and ***neither … nor***:
   - ***Does** either the cat or its kittens need feeding?*
   - *Neither my brother nor I **like** chocolate.*

there is and there are

1. You can use ***there is*** and ***there are*** (or ***there was*** and ***there were***) to say what exists or what is available:
   - ***There is** some paper in the cupboard.*
   - ***There were** no emails in my inbox.*
   - ***Are there** any volunteers?*
   - ***There wasn't** any salt on the table.*

2. When you use these phrases, the **verb** agrees with the **noun** that follows it:
   - *There **is** a stain on the carpet.*
   - *There **were** footprints in the snow.*

 ISBN 978-81-8477-745-1

3 When the phrase is followed by a quantifier, the **verb** agrees with the noun that the quantifier refers to:

- *There **was** lots of work to be done.*
- *There **were** several people on the platform.*
- *Most of the cakes have been eaten, but there **are** a few left.*
- *I've spilt the ink. **Is** there any on the floor?*

Note that the verb does not agree with 'lots' and 'a few' in the first and third examples above.

one of ... who/that ...

1 Phrases such as *one of the things that* or *one of those people who* are followed by a **plural verb** because the verb agrees with the plural noun *things* or *people*:

- *This is one of the things that **annoy** me most.*
- *Tom is one of those people who never **say** exactly what they mean.*
- *One of the boys who **play** in the band has promised to teach me the guitar.*

2 However, the **verbs** outside the relative clause (that is, the clause beginning with *that* or *who*) are **singular** because they agree with one:

- *This **is** one of the things that annoy me most.*
- *One of the boys who play in the band **has** promised to teach me the guitar.*

You will learn more about relative clauses in Unit 64.

PRACTICE

Exercise 1

Choose the correct form of the verb in brackets to fill in the blanks.

1. Some people ______________ coffee to tea. (*prefers/prefer*)
2. The traffic ______________ slowly at this time of day. (*moves/move*)
3. Sally and I ______________ going to the cinema this evening. (*is/are*)
4. There ______________ little to do in the village. (*was/were*)
5. ______________ either of you seen this film before? (*Has/Have*)
6. Four hours ______________ a long time to wait. (*is/are*)
7. ______________ all the houses have gardens? (*Does/Do*)
8. There ______________ a lot of interesting photographs in this book. (*is/are*)
9. Our house, as well as those around it, ______________ badly damaged by the fire. (*was/were*)
10. Bill or I ______________ usually the last to leave. (*am/is/are*)

 ISBN 978-81-8477-745-1

Exercise 2

*Rewrite these sentences in the **present tense**, using the correct **singular** or **plural form** of the verb in bold print.*

1. The water **looked** cloudy. ______________________
2. The children **did** not understand. ______________________
3. Nobody **knew** the answer. ______________________
4. Neither of the clocks **told** the right time. ______________________
5. Mr Jones **drove** to work. ______________________
6. Sally and Jane **slept** in the same room. ______________________
7. The dog **could** run very fast. ______________________
8. Each of the guests **made** a speech. ______________________
9. A few of the cups **had** broken handles. ______________________
10. The machine **put** a lid on each bottle. ______________________

Exercise 3

*In the following sentences, underline the **noun**, **pronoun** or **phrase** that the verb in bold print **agrees** with. The first one has been done to help you.*

1. The man driving the van **was wearing** a baseball cap.
2. Students who listen to their teachers **learn** most.
3. Playing football in the park **is** forbidden.
4. There **was** not a lot of space on the form to write my address.
5. **Is** either of your sisters as talented as you are?
6. The boy and his parents **are** waiting outside.
7. It is one of those things that nobody **knows** for certain.
8. Neither you nor Paul **has** been invited to the wedding.
9. Two of the children who **live** next door go to my school.
10. Some birds, such as penguins and ostriches, **are** unable to fly.

 ISBN 978-81-8477-745-1

Exercise 4

Choose the correct form of the verb in brackets to fill in the blanks in the following passage.

Joe and his family ____________ (*is/are*) moving to a new house. They have asked whether Tom and I ____________ (*am/is/are*) interested in renting their present apartment. We ____________ (*am/is/are*) considering their offer. The apartment ____________ (*is/are*) one of those places that ____________ (*looks/look*) bigger than they actually ____________ (*is/are*). There ____________ (*is/are*) two bedrooms, but both ____________ (*is/are*) small and neither ____________ (*has/have*) a very nice view. Also, the people who ____________ (*lives/live*) in the apartment next door ____________ (*has/have*) a lot of parties, which often ____________ (*lasts/last*) into the early hours of the morning. I think Tom and I will probably stay in our current home. Everyone ____________ (*is/are*) very friendly in the community where we ____________ (*lives/live*), and there ____________ (*is/are*) a lot more space, both inside and outside the house.

Exercise 5: grammar for writing

Write a letter, about 150 words long, telling a foreign friend how Christmas is celebrated in your country. Underline the subjects and put a ring round the verbs, making sure that they agree.

____

____

____

____

____

____

____

____

 ISBN 978-81-8477-745-1

UNIT 36

THE IMPERATIVE AND OTHER MOODS

What do they look like?

Anna **was** bored. She **looked** out of the classroom window and **saw** a flock of birds in the sky. 'I **wish** I **were** a bird,' **thought** Anna. '**Pay** attention, Anna,' **said** her teacher. '**Don't forget** that you **have** an important exam at the end of this term. If you **do not listen**, you **will not learn**.'

What are they?

Verbs have **three moods**. They are the **indicative mood**, **the subjunctive mood** and **the imperative mood**.

- *I **was washing** my hair when the phone **rang**.* (indicative)
- *Jane sometimes wishes she **were** a boy.* (subjunctive)
- ***Peel** the orange but **do not throw** the peel away.* (imperative)

How do you use them?

The indicative mood

The **indicative mood** is the form of the **verb** that you use in most **statements** and **questions**. It always has a **subject**:

- *We **walked** across the bridge.*
- ***Does** this road **lead** to the station?*

The subjunctive mood

1. The **present tense** of the **subjunctive mood** is the **base form** of the verb (without *s* in the third person). It is chiefly used in formal English to say that something is **essential** or **advisable**:
   - *They insisted that she **apologize**.*
   - *I propose that the meeting **be** postponed.*

2. The **past tense** of the **subjunctive mood** is the same as the **past indicative** for all verbs except ***be***. It is chiefly used in the **conditional**, or for **wishes that cannot be fulfilled**:
   - *You would see better if you **wore** your glasses.*
   - *I wish I **had** wings!*

You will learn more about the conditional in Unit 47.

 ISBN 978-81-8477-745-1

3. The **past subjunctive** of *be* is *were* in all persons, singular and plural:

- *If I **were** you, I would sell that car and buy a more reliable one.*
- *The children would be better behaved if their father **were** here.*
- *Grandma wishes she **were** ten years younger.*

The imperative mood

1. You use the **imperative mood** to give **commands** or **instructions**. It is the **base form** of the verb which you use without a subject, often at the beginning of a sentence:

- ***Come** here at once!*
- ***Sit** down and **be** quiet!*
- ***Have** another sandwich.*
- ***Press** the red button on the front of the machine.*

The imperative is often used in **procedures** which you will learn about in Unit 78.

2. When you tell someone **not** to do something, you have to use the auxiliary verb ***do.*** The pattern is *do* + *not* + **base form**, or you can use the contraction *don't*:

- *Do not **remove** this trolley from the supermarket.*
- *Don't **forget** your passport.*

3. You can make an imperative sound more polite by using *please* before it.

- *Please **leave** me alone.*
- *Please **do not touch** the exhibits.*

PRACTICE

Exercise 1

Using verbs in the imperative mood, write a command in the left-hand column that will produce the result in the right-hand column. The first one has been done to help you.

	COMMAND	RESULT
1.	Go to your kennel.	The dog went to its kennel.
2.	____________	He tied the rope to the post.
3.	Please ____________	She passed me the salt.
4.	____________	The girl was kind to her little brother.
5.	Please ____________	We closed the door behind us.
6.	____________	They weren't frightened.
7.	____________	I sat down and stopped talking.
8.	____________	Nobody walked on the grass.

 ISBN 978-81-8477-745-1

Exercise 2

In the following dialogue, say whether the verbs in bold print are in the indicative (Ind), subjunctive (S) or imperative (Imp) mood.

Alice: I **need** ( ) some information about the local car factory for a school project. I **wish** ( ) Grandpa **were** ( ) still alive. He **worked** ( ) there for many years, didn't he?

Dad: **Don't worry** ( ) – you **can find** ( ) plenty of information on the Internet. **Shall I show** ( ) you how?

Alice: Yes, please.

Dad: OK, first **switch** ( ) the computer on.

Alice: That **is** ( ) easy enough – if only everything **were** ( ) so simple!

Dad: Now **click** ( ) that icon at the bottom of the screen. It **will take** ( ) you straight into the search engine. **Type** ( ) the name of the car factory into the box, then **press** ( ) the 'Enter' key.

Alice: Wow, there **are** ( ) lots of websites here with useful information. Thanks, Dad!

Exercise 3: grammar for writing

Write a set of 'kitchen rules' for your house using at least eight verbs in the imperative mood. When you have finished, underline the imperative verbs.

____

____

____

____

 ISBN 978-81-8477-745-1

UNIT
37

GERUNDS

What do they look like?

The school has many different clubs. Do you like **making** things? If so, you can join the craft club. **Swimming** is the main activity of the water-sports club, but they also do other things such as **sailing**. With the Scout troop, you can go **camping**. Tents are provided. All you need is a **sleeping** bag.

A **gerund** (sometimes called a **verbal noun**) looks exactly the same as the **present participle** (the *ing* participle) of a verb, which you learnt about in Unit 3:

- *The boys were **walking** to school.* (present participle)
- ***Walking** to school is an easy way to take daily exercise.* (gerund)

How do you use them?

1 You can use a **gerund** as the **subject** of a **verb**:

- ***Smoking is** banned on all flights.*
- ***Running is** a good way to keep fit.*

2 A gerund can also be the **object** of a **verb**:

- *Jim **loves walking**.*
- *I **hate sewing**.*
- *It has **stopped raining**.*
- *This sock **needs darning**.*

3 A gerund can be the **object** of a **preposition**:

- *Think **before deciding**.*
- *Michael insisted **on paying**.*
- *You're good **at drawing**.*
- *There's no excuse **for lying**.*

4 A gerund can be the **complement** of a **linking verb**:

- *The cat's favourite occupation **was sleeping**.*
- *Looking at another player's cards **is cheating**.*

Do not confuse this use of the gerund with a **present participle** which can also follow the **auxiliary verb *be***.

- *The cat **was sleeping**.* (present participle)
- *One of the players **is cheating**.* (present participle)

 ISBN 978-81-8477-745-1

5. You can use a gerund **like an adjective** before another **noun**:
   - *Have you brought your **swimming** **costume**?*
   - *The **washing** **machine** is broken.*

6. A gerund can be followed by an **object**, an **adverb** or a **prepositional phrase**:
   - ***Eating** **too many sweets** is bad for your teeth.*
   - *We'll gain nothing by **acting** **hastily**.*
   - *Nobody likes **waiting** **in queues**.*

7. You can put a **determiner**, **possessive form** or **adjective** before a gerund:
   - *I didn't enjoy the play — **the** **acting** was not very good.*
   - ***Jane's** **dancing** has improved recently.*
   - ***Noisy** **coughing** spoilt the performance.*

8. In formal English, you should use a **possessive determiner** before the gerund in sentences of the following type:
   - *We did not approve of **their** **changing** the rules.*
   - *Bill's neighbours object to **his** **parking** outside their house.*

   However, in informal English you can use a **personal pronoun** instead:
   - *We did not approve of **them** **changing** the rules.*
   - *Bill's neighbours object to **him** **parking** outside their house.*

Gerund or present participle?

1. It is usually easy to tell the difference between a **gerund** used as part of a **noun phrase** and a **present participle** used as part of a **verb phrase**:
   - ***Taking** **photographs** is easy with my new digital camera.* (gerund)
   - *The tourists **were** **taking** photographs.* (present participle)

2. However, it can be difficult to tell the difference between a **gerund** and a **present participle** when they are used as **adjectives** before **nouns**:
   - *I couldn't find my **sleeping** **bag**.* (gerund = *my bag for sleeping in*)
   - *I didn't want to disturb the **sleeping** **baby**.* (present participle = *the baby who was sleeping*)

3. If the ***ing*** form is used adjectivally after the **noun**, it must be a **present participle**, not a **gerund**:
   - *The **people** **waiting** were becoming impatient.* (present participle)
   - *A **man** **wearing uniform** asked to see my ticket.* (present participle)

 ISBN 978-81-8477-745-1

PRACTICE

Exercise 1

Rewrite the following sentences, replacing the personal pronoun in bold print with a possessive determiner.

1. We appreciated **them** showing us what to do.

2. Alice does not mind **me** using her computer.

3. I told Bill I resented **him** calling me a liar.

4. Our parents are not happy about **us** staying out late.

5. Aunt Jane told the owner of the cat that she objected to **it** digging in her garden.

6. Don't your neighbours dislike **you** playing music so loud?

7. The boss does not approve of **us** making personal telephone calls.

8. I was not surprised at **him** refusing to co-operate.

9. The teacher would not agree to **me** leaving early.

10. They were annoyed at **you** wasting the money.

Exercise 2

Say whether the ing form is a gerund (G) or a present participle (P).

1. Janet is fond of **teasing** people. ( )
2. The children were **playing** in the garden. ( )

 ISBN 978-81-8477-745-1

3. We had a **spelling** test yesterday. ( )
4. The man **sitting** by the fire is my grandfather. ( )
5. The soldiers pursued their **fleeing** enemies. ( )
6. I apologize for **being** late. ( )
7. Was Jack **telling** the truth? ( )
8. Is **wearing** school uniform compulsory? ( )
9. Sam loved **working** on the farm. ( )
10. **Having** nothing to say, I remained silent. ( )

Exercise 3

Underline all the gerunds in the following passage.

Jack had been reading an article about heart disease. He decided that he should take more exercise. Walking around the house was not enough. The sun was shining outside, so there was no excuse for sitting around indoors. He went upstairs to find his running shorts. They needed washing, so he looked for something else to wear. Hanging in the wardrobe was an old pair of jogging pants. Jack put them on and went downstairs. He opened the front door and looked anxiously at the darkening sky. The sun had stopped shining, and it had started raining. Jack changed his mind about going for a run that day. There was no point in getting wet unnecessarily. Waiting another day to start his new exercise regime would do him no harm, would it?

Exercise 4: grammar for writing

Write a short passage on the subject of hobbies and pastimes, about 120 words long. Your passage should contain at least ten gerunds, used in as many different ways as possible.

 ISBN 978-81-8477-745-1

UNIT 38

THE INFINITIVE

What does it look like?

If you want **to become** a teacher, you must **work** hard at school. You need **to pass** all your exams so that you can **go** to university. It is also important **to be** the right kind of person – someone who enjoys helping children **learn**.

The **infinitive** takes two forms:

1. The **bare infinitive** is the **base form** of the verb, for example:

   be ***go*** ***come*** ***talk*** ***break*** ***respect*** ***educate***

2. The ***to*-infinitive** is the **base form** of the verb with **to** before it, for example:

   to be ***to go*** ***to come*** ***to talk*** ***to break*** ***to respect*** ***to educate***

How do you use it?

The bare infinitive

1. You use the **bare infinitive** after the **primary auxiliary verb *do***:
   - ***Do*** *you* ***know*** *Sam?*
   - *It* ***does*** *not* ***work****.*

2. You also use the **bare infinitive** after **modal verbs** and the **semi-modal verb *need***:
   - ***Can*** *you* ***swim****?*
   - *It* ***might rain*** *later.*
   - *You* ***need****n't* ***alter*** *the arrangements for my sake.*

3. You use the **bare infinitive** after the verbs ***let*** and ***make*** (meaning 'force' or 'cause'):
   - *Just* ***let*** *me* ***think****.*
   - *Mum* ***made*** *me* ***confess*** *the truth.*

4. You also use the **bare infinitive** after some **sensing** verbs:
   - *I* ***saw*** *her* ***cross*** *the street.*
   - *We* ***felt*** *the ground* ***shake****.*
   - *She* ***heard*** *him* ***speak****.*

 ISBN 978-81-8477-745-1

5. You can use the **bare infinitive** or the ***to*-infinitive** after the verb ***help***:
   - *I **helped** Jane **count** the votes.*
   - *I **helped** Jane **to count** the votes.*

The *to*-infinitive

1. You use the ***to*-infinitive** after the **semi-modal verbs *ought* and *used***:
   - *They **ought** **to apologize**.*
   - *Dad **used** **to cycle** to work.*
2. You use the ***to*-infinitive** after ***need*** when it is used as a **main verb**:
   - *Do we **need** **to bring** a packed lunch?*
   - *Someone **needs** **to mend** this fence.*
3. You can also use the ***to*-infinitive** after many other **main verbs**:
   - *I **want** **to win**.*
   - *We **intend** **to complain**.*
   - *David and I **agreed** **to meet** at 4 o'clock.*
   - *Joe has **decided** **to train** as a doctor.*
   - ***Try** **to keep** calm.*
   - *They **seem** **to like** my idea.*
4. Some **verbs** have an **object** before the ***to*-infinitive**:
   - ***Remind** **me** **to buy** more noodles.*
   - *I **forbid** **you** **to use** my car.*
5. You can use the ***to*-infinitive** after certain **adjectives**, for example:
   - *Julie was **afraid** **to cross** the road.*
   - *I'm so **glad** **to see** you.*
   - *The boys are all **keen** **to be** in the team.*
   - *They were **eager** **to hear** the latest news.*
   - *Dan is **likely** **to win**.*
6. You can also use the ***to*-infinitive** after certain **nouns**, for example:
   - *I've no **desire** **to be** famous.*
   - *We need **time** **to think**.*
   - *Jim's **decision** **to retire** surprised everyone.*
   - *We have several **problems** **to discuss**.*
7. You sometimes use the ***to*-infinitive** after ***wh*-words**:
   - *Sue asked Joe **where** **to put** the books.*
   - *I didn't know **what** **to do**.*
   - *Tell me **when** **to stop**.*
8. You can make a ***to*-infinitive** negative by putting ***not*** before it:
   - *I prefer **not** **to drive** at night.*
   - *We were anxious **not** **to be** late.*

 ISBN 978-81-8477-745-1

PRACTICE

Exercise 1

*Fill in the blanks with the **bare infinitive** or the **to-infinitive** of the verb in brackets.*

1. Jane asked the teacher ______________ her. (*help*)
2. Joe's parents won't let him ______________ the karate club. (*join*)
3. I noticed Sam ______________ something to his friend. (*pass*)
4. The winner has ______________ a speech. (*make*)
5. You don't need ______________ this shirt. (*iron*)
6. The baby wouldn't ______________ crying. (*stop*)
7. Who taught those girls ______________? (*dance*)
8. Need I ______________ to this email? (*reply*)
9. That chair ought ______________ in the dining room. (*be*)
10. The dog wants ______________ outside. (*go*)

Exercise 2

*Write sentences on any subject containing the given **infinitives**.*

1. (*to eat*) ____
2. (*win*) ____
3. (*sink*) ____
4. (*to change*) ____
5. (*find*) ____
6. (*to open*) ____
7. (*to live*) ____
8. (*break*) ____
9. (*see*) ____
10. (*to stay*) ____

 ISBN 978-81-8477-745-1

Exercise 3

In the following passage, underline all the to-infinitives and put a ring round all the bare infinitives.

Jack: You had an interview this morning, didn't you? When do you expect to find out whether you have got the job?

Tom: I hope to hear by the end of the week. They had a few more candidates to interview after me, but they said they would tell everyone their decision as soon as possible.

Jack: That's good. It's horrible having to wait for news like that.

Tom: I'm trying not to think about it. I really want the job, but I must not be too optimistic.

Jack: Why don't you come fishing with me? That will help to take your mind off it.

Tom: Thanks. I'll bring some sandwiches, and we can have a picnic lunch.

Jack: That's an excellent idea. And don't forget your fishing rod!

 ISBN 978-81-8477-745-1

UNIT 39

PHRASAL VERBS

What do they look like?

The passengers boarded the plane and **sat down** in their seats. Before the plane **took off**, they were shown how to **put on** their lifejackets in an emergency. They were also warned that the plane might **run into** some turbulence. During the flight, the stewardesses **waited on** them, bringing them everything they **asked for**.

What are they?

A **phrasal verb** is a **verb** used with one or more **adverbs** or **prepositions**, which often give it a special meaning:

- *What do you want to be when you **grow up**?* (grow up = 'become an adult')
- *We **ran into** a serious problem.* (run into = 'encounter')
- *I refuse to **put up with** their bad behaviour.* (put up with = 'endure')

Do not confuse a **phrasal verb** with a **verb phrase** (see Unit 40).

How do you use them?

1. The simplest form of phrasal verb consists of **verb** + **adverb**:
   - *They were away from home when the fire **broke out**.* (break out = 'begin')
   - *I'm afraid a problem has **come up**.* (come up = 'occur')

2. Another form consists of **verb** + object + **adverb**:
   - *Please **put** your books **away**.*
   - *I **switched** the television **off**.*
   - *Mrs Jones has arrived. I'll **show** her **in**.*

   If the object is a noun or noun phrase, you can change the order to **verb** + **adverb** + object:
   - *Please **put away** your books.*
   - *I **switched off** the television.*

   However, if the object is a personal pronoun, you cannot change the order. You cannot write ***I'll show in her***.

 ISBN 978-81-8477-745-1

3. A third form of phrasal verb consists of **verb** + preposition + object:
   - *The caterpillar **changed** into a butterfly.*
   - ***Turn** off the expressway at the next junction.*

   You cannot put the object before the preposition. You cannot say ***Turn the expressway off***.

4. Another form consists of **verb** + **adverb** + preposition + object:
   - *John **fell out** with his best friend.* (*fall out with* = *'quarrel with'*)
   - *The hotel did not **live up** to its reputation.* (*live up to* = *'be as good as'*)

   You cannot move the object in sentences like these.

Adverb or preposition?

1. Some words can be used both as an **adverb** and as a **preposition**. They include:

   about, across, after, before, by, down, in, off, on, out, over, through, to, up

   - *The patient may not pull **through**.* (adverb; *pull through* = 'recover')
   - *I may not get **through** the exam.* (preposition; *get through* = 'pass')

2. If the word is not immediately followed by a noun, pronoun or noun phrase, it is most likely to be an **adverb**:
   - *They watched the helicopter take **off**.* (*take off* = 'leave the ground')
   - *The missing key turned **up** in Dad's briefcase.* (*turn up* = 'be found')

3. If the word is immediately followed by a personal pronoun, it is most likely to be a **preposition**:
   - *The police ran **after** them.*
   - *I took **to** him straight away.* (*take to* = 'like')

4. If the word is immediately followed by a noun or noun phrase, it may be an **adverb** or a **preposition**:
   - *What is the best way to put **across** this message?* (adverb; *put across* = 'communicate')
   - *I came **across** a mistake in the book.* (preposition; *come across* = 'find')

   To find out whether the word is an adverb or a preposition, try putting it after the noun or noun phrase. If you can change the order in this way, the word is an adverb:
   - *What is the best way to put this message **across**?*

   If you cannot change the order in this way, the word is a preposition. (You cannot say ***I came a mistake across***.)

 ISBN 978-81-8477-745-1

5. If there are two words after the verb, the first is probably an **adverb** and the second a **preposition**:
   - *We have run* ***out of*** *milk.* (*run out of* = 'use up all of')
   - *The robbers thought they had got* ***away with*** *the crime.* (*get away with* = 'escape punishment for')

You will learn more about adverbs and prepositions in Chapters 6 and 7.

PRACTICE

Exercise 1

Say whether the words in bold print are adverbs (A) or prepositions (P).

1. The air grew cooler after the sun went **down** ( ).
2. He knows he can count **on** ( ) us to help him.
3. Have you signed **up** ( ) for the marathon?
4. They were ordered to hand **over** ( ) their weapons.
5. Mr Brown doesn't get on **with** ( ) his next-door neighbour.
6. We have not yet started **on** ( ) our new project.
7. The road passes **through** ( ) a long tunnel.
8. The baby bird fell **out** ( ) of the nest.
9. The farmer came **across** ( ) some old coins while ploughing his field.
10. Don't forget to turn **off** ( ) the light.

Exercise 2

Choose a verb from box A and an adverb or preposition from box B to make a phrasal verb with the given meaning. Use each word only once.

A: break	carry	give	go	look	set	tell	throw
B: about	**away**	**back**	**down**	**into**	**off**	**on**	**up**

MEANING	PHRASAL VERB
1. continue	________
2. stop working	________
3. get rid of	________
4. investigate	________

 ISBN 978-81-8477-745-1

5. scold ______________
6. return ______________
7. stop trying ______________
8. start ______________

Exercise 3

*Fill in each blank in the following passage with an **adverb** or **preposition** from the box. You will have to use some of the words more than once.*

at	away	back	down	in	off	on	out	up

My alarm clock went ______________ at six o'clock. I woke ______________ and looked ______________ the time. At first, I couldn't remember why I had to get ______________ so early. Then it came ______________ to me. I was going on a trip with my friend Joe and his parents. We had to set ______________ early to avoid getting held ______________ in the traffic. I got ______________ of bed, had a shower and put ______________ my favourite T-shirt and jeans. Then I went downstairs to make myself some breakfast. While I was doing so, I switched ______________ the radio to find ______________ what was going ______________ in the world. There was no interesting news, so I turned the radio ______________ and sat ______________ to eat my breakfast. At seven o'clock, a large silver car pulled ______________ outside the house. It was Joe and his parents. I ran ______________ to the car and climbed ______________, and we drove ______________.

Exercise 4

*Complete the following responses by filling in the blanks with suitable **phrasal verbs**.*

1. 'It's warm in here.' 'Why don't you ______________ your jacket?'
2. 'I can't see what I'm doing.' 'I'll ______________ the lamp.'
3. 'The park is a mess.' 'Let's ______________ some of this litter and put it in the bin.'
4. 'Where's Mum?' 'She has a headache, so she's gone to ______________ on her bed.'
5. 'I've finished my essay.' 'Now ______________ what you've written and correct any mistakes.'
6. 'Have you fixed my bike yet?' 'No. If you ______________ in about half an hour, it should be ready then.'

 ISBN 978-81-8477-745-1

UNIT 40

VERB PHRASES AND PARTICIPIAL PHRASES

What do they look like?

Kate **had entered** a crossword competition. She **was waiting** to hear if she **had been awarded** first prize – a trip to Florida. One day, a large white envelope **addressed to Kate** came through the letterbox. **Trembling with excitement**, she tore it open. 'Congratulations,' it said, 'you **have won** … a free copy of our puzzle magazine!'

What are they?

1 A **verb phrase** is a word group that makes up the verb in a sentence. It consists of one or more **auxiliary verbs** followed by a **main verb** in the form of a **participle** or the **infinitive**:

- *They **were eating** their lunch.*
- *Sally **has broken** her arm.*
- *The bus **will leave** at 10.30.*
- *We **had been waiting** for several hours.*
- *The money **might have been stolen** by one of the servants.*

Do not confuse a **verb phrase** with a **phrasal verb** (see Unit 39).

2 A **verb phrase** can be 'interrupted' by another word or word group, such as ***not***, an **adverb**, or the **subject** of a question:

- *We **did not notice** any difference.*
- *Mum **has always liked** cats.*
- ***Could** the flight **have been delayed**?*

3 A **participial phrase** is a word group that begins with a **present participle** (sometimes called an ***-ing* participle**) or a **past participle** (sometimes called an ***-ed*/*-en* participle**):

- *Tom spoke to the woman **standing behind the counter**.*
- ***Running to catch the bus**, she tripped and fell.*
- *A man **dressed in black** opened the door.*
- ***Disappointed with the result**, I tried again.*

4 There may be an **adverb** or a **conjunction** before the participle:

- *She received a **neatly written** letter from her young nephew.*
- ***While taking a shower**, I noticed a rash on my leg.*

 ISBN 978-81-8477-745-1

How do you use them?

Verb phrases

1 In earlier units of this chapter, you learnt about using auxiliary verbs to 'help' main verbs. Verb phrases containing ***be*** and ***have*** are used for the **continuous** and **perfect** tenses (which you will learn more about in the next chapter) and the **passive** voice:

- *It **is raining** again.* (continuous)
- *Tom **has lost** his mobile phone.* (perfect)
- *The floor **had been polished** until it shone.* (passive)

2 Verb phrases containing the primary auxiliary verb ***do*** are used for **questions** and **negative statements**:

- ***Does** this book **belong** to you?*
- *The birds **did** not **eat** the seeds I gave them.*

3 Verb phrases containing the modal auxiliary verbs (***will***, ***shall***, ***would***, ***should***, ***can***, ***could***, ***may***, ***might***, ***must***) are used for various purposes:

- *She **will** never **return**.*
- *This new lamp **should make** the room look brighter.*
- ***May** I **sit** here?*
- *You **must have been dreaming**.*

Participial phrases

1 You can use a **participial phrase** like an adjective, before or after a **noun**:

- *The tourists took shelter from the **rapidly worsening** **storm**.*
- *The treasure is buried at the **place** **marked with a cross on the map**.*

2 You can use a **participial phrase** as the **complement** of a **linking verb**:

- *The light **was** **too dazzling to look at**.*
- *You **seem** **dissatisfied with the arrangement**.*

3 You can use a **participial phrase** at the beginning of a sentence to say something about the **subject** of the verb that follows:

- ***Having no children**, **the old man** left all his money to charity in his will.*
- ***Shaking with fury**, **Joe** stormed out of the room.*
- ***Built of concrete and glass**, **the new building** does not fit in with its surroundings.*
- ***Born in London**, **Alice** emigrated to Australia with her family at the age of seven.*

Do not make the mistake of using a **participial phrase** that refers to the **object** of the verb that follows. You cannot say, for example: ***Built of concrete and glass**, most people do not like **the new building**.* This error is sometimes called a **hanging participle** or a **dangling participle**.

 ISBN 978-81-8477-745-1

4. The **participial phrase** sometimes talks about an activity taking place at the same time as the main action of the sentence, or just before it:
   - ***Taking a piece of paper from the rack**, she sat down to write her note.*
   - ***When planning a meal**, you should include several different types of food.*
   - ***Tempted by the cheese**, the mouse stepped on to the trap.*
   - ***Though irritated by his remark**, I said nothing.*

5. A **participial phrase** can also come at the end of a sentence:
   - *Joe was standing on the other side of the road **waving his arms**.*
   - *The thief ran away, **closely followed by a policeman**.*

PRACTICE

Exercise 1

Say whether each sentence contains a verb phrase (VP) or a participial phrase (PP), and underline the phrase.

1. We have spent all our money on food. ( )
2. John said he had not been waiting long. ( )
3. Give this book to the boy standing by the door. ( )
4. Frightened by the noise, the dog ran away. ( )
5. Will Tom be coming to your party? ( )
6. This work is very tiring. ( )
7. The two men accused of the crime entered the courtroom. ( )
8. This book was written by one of my favourite authors. ( )
9. The children ran home, laughing all the way. ( )
10. The letter had been sent to the wrong address. ( )

Exercise 2

Fill in the blanks with the present or past participle of the verb in brackets.

Jack was in his bedroom, ______________ (*put*) away his clothes and games. He would rather have been outside ______________ (*play*) football with his friends, but his mother had ______________ (*tell*) him to tidy his room instead. She said she was ______________ (*tire*) of having to step over all the things ______________ (*lie*) on the floor when she came in to clean the room. ______________ (*pick*) up a T-shirt, Jack

 ISBN 978-81-8477-745-1

noticed something small and shiny on the carpet. It looked a bit like one of the earrings _______________ (*wear*) by a girl in his class. But she had never _______________ (*visit*) his house, so what was it _______________ (*do*) there? _______________ (*puzzle*) by this discovery, he took the earring to show his mother. She was _______________ (*delight*) to see what he was _______________ (*hold*) in his hand. 'You've _______________ (*find*) my missing earring!' she cried. 'I thought I had _______________ (*lose*) it forever!'

Exercise 3

Rewrite each pair of sentences as a single sentence beginning with a **participial phrase**. *The first one has been done to help you.*

1. Anna wanted to find out more. She looked for information on the Internet.
   Wanting to find out more, Anna looked for information on the Internet.
2. I had spent my bus fare. I had to walk home.
   ____
3. He was confused by the instructions. He asked for help.
   ____
4. Sally read the essay again. She noticed a spelling mistake.
   ____
5. The man was dressed in a wetsuit. He dived off the boat.
   ____
6. I am afraid of flying. I never travel by air.
   ____
7. The words are written in tiny letters. They are hard to read.
   ____
8. They needed a rest. They sat down on a bench.
   ____
9. She grabbed my arm. She begged me to help her.
   ____
10. Grandpa was born in England. He moved to Singapore in 1970.
    ____
11. The house was badly damaged by the fire. It is no longer fit to live in.
    ____
12. Joe is very good at football. He expected to be picked for the team.
    ____

 ISBN 978-81-8477-745-1

5 TENSES AND ASPECTS

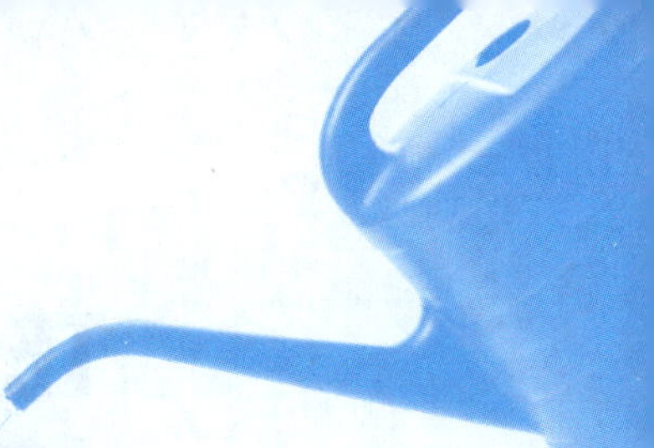

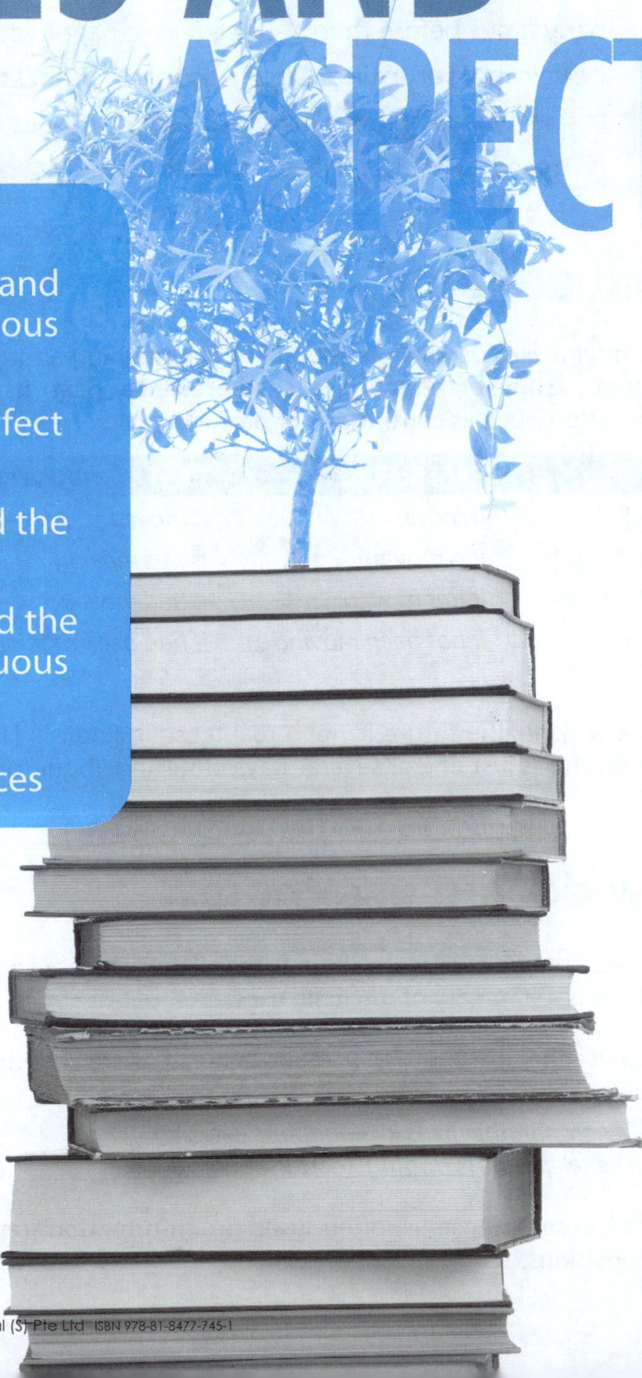

 ISBN 978-81-8477-745-1

UNIT 41

TENSES AND ASPECTS

What do they look like?

The volcano **has erupted** twice since I was born. It **had erupted** many times before then. Whenever we hear a loud noise, we fear the volcano **is erupting.** When it **erupts**, red-hot lava streams down its sides. The last time it **erupted**, several villages were completely destroyed. Scientists believe it **will erupt** again soon.

What are they?

The form of a verb or verb phrase tells you something about the action. Its **tense** tells you about the **time** of the action (such as **present** or **past**). Its **aspect** tells you about the **kind** of action (such as **continuous** or **perfect**):

	PRESENT	PAST	FUTURE
SIMPLE	*it moves*	*it moved*	*it will move*
CONTINUOUS	*it is moving*	*it was moving*	*it will be moving*
PERFECT	*it has moved*	*it had moved*	*it will have moved*
PERFECT CONTINUOUS	*it has been moving*	*it had been moving*	*it will have been moving*

Strictly speaking, the **future** is not a real tense in English. Using ***will*** or ***shall*** with the **bare infinitive** is just one of several ways of talking about future time, as you will learn in Unit 46.

How do you use them?

In Units 42 to 46, you will learn about using all these tenses and aspects in many different ways. Here is a summary of the main uses.

1 You use the **present** to talk about things that are **true now** or that are **happening now**:

- *My grandfather **lives** in Singapore.* (simple)
- *The telephone **is ringing**.* (continuous)

The present tense is often used in **information reports**, **explanations** and **expositions**.

 ISBN 978-81-8477-745-1

2. You use the **past** to talk about things that are **no longer true** or **no longer happening**:
   - *My grandfather **lived** in China many years ago.* (simple)
   - *The telephone **had been ringing for some time**.* (perfect continuous)

   The past tense is often used in **personal recounts, factual recounts** and **narratives**.

3. You use the **future** to talk about things that are **not yet true** or **not yet happening**:
   - *I **shall wear** my new dress for Jane's wedding.* (simple)
   - *By the end of the course, you **will have learnt** how to program a computer.* (perfect)

4. You use **simple** verbs for **single or regular actions**:
   - *I **wash** my hair every day.* (present)
   - *Tom **rang** the doorbell.* (past)

5. You use **continuous** verbs for **ongoing activities**:
   - *I **am washing** my hair.* (present)
   - *Miss Jones **will be teaching** you English.* (future)

6. You use **perfect** verbs for **completed actions**:
   - *Mr Lee **has written** several books on the subject.* (present)
   - *They **had walked** more than twenty kilometres.* (past)

7. You use **perfect continuous** verbs for **activities that are or were ongoing up to a particular time**:
   - *They **had been hoping** that he would change his mind.* (past)
   - *At the end of next month, I **will have been working** here for two years.* (future)

PRACTICE

Exercise 1

Say whether the verb in bold print is in the present (Pr), past (Pa) or future (F).

1. Alice **ran** ( ) all the way home.
2. The plants **will need** ( ) watering.
3. The children **are playing** ( ) in the garden.
4. I **have broken** ( ) my arm.
5. My favourite band **will be playing** ( ) at the concert.
6. Nobody **had told** ( ) Mary about the party.

 ISBN 978-81-8477-745-1

7. You **press** ( ) this button to switch the computer on.
8. Jack **was writing** ( ) a letter to his aunt.
9. Phone me at six o'clock – I **shall have finished** ( ) my homework by then.
10. The twins **have been making** ( ) cards for their mother's birthday next week.

Exercise 2

Fill in the blanks with the correct form of the verb in brackets. The required tense and aspect is given at the end of the sentence.

1. Someone ______________ (*steal*) Joe's bicycle. (*past perfect*)
2. I ______________ (*learn*) to play the violin. (*present continuous*)
3. Tears ______________ (*run*) down her cheeks. (*past continuous*)
4. The dog ______________ (*eat*) all the sausages. (*present perfect*)
5. We ______________ (*listen*) to the news on the radio. (*present perfect continuous*)
6. The police ______________ (*arrest*) three of the protesters. (*simple past*)
7. The robbers ______________ (*hide*) in a disused barn. (*past perfect continuous*)
8. Jenny ______________ (*be*) a member of the basketball team. (*simple present*)
9. The patient ______________ (*make*) a full recovery. (*simple future*)
10. She ______________ (*spend*) all her money by the end of the holiday. (*future perfect*)

Exercise 3

Fill in the blanks with the correct form of the verb wash*, using it once in each* aspect *of the* present *and* past tenses.

1. Jane is in the bathroom. She ______________ her hair.
2. Jane ______________ her hair yesterday.
3. Jane ______________ her hair when the phone rang.
4. Jane ______________ her hair every day.
5. Jane ______________ her hair and there was water all over the bathroom floor.

 ISBN 978-81-8477-745-1

6. Jane ______________ her hair but she hasn't dried it yet.

7. Jane ______________ her hair the day before.

8. Jane ______________ her hair with this shampoo for months.

Exercise 4

Fill in the blanks with the correct form of **be** *or* **have**. *Notice that there are sometimes two blanks to be filled.*

Sue: I ______________ looking forward to next weekend. I ______________ arranged to meet my cousin Jack at a coffee bar in town. I ______________ not seen him for more than ten years because he ______________ ______________ working abroad.

Jane: He will probably ______________ changed a lot. How will you recognize him?

Sue: He will ______________ wearing a bright red jumper, which Mum sent him for his birthday last year. She ______________ ______________ knitting it for ages, and ______________ originally planned to give it to my father. However, by the time it ______________ finished, Dad ______________ put on a lot of weight, and the jumper was too small for him!

Exercise 5: grammar for writing

Write a short narrative, about 120 words long, called 'A Rainy Day'. Your story should contain at least one verb in each aspect of the present and past tenses.

____

____

____

____

____

____

 ISBN 978-81-8477-745-1

UNIT 42

THE SIMPLE PRESENT AND THE PRESENT CONTINUOUS

What do they look like?

The coastline **is changing**, little by little, all the time. The cliffs **are being eroded** by the sea. Each time a wave **hits** the rock face, it **removes** a few particles or lumps of stone. Large caves **are formed** in this way. Sometimes, the land above them **collapses** and **is swept** away.

Construction of the simple present tense

active: **base form**, with ***s*** added for the third person singular (see Unit 24)

passive: ***am/is/are*** + **past participle**

Construction of the present continuous

active: ***am/is/are*** + **present participle**

passive: ***am/is/are*** + ***being*** + **past participle**

How do you use them?

1. You use the **simple present tense** to talk about something that happens **always**, **regularly**, **sometimes** or **never**:
   - *I **have** a shower every morning.*
   - *The rubbish **is collected** twice a week.*

2. The **simple present** is used to state **timeless facts that will never change**:
   - *The earth **goes** round the sun.*
   - *Dolphins **are** mammals.*

3. You can also use the **simple present** to state **something that is currently true** but may not always be true:
   - *Tim **is** a lawyer.*
   - *Our new house **has** no garage.*

4. You use the **simple present** with 'thinking' verbs, for example in **expositions**:
   - *I **believe** that all people should be treated equally.*
   - *I **agree** with you entirely.*

 ISBN 978-81-8477-745-1

5. The **simple present** is occasionally used in **recounts** to talk about **events as they happen**:
   - *Thomas **passes** the ball to Lee, who **throws** it into the net.*
   - *I **walk** into the room and everyone **shouts** 'Surprise!'*

6. You can also use the **simple present** to talk about **things that have been scheduled for the future**:
   - *The train **departs** in five minutes.*
   - *The president **retires** next year.*

7. You use the **present continuous** to talk about **things that are going on or happening now**:
   - ***Are** you **listening** to me?*
   - *A new office block **is being built** in the city centre.*

8. You use the **present continuous** for **temporary situations and activities**:
   - *Gary **is living** with us until his apartment is ready to move into.*
   - *We **are looking** after the twins while their parents are away.*

9. You can also use the **present continuous** to talk about **future plans or arrangements**:
   - *My cousins **are coming** to stay with us next week.*
   - *Jack **is taking** his little sister to the park this afternoon.*

   You will learn more about using the simple present and present continuous for future time in Unit 46.

PRACTICE

Exercise 1

Use the verbs provided in the simple present or present continuous, as you think suitable. You may have to use passives.

1. Everyone ________________ (*know*) that penguins cannot fly.
2. Alice ________________ (*look*) for an apartment in the city centre.
3. The twins ________________ (*have*) a party next Saturday.
4. Champagne ________________ (*make*) in France.
5. The cuckoo ________________ (*lay*) its eggs in other birds' nests.
6. We will have to go by bus because our car ________________ (*repair*).
7. Who ________________ (*cook*) dinner this evening?
8. Elections ________________ (*hold*) every two years.

 ISBN 978-81-8477-745-1

Exercise 2

In the following sentences, fill one blank with the ***simple present*** *and the other with the* ***present continuous*** *of the verbs provided.*

1. Mum ______________ (*drive*) to work when it ______________ (*rain*).
2. I ______________ (*tell*) the truth, but nobody ______________ (*believe*) me.
3. Peter ______________ (*try*) to lose weight, so he ______________ (*run*) round the park every morning.
4. 'Who ______________ (*want*) to play football?' 'Not me, I ______________ (*eat*) my lunch.'
5. The students ______________ (*be*) upset because their favourite teacher ______________ (*leave*).
6. I ______________ (*think*) we ______________ (*go*) the wrong way.

Exercise 3

Fill in the blanks with the verbs provided in the ***simple present*** *or the* ***present continuous****.*

Mum: Hurry up, Sally. Dad and I ______________ (*wait*) for you.

Sally: I ______________ (*be*) nearly ready. I ______________ (*try*) to find my jacket. Have you seen it anywhere?

Mum: It ______________ (*clean*). You'll have to wear something else.

Sally: I've also lost my handbag.

Dad: What does it look like?

Sally: It ______________ (*make*) of black leather, and it ______________ (*have*) a long shoulder strap.

Dad: It ______________ (*lie*) on the table here in the hall, where we ______________ (*stand*). Come on! The bus ______________ (*leave*) in five minutes, and we mustn't miss it.

Mum: I told Grandma we'd be there by twelve o'clock, and you ______________ (*know*) she always ______________ (*worry*) if we ______________ (*be*) late.

 ISBN 978-81-8477-745-1

UNIT
43

THE PRESENT PERFECT AND THE PRESENT PERFECT CONTINUOUS

What do they look like?

The suspected terrorist **has been living** in the flat for several months. The police **have been keeping** him under surveillance, though he doesn't realize they **have been watching** him. His neighbours **have been questioned** about him, and one of them **has provided** some useful information.

Construction of the present perfect

active: ***has/have*** **+ past participle**

passive: ***has/have*** **+** ***been*** **+ past participle**

Construction of the present perfect continuous

active: ***has/have*** **+** ***been*** **+ present participle**

passive: ***has/have*** **+** ***been*** **+** ***being*** **+ past participle**

(The passive of the present perfect continuous is not often used because it is a rather long, clumsy verb phrase.)

How do you use them?

1 You use the **present perfect** for **past events that affect or explain the present situation**:

- *I **have lost** my address book, so I can't give you Sue's new address.*
- *Tom is feeling depressed because he **has failed** his driving test.*

2 You also use the **present perfect** for **situations that began in the past and still exist**:

- *Grandma **has lived** in this house since she was a girl.*
- *This path **has** always **been used** as a public right of way.*

3 You can use the **present perfect** to talk about **individual or repeated events in the past**, especially things that happened at an **unspecified time in the recent past**:

- *Our visitors **have arrived**.*
- *I **have seen** this film three times before.*

 ISBN 978-81-8477-745-1

4. The **present perfect** is used with ***already***, ***yet*** and ***just***:
   - *The money **has** already **been spent**.*
   - ***Have** you **made** any holiday plans yet?*
   - *Harry **has** just **phoned** to invite us to his party.*

5. You use the **present perfect continuous** for **ongoing activities that began in the past and are still continuing**:
   - *David **has been trying** to fix my computer, but he hasn't succeeded yet.*
   - *I **have been working** in the garden all morning — I need a break!*

PRACTICE

Exercise 1

*Use the verbs provided in the **present perfect** or **present perfect continuous**, as you think suitable. You may have to use passives.*

1. Tom ____________ (*buy*) a new motorbike.
2. Aunt Jane ____________ (*cook*) all morning, so I hope you're hungry!
3. The missing necklace ____________ (*find*).
4. Anna says she ____________ (*read*) all the books on these shelves.
5. I don't know what you ____________ (*do*) in these jeans, but they're filthy!
6. The rain ____________ (*stop*) at last.
7. Several useful ideas ____________ (*put*) forward.
8. The dog ____________ (*dig*) in the flower bed again.

Exercise 2

*Fill in the blanks with the **present participle** or **past participle** of the verbs provided to form active or passive verbs in all aspects of the present tense.*

Our computer broke down last week. It is ____________ (*use*) by the whole family, so everyone has ____________ (*miss*) it. However, it has now been ____________ (*mend*), and I have been ____________ (*catch*) up with my schoolwork. I am ____________ (*design*) a website for our school orchestra. Some of the players have ____________ (*write*) articles about their instruments. The site is ____________ (*illustrate*) with photographs that have been ____________ (*take*) by parents at school concerts. I have been ____________ (*play*) the trumpet in the orchestra for two years, and I am also ____________ (*learn*) the trombone. My teacher is ____________ (*call*) Mr Jackson. He is the most brilliant trumpeter I have ever ____________ (*hear*). I don't think I will ever be able to play as well as him.

 ISBN 978-81-8477-745-1

UNIT 44

THE SIMPLE PAST AND THE PAST CONTINUOUS

What do they look like?

There **was** an accident on the expressway yesterday evening. A car **collided** with a truck, and four other vehicles **crashed** into them. It **was raining** heavily, and people **were driving** too fast. Two people **were killed** in the accident. One of them **died** as he **was being cut** from the wreckage of his car.

Construction of the simple past tense

active: **simple past** form (ending with ***-ed*** in regular verbs; see Unit 24)
passive: ***was/were*** + **past participle**

Construction of the past continuous

active: ***was/were*** + **present participle**
passive: ***was/were*** + ***being*** + **past participle**

How do you use them?

1 You use the **simple past tense** to talk about things that happened in the past, whether a long time ago or very recently:

- *Dr Johnson's famous dictionary **was published** in 1755.*
- *I **bought** a new camera last week.*

2 The **simple past** is the normal tense for completed actions in **narratives** and **recounts**:

- *The Lilliputians **fastened** Gulliver to the ground with ropes.*
- *The man **was attacked** on his way home from work.*

 ISBN 978-81-8477-745-1

3. The **simple past** is used for an **activity that was ongoing but has now stopped:**
   - *My elder sister **attended** this school for six years.*
   - *Joe **lived** with his parents until he got married.*

4. You use the **past continuous** for the **situation that was ongoing** when a certain **single action** took place:
   - *I **was doing** a tricky job on my computer **when a power cut destroyed all my data.***
   - ***The telephone rang** just as the meal **was being served**.*

5. The **past continuous** is also used for an **activity that was ongoing at a certain point in the past**:
   - *I **was basking** in the sun on a Cretan beach **this time last week**.*
   - ***At half past eight**, Sam **was eating** his breakfast.*

6. In some cases, such as descriptive passages in stories, only the **ongoing situation** is mentioned:
   - *A dog **was barking** somewhere along the street.*
   - *The cliffs **were being eroded** by the sea.*

PRACTICE

Exercise 1

*Use the regular verbs provided in the **simple past** or **past continuous**, as you think suitable. You may have to use passives.*

1. The horse ______________ (*jump*) over the fence and galloped away.
2. I couldn't sleep because my brother ______________ (*snore*) loudly.
3. The injured player ______________ (*carry*) off the field on a stretcher.
4. Do you know who ______________ (*paint*) this picture?
5. Sally ______________ (*wait*) at the bus stop when it began to rain.
6. Only one student ______________ (*answer*) all the questions correctly.
7. The man did not realize he ______________ (*deceive*).
8. The audience ______________ (*clap*) their hands at the end of the show.

 ISBN 978-81-8477-745-1

Exercise 2

Use the irregular verbs provided in the ***simple past*** *or* ***past continuous****, as you think suitable. You may have to use passives.*

1. The sun ______________ (*shine*) and the sky was blue.
2. This book ______________ (*write*) by one of my favourite authors.
3. The soldiers ______________ (*fight*) bravely and won the battle.
4. We lived in a caravan while our new house ______________ (*build*).
5. The plane ______________ (*fly*) over the ocean when one of its engines failed.
6. The train ______________ (*leave*) the station at 10.50.

Exercise 3

In the following sentences, fill one blank with the ***simple past*** *and the other with the* ***past continuous*** *of the verbs provided.*

1. The doorbell ______________ (*ring*) as I ______________ (*dress*) to go out.
2. Sue ______________ (*have*) a shower when Jack ______________ (*phone*).
3. Tom ______________ (*feel*) cold, so he ______________ (*zip*) up his jacket.
4. The police officer ______________ (*ask*) the man where he ______________ (*go*).
5. The building ______________ (*use*) as a hospital by the people who ______________ (*live*) in the village at that time.
6. The fault ______________ (*discover*) while the car ______________ (*service*).

Exercise 4

Fill the blanks with the verbs provided in the ***simple past*** *or the* ***past continuous****.*

I ______________ (*spend*) last weekend with my cousin Leo and his family. I ______________ (*arrive*) on Friday evening and ______________ (*greet*) by Leo, who ______________ (*look*) rather tired. I ______________ (*understand*) why. His four young children ______________ (*run*) about everywhere. They ______________ (*chase*) by a large dog, which ______________ (*bound*) up to me and ______________ (*put*) its paws on my chest. I ______________ (*offer*) to take the children out the next day, to give Leo and his wife a bit of a rest.

 ISBN 978-81-8477-745-1

UNIT 45

THE PAST PERFECT AND THE PAST PERFECT CONTINUOUS

What do they look like?

I **had been using** the computer for nearly an hour when the screen went blank. This **had happened** once before. On that occasion, the fault **had been fixed** by one of my father's friends. He **had been staying** with us for a few days while his house was being decorated. He **had been** a very useful guest!

Construction of the past perfect

active: ***had*** **+ past participle**

passive: ***had*** **+** ***been*** **+ past participle**

Construction of the past perfect continuous

active: ***had*** **+** ***been*** **+ present participle**

passive: ***had*** **+** ***been*** **+** ***being*** **+ past participle**

(The passive of the past perfect continuous is not often used, because it is a rather long, clumsy verb phrase.)

How do you use them?

1. You use the **past perfect** to mention something that **happened before** an action or event in the **simple past**:
   - *The bus **had** already **left** by the time I **reached** the bus stop.*
   - *The villagers who **had lost** their homes in the earthquake **were given** food and blankets.*

2. You sometimes use the **past perfect** in indirect speech. It can replace the **present perfect** or the **simple past** in direct speech:

DIRECT SPEECH	INDIRECT SPEECH
Tom said, 'I *have lost* my watch.'	Tom said that he ***had lost*** his watch.
Sue said, 'I *saw* Mike at the cinema.'	Sue said that she ***had seen*** Mike at the cinema.

 ISBN 978-81-8477-745-1

3 You use the **past perfect continuous** to talk about activities that **were ongoing until** an action or event in the simple past:

- *We **had been walking** for about an hour when the storm broke.*
- *Grandpa died on Friday — he **had been getting** progressively weaker.*

4 You sometimes use the **past perfect continuous** in indirect speech. It can replace the present perfect continuous or the past continuous in direct speech:

DIRECT SPEECH	INDIRECT SPEECH
Joe said, 'I *have been waiting* for hours.'	Joe said that he ***had been waiting*** for hours.
Kate said, 'I *was trying* to help.'	Kate said that she ***had been trying*** to help.

You will learn more about indirect speech in Unit 71.

PRACTICE

Exercise 1

Use the verbs provided in the past perfect or past perfect continuous, as you think suitable. You may have to use passives.

1. The police finally arrested the man they ______________ (*follow*) for several days.
2. The house was falling down, and several of the windows ______________ (*smash*) by vandals.
3. The teacher read out to the class what I ______________ (*write*) on her card.
4. Billy thought everyone ______________ (*forget*) his birthday.
5. It ______________ (*rain*) since the early hours of the morning.
6. The little girl was crying because she ______________ (*break*) her favourite toy.
7. The passengers found out that their flight ______________ (*cancel*).
8. She realized that she ______________ (*drive*) in the wrong direction for the past hour.
9. Mr Brown ______________ (*retire*) a few years earlier.
10. They ______________ (*offer*) half a million dollars for the house, but they did not want to sell it.

Exercise 2

Rewrite the following sentences in indirect speech.

1. Jane said, 'Ben spilt the ink.'

____

2. 'The cat has been chasing the birds,' said Mrs Green.

____

 ISBN 978-81-8477-745-1

3. The newsreader announced, 'Someone has shot the president.'

____

4. A police spokesman said, 'The robbers were wearing masks.'

____

5. 'The wrong date was printed on the invitations,' explained Jack.

____

6. 'The concert has been cancelled,' Mr Lee told us.

____

7. 'The alarm did not go off,' I explained.

____

8. Carol said, 'The bank has been robbed.'

____

9. 'It was snowing in England,' Joe told me.

____

10. Dad announced, 'I have written to the bank manager.'

____

Exercise 3

Say whether the verbs in bold print are in the simple past (SP), past continuous (PC), past perfect (PP) or past perfect continuous (PPC).

Harry **was feeling** ( ) absolutely exhausted. He **was** ( ) a nurse and he **had** just **worked** ( ) a double shift. An emergency **had occurred** ( ) and Harry **had been asked** ( ) to do an extra spell of duty. The town **had been hit** ( ) by a severe flu epidemic. It **was estimated** ( ) that about a third of all the residents **were suffering** ( ) from the bug. Many companies **had been** badly **affected** ( ) because so many people **were** ( ) absent. Doctors **pleaded** ( ) with people to seek medical help only if they were seriously ill. Patients with mild symptoms **had been calling** ( ) surgeries and asking for appointments. The hospitals **were overflowing** ( ) with flu victims. People who **had been waiting** ( ) for months to have routine operations **had received** ( ) letters saying that their operation **had been cancelled** ( ).

Exercise 4: grammar for writing

Write a short passage, about 120 words long, with the title 'An Important Visitor'. Your passage should contain eight or more verbs in the past perfect or past perfect continuous (at least three of each). When you have finished, underline all the past perfect phrases and put a ring round all the past perfect continuous phrases.

 ISBN 978-81-8477-745-1

UNIT 46

THE FUTURE

What does it look like?

'I **am resigning** from the council,' said Jack. 'There **is** a council meeting tomorrow, and I **will announce** my retirement then. I **am going to buy** a boat — this time next year I **will be sailing** around the world. My son **is about to graduate** from university, and he **will come** with me.'

Different ways of talking about future time

1 There are various ways of using verbs to talk about the future. The most common of these is with ***will*** or ***shall*** and the **bare infinitive** (the **base form**) of the verb:
active: ***will/shall*** **+ bare infinitive**
passive: ***will/shall*** **+** ***be*** **+ past participle**
continuous: ***will/shall*** **+** ***be*** **+ present participle**
perfect: ***will/shall*** **+** ***have*** **+ past participle**
perfect continuous: ***will/shall*** **+** ***have*** **+** ***been*** **+ present participle**

As you learnt in Unit 29, ***will*** can be used for all persons, and ***shall*** is sometimes used for the first person.

2 You can also use ***be going*** with a **to-infinitive** to talk about the future:
- *According to the weather forecast, it* ***is going*** *to rain this afternoon.*
- ***Are*** *you* ***going*** *to accept their offer?*

3 You can also use ***be about*** with a **to-infinitive** to talk about the future:
- *The train* ***is about*** *to leave.*
- *We* ***are about*** *to move house.*

4 As you learnt in Unit 42, the **simple present** and the **present continuous** sometimes have a future meaning:
- *The new law* ***comes*** *into operation next month.*
- *I will phone you when I* ***arrive****.*
- *What* ***are*** *you* ***wearing*** *for the dance?*

 ISBN 978-81-8477-745-1

How do you use them?

1. You can use any of these methods to talk about **plans or intentions:**
   - *A representative of the company* ***will meet*** *you at the airport.*
   - *The house* ***is going to be demolished****.*
   - *The president* ***is about to make*** *a speech.*
   - *The shop* ***closes*** *at five o'clock today.*
   - *I* ***am buying*** *Mum some flowers for her birthday.*

   You use ***be about*** for things in the **immediate future.**
   You use the **simple present** for things that have been **formally scheduled.**
   You use the **present continuous** for things that are **more informal or less definite.**

2. You can also use ***will/shall*** or ***be going*** to make **predictions:**
   - *Hurry up, or you* ***will miss*** *the bus!*
   - *This project* ***is going to be*** *a lot of fun.*

3. You use the **continuous** form of ***will/shall*** to talk about **ongoing activities planned for the future.**
   - *Get off the bus at the Town Hall — I* ***will be waiting*** *at the bus stop.*
   - *My niece* ***will be accompanying*** *me on my travels.*

4. You use the **perfect** form of ***will/shall*** for **things expected to be done by a particular time:**
   - *When you get this message I* ***shall have left*** *the country.*
   - *You can collect the car next Tuesday — we* ***will have repaired*** *it by then.*

5. You use the **perfect continuous** form of ***will/shall*** for **ongoing activities ending at a particular time in the future:**
   - *By the end of term, Mr Green* ***will have been teaching*** *for 40 years.*
   - *By the time they reach England, they* ***will have been travelling*** *for nearly 24 hours.*

The future in the past

You sometimes need to say what was in the **future** at some time in the **past.** Examples include indirect speech, or talking about plans that have changed. For these purposes, you use ***would*** instead of ***will/shall***, or past forms of ***be going*** and ***be about***:

- *Tom said he* ***would meet*** *me at the station.*
- *I thought the sun* ***would be shining****.*
- *She asked when we* ***were going to announce*** *the winner.*
- *The robbers* ***were going to sell*** *the jewels to a foreign dealer.*
- *He* ***was about to dive*** *into the water when he noticed the shark.*

You will learn more about indirect speech in Unit 71.

 ISBN 978-81-8477-745-1

PRACTICE

Exercise 1

Use the verbs provided in the **future** *with* **will***. You may have to use some* **passive***,* **perfect** *or* **continuous** *forms.*

1. You ______________ (*regret*) that decision.
2. Sally ______________ (*enjoy*) the dinner. She ______________ (*sit*) beside my cousin Tony, who has a great sense of humour.
3. This joke ______________ (*make*) you laugh.
4. We ______________ (*be*) late. The show ______________ (*end*) by the time we arrive!
5. The building work ______________ (*take*) about four more months.
6. Our class ______________ (*study*) Shakespeare's 'Hamlet' this term.
7. In another hour, the sun ______________ (*set*).
8. The prizes ______________ (*award*) by the mayor.
9. This time tomorrow we ______________ (*fly*) over the Atlantic Ocean.
10. I hope the judges ______________ (*impress*) by my performance.

Exercise 2

Fill in the blanks with **about** *or* **going***, as appropriate.*

1. Can I phone you back later? I am ______________ to eat my lunch.
2. Mum is ______________ to be very angry when she finds out.
3. I thought you were ______________ to buy a new computer.
4. The plane was ______________ to take off when one of the passengers had a heart attack.
5. Tom is ______________ to help us with the decorating.
6. Look out! You are ______________ to step in a puddle!
7. The man opened his mouth as if he was ______________ to speak.
8. I am ______________ to complain to the manager.
9. Alice was ______________ to sell her boat, but she changed her mind.
10. We were told to leave the shop because it was ______________ to close.

 ISBN 978-81-8477-745-1

Exercise 3

In the following passage, underline all the verbs and verb phrases that have a future meaning. Take care to underline any infinitives or participles that form part of the phrase.

When I grow up I am going to be a doctor. I will travel around the world treating sick people in developing countries. By that time, cures will have been found for many of today's fatal diseases. People in the developed world will be living longer, healthier lives, so they will not require my help. I am about to start my third year at secondary school. There are important exams at the end of this year, and I am going to work hard, especially in science. I will need to get good grades in biology and chemistry if I want to study medicine at university. It is a difficult subject, and they will accept only the most promising students.

Exercise 4: grammar for writing

Write a short passage, about 100 words long, describing a trip you are planning to make in the future.

 ISBN 978-81-8477-745-1

UNIT 47

CONDITIONAL SENTENCES

What do they look like?

Mr Jones will give us ten dollars each **if we tidy up his garden**. We won't get anything **unless all the weeds are gone**. He said that **if he were less busy**, he would do it himself. I'm sure he will give us the money – he wouldn't have made the offer **if he hadn't meant it**.

What are they?

1 **Conditional sentences** contain **clauses** introduced by ***if*** or a similar connector (such as ***unless***):

- ***If*** *I knew their address, I would write to them.*
- *Contact us* ***if*** *you want further information.*
- *The cat will not scratch you* ***unless*** *you annoy it.*

2 There are three types of **conditional sentences**, called **first conditional** (or **present conditional**), **second conditional** (or **hypothetical conditional**) and **third conditional** (or **past perfect conditional**):

- *If he apologizes, I will forgive him.* (first conditional)
- *If he apologized, I would forgive him.* (second conditional)
- *If he had apologized, I would have forgiven him.* (third conditional)

How do you use them?

First conditional

1 **First conditional** sentences express a **real possibility**. You are stating the **likely** result (in the main clause) of some future event (in the ***if*-clause**):

- *Everything will be all right* ***if we keep calm and don't panic.***
- ***If it rains,*** *the trip will be cancelled.*
- *Don't put your hand up* ***unless you know the answer.***

Notice that the ***if*-clause** can come before or after the main clause.

2 The verb in the **main** clause is usually in the future or the imperative, and the verb in the ***if***-clause is usually in the **simple present**:

- *I will scream if you* ***come*** *any nearer.*
- *If you* ***need*** *help, phone this number.*
- *You will not be allowed to work here unless you* ***apply*** *for a permit.*

 ISBN 978-81-8477-745-1

Second conditional

1. **Second conditional** sentences express a **hypothetical possibility**. You are stating what would happen (in the **main clause**) if some **unlikely** event occurred (in the ***if*-clause**):
   - ***Tom would get better grades if he worked harder.***
   - ***If I had more money, I would buy a bigger house.***

2. The verb in the **main** clause is usually the modal auxiliary ***would*** followed by a **bare infinitive**. The verb in the ***if***-clause usually has the same form as the **simple past**:
   - *I **would join** a choir if I **had** a good voice.*
   - *If Jack **shaved** off his beard he **would look** younger.*

3. When the event in the ***if***-clause is **impossible**, the verb is in the **past subjunctive**. As you learnt in Unit 36, the past subjunctive has the same form as the simple past for all verbs except ***be***. For the verb ***be*** you use ***were*** in all persons, singular and plural:
   - *If your grandmother **were** still alive, you **would be** able to ask her about your ancestors.*
   - *I **would buy** a warmer coat if I **were** you.*

Third conditional

1. **Third conditional** sentences express an **unreal possibility in the past, which cannot be changed**. The **main clause** states what would have happened if the circumstances mentioned in the ***if*-clause** had been different:
   - ***The boy would have drowned if you hadn't pulled him out of the water.*** (but you did pull him out, so he didn't drown)
   - ***If she had looked at the map, she would not have got lost.*** (but she didn't look at the map, so she did get lost)

2. The verb in the **main** clause is usually ***would have*** followed by a **past participle**. The verb in the ***if***-clause usually has the same form as the **past perfect**:
   - *The bridge **would have collapsed** if the truck **had attempted** to cross it.*
   - *If I **had known** you were in town, I **would have invited** you to lunch.*

 ISBN 978-81-8477-745-1

PRACTICE

Exercise 1

Say whether the sentences are in the first conditional (1), second conditional (2) or third conditional (3).

1. I would not have passed the exam if you hadn't given me extra lessons. ( )
2. She will die unless she receives these drugs immediately. ( )
3. If they had been wearing brighter clothing, they would have been spotted and rescued. ( )
4. What adventures we would have if we were able to fly! ( )
5. You would be bored if you didn't have plenty to do. ( )
6. If you see anything suspicious, tell the police. ( )
7. If the fire alarm rings, leave the building immediately. ( )
8. He would not have eaten the berries if he had known they were poisonous. ( )
9. If I had a better camera, I would take more photos. ( )
10. The flight will be cancelled if the fog does not clear. ( )

Exercise 2

Rewrite the following sentences in the second or third conditional, as indicated. The first one has been done to help you.

1. If you eat more slowly, you will not get indigestion.

   (*second*) *If you ate more slowly, you would not get indigestion.*

2. Sue will call us if she manages to get tickets.

   (*third*) ______________________________

3. If the meeting finishes on time, I will be home at six.

   (*third*) ______________________________

4. He will buy some new jeans if he has enough money.

   (*second*) ______________________________

5. The grapes would ripen more quickly if there was more sunshine.

   (*third*) ______________________________

 ISBN 978-81-8477-745-1

6. If they bring all their children, we will not have enough beds.

   (*second*) ____________________

7. The plants will die if I do not water them.

   (*second*) ____________________

8. If there is a lot of traffic, we will be late.

   (*third*) ____________________

9. The birds will eat the food if they are hungry.

   (*second*) ____________________

10. If I spot any errors, I will correct them.

    (*third*) ____________________

Exercise 3

Fill in the blanks with will, would, had, have, was *or* were, *as appropriate.*

Carol: Look at this cake. It's a disaster! It __________ not __________ been a problem if I __________ just baked it for myself. But Tom's parents are coming to tea. I have never met them before. If they see what a hopeless cook I am they __________ not get a very good first impression. I __________ bake another cake if I __________ enough ingredients, but I don't. What am I going to do?

Lucy: If I __________ you, I __________ cut off the top of the cake, where it has sunk in the middle, and cover it with icing.

Carol: Nobody __________ get a very big piece if I do that.

Lucy: If the cake is really awful, that __________ not be a bad thing!

Carol: I hope Tom will be home soon. He said he __________ ring me if he __________ going to be late.

Lucy: Here he comes now. And he seems to be carrying a large cake box. I think your problem is solved!

 ISBN 978-81-8477-745-1

6 ADVERBS

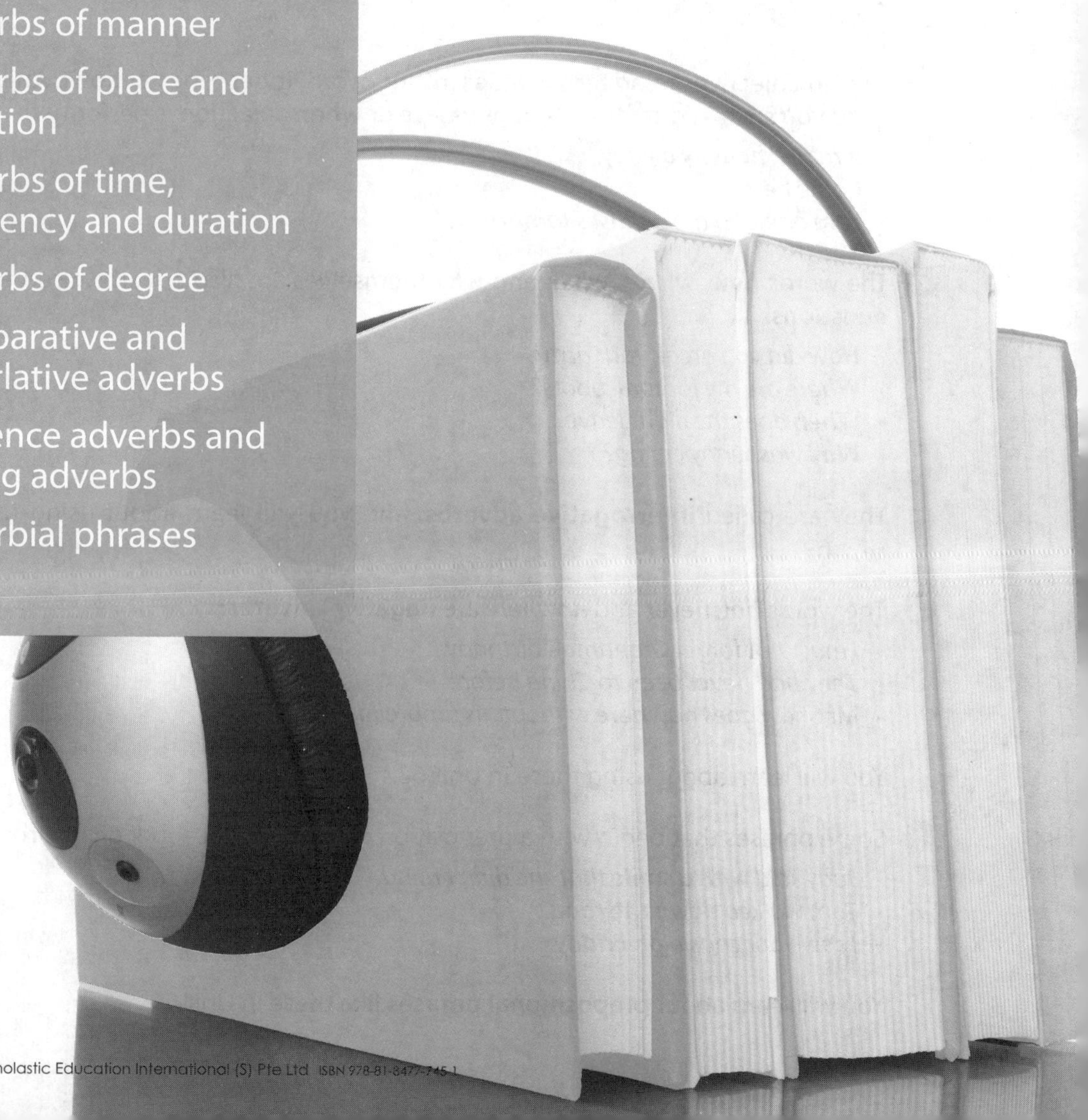

 ISBN 978-81-8477-745-1

UNIT 48

ADVERBS

What do they look like?

The children are **very** excited. They are flying to China **tomorrow** to visit their grandparents, and they have **never** been on a plane **before**. Tom, the eldest, is **constantly** asking his parents about China. His mother was born **there**, so she can answer most of his questions. She grew **up** in Beijing, the capital of the country.

What are they?

1 Like an adjective, an **adverb** is a **describing** word. It describes **actions**. An adverb gives you such information as **how, where** or **when** an action is performed:

- *It rained **heavily** all day.*
- *Come **here**!*
- *I am going to the dentist's **tomorrow**.*

2 The words ***how***, ***where***, ***when*** and ***why*** themselves are also adverbs, used to form **questions**:

- ***How** did you break your arm?*
- ***Where** are my football boots?*
- ***When** does the flight leave?*
- ***Why** was Jenny crying?*

They are called **interrogative adverbs**, and you will learn about using them in Unit 69.

3 The words ***not***, ***never*** and ***nowhere*** are **negative adverbs**:

- *I must **not** forget Grandma's birthday.*
- *They had **never** been to China before.*
- *Mr Shaw goes **nowhere** without his umbrella.*

You will learn about using these in Unit 68.

4 Some phrases that begin with a preposition can also do the work of adverbs:

- *Judy said **with a smile** that she didn't mind.*
- *Tom walked **down the road**.*
- *I saw your cousin **on Friday**.*

You will learn about **prepositional phrases** like these in Unit 56.

 ISBN 978-81-8477-745-1

5. Other types of phrases and clauses can also do the work of adverbs:
   - *We had a quarrel **last week**.*
   - ***Shaking with fear**, she opened the door.*
   - ***Although it was late**, I phoned my parents.*

   All the words and word groups that do the work of adverbs belong to a class called **adverbials**.

How do you use them?

1. **Adverbs** are mainly used with verbs. They tell you such things as the **manner**, the **place** or the **time** of the action represented by the verb:
   - *Emily **dances gracefully**.* (manner)
   - *We **have lived here** for six years.* (place)
   - *The train **arrived late**.* (time)
2. Some short **adverbs** are used to form **phrasal verbs**, which you learned about in Unit 39:
   - *Joe **took off** his jacket.*
   - *Everyone **stood up** when the president entered.*
3. You can also use an **adverb** to say more about an adjective:
   - *I am reading a **very interesting** book.*
   - *The patient is **seriously ill**.*
4. An **adverb** can even describe another adverb:
   - *Our team did **extremely well**.*
   - *You are speaking **too quietly**.*
5. Some **adverbs** comment on a whole clause or sentence, indicating the **attitude** of the person making the statement:
   - ***Frankly**, I think you're making a big mistake.*
   - *We didn't win a prize, **unfortunately**.*
6. **Adverbs** are sometimes used as **connectors**, to link clauses or sentences:
   - *She thought he was lying; **however**, she said nothing.*
   - *John is late. **Perhaps** his car has broken down.*

 ISBN 978-81-8477-745-1

Where do you put them?

Adverbs can come in various **positions** in a sentence.

1. You can put an **adverb** at the **beginning** of a sentence:
   - ***Soon*** *we were on our way to Bangkok.*
   - ***Eventually*** *the police found what they were looking for.*

2. You can put an **adverb** at the **end** of a sentence:
   - *He thanked me* ***politely****.*
   - *I'll phone her* ***tomorrow****.*

3. You can put some **adverbs** in the **middle** of a sentence, **before** the **verb**, **adjective** or **adverb** they describe:
   - *Michael* ***rarely visits*** *his grandparents.*
   - *The girl was wearing a* ***rather old-fashioned*** *dress.*
   - *He sent me a* ***very neatly*** *written letter.*

   However, if the **adverb** is ***enough***, it comes **after** the **adjective** or **adverb** it describes:
   - *Is the water* ***warm enough*** *to swim in?*
   - *He does not play* ***well enough*** *to join the band.*

   And if the **verb** is ***be***, the **adverb** comes **after** it:
   - *She* ***was often*** *bad-tempered in the morning.*
   - *The weather* ***is usually*** *colder than this in February.*

4. In a **verb phrase**, you often put the **adverb** between the **auxiliary verb** and the **main verb**:
   - *You* ***can sometimes find*** *good bargains at the market.*
   - *The horses* ***were badly treated*** *by their owner.*

How do you form them?

1. Many adverbs, especially **adverbs of manner**, are formed by adding ***ly*** to an **adjective**.

patient → *patiently*	*helpful* → *helpfully*	*safe* → *safely*

   - *Your handwriting is very* ***neat****.* (adjective)
   - *You write very* ***neatly****.* (adverb)

   If the adjective ends in *e*, you usually do not drop this letter before adding ***ly***. However, there are a few exceptions to this rule:

true → *truly*	*whole* → *wholly*

 ISBN 978-81-8477-745-1

And if the adjective ends in a consonant followed by ***le***, you change the ***e*** to ***y*** to form the adverb:

gentle → *gently*	*comfortable* → *comfortably*	*simple* → *simply*

If the adjective ends in **y**, you usually change the **y** to **i** before adding ***ly***:

funny → *funnily*	*happy* → *happily*	*busy* → *busily*

If the adjective ends in ***ic***, you usually add ***ally*** to form the adverb:

basic → *basically*	*romantic* → *romantically*	*tragic* → *tragically*

If the adjective ends in ***ll***, you just add ***y*** to form the adverb:

full → *fully*	*shrill* → *shrilly*

2 Some **adverbs** have the same form as **adjectives** ending in ***ly***:

- *They caught an **early** train.* (adjective)
- *They left **early**.* (adverb)
- *This is a **monthly** magazine.* (adjective)
- *The magazine is published **monthly**.* (adverb)

3 Some **adverbs** have the same form as **adjectives** that do not end in ***ly***:

- *Anne drives a **fast** car.* (adjective)
- *Anne was driving too **fast**.* (adverb)
- *We were given **free** tickets for the trip.* (adjective)
- *The tickets allowed us to travel **free**.* (adverb)

Some of these adverbs have two forms, one with ***ly*** and one without, often with different meanings:

- *The tickets allowed us to travel **free**.* (= without paying)
- *The ink is not flowing **freely**.* (= without restriction)
- *They flew **direct** to London.* (= without changing planes)
- *They went **directly** to the police station.* (= immediately)

4 There are many other adverbs that do not end in ***ly***:

- *Tom picked **up** his schoolbag.*
- *I **often** watch the news on television.*
- *The exam was **quite** easy.*

5 The adjective ***good*** has the irregular adverb ***well***:

- *Mary is **good** at tennis.*
- *Mary plays tennis **well**.*

 ISBN 978-81-8477-745-1

PRACTICE

Exercise 1

Put a ring round the word that the adverb in bold print describes. The first one has been done to help you.

1. The deer (ran) **away** when it heard our footsteps.
2. Jill looked **very** glad to see us.
3. They stayed **indoors** because it was raining.
4. The man **rather** rudely asked us to leave.
5. I **stupidly** forgot to take my keys with me.
6. You must hand your essays **in** by Friday at the latest.
7. The plane rose **high** above the clouds.
8. Are these boots big **enough** to fit you?

Exercise 2

Say whether the word in bold print is being used as an adverb (adv) or as an adjective (adj).

1. A **high** fence surrounded the garden. (   )
2. Council meetings are held **monthly** in the town hall. (   )
3. Some of the guests arrived **late**. (   )
4. The music was too **loud**. (   )
5. There is a **daily** bus service to the museum. (   )
6. The men worked **hard** all day. (   )

Exercise 3

Underline all the single-word adverbs in the following passage.

'We do not have enough milk for breakfast,' said Mrs Simpson. 'Could one of you run quickly to the corner shop and get some?' 'I'll go,' said Betty eagerly. The sun was shining brightly, and Betty hated being indoors in fine weather. She picked up some money and ran out. Unfortunately, there was no milk at the corner shop, 'The delivery truck has broken down,' said the shopkeeper apologetically. 'A replacement truck is on its way, but it has not arrived yet.' Betty had to go back empty-handed. 'Where is the milk?' asked her mother. Betty explained what had happened. Her mother was rather upset, but she thanked Betty for going to the shop.

 ISBN 978-81-8477-745-1

UNIT 49

ADVERBS OF MANNER

What do they look like?

It was raining **heavily**, so Kate **sensibly** decided to take the bus to school. She ran to the bus stop as **fast** as she could, **carelessly** stepping in a large puddle on the way. The water splashed the trousers of a passer-by, who glared **angrily** at her. She smiled **apologetically** and ran on.

What are they?

1 **Adverbs of manner** tell you the **way** an action is performed. They answer the question ***how?*** You can use adverbs of manner to make **narratives** and **recounts** more interesting.

- *Tom **gently** rocked the sleeping baby in his arms.*
- *The waves crashed **violently** against the rocks.*

2 Some **adverbs** of **manner** have the same form as **adjectives**:

- *You have spelt my name **wrong.*** (adverb)
- *That is the **wrong** answer.* (adjective)
- *She threw the ball as **high** as she could.* (adverb)
- *We climbed a **high** mountain.* (adjective)

How do you use them?

1 You often put an **adverb of manner** ending in *ly* after the **verb** it describes:

- *The phone **rang** **suddenly**.*
- *The children **were playing** **happily** in the garden.*

2 You can sometimes put the **adverb** before the **verb** (or the **main verb** in a verb phrase) for emphasis:

- *The phone **suddenly** **rang**.*
- *The children **were** **happily** **playing** in the garden.*

3 If the verb has an object, the **adverb** comes either **after** the **object** or **before** the **verb**, not between them:

- *The boy **thanked** **us** **politely**.*
- *I **carefully** **removed** **the label** from the jar.*

 ISBN 978-81-8477-745-1

4. In narratives and recounts, it is sometimes effective to put the **adverb** at the **beginning** of the sentence:
   - ***Suddenly** the phone rang.*
   - ***Reluctantly** he let the doctor examine his wound.*

5. Some **adverbs of manner** do not end in ***ly***. These adverbs go after the verb (and its object):
   - *I'm studying **hard** for my exams.*
   - *Sue played her solo **well**, and everyone applauded.*

6. You can also use an **adverb of manner** before a **past participle used as an adjective**:
   - *a **carefully** written essay*
   - *a **neatly** folded sheet.*
   - *a **well**-dressed young man.*
   - *a **hard**-fought battle*

   You link the two words with a hyphen if the adverb does not end in ***ly***.

PRACTICE

Exercise 1

Fill in the blanks with the correct adverb of manner formed from the adjective provided.

1. The birds were ______________ building their nests. (*busy*)
2. They have not ______________ announced their engagement yet. (*official*)
3. The alarm rang ______________, breaking the silence. (*shrill*)
4. The clown was ______________ dressed in baggy striped trousers. (*comic*)
5. James did ______________ in all his exams. (*good*)
6. I ______________ asked them to make less noise. (*polite*)
7. The boy slipped ______________ out of the room. (*silent*)
8. Please try to write more ______________. (*legible*)
9. Carol smiled ______________ and said nothing. (*mysterious*)
10. He did not ______________ understand what he was supposed to do. (*full*)

 ISBN 978-81-8477-745-1

Exercise 2

*Rewrite the following sentences, putting the given **adverb of manner** in the correct position **after** the verb (and its object, if it has one).*

1. I wrapped the ornament in tissue paper. (*carefully*)

   ____

2. The trees were blowing in the gale. (*wildly*)

   ____

3. Sally waved from the train window. (*cheerfully*)

   ____

4. The children ate their supper. (*hungrily*)

   ____

5. He strode down the road. (*purposefully*)

   ____

6. Tom wrote his name at the top of the page. (*neatly*).

   ____

7. The van drove away. (*slowly*)

   ____

8. The men have been working all day. (*hard*)

   ____

9. Grandma spoke to the little boy. (*kindly*)

   ____

10. She pinched her brother on the arm. (*playfully*)

    ____

Exercise 3

*Use the **adverbs of manner** in the box to fill in the blanks in the following passage.*

crossly	deliberately	elegantly	energetically
enthusiastically	excitedly	gradually	lazily
noisily	slowly	spectacularly	suddenly

 ISBN 978-81-8477-745-1

I was walking __________ along the promenade, looking at the people on the beach. Some were __________ sunbathing, others were __________ exercising or splashing __________ in the sea. __________ I spotted a dolphin in the water, then another and another. They kept rising __________ out of the water, __________ curving their backs and flicking their tails. It was as if they were __________ putting on a show for everybody. __________ other people began to notice the dolphins. 'Look!' cried a little boy __________, tugging at his mother's sleeve. 'What's the matter?' she said rather __________. Then she saw the dolphins and smiled. Eventually the dolphins swam away, and everybody on the beach applauded __________.

Exercise 4

Rewrite the following sentences using adverbs of manner. The first one has been done to help you.

1. Joe is a neat writer. *Joe writes neatly.*
2. Anne is a brilliant player. __________
3. He was a brave fighter. __________
4. She is a reckless driver. __________
5. Tom is a fast runner. __________
6. I am a clumsy dancer. __________
7. Jane is a good singer. __________
8. He is a slow walker. __________
9. They are hard workers. __________
10. She was a shameless liar. __________

Exercise 5: grammar for writing

Write a short narrative called 'An Anxious Mother', about 100 words long, using ten different adverbs of manner. When you have finished, underline these adverbs.

 ISBN 978-81-8477-745-1

UNIT 50

ADVERBS OF PLACE AND DIRECTION

What do they look like?

'Have you seen my car keys?' called Alan. 'I've looked **everywhere**, but I can't find them.' 'They're **here** in the bedroom,' replied his wife. Alan raced **upstairs**, picked **up** the keys and kissed his wife goodbye. Then he ran **back** down the stairs and left the house. He got into his car and drove **away**.

What are they?

1 **Adverbs of place** and **direction** tell you about **position** and **movement**. They answer the question ***where?***:

- *Mr Jones lives **here**.*
- *These weeds grow **everywhere**.*
- *Please take the rubbish **outside**.*
- *They went **away** and never came **back**.*

2 Some **adverbs of place** and **direction** have the same form as **prepositions**. They include:

above, across, along, behind, below, by, down, in, off, on, over, past, through, under, up

- *She came **across** to speak to me.* (adverb)
- *She walked **across** the bridge.* (preposition)
- *He put **up** a notice saying 'Keep out'.* (adverb)
- *He climbed **up** the ladder.* (preposition)

In Unit 39, you learnt how to tell the difference between adverbs and prepositions in **phrasal verbs**.

How do you use them?

1 An **adverb of place** or **direction** usually comes after the verb it describes:

- *The birds flew **away**.*
- *Dad sometimes goes **there** on business.*

 ISBN 978-81-8477-745-1

2 If the verb has an object, the **adverb** usually comes **after** the object:

- *Please leave your muddy boots **outside**.*
- *Mum told the children to put their toys **away**.*

However, if the **adverb** is part of a **phrasal verb** (see Unit 39), you can sometimes put it before the object:

- *Mum told the children to put **away** their toys.*
- *Switch **off** the light when you leave the room.*

3 An **adverb of place** or **direction** usually comes **before** an adverb of time:

- *Sit **down** immediately!*
- *I'm going **home** tomorrow.*

4 In conversation and some types of written text (such as narratives and poetry), you occasionally put an **adverb of place** or **direction** at the **beginning** of a sentence, for emphasis or effect:

- ***Here** she comes!*
- ***Off** they went to search for the treasure.*

If the subject of the verb is a noun or noun phrase, not a pronoun, you put it **after** the verb. This is called **inversion**:

- ***Here** comes the bus!*
- ***Off** went James and John to search for the treasure.*

5 Some **adverbs of place** can be used like an adjective after a noun phrase:

- *The apartment **upstairs** is empty.*
- *The car rolled over, but the people **inside** were not badly hurt.*

PRACTICE

Exercise 1

Underline the adverbs of place or direction in the following sentences. There may be more than one adverb in some of the sentences.

1. There was no bridge over the river, so we had to swim across.
2. Sam took off his jacket and hung it on a peg.
3. They went in and sat down.
4. I had been there for more than an hour.
5. Kate ran downstairs and into the lounge.
6. Did you go anywhere interesting on holiday this year?

 ISBN 978-81-8477-745-1

7. Come back here at once!
8. The boy stood up and offered the woman his seat.
9. Jane went home and told her parents what had happened.
10. The teacher took my phone away and put it on her desk.

Exercise 2

Say whether the words in bold print are adverbs (A) or prepositions (P).

1. Stop writing and put your pens **down**. ( )
2. A large bird flew **over** our heads. ( )
3. Mrs Lee took a book **off** the shelf. ( )
4. I put **up** a poster on the wall. ( )
5. Sue went **round** to her friend's house. ( )
6. Animals should not have to live **in** cages. ( ).
7. The president waved as his car drove **past**. ( )
8. I switched **on** the television to watch the news. ( )
9. We walked **along** the path by the river. ( )
10. This is the rock which the snake was hiding **under**. ( )

Exercise 3

Fill in each blank in the following passage with a suitable adverb of place or direction. There may be more than one correct answer, but you should not use the same adverb twice.

Mrs Jones picked ______________ her handbag and set ______________ for the post office. It was cold ______________, so she went ______________ and put ______________ a jacket. She did not have far to go, and she walked briskly ______________, hoping that the post office would be warm ______________. When she got ______________, she realized that she had forgotten something important: the parcel she wanted to post. She had left it ______________ on the table in the hall. Running ______________ to collect it, she tripped and fell ______________. A man on the other side of the road came ______________ to help her. She was not hurt, but she felt very foolish, and extremely annoyed with herself.

 ISBN 978-81-8477-745-1

UNIT 51

ADVERBS OF TIME, FREQUENCY AND DURATION

What do they look like?

Tomorrow, I am going to the school fancy-dress ball. It is held **annually,** at the end of the school year. The tradition began thirty years **ago,** when our current principal was **still** a student here. She **briefly** considered cancelling this year's ball, but many students protested because they had **already** started making their costumes.

What are they?

1. **Adverbs of time** answer the question ***when?***:
   - *The train will arrive **soon**.*
   - *I went to the cinema **yesterday**.*

2. **Adverbs of frequency** answer the question ***how often?***:
   - *Tom visits his grandparents **weekly**.*
   - *The dog **rarely** bites anyone.*

3. **Adverbs of duration** answer the question ***for how long?***:
   - *Sandra stopped **briefly** to look in a shop window.*
   - *The hospital may have to close **permanently**.*

4. Some **adverbs of time**, **frequency** and **duration** have the same form as **adjectives** or **prepositions:**
   - *We arrived **early** and had to wait.* (adverb)
   - *She spent her **early** life in Japan.* (adjective)
   - *Fresh milk is delivered **daily**.* (adverb)
   - ***Daily** exercise is good for you.* (adjective)
   - *I bought this T-shirt on holiday and I haven't worn it **since**.* (adverb)
   - *Aunt Julie hasn't been in a plane **since** 1994.* (preposition)
   - *Have you seen this film **before**?* (adverb)
   - *Sue always gets nervous **before** an exam.* (preposition)

 ISBN 978-81-8477-745-1

How do you use them?

1 Some **adverbs of time, frequency** and **duration** most often come after the verb or at the **end** of the sentence:

- *The new supermarket will open **shortly**.*
- *Our staff are paid **monthly**, on the 25th of the month.*
- *Have you been waiting **long**?*

2 Some **adverbs of time** and **frequency** most often come **before** the verb (or the main verb in a verb phrase):

- *We **finally** agreed on a name for the product.*
- *They had **already** left.*
- *The birds **often** wake us up in the morning.*
- *Mrs Kim **seldom** leaves her house.*

Some **adverbs of duration** can also have this position:

- *They are **temporarily** living in a caravan.*

3 Some **adverbs of time** and **frequency** can be used at the **beginning** of the sentence:

- ***Yesterday** we collected the keys to the new apartment.*
- ***Sometimes** the school lunches are almost inedible.*

4 The adverb ***ago*** always follows an expression of time and a verb in the simple past:

- *I started this job three months **ago**.*
- *Most of the houses were built more than two hundred years **ago**.*

5 The adverb ***since*** is used with a verb in one of the perfect tenses:

- *He had disappeared in 2004 and nobody had seen him **since**.*
- *She couldn't speak the language when she first arrived, but she has **since** learnt a few words and phrases.*

PRACTICE

Exercise 1

Say whether the adverb in bold print is an adverb of time (T), frequency (F) or duration (D).

1. Jack **sometimes** helps his mother with the gardening. ( )
2. Have you ironed my shirt **yet**? ( )
3. You should **always** wear a helmet when cycling. ( )
4. Sally had not been working there **long** when she was promoted. ( )

 ISBN 978-81-8477-745-1

5. I have **often** envied people who are good at sport. ( )

6. We **briefly** considered moving to the coast. ( )

7. Paul can sleep in Joe's room **tonight**. ( )

8. The plane should be arriving **shortly**. ( )

9. The road will be closed **temporarily** while the surface is being repaired. ( )

10. My brother is **rarely** ill. ( )

Exercise 2

Rewrite the following sentences, putting the given ***adverbs*** *in the correct position* ***before*** *the verb (or the main verb in a verb phrase).*

1. We will reach our destination. (*soon*)

____

2. They solved the problem. (*finally*)

____

3. John is complaining about his unfair treatment. (*still*)

____

4. I've passed my driving test. (*just*)

____

5. Dad played tennis twenty years ago. (*last*)

____

6. Alice has had a bad cold. (*recently*)

____

7. The hall is used for concerts. (*occasionally*)

____

8. Grandma has lived in this house. (*always*)

____

9. My sister and brother had eaten their breakfast. (*already*)

____

 ISBN 978-81-8477-745-1

10. Jane goes for a run before breakfast. (*often*)

____

Exercise 3

Use the adverbs in the box to fill in the blanks in the following passage.

ago	already	before	eventually	late
recently	soon	still	then	yesterday

I had an appointment at the allergy clinic of our local hospital ____________. I had ____________ been there several times ____________, so I thought I knew where to go. However, when I got there, I discovered that the clinic had ____________ moved to a different part of the building. A hospital porter told me which way to go, and I ____________ found the right place. By ____________ I was late for my appointment. 'You should have been here ten minutes ____________,' said the receptionist. 'Fortunately, the doctor also arrived ____________ this morning, and he is ____________ treating the patient before you. Take a seat and he will see you as ____________ as he can.'

Exercise 4

Complete the following sentences with an appropriate activity, such as 'go to bed early' or 'forget to do my homework'.

1. I always ______________________________________.
2. I usually ______________________________________.
3. I often ______________________________________.
4. I sometimes ______________________________________.
5. I never ______________________________________.

 ISBN 978-81-8477-745-1

UNIT 52

ADVERBS OF DEGREE

What do they look like?

Alice is **rather** shy and she speaks **very** quietly. It is **quite** difficult to hear what she is saying — you **really** have to listen **hard**. Her friend Emma is **completely** different. She speaks **so** loudly that **absolutely** everyone can hear her, and it can be **extremely** difficult to get her to stop talking.

What are they?

Adverbs of degree answer the question ***how much?*** They increase or reduce the force of the word they describe:

- *That's a **remarkably** difficult question to answer.*
- *I **strongly** recommend the new Thai restaurant.*
- *The work went **reasonably** smoothly.*
- *The villagers had **almost** nothing to eat.*

How do you use them?

1. **Adverbs of degree** are most often used with adjectives. You put the adverb **before** the adjective it describes:
   - *They were **very** apologetic.*
   - *We had **pretty** good weather for our holiday.*
   - *What you suggest is **totally** impossible.*

2. **Adverbs of degree** are also used with other adverbs. You put the adverb of degree **before** the adverb it describes:
   - *You should dress **particularly** smartly for an interview.*
   - *We are all trying **very** hard.*
   - *He knew **perfectly** well that she couldn't swim.*

 ISBN 978-81-8477-745-1

3. You can use some **adverbs of degree** with **verbs**. The adverb often comes **before** the **verb** (or the **main verb** in a verb phrase):
   - *The new shopping centre has **completely** **ruined** our view.*
   - *The library was **entirely** destroyed by the fire.*
   - *I **rather** **hoped** he would change his mind.*
   - *That **considerably** **alters** the situation.*

4. However, the **adverb** can sometimes come **after** the **verb** (and its object). The adverbs ***much*** and ***little*** usually come in this position:
   - *That **alters** the situation **considerably**.*
   - *We **have progressed** **little** during the past week.*
   - *I **do** not **watch** television **much**.*

5. A few **adverbs of degree** can also be used before an **indefinite pronoun**:
   - ***Nearly*** ***everyone*** *thought it was a good idea.*
   - *Sally saw **hardly** **anybody** she knew.*
   - *I know **absolutely** **nothing** about computers.*

6. The adverbs ***as***, ***so***, ***too*** and ***very*** can be used before some **quantifiers**, as well as before **adjectives** and other **adverbs**:
   - *Take **as** **many** sweets as you want.*
   - *We ran **as** **fast** as we could.*
   - *There's **so** **little** anyone can do to help.*
   - *John watches **too** **much** television.*
   - *I was **too** **exhausted** to walk any further.*
   - ***Very*** ***few*** *people like going to the dentist's.*

7. The adverb ***only*** can be used with many word classes. You should always try to put it as close as possible to the **word it describes**:
   - ***Only*** ***Jane*** *speaks Japanese.* (= nobody else speaks Japanese)
   - *Jane **only** **speaks** Japanese.* (= she cannot read or write Japanese)
   - *Jane speaks **only** **Japanese**.* (= she cannot speak any other language)

PRACTICE

Exercise 1

Fill in the blanks with the correct adverb of degree formed from the adjective provided.

1. Are you ______________ sure you want to come? (*complete*)
2. The new buildings have ______________ altered the appearance of the town centre. (*total*)
3. I am ______________ aware of the problems. (*full*)

4. They ________________ agreed with our suggestion. (*entire*)
5. The wedding was a ________________ wonderful occasion. (*true*)
6. Tom is ________________ certain that he locked the door. (*absolute*)
7. The two words are spelt ________________ differently. (*slight*)
8. Aunt Julie's health has ________________ improved since she moved to the coast. (*considerable*)

Exercise 2

In the following sentences, all the adverbs of degree are in bold print. Put a ring round the word that each adverb describes.

1. The book is **too** big to fit on this shelf.
2. The village has changed **considerably** since I was last here.
3. Jane was **rather** embarrassed to receive **so** much praise.
4. I recognized **hardly** anyone in the room.
5. The children were behaving **particularly** well that day.
6. Our new teacher is **very** stern and smiles **little**.
7. There were **only** two cakes on the plate.
8. David does not like football **much**.
9. The rabbit's eyes were **as** black as coal.
10. The weather improved **greatly** during the second week of our holiday.

Exercise 3

Underline all the adverbs of degree in the following passage.

Fred and Bill are identical twins. Nearly everyone they meet finds it completely impossible to tell them apart. They are so alike that their own parents sometimes muddle them up. However, the twins are also remarkably different in many ways. Fred is a keen student and works very hard at school. Bill is as clever as his brother, but he is too lazy to do as much work as he should. He likes only one subject, and that is art. He has painted some absolutely beautiful pictures of the countryside around his home. Fred does not like art much, though he is quite good at it. He prefers maths and science, and hopes to study medicine at university eventually.

 ISBN 978-81-8477-745-1

UNIT 53

COMPARATIVE AND SUPERLATIVE ADVERBS

What do they look like?

A car engine works **best** when it is warm. It runs **more smoothly** than when it is cold. It also seems to go **faster**, because you can accelerate **more easily**. The engine functions **most efficiently** if it is regularly serviced, which means you can drive **further** on a tankful of fuel.

Like adjectives, many adverbs have three forms: the **positive**, the **comparative** and the **superlative**. The normal base form of the adverb is the **positive**. The **comparative** and **superlative** forms are used in comparisons.

POSITIVE	COMPARATIVE	SUPERLATIVE
fast	*faster*	*fastest*
early	*earlier*	*earliest*
easily	*more easily*	*most easily*
well	*better*	*best*

How do you form them?

1. Short adverbs that are not formed by adding *ly* to an adjective have a **comparative** form ending in *er* and a **superlative** form ending in *est*:

loud	*louder*	*loudest*
hard	*harder*	*hardest*

2. For adverbs that are formed by adding *ly* to an adjective, you use *more* to form the **comparative** and *most* to form the **superlative**. These words come before the adverb:

strongly	***more** strongly*	***most** strongly*
comfortably	***more** comfortably*	***most** comfortably*

 ISBN 978-81-8477-745-1

3. Some adverbs have **irregular** comparative and superlative forms:

well	***better***	***best***
badly	***worse***	***worst***
far	***further***	***furthest***
little	***less***	***least***
much	***more***	***most***

How do you use them?

1. You use the **comparative** form of an adverb when comparing **one** action, or the way it is done, with **another**:
   - *You will have to try **harder**.*
   - *An electric light shines **more brightly** than a candle.*

2. You use the **superlative** form, usually with ***the***, when comparing **three or more** items:
   - *All the boys tried hard, but James tried **the hardest**.*
   - *The sun shines **the most brightly** of all sources of light.*

3. You can also form **comparatives** with ***less*** and **superlatives** with ***least***:
   - *Our grandchildren visit us **less often** now.*
   - *Sally was dressed the **least smartly** of all the girls.*

4. You use the **positive** form of the adverb in comparisons with ***as***:
   - *I can run **as fast** as you.*
   - *We don't spend our money **as extravagantly** as some other people do.*

5. You use the **comparative** form of the adverb in comparisons with ***than***:
   - *Jane did **better than** Sue in the exam.*
   - *You can cook **more efficiently** with gas **than** with electricity.*

PRACTICE

Exercise 1

Fill in the blanks with a suitable superlative adverb. The first one has been done to help you.

1. All the girls have neat handwriting, but Mary writes the *most neatly*.
2. All the guests arrived early, but Mr Brown arrived the ____________.
3. All the boys wear smart clothes, but Sam dresses the ____________.

 ISBN 978-81-8477-745-1

4. All the contestants sang well, but the winner was the one who sang the ______________.

5. All the children have quiet voices, but Alice speaks the ______________.

6. All the pets behaved badly, but my dog behaved the ______________.

7. All the cars went fast, but the blue car went the ______________.

8. All the buses run frequent services, but the bus to the station runs the ______________.

9. All the soldiers were courageous, but Jack Robinson fought the ______________.

10. All the clocks have loud alarms, but this one rings the ______________.

Exercise 2

Fill in the blanks in the second sentence with a suitable comparative adverb, using the information given in the first sentence. The first one has been done to help you.

1. Bill cycled seven kilometres and Simon cycled ten kilometres.

   Simon cycled *further* than Bill.

2. Kate goes to the gym every day but Sue goes only three times a week.

   Sue goes to the gym ______________ ______________ than Kate.

3. Jim passed the test fairly easily and Ken passed it very easily.

   Ken passed the test ______________ ______________ than Jim.

4. The red car was going at 50 kph and the blue car was going at 70 kph.

   The blue car was going ______________ than the red car.

5. Emma doesn't like dancing much but Jane likes it very much.

   Jane likes dancing ______________ than Emma does.

6. Ben waited an hour and Dave waited two hours.

   Dave waited ______________ than Ben.

7. Mary's holidays start on 6 June and Carol's start on 10 June.

   Carol's holidays start ______________ than Kate's do.

8. I worry a little about exams and Alan worries a lot.

   I worry ______________ about exams than Alan does.

 ISBN 978-81-8477-745-1

9. There was not much wind when we set sail, but it increased at lunchtime.

   The wind blew ______________ in the afternoon than it did in the morning.

10. There was a bit of light rain on Monday and it poured with rain on Tuesday.

   It rained ______________ on Tuesday than it did on Monday.

Exercise 3

Fill in the blanks in the following passage with a comparative or superlative adverb formed from the given adjective.

'You didn't play very well today,' said the football coach. 'You need to play much ______________ (*good*) if you're going to win next week. Your opponents are kicking the ball ______________ (*skilful*) than any of you.' He went on to say, even ______________ (*firm*), 'Tomorrow I will hold trials for next week's team. I am looking for those players who can run the ______________ (*fast*) and kick the ball the ______________ (*far*). You all need to train ______________ (*strenuous*) and some of you need to get to the football field ______________ (*early*). Being late shows a lack of commitment which I will not tolerate.' The team listened to their coach ______________ (*attentive*) than usual. They were all aware of their recent poor performance. Joe Green, the goalkeeper, felt that he had played the ______________ (*bad*) of all. He vowed to try much ______________ (*hard*) in future.

Exercise 4: grammar for writing

Write a short passage, about 100 words long, comparing the skills and abilities of some of your friends or classmates. Your passage should contain at least three comparative adverbs and at least three superlative adverbs.

____

____

____

____

____

____

____

 ISBN 978-81-8477-745-1

UNIT 54

SENTENCE ADVERBS AND LINKING ADVERBS

What do they look like?

Tom was involved in a bicycle accident. **Fortunately**, he wasn't badly hurt, but his parents were concerned, **naturally**. He didn't tell them, **however**, that he had been fooling around on his bike and **consequently** fell off. **Perhaps** he will be a bit more careful next time he goes cycling!

What are they?

Sentence adverbs and **linking adverbs** do not describe a particular verb, adjective or other adverb in a sentence. They refer to a **whole clause** or **sentence**.

1. A **sentence adverb** makes a **comment on a statement**. It often shows the **attitude** of the person who is speaking or writing:
   - ***Sadly,*** *all the plants died.*
   - *They* ***probably*** *didn't want to make a fuss.*

2. A **linking adverb** is used as a **connector**. It **links clauses or sentences** by showing that the information they contain is related in some way:
   - *The scheme is impractical;* ***besides****, we can't afford it.*
   - ***First*** *you peel the potatoes.* ***Then*** *you cut them into thin slices.*

How do you use them?

Sentence adverbs

1. **Sentence adverbs** often come at the **beginning** of the statement, usually separated by a comma, as an introduction to what follows:
   - ***Fortunately****, no damage has been done.*
   - ***Naturally****, parents want their children to do well.*

 ISBN 978-81-8477-745-1

2 You can also put **sentence adverbs** at the **end** of the statement, again separated by a comma:

- *No damage has been done, **fortunately**.*
- *Parents want their children to do well, **naturally**.*

3 **Some sentence adverbs** can come in the **middle** of the statement. You usually put them **before** the verb, without commas:

- *I **luckily** remembered where I had put my keys.*
- *She **actually** prefers classical music to rock music.*

4 In a positive statement with a verb phrase, you put the **sentence adverb after** the first auxiliary verb:

- *They will **probably** be late.*
- *I have **definitely** seen this film before.*
- *He had **actually** been hoping that they would refuse the offer.*

5 However, in a negative statement with the contraction *n't*, you put the **sentence adverb before** the verb phrase:

- *They **probably** won't mind.*
- *I **definitely** haven't seen this film before.*

Linking adverbs

1 **Linking adverbs** most often come at the **beginning** of the clause or sentence, usually separated by a comma. They often make a connection with what has already been said:

- *Sally's computer broke down. **Consequently**, she was not able to finish her homework.*
- *We could go to a restaurant; **alternatively**, we could invite a few friends for dinner here.*

2 You sometimes put **linking adverbs** at the **end** of the clause or sentence, with or without a comma:

- *We've had a few problems, but it's been a successful venture **altogether**.*
- *'I'm not going out tonight.' 'Can I borrow your jacket, **then**?'*

3 You can also put some **linking adverbs** in the **middle** of the clause or sentence, with or without commas around them:

- *Something may go wrong. I have **therefore** made some emergency arrangements.*
- *Joe likes animals. He does not, **however**, have any pets of his own.*

4 **Linking adverbs** are used for many different purposes, such as showing **sequence**, **addition**, or **contrast**:

- *I had a shower, **then** I got dressed.* (sequence)
- *Jane is a very good tennis player. She plays squash and badminton **too**.* (addition)
- *Uncle Jack does not have much money. **However**, he always buys me a birthday present.* (contrast)

You will learn more about using these and other **connectors** in Chapter 8.

 ISBN 978-81-8477-745-1

PRACTICE

Exercise 1

Choose the more suitable sentence adverb *from those provided to fill in the blanks.*

1. ______________, Harry had a spare key for the padlock. (*Fortunately*, *Frankly*)
2. ______________, the thief will soon be caught. (*Generally*, *Hopefully*)
3. ______________, Jane is a very talented musician. (*Clearly*, *Definitely*)
4. ______________, someone else asked me the same question earlier. (*Coincidentally*, *Obviously*)
5. ______________, the return ticket is cheaper than the single ticket. (*Confidentially*, *Surprisingly*)
6. ______________, Dad was not pleased with my exam results. (*Luckily*, *Predictably*)
7. ______________, I have never been skiing before. (*Actually*, *Unfortunately*)
8. ______________, everyone was shocked to hear the bad news. (*Naturally*, *Probably*)

Exercise 2

Rewrite the following sentences, putting the given adverbs *before the correct part of the verb phrase (not at the beginning of the sentence).*

1. She doesn't want anyone to know she might be leaving. (*naturally*)

   ____

2. I was expecting you to say no. (*actually*)

   ____

3. The work will be finished by Thursday. (*definitely*)

   ____

4. Dad won't notice the dent in the car door. (*hopefully*)

   ____

5. They had been following us for some time. (*apparently*)

   ____

6. This isn't the best time to ask Dad for a loan. (*probably*)

   ____

 ISBN 978-81-8477-745-1

7. I have forgotten to bring my mobile phone. (*unfortunately*)

____

8. The woman was lying. (*obviously*)

____

9. The word is used as a connector. (*generally*)

____

10. We need a larger house. (*clearly*)

____

Exercise 3

Use the linking adverbs in the box to fill in the blanks in the following passage.

also	besides	consequently	firstly	however
nevertheless	perhaps	secondly	then	therefore

Our sales figures have not been very good this year. ______________, we will not be paying any of our staff a bonus. I don't want to sound too gloomy, ______________. There are bound to be disappointing years from time to time; ______________, many other companies are struggling at the moment. ______________, we must make a big effort to improve our sales in the coming year. We must ______________ think about ways of cutting costs. The task before us is ______________ a double one. ______________, we must try to find ways of persuading people to buy our products, rather than those of our competitors. (______________ the marketing department will have some good ideas about how to do this.) ______________, we must work more efficiently, so that our goods cost less to produce. We will ______________ be able to sell more of them at lower prices.

Exercise 4: grammar for writing

Write a short passage, about 100 words long, describing a day when everything went wrong. Your passage should contain at least four sentence adverbs and at least four linking adverbs. When you have finished, underline all the sentence adverbs and put a ring round all the linking adverbs.

____

____

 ISBN 978-81-8477-745-1

UNIT 55

ADVERBIAL PHRASES

What do they look like?

Last weekend, Anna **very reluctantly** began clearing out her wardrobe. She took an old jacket **off a hanger**. She liked it **a lot** but hadn't worn it **for ages** because it was **far too** tight. 'I could give it **to my sister**,' she thought. '**On the other hand**, it might be best to throw it **in the bin**.'

What are they?

An **adverbial phrase** is any set of words that does the work of an adverb:

- *Sally has been working **too hard**.*
- *I'll see you **this evening**.*
- *Mum was **at work** when the parcel arrived.*
- ***To be honest**, I was quite relieved.*

What are they made up of?

1. An **adverbial phrase** can consist simply of **two adverbs**, the first of which is often an **adverb of degree**:
   - *George was walking **very quickly**.*
   - ***Quite frankly**, I think they should pay for the repair.*

2. Sometimes, there is more than one **adverb of degree**, making an **adverbial phrase** of at least three words:
   - *George was walking **far too quickly**.*
   - *They treat some criminals **much more leniently** than others.*

3. Some **adverbial phrases** consist of **one** adverb of place or time followed by **another**:
   - *When did you get **back home**?*
   - ***Just then** the telephone rang.*

 ISBN 978-81-8477-745-1

4 The most common type of **adverbial phrase** begins with a **preposition**:

- *I hung my coat* ***on the peg.***
- *The play starts* ***at seven o'clock.***
- *Your slippers are* ***under your bed.***
- ***In a way,*** *I was quite pleased.*

These are also called **prepositional phrases**, and you will learn more about them in Unit 56.

5 An **adverbial phrase** can also have the form of a **noun phrase**:

- *They are getting married* ***next year.***
- *She has been crying* ***all afternoon.***
- *I found the work* ***a bit*** *boring.*

6 Some **adverbial phrases** consist of two **adverbs**, **nouns** or **pronouns** linked by a **preposition** or **conjunction**:

- *The boat bobbed* ***up and down.***
- *He rolled* ***head over heels.***
- *Stand* ***back to back.***
- *Disasters came* ***one after another.***
- ***Little by little*** *we cleared up the mess.*

How do you use them?

1 An **adverbial phrase** can be used as an **adverb of manner**:

- *Our team played* ***fairly well,*** *but the other team played better.*
- *Kate pulled the handle* ***with all her strength.***

2 It can be used as an **adverb of place** or **direction**:

- *Go and stand* ***over there.***
- *The boys walked* ***through the forest.***

3 It can be used as an **adverb of time, frequency** or **duration**:

- *I had posted the letter* ***the day before.***
- *Grandma has a medical check-up* ***twice a year.***
- *He has been working here* ***for six months.***

4 It can be used as an **adverb of degree**:

- *I like this* ***very much.***
- *She felt* ***a great deal*** *happier when she heard the good news.*

5 It can be used as a **sentence adverb**:

- *They gave the job to the wrong person,* ***in my opinion.***
- ***To be fair,*** *he hadn't had much time to learn his lines.*

 ISBN 978-81-8477-745-1

6. It can be used as a **linking adverb**:
   - *You could easily take more exercise.* ***For example****, you could walk or cycle to school.*
   - *I'm a bit short of money;* ***in other words****, I can't afford to go.*

7. An **adverbial phrase** can also be used as the **complement** of a linking verb:
   - *Your dinner is* ***in the microwave****.*
   - *Those two chairs look* ***out of line****.*

PRACTICE

Exercise 1

Fill in the blanks with one word from each box to form adverbial phrases. Use each word only once.

A:				
all	almost	for	in	last
quite	rather	strangely	up	very

B:				
day	down	enough	everywhere	example
foolishly	honestly	kindly	night	out

1. They treated us __________ __________ and bought us lots of presents.
2. Stop running __________ and __________ in your muddy shoes.
3. Sally knew she had behaved __________ __________.
4. I had a very odd dream __________ __________.
5. __________ __________, nobody noticed that anything was wrong.
6. The children were jumping __________ and __________ with excitement.
7. __________ __________, I'd rather read a book than watch rubbish like this on TV.
8. Jane had looked __________ __________ for her missing ring.
9. It has been raining __________ __________.
10. You could do more to help; you could offer to cook a meal, __________ __________.

 ISBN 978-81-8477-745-1

Exercise 2

*Choose **adverbial phrases** from the box to fill in the blanks in the following passage.*

at eleven o'clock	just in time
at the gym	last Saturday morning
at the weekend	quite often
from the recreation ground	to the bathroom
in a helicopter	very quickly
in bed	with me

I was still lying ______________ when my friend Sue phoned ______________. I had been happily thinking that I would spend the morning ______________, swimming and exercising. I ______________ go there ______________. But Sue had other plans for me. 'Hey,' she said, 'I've won a ride ______________ and I can bring a friend ______________. The helicopter takes off ______________ at half past eleven, so I'll meet you there ______________. It was already ten o'clock, so I raced ______________ and ______________ got washed and dressed. I caught a bus to the recreation ground and arrived ______________.

Exercise 3: grammar for writing

*Write a short narrative, about 100 words long, called 'The Empty House'. Your passage should contain at least ten **adverbial phrases**. When you have finished, underline all the adverbial phrases.*

____

____

____

____

____

____

____

____

 ISBN 978-81-8477-745-1

7 PREPOSITIONS

 ISBN 978-81-8477-745-1

UNIT 56

PREPOSITIONS

What do they look like?

I went **to** the newsagent's **for** a magazine. There was a long queue, so I stood **at** the back and waited. The woman **in front of** me had two young children **with** her. They were getting impatient. Some people who had come **into** the shop **after** me gave up waiting and left.

What are they?

1. **Prepositions** are **short words** that **link** other words or phrases within a sentence. They often show the **relationship** that exists between people and things:
   - *The cat sat* ***on*** *the mat.*
   - *He walked* ***towards*** *the door.*
   - *I often go running* ***before*** *breakfast.*
   - *Most people wash their hair* ***with*** *shampoo.*
   - *James is older* ***than*** *Peter.*
   - *She will drink anything* ***except*** *cola.*

2. Some prepositions are made up of **more than one word**. They are called **complex prepositions**:
   - *I've read* ***as far as*** *page 28.*
   - *A stranger came* ***up to*** *me and asked the time.*

   Many complex prepositions consist of adverb + **preposition**:
   - *Keep* ***away from*** *the electric fence.*
   - *A large dog ran* ***out of*** *the house.*

   Some consist of **preposition** + noun + **preposition**:
   - *Sally's desk is* ***in front of*** *mine.*
   - *I put a plate* ***on top of*** *the dish.*

 ISBN 978-81-8477-745-1

How do you use them?

1 A **preposition** always has an **object** which usually comes after it. The object of a preposition is most often a **noun**, **noun phrase** or **pronoun**:

- *We travelled home **by** bus.*
- *I haven't seen Tom **since** January.*
- *Carol works **at** the local supermarket.*
- *The man took a pen **out of** his pocket.*
- *These flowers are **for** you.*
- *Alice gets on well **with** everyone.*

2 The **object** of a **preposition** can also be an *ing* form (a **gerund**):

- *Joe is good **at** drawing.*
- *They suspected her **of** cheating.*

3 A **preposition** followed by its **object** is called a **prepositional phrase**:

- *I sat **on** the sofa.*
- *The children went shopping **with** their parents.*

4 A **prepositional phrase** often does the work of an **adverb**, telling you more about the action of a **verb**:

- *The horse jumped **over the fence**.*
- *He put the letter **in his pocket**.*

These are also called **adverbial phrases**, which you learnt about in Unit 55.

5 A **prepositional phrase** can also do the work of an **adjective**, telling you more about a **noun**:

- *The maps **on this wall** are very old.*
- *I saw a man **with black hair**.*

These are also called **adjectival phrases**, which you learnt about in Unit 22.

6 A **prepositional phrase** can be the **complement** of a **linking verb**:

- *Dad is **in the kitchen**.*
- *Joan felt **out of place**.*

7 You sometimes use two or more **prepositional phrases** one after another:

- *We travelled **to the airport** | **in a taxi**.*
- *Give your ticket **to the man** | **in uniform** | **at the main door**.*

8 You sometimes put a **prepositional phrase** at the beginning of a sentence for **emphasis**, or to **vary** the way sentences are written in a narrative or recount:

- ***Above the fireplace** there was a portrait of his grandfather.*
- ***Since 1990** she has lived alone.*

 ISBN 978-81-8477-745-1

Prepositions separated from their objects

There are a few circumstances in which a **preposition** may become separated from its **object**. In these cases the preposition often comes at the end of the clause or sentence, 'looking back' to its object.

1 A **preposition** can come at the end of some spoken questions beginning with a *wh*-word. The **object** of the preposition is the ***wh*-word** or the **noun phrase** it introduces:

- ***What*** *is this dial used* ***for****?*
- ***Whose team*** *are you* ***in****?*
- ***Who*** *did they get the information* ***from****?*
- ***Which department*** *should I send my complaint* ***to****?*

In more formal written English, the **preposition** comes at the beginning of the question, before the ***wh*-word**:

- ***From whom*** *did they obtain the information?*
- ***To which department*** *should I address my complaint?*

Remember that you must use ***whom*** rather than ***who*** directly after a preposition.

2 A **preposition** can also come at the end of an indirect question containing a **wh-word**:

- *David couldn't decide* ***which film*** *to go* ***to****.*
- *I've never been to this museum before — tell me* ***what*** *I should look* ***at****.*

3 A **preposition** stays with a verb when its **object** becomes the **subject** of a **passive sentence**:

- ACTIVE: *The emperor slept* ***in this bed****.*
- PASSIVE: ***This bed*** *was slept* ***in*** *by the emperor.*
- ACTIVE: *You can see* ***through transparent materials****.*
- PASSIVE: ***Transparent materials*** *can be seen* ***through****.*

4 A **preposition** sometimes stays with a ***to*-infinitive** when its **object** comes earlier in the sentence:

- *I'm looking for* ***something to write with****.*
- *Bring* ***a cushion to sit on****.*
- ***The stream*** *was too wide* ***to jump over****.*

 ISBN 978-81-8477-745-1

PRACTICE

Exercise 1

*In the following sentences, underline the **object** of the **preposition** in bold print.*

1. Julie sat **beside** the fire.
2. Don't go out **without** your sunhat.
3. Which shelf should I put this book **on**?
4. How dare you accuse me **of** stealing!
5. Peter didn't have anyone to talk **to**.
6. **In** her hand she held a large black umbrella.
7. We climbed **over** the fence **into** the garden.
8. The man **with** a gold chain **around** his neck is the mayor.
9. The slope was too steep to cycle **up**.
10. The ring Sally was looking **at** was very expensive.

Exercise 2

*Fill in each blank with a suitable **preposition**. Do not use any complex prepositions, and do not use the same preposition more than once.*

1. The boys hid ______________ the door.
2. We have lived here ______________ 2006.
3. David goes ______________ the gym ______________ Tuesdays and Thursdays.
4. I took a cloth ______________ the drawer and laid it ______________ the bowl, to keep the flies out.
5. Sue felt better ______________ discussing the matter ______________ her mother.
6. These flowers are ______________ my aunt, who is ______________ hospital.
7. Alice fell ______________ the stairs and hurt her ankle.
8. You should always wash your hands ______________ handling food.
9. We watched an interesting programme ______________ space travel.
10. This chair is more comfortable ______________ that one.

 ISBN 978-81-8477-745-1

Exercise 3

Underline all the complex prepositions in the following passage and put a ring round all the other prepositions.

Jane walked into the lounge and stood by the window. She looked around the room at all the valuable things her aunt had collected over the years. An embroidered screen stood in front of the fireplace. The shelves on the wall were filled with ornaments, pictures and old books. On top of the sideboard there was an antique porcelain vase. Jane could see nothing in the room that was new, except for a copy of the latest novel by her aunt's favourite author. She turned to look out of the window. All the land she could see belonged to her aunt. There was a huge garden, with orchards and fields beyond it. Jane's aunt was a very rich woman, but she was lonely and unhappy in spite of her wealth. She liked nothing better than having a visit from one of her nieces or nephews, and Jane was her favourite.

Exercise 4: grammar for writing

Write a short passage, about 120 words long, describing part of a typical day in your life. The passage should contain at least 15 different prepositions. When you have finished, underline all the prepositions. Take care not to underline any adverbs by mistake.

 ISBN 978-81-8477-745-1

UNIT
57

PREPOSITIONS OF SPACE AND TIME

What do they look like?

Sally cycled **to** the station **on** her new bike. She was meeting her grandmother, whose train arrived **at** ten o'clock. Sally leant her bike **against** the railings **outside** the station and went **on to** the platform. Her grandmother got **off** the train looking rather tired. She had been travelling **for** more than five hours.

How do you use them?

1. You can use **prepositions of space** to indicate **position** or **direction**. The object of a **preposition of position** is the place where someone or something is. A **preposition of direction** is used with a verb of movement:
    - *Dad hung the picture **above** the fireplace.* (position)
    - *A delivery van was parked **behind** our car.* (position)
    - *We live **in** a small apartment.* (position)
    - *They walked **towards** the gate.* (direction)
    - *The rabbit ran **down** a hole.* (direction)
    - *A cold wind was blowing **from** the east.* (direction)

2. Many **prepositions of space** can indicate both **position** and **direction**, in different contexts:
    - *How many people were **aboard** the train?* (position)
    - *The passengers climbed **aboard** the boat.* (direction)
    - *I found my missing slipper **under** the bed.* (position)
    - *The spider crawled **under** the mat.* (direction)
    - *There is a bridge **across** the river.* (position)
    - *We rowed **across** the river.* (direction)

3. You use **prepositions of time** to talk about something that **happens at a particular moment** or something that **lasts for a particular period**:
    - *The birds start singing **before** sunrise.*
    - *The car won't be ready **until** Friday.*
    - *We visited several museums **during** our holiday.*
    - *My grandparents have lived in Taiwan **since** their retirement.*

 ISBN 978-81-8477-745-1

4. The **object** of a **preposition of time** is often a date, a time, or a number of hours, days, etc.:
   - *My sister was born **in** 2008.*
   - *The bus arrived **at** half past ten.*
   - *He had been waiting **for** two hours.*

   The words ***past*** and ***to***, used in telling the time, are also prepositions.

5. Some prepositions can be a **preposition of space** in one context and a **preposition of time** in another context:
   - *The bird perched **on** a branch.* (space)
   - *I always have a party **on** my birthday.* (time)
   - *I picked up the purse and ran **after** its owner.* (space)
   - *The boys felt tired **after** their game of football.* (time)
   - *We flew **from** Singapore **to** Beijing.* (space)
   - *The museum is open **from** Monday **to** Friday.* (time)

6. Some prepositions of **space** and **time** are **complex prepositions**:
   - *I took the dictionary **out of** the bookcase.*
   - *The faster walkers were a long way **ahead of** the others.*
   - *Keep **away from** the edge of the canal.*
   - *I had to make a speech **in front of** the whole school.*
   - *I'll come with you **as far as** the crossroads.*
   - *He had worked in a bank **up to** 2005.*

PRACTICE

Exercise 1

Say whether the prepositions in bold print are prepositions of position (P), direction (D) or time (T).

1. I like to take my holidays **in** the spring. ( )
2. A plane flew **over** the treetops. ( )
3. The secretary made notes **during** the meeting. ( )
4. I'll meet you **outside** the cinema. ( )
5. Uncle Jack went **to** England on business. ( )
6. Please hand in your essays **before** Friday. ( )
7. I sat **beside** my best friend. ( )
8. A squirrel ran **up** the tree. ( )
9. The picture **on** the wall was painted by my aunt. ( )
10. I have not seen Tom and Sue **since** their wedding. ( )

 ISBN 978-81-8477-745-1

Exercise 2

*Rewrite the following sentences, replacing the **preposition** in bold print with one that has the opposite meaning. Put a ring round the new preposition. The first one has been done to help you.*

1. The children ran **into** the house. *The children ran out of the house.*
2. I walked **down** the stairs. ______________________________
3. Sue took the dog for a walk **after** lunch. ______________________________
4. Tom was standing **behind** Peter. ______________________________
5. We took a taxi **to** the airport. ______________________________
6. A snake crawled **over** the rock. ______________________________
7. I wrote my name **above** the picture I had drawn. ______________________________
8. She moved her chair **towards** the table. ______________________________
9. The man stepped **on to** the bus. ______________________________
10. We arranged to meet **inside** the restaurant. ______________________________

Exercise 3

*Use the **prepositions** in the box to fill in the blanks in the following passage. Use each word only once.*

across	at	before	between	for	in	into
near	on	off	over	since	to	towards

Tom and I had decided to spend the day ______ an island ______ a lake ______ my parents' holiday cottage. They have owned the cottage ______ 2002, but they don't use it very often. We had arranged to meet there ______ 10 o'clock. However, I was late and Tom arrived ______ me. 'I have been waiting ______ nearly an hour,' he said crossly. 'Sorry,' I replied. We made our way ______ the lake and hired a rowing boat. Stepping ______ the jetty ______ the boat, we discussed who would do the rowing. Tom volunteered, and soon the boat was moving ______ the lake ______ the island. I put my arm ______ the side, letting the water run ______ my fingers. It was very cold. 'I don't think we'll be going swimming today,' I said.

 ISBN 978-81-8477-745-1

UNIT 58

PREPOSITIONS WITH OTHER USES

What do they look like?

We had a discussion **about** school uniform last week. I am **in favour of** it. Having to wear school uniform makes life easier **for** students **with** poor parents, who cannot afford to buy them expensive clothes. **Without** school uniform, the differences **between** rich and poor students would be much more obvious.

How do you use them?

Prepositions can be used for many different purposes.

1. Some prepositions indicate the **purpose** or **means** of doing something:
   - *I use this pen **for** writing letters.*
   - *The letters are sorted **by** machine.*
   - *He cut up the meat **with** a sharp knife.*
   - *How did you get into the apartment **without** a key?*

2. Some indicate **possession**, **having** or **belonging**:
   - *The lid **of** the box is broken.*
   - *A girl **with** dark hair was standing by the door.*
   - *I never go out **without** an umbrella.*
   - *Where is the key **to** this cupboard?*
   - *This is a quotation **from** Shakespeare's 'Hamlet'.*

3. They can show that one person or thing **accompanies** another:
   - *Jane went to the cinema **with** Sam.*
   - *Children under twelve will not be admitted **without** an adult.*

4. They can also indicate the **subject** of something:
   - *I watched an interesting documentary **about** climate change.*
   - *Mr Brown gave a talk **on** photography.*
   - *They had an argument **over** the bill.*
   - *Thank you for your enquiry **concerning** the post of school secretary.*
   - *I wrote to the council **with regard to** the potholes in the road.*

 ISBN 978-81-8477-745-1

5 Some prepositions are used for **comparison** or **contrast**:

- *Your house is bigger* ***than*** *ours.*
- *Jim is nearly as tall* ***as*** *his father.*
- *That sounds* ***like*** *thunder.*
- *Alice loves jazz,* ***unlike*** *the rest of her family.*
- *What is the difference* ***between*** *a transitive verb and an intransitive verb?*
- *The hotel was expensive* ***compared with*** *the one where we stayed last year.*

6 Some show **support** or **opposition**:

- *Twenty people voted* ***for*** *the proposal and sixteen voted* ***against*** *it.*
- *Are you* ***in favour of*** *capital punishment?*
- *I agree* ***with*** *everything the speaker said.*

7 Some prepositions indicate that something is **not included**:

- *The shop is open every day* ***except*** *Monday.*
- *I've packed everything* ***but*** *my walking boots.*
- *She has no friends* ***apart from*** *us.*
- *What interests do you have* ***besides*** *playing computer games?*

8 Others indicate **addition**:

- *You will receive 500 dollars a week,* ***plus*** *a productivity bonus.*
- *He owns an apartment in the city* ***as well as*** *a large country house.*
- *She has to look after her little sister,* ***in addition to*** *her other commitments.*

9 They can refer to **giving** or **receiving**:

- *I handed my essay* ***to*** *the teacher.*
- *Tom bought a box of chocolates* ***for*** *his mother.*
- *Some students receive a grant* ***from*** *the government.*

10 They can also refer to **sharing** or **dividing**:

- *The thieves shared the money* ***among*** *themselves.*
- *This is a secret* ***between*** *you and me.*
- *Divide 20* ***by*** *5.*
- *I cut the cake* ***into*** *six pieces.*
- *Half* ***of*** *the land belongs to our neighbour.*

11 Some prepositions give a **reason**:

- *His poor performance was entirely* ***due to*** *his own laziness.*
- *Aunt Mary was advised to give up driving* ***because of*** *her failing eyesight.*
- *He agreed to help them* ***out of*** *pity.*
- *I failed the exam* ***through*** *sheer carelessness.*

12 Some indicate **concession**:

- *Joe agreed to help,* ***despite*** *his reservations about the wisdom of the plan.*
- *She managed to make herself heard* ***in spite of*** *the noise outside.*

 ISBN 978-81-8477-745-1

PRACTICE

Exercise 1

Choose the correct ***prepositions*** *to fill in the blanks.*

1. There is little difference ______________ (***among/between***) the two books.
2. The tablecloths are embroidered ______________ (***by/with***) hand.
3. The children were fighting ______________ (***on/over***) their toys.
4. Everyone ______________ (***despite/except***) Peter had brought a packed lunch.
5. Many people are ______________ (***against/without***) lowering the voting age.
6. The windscreen ______________ (***of/to***) the car was broken.
7. This picture was painted ______________ (***about/by***) my brother.
8. I mainly use the computer ______________ (***for/in***) schoolwork.
9. My feet are not as big ______________ (***as/than***) yours.
10. They had been robbed by a man ______________ (***of/with***) a gun.

Exercise 2

Complete each sentence with a ***prepositional phrase*** *formed by taking one word from each box. Do not use the any word more than once.*

A: about by for from in into than to with without

B: Dad laughter lemons mistake pain shelter slices stopping success whales

1. I borrowed some money ______________.
2. The clown tripped over and the audience roared ______________.
3. We have to write an essay ______________.
4. The cook put sugar in the soup instead of salt, ______________.
5. Simon ran all the way home ______________.
6. Jane trod on a drawing pin and screamed ______________.
7. It began to rain, so everyone ran ______________.

 ISBN 978-81-8477-745-1

8. Oranges are much sweeter ______________.

9. Hard work is the key ______________.

10. Mum cut the loaf ______________.

Exercise 3

Fill in each blank in the following dialogue with a suitable ***preposition****.*

Jane: Do you like this necklace? I saw it ______________ the window ______________ the jeweller's shop this morning. I went in and bought it straight away. I thought I could give it ______________ Sue ______________ her birthday next week.

Lucy: It's a lovely necklace, but Sue already has one exactly the same ______________ that. She got it ______________ her parents ______________ passing her exams last term.

Jane: Never mind, I'll keep it myself. It will look great ______________ my new dress. However, if Sue invites me ______________ her birthday party, I'd better put something else ______________ my neck. We don't want to find ourselves wearing identical necklaces!

 ISBN 978-81-8477-745-1

UNIT 59

COLLOCATING PREPOSITIONS

What do they look like?

Tom is very **keen on** science. He is also **fond of** geography, though he is not particularly **good at** it. His friend Bill has no **interest in** science. He says he doesn't understand it, but this is because he never **listens to** the teacher properly. Art is his favourite subject, and he **has entered for** several painting competitions.

How do you use them?

Certain **adjectives, nouns** and **verbs** are used with particular **prepositions.** When two words are often used together, you can say that they **collocate** with each other.

1. Here are some examples of **adjectives** (and **past participles**) used with their customary **prepositions**:
   - *I am very **bad at** maths.*
   - *Paul is **good at** making models.*
   - *Who is **responsible for** cleaning the bedrooms?*
   - *I feel **sorry for** people who have no friends.*
   - *Our new house is quite **different from** our old one.*
   - *Many doctors are **interested in** alternative medicine.*
   - *Are you **afraid of** the dark?*
   - *Helen was **ashamed of** her lack of knowledge.*
   - *We became **aware of** a strange sound.*
   - *Sam is very **fond of** his little sister.*
   - *The bucket was **full of** sand.*
   - *My parents are quite **proud of** my achievements.*
   - *I am **tired of** answering questions.*
   - *Dan was never **keen on** football.*
   - *I am **allergic to** peanuts.*
   - *Alice is **married to** a naval officer.*
   - *His new book is **similar to** his last one.*
   - *Our eyes gradually became **accustomed to** the dark.*
   - *My grandfather is **used to** being obeyed.*
   - *Are you **pleased with** your new apartment?*
   - *There is something **wrong with** this computer.*

 ISBN 978-81-8477-745-1

2. Here are some examples of **nouns** used with their customary **prepositions**:

- *James has an **aptitude for** engineering.*
- *There is no **cure for** this illness.*
- *I felt great **pity for** the victims of the earthquake.*
- *Sue's **talent for** music became apparent at an early age.*
- *I have **faith in** their ability to solve the problem.*
- *As a child Sophie had no **interest in** dolls.*
- *What was the **cause of** the riot?*
- *There was a **hint of** sarcasm in her voice.*
- *Owing to **lack of** time, there will be no choir practice today.*
- *Is there any **proof of** her guilt?*
- *Many people are in favour of a **ban on** smoking in public places.*
- *My warning had no **effect on** him.*
- *I have an **allergy to** wheat flour.*
- *Is there an **alternative to** this method?*
- *This word is an **exception to** the usual spelling rule.*
- *Is population growth a **threat to** the environment?*

3. Here are some examples of **verbs** used with their customary **prepositions**:

- *Are you **entering for** the art competition?*
- *We're **searching for** a solution.*
- *Who **paid for** the meal?*
- *There are lots of styles to **choose from**.*
- *Lisa is **recovering from** pneumonia.*
- *Peter was **suffering from** depression.*
- *I don't **believe in** miracles.*
- *A caterpillar **changes into** a butterfly.*
- *The empty office has been **turned into** an apartment block.*
- *Sue **accused** me **of** lying.*
- *We don't **approve of** the trade in ivory.*
- *The band **consists of** two guitarists, a drummer and a singer.*
- *The room **smelt of** flowers.*
- *Her family **depends on** her for everything.*
- *I **insisted on** paying for the coffee.*
- *I'm sure we can **rely on** you.*
- *Please will you **attend to** these matters?*
- *Do these socks **belong to** you?*
- *Poverty does not necessarily **lead to** crime.*
- *We were **listening to** the radio.*
- *I don't **object to** hard work.*
- *How did she **react to** the suggestion?*
- *Who were you **referring to**?*
- *Parents should never **resort to** violence.*
- *I don't **agree with** you at all.*
- *Miss Brown will **deal with** any questions you may have.*
- *Have you **finished with** my calculator yet?*

 ISBN 978-81-8477-745-1

4. Some **words** collocate with different **prepositions** in different contexts:
   - *Dad seems rather annoyed **with** me.*
   - *She was annoyed **by** their rude remarks.*
   - *The chairs are made **of** plastic.*
   - *The soup was made **with** fresh vegetables.*
   - *I apologize **for** not recognizing you.*
   - *You must apologize **to** your father.*
   - *The neighbours complained **about** the noise.*
   - *The dissatisfied customers complained **to** the manager.*
   - *Have you heard **about** Joe's accident?*
   - *I've never heard **of** that author.*
   - *He reminds me **of** someone I used to know.*
   - *You'd better remind me **about** my hospital appointment.*

5. Phrasal verbs, which you learnt about in Unit 39, sometimes consist of **verb** + **preposition**:
   - *The ship ran **into** a storm.*
   - *I came **across** a photo of my great-grandfather.*
   - *The police were looking **for** a stolen car.*
   - *Anne takes **after** her mother in many ways.*

PRACTICE

Exercise 1

Choose the correct prepositions to fill in the blanks.

1. Our boots were full ____________ (*of/with*) water.
2. I'm looking ____________ (*after/for*) my missing key.
3. Joe is very keen ____________ (*at/on*) photography.
4. She apologized ____________ (*for/to*) offending me.
5. The doctor said there was nothing wrong ____________ (*in/with*) Dad's heart.
6. The crown was made ____________ (*of/with*) solid gold.
7. Pay increases have an indirect effect ____________ (*for/on*) prices.
8. While digging in the garden, Anna came ____________ (*across/over*) some old coins.
9. Carol seemed pleased ____________ (*about/with*) the present I bought her.

 ISBN 978-81-8477-745-1

10. He may never recover ______________ (*from/of*) this illness.

11. The rash could be caused by an allergy ______________ (*for/to*) the soap you use.

12. My parents do not approve ______________ (*of/with*) my choice of career.

Exercise 2

*Fill in the blanks with an adjective or a verb from box **A** and a preposition from box **B**. Use each word only once.*

A: accused	annoyed	heard	insisted	interested
looked	shouted	suffered	turned	used

B: about	at	for	from	in	into	of	on	to	with

1. The witch ______________ the prince ______________ a frog.
2. Joan was ______________ ______________ her sister for forgetting her birthday.
3. I have only just ______________ ______________ the assassination of the president.
4. He was not ______________ ______________ being treated so rudely.
5. The teacher ______________ us ______________ cheating.
6. They ______________ ______________ helping with the washing-up.
7. Tom ______________ everywhere ______________ the missing key.
8. I am not at all ______________ ______________ photography.
9. Mum ______________ ______________ asthma when she was a child.
10. The farmer ______________ ______________ the children for trampling on his crops.

Exercise 3

Use the **prepositions** *in the box to fill in the blanks in the following passage. You will have to use some of them more than once.*

about	after	by	during	for	in	of	on	to	with

Residents are complaining ____________ the teenagers who gather ____________ the children's playground ____________ the evening. There have been no reports ____________ the young people doing any damage ____________ the equipment there. However, some of the older residents feel that the presence ____________ the teenagers presents a threat ____________ the community. They are afraid ____________ being attacked ____________ them. Consequently, they are asking ____________ a ban ____________ the use ____________ the park ____________ 6 p.m. Others do not agree ____________ this idea. Margaret Watson, who is fond ____________ young people, thinks that the best way ____________ solving the problem would be to provide the teenagers ____________ better leisure facilities. She has written ____________ the council suggesting this, but they seem to have no interest ____________ dealing ____________ the matter.

Exercise 4: grammar for writing

Write a short passage, about 100 words long, on a subject related to health. Your passage should contain at least two examples each of prepositions collocating with adjectives, nouns and verbs. When you have finished, underline these words and their collocating prepositions.

____

____

____

____

____

____

 ISBN 978-81-8477-745-1

8 CONNECTORS & CLAUSES

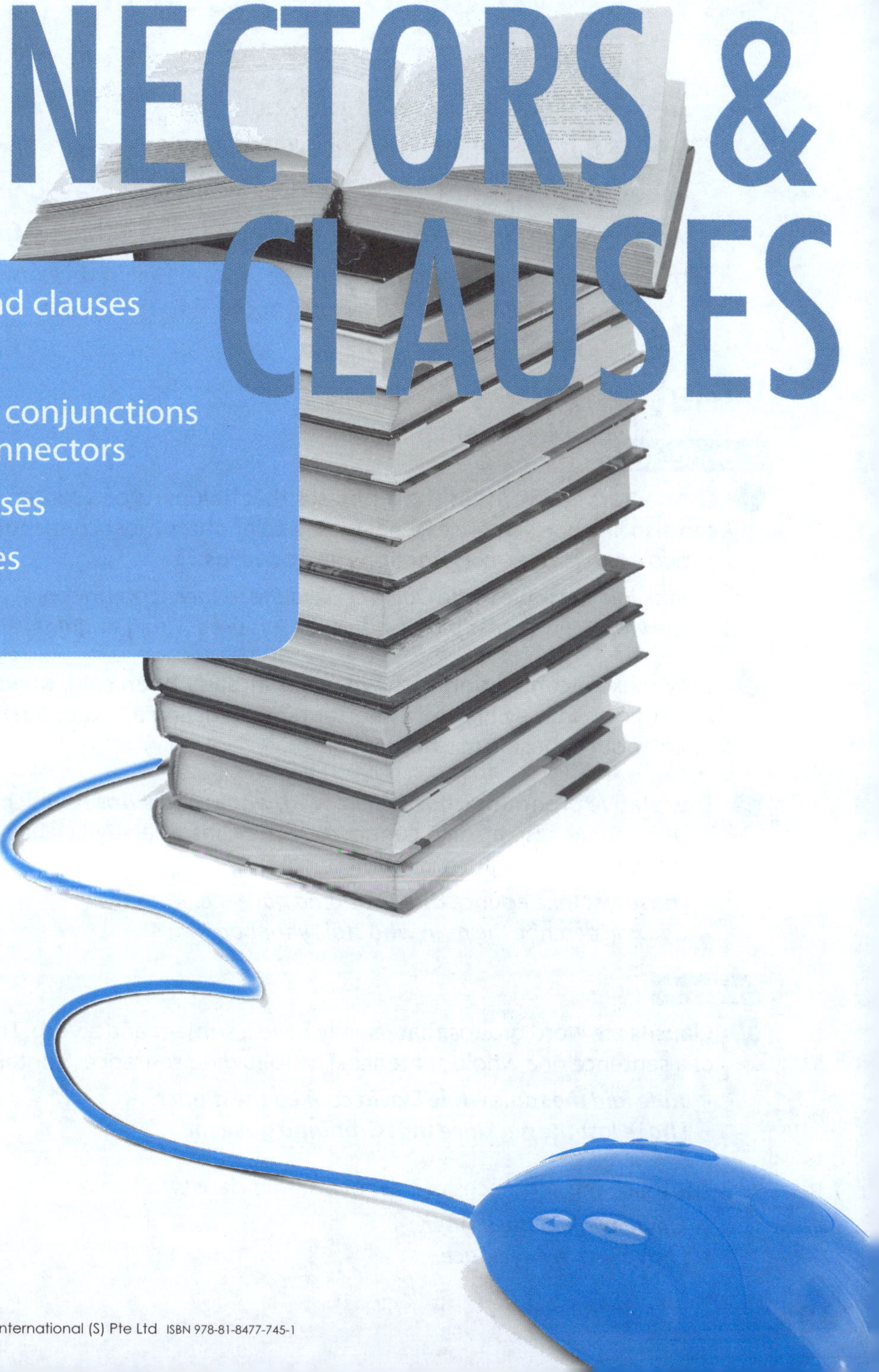

 ISBN 978-81-8477-745-1

UNIT 60

CONNECTORS AND CLAUSES

What do they look like?

Fred was upset **because** his car would not start. He looked at the engine **but** everything seemed OK. **However**, he didn't know much about **how cars worked**, **so** he decided to ask his neighbour Ben, **who was a car mechanic**. Ben discovered two problems: **firstly**, the battery was flat **and secondly**, there was no fuel in the tank.

What are they?

Connectors

1. **Connectors** are words or short phrases that **link** parts of a sentence together. They can also link one sentence or paragraph to another. Most connectors belong to one of two word classes, **conjunctions** and **adverbs**:
   - *Jane laid the table **while** David cooked the dinner.* (conjunction)
   - *The word 'news' looks plural; **however**, it is used with a singular verb.* (adverb)

2. They make a **connection** with **what has already been said**, or with **what follows**. For this reason they play an important role in giving a text **cohesion**. You will learn more about cohesion in Chapter 10.

3. The **relative pronouns** (***that***, ***which***, ***who***, ***whom*** and ***whose***), which you learnt about in Unit 15, can also act like connectors. They link a relative clause to the rest of the sentence:
   - *I have lost the necklace **that** Grandma gave me.*
   - *Can you describe the man **who** stole your bag?*

Clauses

1. **Clauses** are word groups that usually have a **subject** and a **verb**. They can form part of a sentence or a whole sentence. The following sentences contain two clauses:
   - ***Jane laid the table while David cooked the dinner.***
   - ***I have lost the necklace that Grandma gave me.***

   The following sentences consist of a single clause:
   - ***David cooked the dinner.***
   - ***I have lost my necklace.***

 ISBN 978-81-8477-745-1

2. The main difference between a **clause** and a **phrase** is that a phrase does not have a subject and a verb. It does the work of a particular word class: a noun (see Unit 7), an adjective (see Unit 22), a verb (see Unit 40) or an adverb (see Unit 55):
   - *Mary left* ***at eight o'clock***. ('at eight o'clock' is a phrase)
   - *Mary left* ***before I arrived***. ('before I arrived' is a clause)

How do you use connectors?

Connectors can be used for many different purposes. Here are some of the most important ones.

1. The following words and phrases can be used to introduce an **additional** item or point:

   and, in addition, in addition to, together with, as well as, as well, also, too, what's more, moreover, furthermore, besides

   - *I cannot bath the baby* ***and*** *cook the dinner at the same time!*
   - *The location of the apartment is not ideal.* ***Moreover***, *the rent is very expensive.*
   - *John is coming to the party. Simon will come* ***too***, *if he gets home from work in time.*

2. The following connectors, most of which are **linking adverbs**, can be used to **list** items, points or actions:

   first, second, third, firstly, secondly, thirdly, in the first place, then, next, finally

   - *We have two problems:* ***firstly***, *we don't have enough time;* ***secondly***, *we don't have enough money.*
   - *Everything went wrong.* ***First*** *it began to rain,* ***then*** *I fell over in the mud,* ***next*** *I dropped the map and* ***finally*** *a gust of wind blew my hat off.*

3. The following, which are a mixture of **conjunctions** and **adverbs**, can be used to show a **sequence** of events, or how things are connected in **time**:

   before, after, while, when, whenever, as, as soon as, since, until, then, later, previously, meanwhile, at first, eventually

   - *Look both ways* ***before*** *you cross the road.*
   - *I'll make a pot of tea* ***as soon as*** *the kettle boils.*
   - *Tom hasn't seen Sarah* ***since*** *he left school.*
   - *I waited patiently,* ***then*** *I rang the doorbell again.*

4. The connectors ***where*** and ***wherever*** refer to **place**:
   - *You can sit* ***where*** *you like.*
   - *We received a warm welcome* ***wherever*** *we went.*

5. The connectors ***as*** and ***than*** are used in **comparisons**:
   - *The weather was hotter in Egypt* ***than*** *it was in Malta.*
   - *James doesn't sing as well* ***as*** *Martin does.*

 ISBN 978-81-8477-745-1

6 Some connectors can indicate **contrast**, for example:

but, although, though, however, nevertheless, yet, whereas, on the other hand, on the contrary

- *The work was difficult **but** rewarding.*
- *Simon is not very good at maths; **however**, he tries very hard.*
- *This is not the ideal solution. **On the contrary**, it will probably make the problem worse.*

7 The following connectors can be used to make a **concession**:

even though, even if, while, admittedly, granted, however, anyway

- *She feels tired all the time, **even though** she gets plenty of sleep.*
- ***Admittedly**, he is a mischievous child, but he has a great sense of humour.*
- *I could have made more effort. **Anyway**, it's too late now.*

8 Some connectors can introduce a **reason** or **cause**, for example:

because, as, since

- *I left the party early **because** I wasn't enjoying myself.*
- ***As** it was raining we took a taxi home.*

9 Others can report a **result** or **effect**, for example:

therefore, consequently, so, as a result, thus, so … that, such … that

- *Bill felt unwell, **so** he went to see the doctor.*
- *Sally had not been paying attention. **Consequently**, she did not know what to do.*
- *Some people have **such** poor eyesight **that** they have to wear glasses all the time.*

10 The following connectors can be used to state a **purpose**:

so, so that, in order to, in order that, so as to

- *Dad put on his glasses **in order to** read the instructions.*
- *Stand up straight **so that** I can measure how tall you are.*

11 The following can be used to make an **inference** or draw a **conclusion**:

otherwise, in that case, then

- *You had better take a map. **Otherwise**, you might get lost.*
- *'Sam lived in London for ten years.' 'He must speak good English, **then**.'*

12 Some connectors can introduce a **condition**, for example:

if, unless, provided that, providing that

- *You can come with us, **provided that** you don't make a nuisance of yourself.*
- *I won't phone you **unless** I'm going to be late.*
- ***If** you don't understand something, ask your teacher to explain it.*

 ISBN 978-81-8477-745-1

13 Some can express **choice**, for example:

or, either … or, neither … nor, alternatively, instead

- *I can't decide whether to study history **or** geography at university.*
- *We could go to the cinema. **Alternatively**, we could stay at home and watch TV.*

14 The following connectors can be used to give more **specific** information, an **example** or an **explanation**:

for example, for instance, such as, namely, specifically, more accurately, that is, that is to say, in other words

- *You could give your mother a bit more help; **for example**, you could do some of the housework.*
- *There's a major problem: **namely**, lack of cash.*
- *She is a vegetarian. **That is**, she doesn't eat meat or fish.*

15 The following can be used **in summing up**:

altogether, all in all, overall, to sum up, in conclusion, in short, anyhow, therefore

- *We've had our problems, but it has been a successful venture **overall**.*
- ***To sum up**, if everyone makes a bit of extra effort, the work will be finished on time.*

How do you use clauses?

You use clauses to build sentences.

1 The **main clause** of a sentence expresses the main idea. In the following examples, the **main clause** is in bold print:

- ***The little girl was crying** because she had broken her doll.*
- *If we don't leave soon **we will miss the train**.*
- ***My uncle lives in England**, which is a long way from Singapore!*

A main clause can usually **stand alone** as a sentence in its own right:

- ***The little girl was crying.***
- ***We will miss the train.***
- ***My uncle lives in England.***

2 Some sentences have two (or more) **main clauses**:

- ***The little girl was crying** and **her mother was trying to comfort her.***
- ***My uncle lives in England** but **he sometimes comes to Singapore on business.***

Sentences made up of two or more main clauses are called **compound sentences**, which you will learn more about in Unit 67.

 ISBN 978-81-8477-745-1

3. Some clauses introduced by a **connector** are **dependent** on the main clause. They are called **subordinate clauses**. In the following examples, the **subordinate clause** is in bold print:
   - *The little girl was crying **because she had broken her doll.***
   - ***If we don't leave soon** we will miss the train.*
   - *My uncle lives in England, **which is a long way from Singapore!***

   A subordinate clause **cannot** stand alone as a sentence in its own right. ***If we don't leave soon***, for example, is not a complete sentence.

4. There are three main types of subordinate clauses: **adverbial clauses, relative clauses** and **noun clauses**:
   - *Don't forget to lock the door **when you leave the house**.* (adverbial clause)
   - *The police interviewed the man **whose daughter had disappeared**.* (relative clause)
   - *She told me **that she worked at the bank**.* (noun clause)

   Sentences containing one or more subordinate clauses are called **complex sentences**, which you will learn more about in Unit 67.

5. **Participial phrases** (see Unit 40) are sometimes called **non-finite clauses:**
   - *I found some old photographs **while clearing out the attic**.*
   - ***Disappointed with her exam results,** Jane vowed to work harder.*

PRACTICE

Exercise 1

Say whether the words in bold print make up a clause (C) or a phrase (P).

1. I was disappointed **that I did not win**. ( )
2. Nobody knew **the correct answer**. ( )
3. How did you get **into the apartment**? ( )
4. We'll go to the swimming pool today **if it's open**. ( )
5. Please switch off your mobile phone **before you enter the building**. ( )
6. The snow did not melt **until the end of the winter**. ( )
7. The sales assistant asked us **which computer we wanted to buy**. ( )
8. She will regret this decision **for the rest of her life**. ( )
9. This bed is more comfortable **than the one in my room**. ( )
10. Don't forget to lock the door **when you leave**. ( )

 ISBN 978-81-8477-745-1

Exercise 2

Fill in the blanks with so that *or* in order to*.*

1. Sally turned on the heater ______________ warm the room.
2. I'll pick the strawberries this afternoon ______________ they will be nice and fresh.
3. We leant out of the window ______________ watch the procession.
4. Joe glanced at the last page ______________ see how the story ended.
5. Mary moved the books off the chair ______________ her aunt could sit down.
6. We're moving house ______________ be nearer to the children's school.
7. John took off his boots ______________ he would not make the floor dirty.
8. Close the door gently ______________ it doesn't bang.
9. She is learning English ______________ communicate with foreign visitors to the company.
10. I switched the lamp on ______________ I could see what I was doing.

Exercise 3

Put the connectors *in the box under the correct headings below.*

also	alternatively	altogether	and	before	but
consequently	furthermore	however	in short	instead	later
or	overall	so	therefore	until	whereas

CONTRAST	RESULT	SEQUENCE	CHOICE	SUMMING UP	ADDITION
______	______	______	______	______	______
______	______	______	______	______	______
______	______	______	______	______	______

 ISBN 978-81-8477-745-1

Exercise 4

Fill in the blanks in the following passage with the connectors in the box. Use each word or phrase only once.

after	and	as	either	finally	for example	in order to
next	or	so that	that	which	when	where

Do you know what happens to food ____________ you put it in your mouth? ____________ you chew it, the food is mixed with saliva, ____________ is the liquid inside your mouth. It contains chemicals ____________ begin digesting the food. The process of digestion breaks down food into its smallest parts ____________ the nutrients they contain can be used by your body. ____________, your body needs protein ____________ grow, ____________ vitamins to protect it from disease. ____________ you swallow the chewed-up food it passes through your oesophagus into your stomach, ____________ the digestion process continues. ____________, the muscles in your stomach push the digested food into your intestines. There, the components of this mush ____________ pass into your bloodstream ____________ continue their journey as waste. ____________, the waste parts leave your body.

Exercise 5: grammar for writing

*Write a letter of complaint about a faulty product, about 140 words long, using at least **twelve** different **connectors**. When you have finished, underline all the words and phrases that are connectors.*

____

____

____

____

____

____

____

____

 ISBN 978-81-8477-745-1

UNIT 61

CONJUNCTIONS

What do they look like?

Jane is studying science **and** maths **because** she wants to be an engineer. Her friends want to be teachers **or** nurses, **but** Jane has different ambitions. She has been interested in how things work **since** she was very young. **If** she does well at engineering, she will be able to fix things **when** they go wrong.

What are they?

Conjunctions are connectors that can link words, phrases, clauses or sentences. There are **two main types: co-ordinating conjunctions** (such as ***and***, ***but*** and ***or***) and **subordinating conjunctions** (such as ***while***, ***as***, ***because***, ***if*** and ***so that***):

- *My dog has big ears **and** a long tail.* (co-ordinating conjunction)
- *We stayed indoors **because** it was raining.* (subordinating conjunction)

How do you use them?

Co-ordinating conjunctions

1. You can use **co-ordinating conjunctions** to link **single words**:
   - *The weather was **sunny and warm**.*
   - *My little brother can already **walk and talk**.*
   - *She told them **politely but firmly** to go away.*
   - *I don't like **cabbage or cauliflower**.*

2. They can also link **phrases**:
   - *I heard her go **up the stairs and into her bedroom**.*
   - *The job is **highly dangerous but extremely interesting**.*
   - *You can have **a mixed salad or a selection of cooked vegetables**.*

3. They can also link **clauses**:
   - ***Sue washed the dishes and Bill dried them.***
   - ***Our new house has a large garden but it does not have a garage.***
   - ***The package may arrive tomorrow or it may not come till Friday.***

 ISBN 978-81-8477-745-1

4 **Co-ordinating conjunctions** always link words, phrases or clauses that have the **same grammatical status**. For example, they may link two nouns, or two adjectival phrases, or two main clauses:

- *I don't like **cabbage** **or** **cauliflower**.* (two nouns)
- *The job is **highly dangerous** **but** **extremely interesting**.* (two adjectival phrases)
- ***Sue washed the dishes** **and** **Bill dried them**.* (two main clauses)

They cannot link a noun with an adjective, or an adjectival phrase with an adverbial phrase, or a main clause with a subordinate clause.

Subordinating conjunctions

1 You use a **subordinating conjunction** to introduce a **subordinate clause**:

- *I'll call you **before** **I leave for Beijing**.*
- ***When** **the boat arrived** we climbed aboard.*
- *Mum has suffered from asthma **since** **she was a young girl**.*
- ***If** **the fire alarm rings**, leave the building immediately.*
- *The policeman said **that** **the road was blocked ahead**.*

2 **Some subordinating conjunctions** have the same form as **prepositions**, and are used in a similar way. If the word introduces a **clause** containing a **subject** and **verb**, it is a **conjunction**. If it introduces a **phrase** with no verb, or a single **noun** or **pronoun**, it is a **preposition**:

- *Mum has suffered from asthma **since** she was a young girl.* (conjunction)
- *Mum has suffered from asthma **since** her early childhood.* (preposition)
- *Most people can speak faster **than** they can write.* (conjunction)
- *James speaks faster **than** Bob.* (preposition)
- *I am not as clever **as** you are.* (conjunction)
- *I am not as clever **as** you.* (preposition)

PRACTICE

Exercise 1

Say whether the word in bold print is being used as a conjunction (C) or a preposition (P) in this context.

1. The wind was colder **than** it had been the previous day. ( )
2. Students are not permitted to leave **before** the end of the exam. ( )
3. I have known Bill **since** his marriage to my cousin. ( )
4. They ran home as fast **as** they could. ( )
5. Do not cross the road **until** the light goes green. ( )
6. Grandma was very weak **after** the operation on her heart. ( )

 ISBN 978-81-8477-745-1

Exercise 2

*Complete the following sentences, using a **conjunction** from box A and the rest of the text from box B.*

A: after and before but if or since so

B:	
everyone laughed.	I did not send them an invitation.
he moved to Australia.	she started taking the medicine.
there was no flour in the cupboard.	we are late.
you can wait for the others to arrive.	you go to bed.

1. The clown fell over *and everyone laughed.*
2. Jane wanted to bake a cake ______
3. I knew they could not come ______
4. You should always clean your teeth ______
5. Mum began to feel better ______
6. You can have your lunch now ______
7. I had not seen Uncle Jack ______
8. Our parents will be worried ______

Exercise 3

*In the following passage, underline all the **co-ordinating conjunctions** and put a ring round all the **subordinating conjunctions**.*

John lived on a farm with his parents and his younger sister. While he was a boy, he enjoyed helping his father in the fields. Everyone expected John to become a farmer himself, but he had other ideas. He had visited his cousins in the city, and he thought that life seemed much more exciting there. As he grew older, he spent less time working outside and more time indoors studying. He wanted to do well at school so that he could go to university in the city. If he worked really hard, he could become a lawyer or a doctor. He expected his parents to be angry when he told them about his plans. They were a little disappointed, but they said nothing, because they could see that John had already made up his mind.

 ISBN 978-81-8477-745-1

UNIT 62

CO-ORDINATING CONJUNCTIONS AND SIMILAR CONNECTORS

What do they look like?

Frank, Joe **and** Bill went on a sailing holiday. **Neither** Joe **nor** Bill had ever been in a yacht **or** other sailing boat before, **but** Frank was an experienced sailor. On the first day, there was no wind, **so** they went fishing **instead**. The next day, **however**, the wind was much stronger. **Consequently**, they had a very enjoyable sail.

How do you use them?

Addition

1 The co-ordinating conjunction ***and*** links words, phrases or clauses that go together in some way:

- *The beds are wide, soft **and** comfortable.*
- *He was wearing a denim jacket **and** a baseball cap.*
- *The meal was delicious **and** everyone enjoyed it.*

2 It can introduce an additional item or point:

- *She bought a new camera **and** a case to put it in.*
- *He is rude, lazy **and** selfish.*
- *I must phone the plumber, clean the house, buy some coffee **and** feed the cat.*

3 You sometimes use ***both … and*** as a pair for emphasis:

- ***Both** the car **and** its driver had disappeared.*
- *Sam could **both** read **and** write before he was five.*

For even stronger emphasis, you can use ***not only … but also***:

- *Sam could **not only** read **but also** write before he was five.*
- *The plan was **not only** sensible, **but also** practical.*

4 You can use ***together with***, ***as well as*** or ***in addition to*** instead of ***and*** (or ***both … and***) to add an item. However, you must remember to make the verb agree with the subject in accordance with the rules you learnt in Unit 35:

- *Mary **and** her friend Lucy have offered to help.* (plural verb)
- ***Both** basketball **and** volleyball are played in the gym.* (plural verb)
- *Mary, **together with** her friend Lucy, has offered to help.* (singular verb)
- *Basketball, **as well as** volleyball, is played in the gym.* (singular verb)

 ISBN 978-81-8477-745-1

5. The connectors ***also***, ***too*** and ***as well*** are used in a similar way:
   - *Mary's friend Lucy has offered to help **too**.*
   - *Volleyball is **also** played in the gym.*

6. You can use connectors such as ***moreover***, ***furthermore*** and ***in addition*** to add a point:
   - *The plan is impractical; **furthermore**, it would be far too expensive.*
   - *Working for an American company will give me an opportunity to visit the USA. **In addition**, I will be able to practise my English.*

Contrast

1. The co-ordinating conjunction ***but*** links words, phrases or clauses that have **contrasting** meanings:
   - *Mr Jones has a **relaxed but sensible** attitude to discipline.*
   - *Sue and Jane are **at the same school but in different classes**.*
   - ***I like cabbage but I don't like cauliflower**.*

2. A number of other connectors, such as ***yet***, ***though***, ***however*** and ***whereas***, can also introduce a **contrasting** item or point:
   - *She spoke kindly **yet firmly** to the children.*
   - *Charlie is a nice little boy, **though a rather mischievous one**.*
   - *The puzzle looks impossible to solve; **however**, **it is not as difficult as it seems**.*
   - *I like going to concerts, **whereas my sister prefers going to the theatre**.*

Choice

1. The co-ordinating conjunction ***or*** links words, phrases or clauses that present a **choice** or an **alternative**:
   - *Should we turn **right or left**?*
   - *I can't decide whether to **go to university or get a job**.*
   - ***You can go for a cruise down the river or you can tour the city on an open-topped bus**.*

2. You also use ***or*** between items in negative sentences, instead of ***and***:
   - *The shop sells books and CDs. However, it does not sell magazines **or** stationery.*
   - *The boys have had nothing to eat **or** drink all day.*

3. The pairs ***either … or*** and ***neither … nor*** are used to give more emphasis:
   - *I must have left the keys **either** in the car **or** at the office.*
   - *It's **neither** clever **nor** sensible to throw stones.*

4. You can also use ***neither*** and ***nor*** on their own. When you do this, you must move the **subject** to follow the <u>**verb**</u> (or the <u>**auxiliary verb**</u> in a verb phrase):
   - *Joe could not remember Anna's phone number, **nor <u>could</u> he** find it in the phone book.*
   - *The apartment in North Street was not suitable. **Neither <u>was</u> the one in Station Road**.*

5 The connectors ***alternatively*** and ***instead*** can also be used before or after a **choice** or an **alternative**:

- *You could phone her;* ***alternatively, you could send her a text message.***
- *If you don't want to phone her,* ***you could send her a text message instead.***

Cause and effect

1 The connectors ***so*** and ***therefore*** can be used like co-ordinating conjunctions to link a **cause** or a **reason** to its **effect** or **result**:

- *It was an eye-catching,* ***therefore*** *effective, advertisement.*
- ***These glasses are very fragile, so you must handle them very carefully.***

2 You can use the linking adverb ***consequently*** in a similar way:

- ***Alice did not get much sleep that night. Consequently, she felt very tired the next day.***

You will learn about other connectors used for this purpose, such as ***because*** and ***since***, in Unit 63.

PRACTICE

Exercise 1

Fill in each blank with one of the co-ordinating conjunctions **and**, **but** *or* **or**.

1. What is that noise? Is it somebody singing ______________ a dog howling?
2. Our products are attractive to look at ______________ easy to use.
3. I wanted to buy the book ______________ I did not have enough money.
4. Sue couldn't find her shoes in the wardrobe ______________ under the bed.
5. The day was bright, sunny ______________ warm.
6. We have no milk ______________ sugar.
7. He tried very hard to persuade them, ______________ without success.
8. Michael ______________ Paul are the best players in the team.

 ISBN 978-81-8477-745-1

Exercise 2

*Rewrite the following sentences, inserting **both** or **either** in the correct position.*

1. This method is clean and efficient. ____________________
2. You'll find the milk on the table or in the fridge. ____________________
3. The picture and its frame are very valuable. ____________________
4. We need staff who can work quickly and accurately. ____________________
5. Jane or Peter will help you. ____________________
6. I expect they have lost their way or missed the bus. ____________________
7. She had broken her wrist and her ankle. ____________________
8. You can wait or go home and come back later. ____________________
9. I could not cut the rope with the knife or the scissors. ____________________
10. The law must be fair to those who are guilty and to those who are innocent.

    ____

Exercise 3

Fill in each blank with one of the words from the box. You will have to use some of them more than once.

and	but	furthermore	however	instead
or	so	therefore	too	

It was a wet __________ windy night. I really wanted to spend the evening reading a book __________ watching television, __________ there was absolutely no chance of that. I had to attend a meeting of the local history club at the community centre. I would have loved to ring up __________ say that I couldn't go. __________, I had agreed to give a talk at the meeting, __________ I couldn't let everyone down. __________, I always give my neighbour a lift to the meeting. She doesn't have a car __________ the bus service is very poor. She __________ has no other means of getting there. I sometimes give one of the other members a lift __________, __________ she had already phoned me to say that she was going with her friend __________.

 ISBN 978-81-8477-745-1

UNIT 63

Adverbial clauses

What do they look like?

I took the bus to the theatre **because it was raining**. It went so slowly **that I thought I would be late**. **When I arrived**, I looked around for my friend Jack. He wasn't there, **although we had arranged to meet outside**. **'If he doesn't come soon**,' I thought, 'I will have to go in without him.'

What are they?

Adverbial clauses are **subordinate clauses** that do the work of an **adverb**. They are introduced by **subordinating conjunctions**, such as ***before*** and ***because***. Adverbial clauses are usually divided into nine groups:

1. **Adverbial clauses of time** answer the question ***when?*** They are introduced by the following conjunctions:

   before, after, while, as, as soon as, when, whenever, since, till, until

   - *I usually listen to the radio **while** **I use my exercise bike**.*
   - *Everyone applauded **as** **the speaker left the platform**.*
   - *The traffic will start moving **as soon as** **the light turns green**.*
   - *The roof leaks **whenever** **it rains**.*
   - *The company has grown considerably **since** **I joined it twenty years ago**.*
   - *They sat up talking **until** **the clock struck midnight**.*

2. **Adverbial clauses of place** answer the question ***where?*** They are introduced by the following conjunctions:

   where, wherever, everywhere, anywhere

   - ***Where** **the building had been standing** there was nothing but a crater.*
   - *The crowds followed her **wherever** **she went**.*
   - *You have to learn the rules of chess. You can't move the pieces **anywhere** **you want**!*

3. **Adverbial clauses of manner** answer the question ***how?*** or ***in what way?*** They are introduced by the following conjunctions:

   as, as if, as though, how, however

   - *Thomas never does **as** **he is told**.*
   - *She screamed **as if** **she had seen a ghost**.*
   - *I cooked the eggs **how** **Dad likes them**.*
   - *You may arrange the furniture **however** **you like**.*

 ISBN 978-81-8477-745-1

4 **Adverbial clauses of reason** answer the question ***why?*** They are introduced by the following conjunctions:

because, as, since

- *Jim works hard **because** he wants to do well.*
- *You can lead the way, **since** you know where we're going.*

5 **Adverbial clauses of purpose** also answer the question ***why?*** They are introduced by the following conjunctions:

so, so that, in order that

- *I'll get up early **so** I can catch the 7 o'clock train.*
- *Please write the address clearly **in order that** it can be read by the sorting machine.*

6 **Adverbial clauses of result** are introduced by the conjunction ***that***, linked to ***so*** or ***such*** in the main clause:

- *We had **such** good weather **that** everybody got a suntan.*
- *The birds sing **so** loudly in the morning **that** they wake us up.*

7 **Adverbial clauses of concession or contrast** introduce a fact that makes the statement in the main clause seem rather surprising. They are introduced by the following conjunctions:

although, though, even if, even though, while

- *Helen entered the picture for the competition **although** she wasn't very pleased with it.*
- *She feels exhausted all the time, **even though** she gets plenty of sleep.*
- *Check the answer again, **even if** you are sure it is correct.*
- ***While** we do our very best to be accurate, the occasional error may occur.*

8 **Adverbial clauses of comparison** are also called **comparative clauses**. They are introduced by the conjunction ***than*** (following a **comparative** in the main clause) or the conjunction ***as*** (following the adverb ***as*** in the main clause):

- *A cheetah can run faster **than** an antelope can.*
- *This year's exams weren't **as** difficult **as** last year's were.*

9 **Adverbial clauses of condition** are also called **conditional clauses**. You learnt about these in Unit 47. They are introduced by following conjunctions:

if, as long as, on condition that, provided that, unless

- *I'll call you **if** I manage to get tickets.*
- *You won't be allowed in **unless** you have a ticket.*
- ***Provided that** I pass my exams, I shall be eligible for a university grant.*
- *She accepted my invitation to dinner **on condition that** I let her pay her share.*

 ISBN 978-81-8477-745-1

How do you use them?

1 You can often put adverbial clauses of **time, place, reason, concession** and **condition** before or after the main clause:

- ***After*** *the shops had closed, the street was deserted.*
- *The street was deserted* ***after*** *the shops had closed.*

- ***Everywhere*** *we travelled, we received wonderful hospitality.*
- *We received wonderful hospitality* ***everywhere*** *we travelled.*

- ***As*** *it was late they took a taxi home.*
- *They took a taxi home* ***as*** *it was late.*

- ***Though*** *he is only 55, he has decided to retire.*
- *He has decided to retire,* ***though*** *he is only 55.*

- ***As long as*** *you keep quiet, you may stay here.*
- *You may stay here* ***as long as*** *you keep quiet.*

You usually put a comma after the adverbial clause when it comes first.

2 When you use an adverbial clause of time beginning with ***since***, the **verb** in the main clause must be in one of the perfect tenses:

- *I* ***have changed*** *my mind* ***since*** *we last discussed this.*
- *He* ***had grown*** *a beard* ***since*** *he had left the army.*

3 Adverbial clauses of **manner**, **result**, **purpose** and **comparison** must follow the main clause:

- *Joe was rushing along* ***as though*** *he had a train to catch.*
- *We left the air-conditioning on* ***so that*** *the house would stay cool.*
- *Sally had such sore feet* ***that*** *she could hardly walk.*
- *Harry had made more mistakes* ***than*** *I had.*

4 When you use an adverbial clause of result, you use **so** in the main clause before **adverbs**, some quantifiers (***many***, ***much***, ***few***, ***little***) and **adjectives** that are not followed by nouns:

- *She practised* ***so hard*** *that she was the best player in the orchestra.*
- *She practised for* ***so many*** *hours a day that she was exhausted.*
- *She was* ***so enthusiastic*** *that she practised for three hours a day.*

You use ***such*** in the main clause before **nouns**, the quantifier ***a lot*** and **adjectives followed by nouns**:

- *I had* ***such a headache*** *that I stayed in bed all day.*
- *There is* ***such a lot*** *of work to do that we will be busy for weeks.*
- *The teacher gave the students* ***such easy questions*** *that everyone passed the test.*

 ISBN 978-81-8477-745-1

PRACTICE

Exercise 1

Fill in the blanks with **such** *or* **so**.

1. There was ______________ a huge crowd that we couldn't get across the street.
2. Mum was ______________ worried that she phoned the police.
3. He had ______________ large feet that it was hard to find suitable shoes.
4. There is ______________ little for young people to do that some of them get into trouble.
5. The lid had been screwed on ______________ tightly that I could not remove it.
6. The news was ______________ unexpected that nobody believed it.
7. Sue and Kate are ______________ good friends that they do everything together.
8. We have ______________ a lot of books that we never seem to have enough bookshelves.
9. I was ______________ tired that I could hardly keep my eyes open.
10. We had ______________ nice weather on holiday that we did not want to come home.

Exercise 2

Choose the correct **conjunction** *to fill in the blanks.*

1. We sheltered under a tree ______________ (*after/until*) the rain stopped.
2. I'll phone you ______________ (*if/unless*) I am going to be late.
3. Julie has had her hair cut ______________ (*before/since*) I last saw her.
4. There are plenty of seats. You may sit ______________ (*however/wherever*) you like.
5. Tom left the light on ______________ (*because/though*) he was afraid of the dark.
6. You can borrow my bike ______________ (*as if/as long as*) you ride it carefully.
7. I read a magazine ______________ (*before/while*) I was waiting for the bus.
8. Jane bought the necklace ______________ (*even if/even though*) it was rather expensive.

 ISBN 978-81-8477-745-1

9. The bird flew away ______________ (*as soon as/as long as*) it saw me.

10. I will lend you my calculator ______________ (*when/whenever*) I have finished using it.

Exercise 3

Say whether the adverbial clauses in the following passage are clauses of comparison (Cp), concession (Cc), condition (Cd), place (Pl), purpose (Pu), reason (Rn), result (Rt) or time (T). Then put a ring round the ***connector*** *that introduces each of these clauses.*

I felt worried because I had not done enough revision for my exam ( ). I knew my parents would be very angry if I failed it ( ). Before I went to bed ( ) I set my alarm for 5.30, so I could do some more work before breakfast ( ). Although I was very tired ( ), I found it hard to get to sleep. I was still awake when the hall clock struck two ( ), but I must have fallen asleep soon afterwards. The alarm went off a few hours later and gave me such a shock that I woke up immediately ( ). I reached out to turn off the alarm but all I could find was a glass of water where the clock should have been ( ). I eventually found the clock under the bed and switched off the alarm so that it would not wake the whole family ( ). Then I crept downstairs as quietly as I could ( ) and got on with my work.

Exercise 4: grammar for writing

Write a short narrative or personal recount, about 100 words long, called 'A Busy Day'. Your passage should contain at least five adverbial clauses introduced by different subordinating conjunctions. When you have finished, put a ring round the conjunctions.

____

____

____

____

____

____

____

____

 ISBN 978-81-8477-745-1

UNIT 64

RELATIVE CLAUSES

What do they look like?

Mum took me to the village **where she spent her childhood**. The house **she used to live in** is next door to the village shop. Her old school, **which is now a community centre**, is on the opposite side of the village. She used to walk there with her friend Anna, **whose parents owned the village shop**.

What are they?

Relative clauses are **subordinate clauses** that do the work of an **adjective**. They come after a **noun** or **noun phrase** in the main clause and tell you something about this word or phrase. There are two types of relative clauses: **defining relative clauses** and **non-defining relative clauses**.

1. A **defining relative clause** (sometimes called a **restrictive relative clause**) **identifies** a person or thing in the main clause. A defining relative clause is introduced by one of the **relative pronouns**, which you learnt about in Unit 15. They are:

   that, which, who, whom, whose

   - *A punch is **a tool that makes holes in paper or leather**.*
   - *Can you see **the waiter who took our order**?*
   - *Where is **the girl whose bike has been stolen**?*

2. A **non-defining relative clause** (sometimes called a **non-restrictive relative clause**) **provides extra information** about a person or thing in the main clause. A non-defining relative clause is introduced by one of the following relative pronouns:

   which, who, whom, whose

   - *Go and see **the nurse, who will bandage your leg**.*
   - *I went to visit **my great-uncle, whom I had never met before**.*
   - *We can meet at **the Regent Hotel, which is near the town hall**.*

   Notice that you must put a **comma** before a non-defining relative clause.

 ISBN 978-81-8477-745-1

3. You can also use the words ***where*** and ***when*** to introduce both types of relative clause:
   - *Do you remember **the day** **when** Dad fell into the river?* (defining relative clause)
   - *Maggie went back to **the shop** **where** she had bought the DVD.* (defining relative clause)
   - *I'm going to England at **Christmas**, **when** I'll meet my great-uncle for the first time.* (non-defining relative clause)
   - *We took a taxi to **the Regent Hotel**, **where** we found Jane waiting for us.* (non-defining relative clause)

How do you use them?

1. You can put both types of relative clause in the middle of the **main clause** if they are linked to its **subject**:
   - ***Most of the people** whom we invited **can come**.* (defining relative clause)
   - ***The ring** which James bought me **was not very expensive**.* (defining relative clause)
   - ***Miss Jones**, who teaches English at our school, **is getting married next month**.* (non-defining relative clause)
   - ***This plant**, whose name I have forgotten, **produces bright red berries**.* (non-defining relative clause)

   Notice that you must put **commas** around a **non-defining** relative clause in the middle of a sentence.

2. You can put a **preposition** before ***which***, ***whom*** and ***whose*** in both types of relative clause:
   - *The post **for which** you applied has already been filled.*
   - *Where is the waiter **to whom** we gave our order?*
   - *Mr and Mrs Brown, **in whose** house I stayed, were very kind to me.*

3. You use a **defining relative clause** to give information that is **essential** to the sentence:
   - *The book **that you are looking for** is on the top shelf.*
   - *Children **who tell lies** should be punished.*

   The relative clauses **are needed** to make it clear which book and which children you are talking about. If you omit the relative clause from the second sentence, it sounds as if you think all children should be punished.

4. You use a **non-defining relative clause** to give extra information that is **not essential**:
   - *My favourite film, **which I have seen several times**, is 'The Golden Compass'.*
   - *Michael and Sarah, **whose parents work for a travel agency**, often go abroad on holiday.*

 ISBN 978-81-8477-745-1

These relative clauses **can be omitted** without affecting the overall meaning of the sentences:

- *My favourite film is 'The Golden Compass'.*
- *Michael and Sarah often go abroad on holiday.*

5 You can sometimes omit the relative pronoun at the beginning of a **defining relative clause**:

- *The book **that** you are looking for is on the top shelf.*
- *The book you are looking for is on the top shelf.*
- *Most of the people **whom** we invited can come.*
- *Most of the people we invited can come.*

You cannot do this if the word or phrase that the relative clause refers back to is the **subject** of the verb in the relative clause, as in the following sentences:

- ***The students** who attend this school wear uniform.*
- *I picked up **a coin** that was lying on the ground.*

PRACTICE

Exercise 1

Some of the following sentences would be equally correct without the relative pronoun in bold print. Put a line through those that can be omitted.

1. Would you like to see the photos **that** I took in England?
2. The man to **whom** she spoke did not understand what she said.
3. These biscuits, **which** I bought at the supermarket yesterday, are not very fresh.
4. Mum still knows some of the people **who** she went to school with.
5. The ball **that** Jane found belongs to the boy **who** lives next door.
6. The pen **which** I lent you was a present from my uncle.
7. The principal, **whose** opinion everyone respects, gave me some advice **that** has proved very useful.
8. She refused to marry a man **whom** she hated.

Exercise 2

Rewrite the following pairs of sentences as a single sentence containing a relative clause. There may be more than one correct answer to some of the questions. The first one has been done to help you.

1. Tom bought a book. The book is by Charles Dickens.

   The book that Tom bought is by Charles Dickens.

 ISBN 978-81-8477-745-1

2. My friend lives next door. My friend's name is Sally.

_______________ whose _______________________________________.

3. The men had chainsaws. They were using them to cut down the trees.

_______________________ which _______________________________.

4. I spoke to a sales assistant. She had red hair.

__________________________________ whom ____________________.

5. Joe found the coins in a field. He took his father there.

____ where _______.

6. Miss Williams is my favourite teacher. She teaches us maths.

_______________________ who _________________________________.

7. Joe lent me a pen. I have lost it.

_____________________________________ that __________________.

8. One of the tourists asked an interesting question. The guide did not answer the question.

_______________________ which _______________________________.

9. I saw a man. He was wearing a grey jacket.

__________________________________ whom ____________________.

10. My sister's hair is short and curly. She envies my long, straight hair.

_______________ whose _______________________________________.

Exercise 3

Underline all the defining relative clauses in the following passage and put a ring round all the non-defining relative clauses.

Redlands High, the school my son goes to, was damaged by fire yesterday. The fire started in the school kitchen, where staff were preparing lunch, and spread to the cafeteria and other rooms nearby. Fortunately, the incident happened at a time when the cafeteria is empty. The staff who were working in the kitchen left the building as soon as they heard the fire alarm. My neighbour Margaret Brown, whose son is in the same class as mine, heard about the fire on the local radio. She told me and we drove to the school together to make sure that our boys were all right. They were in the chemistry lab, which is not far from the cafeteria, when the fire broke out. However, they were not in danger. The fire brigade, who had arrived on the scene within minutes, quickly brought the flames under control. The parts of the school which were damaged by the fire will be closed for several weeks.

 ISBN 978-81-8477-745-1

UNIT 65

NOUN CLAUSES

What do they look like?

This article explains **why climate change is a threat to life on earth**. For example, there is a risk **that global warming will cause sea levels to rise**. The article tells us **how we can prevent these problems**. It says **everyone can do something to help**. **What happens next** is up to us!

What are they?

Noun clauses are **subordinate clauses** that do the work of a **noun**, most often as the **object** of a **verb**.

1. **Noun clauses** that are used as the **object** usually follow **verbs of saying and thinking**. They represent people's words and thoughts and are most often used for **indirect speech**, which you will learn more about in Unit 71:
   - *David **announced** **that he was moving house**.*
   - *I **wonder** **why she is angry**?*

2. A **noun clause** can also be the **subject** or **complement** of a **verb** or the **object** of a **preposition**:
   - ***How the thieves got into the building*** ***puzzled*** *the police*. (subject)
   - *Sue's main concern* ***is*** ***that her brother may be in danger***. (complement)
   - *I turned my attention* ***to*** ***what we could have for lunch***. (object of preposition)
   - ***What I want to know*** ***is*** ***where she got the money from***. (subject and complement)

How do you use them?

1. **Noun clauses** that are the **object** or **complement** of a **verb** are often introduced by the word ***that***:
   - *Jim **has told** his parents **that he wants to study medicine**.*
   - *I suddenly **remembered** **that I had a dental appointment**.*
   - *The main problem **is** **that we do not have enough time**.*

2. You can use **noun clauses** in a similar way after some **adjectives** and **nouns**:
   - *Jane was absolutely **certain** **that she had locked the door**.*
   - *The **thought** **that I might have to make a speech** filled me with dread.*

 ISBN 978-81-8477-745-1

3. You can often omit the word ***that*** from the beginning of a **noun clause** that follows a verb or adjective:
   - *Jim has told his parents **he wants to study medicine.***
   - *Jane was absolutely certain **she had locked the door.***

4. A **noun clause** that follows a verb or adjective can also be introduced by ***if***, ***how*** or a word beginning with ***wh***:
   - *I don't know **if I can afford a new jacket.***
   - *The salesman explained **how the machine worked.***
   - *Mum asked us **what we wanted for lunch.***
   - *The question is **whether we should tell them or not.***
   - *I'm not sure **when he will be back.***

   Notice that a noun clause beginning with a question word (such as ***how*** or ***when***) does not have the form of a question. For example, you say '*When **will he** be back?*' but you say '*I'm not sure when **he will** be back.*'

5. These words can also introduce **noun clauses** used as the **subject** of a verb or as the **object** of a preposition:
   - ***What she told me** came as a great surprise.*
   - *We must focus on **how we are going to solve the problem.***

PRACTICE

Exercise 1

In the following sentences, say whether the word that introduces a noun clause (N), a relative clause (R) or an adverbial clause (A).

1. The box was so heavy **that** I could not lift it. ( )
2. Nobody realized **that** Michael had gone. ( )
3. The letter **that** arrived this morning was from the bank. ( )
4. The problem with big cars is **that** they use too much fuel. ( )
5. The woman spoke so quietly **that** we could hardly hear her. ( )
6. I've done all the jobs **that** you asked me to do. ( )
7. Joe has often told me **that** he would like to travel more. ( )
8. The children were having such a good time at the party **that** they did not want to leave. ( )
9. I wrote a review of the book **that** I had just finished reading. ( )
10. The man explained **that** there were no tickets left. ( )

 ISBN 978-81-8477-745-1

Exercise 2

Fill in the blanks with the words in the box. Use each word once only.

how	that	what	when	where	whether	which	who	whose	why

1. I don't know ______________ you managed to do that calculation in your head.
2. Mr Lee explained ______________ I had not been selected for the team.
3. The doctor is not certain ______________ the patient will make a full recovery or not.
4. Can anyone tell me ______________ lunchbox this is?
5. They found out ______________ she lived by following her home.
6. The plan was ______________ one of the boys would distract the woman while the other stole her purse.
7. ______________ you do with the money is entirely up to you.
8. Joe couldn't decide ______________ book to read.
9. She did not say ______________ she was leaving.
10. Mum asked ______________ had broken the vase.

Exercise 3

Underline all the noun clauses in the following sentences. Some of the sentences may contain more than one.

1. Jack explained how a computer works.
2. She said she needed a new outfit for the wedding.
3. I am pleased that they are coming to stay, but I don't know where they will sleep.
4. What my staff do in their own time is none of my business.
5. I expect you won't agree with me when I tell you what I think.
6. Ask the workmen if they would like a cup of tea.
7. The guests were wondering when their dinner would be ready.
8. Why she did not want the money was a mystery to everyone.
9. We could not decide whether we should go or stay.
10. My belief is that he was afraid of making a fool of himself.

 ISBN 978-81-8477-745-1

Exercise 4

Choose the correct word to fill in the blanks in the following passage.

Jane did not understand ______________ (*whether/why*) she had failed her English exam. She was sure ______________ (*if/that*) she had answered all the questions correctly. Her teacher, Mr Johnson, explained ______________ (*what/where*) she had done wrong. He said she had made some serious grammatical errors, and showed her ______________ (*where/why*) these mistakes were. Jane realized ______________ (*that/what*) she would have to work harder at English. She asked Mr Johnson ______________ (*if/how*) he could give her some extra lessons. 'I don't know ______________ (*whether/why*) that will be possible,' he replied. 'I'll have to look at my diary to find out ______________ (*if/when*) I might be free. ______________ (*That/What*) I can do in the meantime, however, is lend you some books that might be useful.' He took the books from his desk and told Jane ______________ (*which/whose*) chapters she should read.

 ISBN 978-81-8477-745-1

9 SENTENCES

 ISBN 978-81-8477-745-1

UNIT 66

SENTENCES

What do they look like?

'What time is it?' asked Joe. His mother looked at the clock. 'It's nearly half past eight,' she replied. 'You'll miss your bus and be late for school if you don't leave soon. Hurry up!' Joe grabbed his schoolbag and left the house. He ran to the bus stop as fast as he could.

What are they?

1 A **sentence** is a group of words that you use to say something. Most sentences have a **subject** and a **verb**:

- ***The audience*** ***applauded***.
- ***It*** ***was raining***.
- ***Jane*** ***kicked*** *the ball.*
- ***Are*** ***you*** *ready yet?*

2 A **sentence** begins with a **capital letter** and ends with a **full stop**, **question mark** or **exclamation mark**:

- *The telephone is ringing.*
- *Where are my car keys?*
- *Stop talking at once!*

3 Sentences can be **positive** or **negative**:

- *I have been to Japan.* (positive)
- *I have* ***never*** *been to Japan.* (negative)
- *Switch the computer off.* (positive)
- *Do* ***not*** *switch the computer off.* (negative)

You will learn more about positive and negative sentences in Unit 68.

4 A **simple sentence** consists of a single clause:

- *I was born in Singapore.*
- *Would you like a cup of tea?*
- *Please stop talking.*

5 A **compound sentence** consists of two or more main clauses linked by a **co-ordinating conjunction**:

- *I was born in Singapore* ***but*** *my parents were born in China.*
- *Would you like a cup of tea* ***or*** *do you prefer coffee?*
- *Please stop talking* ***and*** *listen to me.*

 ISBN 978-81-8477-745-1

6. A **complex sentence** consists of a main clause and one or more **subordinate clauses**:
   - *I was born in Singapore, **which is in Asia**.*
   - *Would you like a cup of tea **when you have finished**?*
   - *Please stop talking **while I explain what I want you to do**.*

   You will learn more about simple, compound and complex sentences in Unit 67.

How do you use them?

1. A **declarative sentence** makes a **statement**. It ends with a full stop:
   - *An elephant has a long trunk.*
   - *I left early because I felt unwell.*

2. An **interrogative sentence** asks a **question**. It ends with a question mark:
   - *Where are the scissors?*
   - *Have you eaten all the grapes I bought yesterday?*

   You will learn more about questions in Unit 69.

3. An **imperative sentence** gives a **command** or an **order**. It usually does not have a subject and it can end with a full stop or an exclamation mark:
   - *Tell me the truth.*
   - *Please come in and sit down.*
   - *Don't talk with your mouth full!*
   - *Go away!*

   You learnt about imperative sentences in Unit 36.

4. An **exclamatory sentence** expresses a **sudden strong feeling**, such as surprise, delight or anger. It ends with an exclamation mark and often has neither a subject nor a verb:
   - *What lovely weather!*
   - *The silly girl!*
   - *Good morning!*

5. As you learnt in Unit 35, the word ***there*** is sometimes used as the subject of a sentence talking about the **existence** of someone or something. The **verb**, however, must **agree** with the **noun phrase** that **follows** it:
   - ***There were two birds** on the fence.*
   - ***Is there any milk** in the fridge?*

   This use of ***there*** is sometimes described as **existential**. Other **verbs** are occasionally used with existential ***there***, especially in formal writing or in stories:
   - ***There remain** three outstanding problems.*
   - ***There** once **lived** a woman who had twenty-five cats.*

 ISBN 978-81-8477-745-1

PRACTICE

Exercise 1

*Read the following sentences. Put a **full stop** at the end of those that are **declarative**, a **question mark** if they are **interrogative**, and an **exclamation mark** if they are **imperative** or **exclamatory**.*

1. What is your name
2. The car has a flat tyre
3. What a pity
4. There are not enough chairs
5. Stop making such a noise
6. Michael laughed
7. Does this scarf belong to you
8. Don't drop that glass bowl
9. How far did you go
10. The box is empty

Exercise 2

*Choose one phrase from each box to complete the following sentences. (Use a verb in the present tense with phrases containing the word **this**.)*

A:				
a hole	a lot	any hope	any mistakes	a rich man
many different ways	no fish	no rain	several accidents	some paint

B:			
at the junction	in a grand house	in my essay	in the pond
in this sock	of success	on his sleeve	since March
to be done	to solve this problem		

1. There were ______________ ______________.
2. There is ______________ ______________.
3. There remains ______________ ______________.
4. There are ______________ ______________.
5. There was ______________ ______________.

 ISBN 978-81-8477-745-1

6. There once lived ______________ ______________.

7. Is there ______________ ______________?

8. There has been ______________ ______________.

9. Were there ______________ ______________?

10. There have been ______________ ______________.

Exercise 3

*Say whether the sentences in the following dialogue are **declarative (D)**, **interrogative (Int)**, **imperative (Imp)** or **exclamatory (E)**.*

Tom: What are you doing ( )?

Kate: I'm clearing all the books and ornaments off these shelves ( ). I'm going to paint the shelves green, to match the new carpet ( ).

Tom: What a good idea ( )! Can I help you ( )?

Kate: Of course ( )! If you pass the things to me, I will put them away in these boxes ( ). Be careful with the china ornaments ( ). They are very fragile ( ).

Tom: You certainly have a lot of books ( ). Have you read them all ( )?

Kate: Certainly not ( )! However, I do intend to read them all eventually ( ).

Tom: How am I going to reach the top shelf ( )?

Kate: Stand on that stool ( ). It should be strong enough to bear your weight ( ). But take care ( )! I don't want you to fall and hurt yourself ( ).

 ISBN 978-81-8477-745-1

UNIT 67

SIMPLE, COMPOUND AND COMPLEX SENTENCES

What do they look like?

Dolphins are mammals, although they live in the sea like fish. Their tail replaces the hind legs of other mammals and they have flippers instead of forelegs. They are closely related to whales and porpoises. Scientist have proved that dolphins are highly intelligent. They are also very gentle creatures which like being with people.

What are they?

1. A **simple sentence** consists of **only one clause**:
   - *Joe has two brothers.*
   - *The play begins at eight o'clock.*
   - *She took her baby to the clinic for a vaccination.*

2. A **compound sentence** consists of **two or more main clauses** linked by a **co-ordinating conjunction** (usually ***and***, ***but*** or ***or***):
   - *Sue dropped the plate **and** it broke in two.*
   - *I went out to buy a newspaper, **but** the shop was shut.*
   - *Would you like to take a shower **or** would you prefer to unpack first?*
   - *Joe waved his arms **and** Jack called for help **but** nobody came to rescue them.*

   As you learnt in Unit 62, some other words can be used like co-ordinating conjunctions:
   - *The baby is asleep, **so** we must not make any noise.*
   - *I am quite good at English, **whereas** my brother's best subject is maths.*

3. A **complex sentence** consists of a **main clause** and **one or more subordinate clauses**:
   - ***I took the shoes back to the shop*** *because they didn't fit*.
   - *If the sun is shining* ***we will eat in the garden***.
   - ***We visited the factory*** *where our mother works*.
   - *While his car was being repaired*, ***Paul read a book*** *that he had brought with him*.

 ISBN 978-81-8477-745-1

How do you form them?

Simple sentences

Here are the most common ways of forming a **simple sentence**.

1. It can have the structure **subject** + **intransitive verb**:
   - ***Everyone departed.***
   - ***The baby is crying.***

2. It can have the structure **subject** + **transitive verb** + **direct object**:
   - ***Birds have feathers.***
   - ***The old man was wearing a ragged coat.***

3. It can have the structure **subject** + **linking verb** + **complement**:
   - ***Sally looked upset.***
   - ***'The Golden Compass' is my favourite film.***

4. It can have the structure **subject** + **intransitive verb** + **adverbial**:
   - ***Paul screamed loudly.***
   - ***The boat was sailing across the lake.***

   An **adverbial** is an adverb or a phrase that does the work of an adverb.

5. It can have the structure **subject** + **transitive verb** + **direct object** + **adverbial**:
   - ***I put my book down.***
   - ***The dog chased the cat up a tree.***

6. It can have the structure **subject** + **ditransitive verb** + **indirect object** + **direct object**:
   - ***Joe gave the puppy a drink.***
   - ***The children have bought their mother a birthday present.***

   You learnt about **transitive, intransitive** and **ditransitive verbs** in Unit 33.

7. If the sentence is **interrogative**, the **subject** follows the first part of the **verb**:
   - ***Is the baby crying?***
   - ***Have the children bought their mother a birthday present?***

8. If the sentence is **imperative**, it does not have a **subject**:
   - ***Put my book down!***
   - ***Give the puppy a drink.***

Compound sentences

1. A compound sentence has the structure **main clause** + **co-ordinating conjunction** + **main clause**:
   - ***I play the piano and my sister plays the violin.***
   - ***The building collapsed but nobody was badly injured.***
   - ***Shall I tell Richard or will you tell him?***

 ISBN 978-81-8477-745-1

2. A **main clause** has the same structure as a **simple sentence**. You can sometimes join two simple sentences with a **co-ordinating conjunction** to form a compound sentence:
   - *Joe is studying. Sue is watching TV.*
   - ***Joe is studying and Sue is watching TV.***
   - *We invited Jim and Jean to the wedding. They couldn't come.*
   - ***We invited Jim and Jean to the wedding but they couldn't come.***

3. If the **subject** of both **main clauses** is the same person or thing, you can often **omit** the subject in the **second** main clause:
   - ***Sally** picked up the cat. **She** stroked it gently.*
   - ***Sally** picked up the cat **and** stroked it gently.*
   - ***The policeman** ran after the thieves. **He** did not catch them.*
   - ***The policeman** ran after the thieves **but** did not catch them.*

Complex sentences

1. A complex sentence has the structure **main clause** + **subordinate clause** (+ subordinate clause):
   - ***Jenny phoned her parents as soon as she arrived.***
   - ***Please tell me what to do.***
   - ***This is the house where my father lived when he was a boy.***

2. The subordinate clause may be an **adverbial clause**, which you learnt about in Unit 63:
   - ***Mrs Brown read a magazine while she was waiting for the train.*** (adverbial clause of time)
   - ***These apples are cheaper than the ones I bought last week.*** (adverbial clause of comparison)

   Some **adverbial clauses** can come before the **main clause**:
   - ***If you smell smoke, you must call the fire brigade immediately.***
   - ***Although they were very tired, they carried on working.***

3. The subordinate clause may be a **relative clause**, which you learnt about in Unit 64:
   - ***I sent a text message to Pat, who responded immediately.***
   - ***Joe did not like the birthday card that I sent him.***

   Some **relative clauses** can come in the middle of the **main clause**:
   - ***The address to which they were sent did not exist.***
   - ***My cousin Jack, who works at the theatre, can get us free tickets for the show.***

4. The subordinate clause may be a **noun clause**, which you learnt about in Unit 65:
   - ***It was quite obvious that he was lying.***
   - ***I wondered what was causing the delay.***

 ISBN 978-81-8477-745-1

PRACTICE

Exercise 1

*Describe the **structure** of the following simple sentences using the abbreviations provided. The first one has been done to help you.*

S = subject	TV = transitive verb	IV = intransitive verb
DV = ditransitive verb	LV = linking verb	DO = direct object
IO = indirect object	C = complement	A = adverbial (adverb or adverbial phrase)

1. The children cycled up the hill. *S + IV + A*
2. Jane was reading a magazine. ____________
3. The building collapsed. ____________
4. Jack told his father the truth. ____________
5. I put the letter in my pocket. ____________
6. My aunt is a doctor. ____________
7. The bus stopped suddenly. ____________
8. The soup smelt delicious. ____________

Exercise 2

Rewrite the following pairs of simple sentences as one compound sentence, using the conjunctions in the box. You should use each word at least once but not more than twice. If you can omit the subject of the second sentence, do so. The first one has been done to help you.

and	but	so	whereas

1. I opened the door. I went in. *I opened the door and went in.*
2. The man called for help. Nobody heard him. ____________
3. The sun was shining. Sally went for a walk. ____________
4. Joe wanted to buy the bike. He did not have enough money. ____________
5. This car runs on petrol. That one uses diesel. ____________
6. A car drove through the puddle. It splashed the people standing at the bus stop.

____

 ISBN 978-81-8477-745-1

7. A spider has eight legs. An insect has only six legs. ______________________

8. The door was open. I went in. ______________________________

Exercise 3

Say whether the sentences in the following passage are simple (S), compound (Cd) or complex (Cx).

Paul's bus was late ( ). He was feeling anxious, because he was on his way to a new job ( ). Arriving late on the first day would not impress his new employers ( ). A bus arrived at the stop, but it was not the right one ( ). Paul looked at his watch ( ). If his bus did not come in the next few minutes, he would certainly be late ( ). He had to be at his desk by nine o'clock, and it was already 8.45 ( ). At that moment, another bus arrived ( ). To Paul's relief, it was the right one this time ( ). He got on, paid his fare and sat down ( ). The building he was heading for was only a ten-minute ride away ( ). However, his office was on the fifth floor ( ). He would have to run up the stairs, as there was no lift ( ). Paul decided that he would try to catch an earlier bus the following day ( )!

Exercise 4: grammar for writing

Write a short passage called 'A Strange Dream', about 100 words long, using a mixture of simple, compound and complex sentences. When you have finished, underline all the main clauses in the compound and complex sentences.

____

____

____

____

____

____

____

 ISBN 978-81-8477-745-1

UNIT 68

NEGATIVE SENTENCES AND CLAUSES

What do they look like?

I went to England last year. **I had never been there before.** The flight took twelve hours and **I did not enjoy it very much.** There was a lot of turbulence, but the pilot said **it was nothing to worry about**. Some people were airsick. **No one ate much of the in-flight meal.**

What are they?

1 A **negative** sentence or clause contains one of the following negative words:

not	never	nowhere	neither	nor
nothing	no one (or nobody)	none	no	

- *You may **not** use this computer.*
- *Dad **never** helps me with my homework.*
- *She had **nothing** to tell us.*
- *There is **no** milk in the fridge.*

2 A negative sentence is the opposite of a **positive** sentence, which does not contain one of these words:

- *You may use this computer.*
- *Dad helps me with my homework.*

Sometimes, a positive sentence has a different **adverb**, **pronoun** or **determiner** in place of the negative one:

- *Dad **always** helps me with my homework.*
- *She had **something** to tell us.*
- *There is **some** milk in the fridge.*

3 A **negative clause** is part of a sentence. The rest of the sentence may be positive:

- ***Jane was not wearing a raincoat**, so she got very wet.*
- *The teacher asked a question **that none of the students could answer**.*
- *I thought **you didn't like popcorn**.*

 ISBN 978-81-8477-745-1

How do you use negative words?

The negative adverb *not* (or *n't*)

1 If the sentence or clause has a verb phrase with one or more auxiliary verbs, you make it **negative** by putting ***not*** or ***n't*** after the first auxiliary verb:

- *You have **not** signed the letter.*
- *We could**n't** find the key.*
- *Michael is**n't** feeling very well.*
- *They had **not** been waiting long.*

You learnt in Chapter 4 about the contraction ***n't***, which you can attach to most auxiliary verbs as an informal replacement for ***not***. Remember the following irregular forms:

will not → ***won't***	***shall not*** → ***shan't***	***can not*** → ***cannot*** or ***can't***

- *The car **won't** start.*
- *I **can't** reach the top shelf.*

2 If the verb **be** in the sentence or clause is used as a main verb, you make it negative by putting ***not*** or ***n't*** after it:

- *They are **not** welcome here.*
- *He was**n't** afraid of the bear.*

3 If the verb is any other main verb in the **simple present** or **simple past**, you make it negative by putting do/does/did + ***not*** (or ***n't***) before the base form:

- *I know the answer.* (positive)
- *I do **not** know the answer.* or *I do**n't** know the answer.* (negative)
- *It tastes like sugar.* (positive)
- *It does **not** taste like sugar.* or *It does**n't** taste like sugar.* (negative)
- *We enjoyed the play.* (positive)
- *We did **not** enjoy the play.* or *We did**n't** enjoy the play.* (negative)

Other negative words

1 You put ***never*** after the first auxiliary verb of a verb phrase, or after ***be*** used as a main verb:

- *Sally has **never** forgotten my birthday before.*
- *They could **never** have foreseen what would happen.*
- *Joe is **never** ready on time.*

2 You put ***never*** before any other main verb in the **simple present** or **simple past**:

- *The dog **never** barks at people it knows.*
- *I **never** saw the stranger again.*

 ISBN 978-81-8477-745-1

❸ If you use ***never***, ***nowhere***, ***nothing***, ***no one*** (or ***nobody***), ***none***, or ***no*** in a sentence or clause, you **must not** add ***not*** to the verb as well:

- *The child has had **nothing** to eat since yesterday.*
- *There is **no** paper in the printer.*
- *She told **nobody** what had happened.*
- *You can borrow this jacket, which I **never** wear.*

You cannot say '*The child has not had nothing …*' or '*There isn't no paper …*', and so on. However, you can rewrite the sentences as follows:

- *The child has **not** had **anything** to eat since yesterday.*
- *There is**n't any** paper in the printer.*
- *She did **not** tell **anybody** what had happened.*
- *You can borrow this jacket, which I do**n't ever** wear.*

❹ You can use ***neither*** and ***nor*** on their own at the beginning of a sentence or clause that follows one containing ***not***. When you do this, you must put the subject after the verb in the second sentence or clause:

- *The key was **not** in her pocket, **nor** was it in the lock.*
- *David did **not** know the answer. **Neither** did anyone else.*

PRACTICE

Exercise 1

Change the following sentences from positive to negative. Use negative words other than not wherever you can.

1. There is some sugar in the bowl.

   ____

2. Jane had been listening to the teacher.

   ____

3. Dad always wears a suit for work.

   ____

4. There is something wrong with this computer.

   ____

5. The boy thanked us for helping him.

   ____

6. Everybody applauded at the end of the show.

   ____

ISBN 978-81-8477-745-1

7. All my friends gave me presents on my birthday.

8. My uncle grows vegetables in his garden.

9. Both of my friends had offered to help.

10. This is a very difficult exercise.

Exercise 2

Rewrite the following sentences using the contraction n't. *The first one has been done to help you.*

1. The children had nothing to do.

   *The children **didn't have anything** to do.*

2. The police found no evidence at the scene of the crime.

3. There is nowhere as beautiful as Scotland.

4. This must never happen again.

5. She likes none of my friends.

6. I saw nobody I recognized.

7. We will never go to that hotel again.

8. Tell no one where you have hidden the key.

 ISBN 978-81-8477-745-1

9. I have read none of these books.

____

10. They had no money and nothing to eat.

____

Exercise 3

Fill in the blanks in the following passage with the negative words in the box. Use each word only once.

never	no	nobody	none	nor	not	nothing	nowhere

A farmer found a strange object in one of his fields. He had ______________ seen anything like it before. ______________ had any of the other farm workers. It looked like a piece of machinery, but it was ______________ a part of any of the farmer's tools or vehicles. He picked up the object and looked at it more closely. There was ______________ printed on it to say where it had come from, or what it was made of. He showed it to some of his friends in the village. ______________ of them knew what it might be. However, one of them had seen something unusual in the sky a few nights earlier. It was a bright light that appeared out of ______________, flew over the village, then disappeared again. He thought it was an alien spacecraft, although ______________ believed him. This object must have fallen from the spacecraft, he said. There was ______________ other possible explanation.

 ISBN 978-81-8477-745-1

UNIT 69

QUESTIONS AND ANSWERS

What do they look like?

Carol: Isn't it a lovely day?

Sue: Yes, it is. It makes a nice change to see the sun, doesn't it?

Carol: It certainly does. Where are you going?

Sue: For a walk in the park. Would you like to come too?

Carol: I'd love to, but unfortunately I have some shopping to do.

How do you use them?

There are several different types of **questions and answers.**

1. A ***yes/no question*** asks for a **positive answer** (***yes***) or a **negative answer** (***no***):
   - ***'Are you ready?'*** ***'Yes.'***
   - ***'Does this computer work?'*** ***'No, it doesn't.'***

2. A ***wh-*****question** asks for **information**:
   - ***'What is the capital of France?'*** ***'Paris.'***
   - ***'How long will it take to get there?'*** ***'About three hours.'***

3. An **alternative question** asks you to make a **choice**:
   - ***'Is this word an adjective, an adverb or a preposition?'*** ***'It's a preposition.'***
   - ***'Would you like tea or coffee?'*** ***'Coffee, please.'***

4. A **rhetorical question** does not need an answer. You sometimes use rhetorical questions in **expositions**, to make a point:
   - *The government has promised to provide free care for the elderly.* ***Who is going to pay for this?*** *The country is already heavily in debt.*
   - *The council has reduced the speed limit throughout the village.* ***Will this solve the problem?*** *There must be a better way.*

5. A **question tag** comes at the end of a statement, usually asking for **confirmation**:
   - *'Those cakes look delicious,* ***don't they?'*** ***'Yes, they do.'***
   - *'You didn't leave the door unlocked,* ***did you?'*** ***'No, of course not.'***

 ISBN 978-81-8477-745-1

How do you form them?

yes/no questions and answers

1 A ***yes/no* question** begins with an **auxiliary verb** or the verb ***be***. The subject follows the first part of the **verb phrase**:

- ***Can*** *John* ***swim****?*
- ***Do*** *the children* ***need*** *any help?*
- ***Should*** *we* ***have notified*** *the authorities?*
- ***Had*** *she* ***been waiting*** *long?*
- ***Was*** *your father* *angry?*

Putting the subject **after** the first part of the verb phrase (or after the verb ***be***) is called **inversion**.

2 The answer to a ***yes/no*** question can be simply ***yes*** or ***no***:

- *'Can John swim?'* ***'Yes.'***
- *'Do the children need any help?'* ***'No.'***

However, it often has the form ***yes*** + pronoun + **verb** or ***no*** + pronoun + **verb** + ***not/ n't***. The **verb** is the usually the same as the one at the beginning of the question. If the verb is in the **third person**, the pronoun in the answer matches the subject of the verb in the question.

- *'****Can*** *John swim?'* ***'Yes, he can.'***
- *'****Had*** *she been waiting long?'* ***'No, she had not.'***
- *'****Do*** *the children need any help?'* ***'No, they don't.'***

If the subject of the **verb** in the question is ***I***, ***you*** or ***we***, you often need a different pronoun (and sometimes a different verb form) in the answer:

- *'****May*** *we sit here?'* ***'Yes, you may.'***
- *'****Are*** *you ready?'* ***'No, I am not.'***

Sometimes the answer does not actually include the word ***yes*** or ***no***:

- *'Should we have notified the authorities?'* ***'I don't think so.'***
- *'Was your father angry?'* ***'He certainly was!'***

3 Some ***yes/no*** questions begin with a **negative verb**. They often expect the answer *yes* (or some other positive answer):

- *'****Aren't*** *those flowers beautiful?' 'Yes, they are.'*
- *'****Wouldn't*** *it* ***have been*** *better to wait?' 'Probably.'*

The negative verb is usually formed with ***n't***, which comes before the subject, as in the examples above. However, in formal English you might want to use ***not*** instead. If you do, you put it **after** the subject:

- ***Would*** *it* ***not have been*** *better to wait?*
- ***Has*** *she* ***not received*** *our letter?*

 ISBN 978-81-8477-745-1

wh-questions

1. A ***wh*-question** begins with one of the following words, which are sometimes called ***wh*-words**:

how, what, when, where, which, who, whom, whose, why

- ***How*** *does this machine work?*
- ***When*** *was the hospital built?*
- ***Why*** *haven't you done your homework?*

The ***wh*-word** may have **another word or phrase** before or after it:

- ***To whom*** *should I address the letter?*
- ***How far*** *is it to the station?*
- ***Which of these pictures*** *do you prefer?*

2. You usually form the rest of a ***wh***-question in a similar way to a ***yes/no*** question, with the **subject** after the first part of the **verb phrase**:

- *Where* ***should I put*** *my coat?*
- *What* ***have the workmen been doing*** *all day?*
- *Whose* ***are these books****?*
- *Why* ***didn't she ask*** *for help?*

3. However, the ***wh*-word** itself (or the phrase it introduces) is sometimes the **subject** of the sentence. In questions like these, the **subject** comes before the **verb** or the whole **verb phrase**:

- ***Who has been sleeping*** *in my bed?*
- ***What could have happened*** *to them?*
- ***Which car uses*** *the least fuel?*

4. The answer to a ***wh*-question** is always a piece of information, never ***yes*** or ***no***:

- *'When was the hospital built?'* ***'In 1982.'***
- *'Whose are these books?'* ***'They belong to my sister.'***
- *'Why haven't you done your homework?'* ***'Because I didn't have time.'***

Notice that the answer is often not a full sentence.

Alternative questions

1. **Alternative questions** are formed like ***yes/no*** **questions**. They include the conjunction ***or*** to offer a **choice** of **two or more things**:

- *Is a whale* ***a fish or a mammal****?*
- *Would you like* ***milk, water or fruit juice****?*
- *Shall we* ***go by bus or call a taxi****?*

2. The answer to an **alternative question** is the **thing selected** from the choice offered:

- *'Is a whale a fish or a mammal?'* ***'A mammal.'***
- *'Would you like milk, water or fruit juice?'* ***'Fruit juice, please.'***
- *'Shall we go by bus or call a taxi?'* ***'Let's call a taxi.'***

 ISBN 978-81-8477-745-1

Question tags

1 A **question tag** can be positive or negative. **Positive question tags** have the structure **verb** + **pronoun**. They refer back to a **negative verb** in the statement, and the **subject** of this verb:

- *You* ***are*** ***not*** *feeling nervous,* ***are*** *you?*
- *People generally* ***don't*** *like being teased,* ***do*** *they?*

Negative question tags have the structure **verb** + ***n't*** + **pronoun**. They refer back to a **positive verb** in the statement, and the **subject** of this verb:

- *Jane* ***is*** *your cousin,* ***isn't*** *she?*
- *The town centre* ***has*** *changed a lot during the past few years,* ***hasn't*** *it?*

2 If the verb in the statement is in the **simple present** or **simple past**, the question tag uses ***does, do*** or ***did***:

- *The room* ***looks*** *nice,* ***does****n't it?*
- *They* ***offered*** *to pay for the damage,* ***did****n't they?*

3 If the verb in the statement is ***am/is/are/was/were***, the question tag usually contains the same form of the verb:

- *The ending of the play* ***was*** *a bit disappointing,* ***was****n't it?*
- *These dishes* ***are*** *not for sale,* ***are*** *they?*

4 If the verb in the statement is a **verb phrase**, the question tag usually contains its **first auxiliary verb** (or a negative contraction of this verb):

- *He* ***should*** *have apologized,* ***should****n't he?*
- *You* ***have****n't been drinking this water,* ***have*** *you?*
- *The students at that school* ***do****n't wear uniform,* ***do*** *they?*
- *Mary* ***will*** *help,* ***wo****n't she?*

5 However, you cannot use ***am*** with ***n't*** in a question tag. You have to say ***aren't I*** or ***am I not***:

- *I* ***am*** *taller than Joe,* ***aren't I****?*
- *I* ***am*** *wearing an officer's uniform,* ***am I not****?*

6 The **answer** to a statement with a question tag has the same structure as a ***yes/no*** answer. If the answer includes a **pronoun** and **verb**, these are the same as those used in the question tag for verbs in the **third person**:

- *'The ending of the play was a bit disappointing,* ***was****n't it?' 'Yes, it* ***was****.'*
- *'Jane likes ice-cream,* ***does****n't she?' 'No, she* ***does****n't.'*

However, if the **verb** in the question tag is in the **first or second person**, you often need a different **pronoun** (and sometimes a different verb form) in the answer:

- *'You haven't been drinking this water,* ***have*** *you?' 'No, I* ***have****n't.'*
- *'I was the best player,* ***was****n't I?' 'Yes, you* ***were****.'*

Question tags and short answers are a form of **ellipsis**. You will learn more about this in Unit 75.

 ISBN 978-81-8477-745-1

PRACTICE

Exercise 1

Say whether the following questions are yes/no questions (Y/N), wh-questions (Wh) or alternative questions (A).

1. How are we going to get all this work done? ( )
2. Shall I accept the offer or refuse it? ( )
3. Are you coming with us? ( )
4. May I leave my suitcase here? ( )
5. Why didn't she scream or call for help? ( )
6. Wouldn't you prefer a cup of tea? ( )
7. Is this your jacket or Michael's? ( )
8. Where can I find a pair of scissors? ( )
9. Does anyone want anything to eat or drink? ( )
10. Did you buy those curtains or make them yourself? ( )

Exercise 2

Fill in the missing question tags at the end of the following sentences, using contractions wherever possible.

1. You have done your homework, ______________?
2. Michael doesn't wear glasses, ______________?
3. She should have warned us, ______________?
4. Dad will pay the bill, ______________?
5. The door wasn't locked, ______________?
6. I am your best friend, ______________?
7. The children like cola, ______________?
8. That isn't your new camera, ______________?
9. We could catch a later train, ______________?
10. Sally didn't have a piece of cake, ______________?

 ISBN 978-81-8477-745-1

Exercise 3

Fill in each blank in the following dialogue with the correct wh-word. Do not use the same word more than once.

Carol: _______________ are you doing, Mum?

Mum: I'm unpacking my shopping. Will you help me put everything away?

Carol: OK. _______________ should I put these cans of soup?

Mum: In the cupboard by the fridge.

Carol: _______________ shelf do they go on?

Mum: It doesn't really matter – put them wherever there's room.

Carol: _______________ have you bought so much food?

Mum: I've invited Uncle Jack and Aunt Mary for the weekend. You know what large appetites they have!

Carol: _______________ are they coming?

Mum: They'll probably arrive on Friday evening.

Carol: _______________ bedroom will they sleep in?

Mum: They can use Jack's room, because he's going away with one of his friends.

Carol: I didn't know that. He never tells me anything. _______________ is he going with, and _______________ long will he be away for?

Mum: He's going on a sailing holiday with Peter for a week.

 ISBN 978-81-8477-745-1

UNIT 70

PUNCTUATION MARKS

What do they look like?

Sue was struggling with her English homework; it was not her favourite subject. She asked her great-aunt (who was staying with the family) for help. 'What do these words have in common: jump, wish, ride and waste?' asked Sue. 'That's easy!' replied her great-aunt. 'Each one belongs to two word classes — they're all both nouns and verbs.'

What are they for?

You use **punctuation marks** in written text, chiefly to indicate breaks **within** sentences or **between** sentences. They help to **make the meaning clear**.

Some punctuation marks indicate a **stop** at the end of a sentence. These are:

1. the **full stop** (.), which you put at the end of **declarative** sentences and some **imperative** sentences:
   - *The dog ran away.*
   - *Please close the door.*
2. the **question mark** (?), which you put at the end of **interrogative** sentences and other **questions**:
   - *What time is it?*
   - *Jane is very attractive, isn't she?*
   - *'I need some black paint.' 'What for?'*
3. the **exclamation mark** (!), which you put at the end of **exclamatory** sentences and some **imperative** sentences:
   - *What a mess!*
   - *Come here at once!*

 ISBN 978-81-8477-745-1

Some punctuation marks indicate a **pause** in the middle of a sentence. These are:

1. the **comma** (,), which you use to **separate** clauses or items in lists:
   - *If it rains, the party will be held indoors.*
   - *France, Italy, Germany and Spain are all countries in Europe.*
2. the **semi-colon** (;), which you use to **link** two sentences that are closely connected in meaning:
   - *My old jeans have holes in the knees; I need a new pair.*
   - *Tom failed the exam; he had not done enough revision.*
3. the **colon** (:), which you use to **introduce** a list or a piece of dialogue in a play:
   - *You will need the following ingredients: flour, sugar, eggs and butter.*
   - *Carol: Did you enjoy your trip to the museum?*
     Jack: Yes, I saw lots of interesting things there.

Some punctuation marks are used for other purposes, such as:

1. **quotation marks** (' ' or " "), also called **inverted commas**, which you use in pairs for **direct speech**, or to draw attention to a particular word:
   - *'Where are you going?' asked Mary.*
   - *The word 'light' has many different meanings.*
2. the **apostrophe** ('), which you use in **possessive forms** and **contractions**:
   - *That is my sister's bedroom.*
   - *He didn't know the answer.*
3. the **hyphen** (-), which **links** words in some compound nouns, numbers and fractions:
   - *Richard is my brother-in-law.*
   - *Seventy-five per cent is the same as three-quarters.*
4. the **dash** (—), which **introduces** or **encloses** a piece of extra information:
   - *This is a digital camera — it doesn't use film.*
   - *Alan chose the steak — the most expensive item on the menu — and Jane chose the vegetarian dish.*
5. **brackets** ( ), also called **parentheses**, which you use in pairs **around** a piece of extra information:
   - *The ship narrowly avoided colliding with a dinghy (a small sailing boat).*
   - *Alan chose the steak (the most expensive item on the menu) and Jane chose the vegetarian dish.*
6. **ellipsis points** or **dots** (...), which show that something is **omitted** or **unfinished**:
   - *The rules clearly say that 'Dogs are not allowed ... on the beach.'*
   - *However, if you would rather stay at home ...*

 ISBN 978-81-8477-745-1

How do you use them?

The full stop (.)

1 You put a **full stop** at the **end** of a declarative sentence or an imperative sentence that does not show strong feeling:

- *I picked up the jar and read the instructions on the label.*
- *Switch off the lights before you leave the room.*

2 You sometimes use a **full stop** to show that a word or name has been shortened:

- *The letter was dated 15 Oct. 2008.*
- *The Harry Potter books were written by J. K. Rowling.*

The question mark (?)

1 You put a **question mark** at the **end** of an interrogative sentence or other question. It represents the way a speaker's voice rises when they expect an answer:

- *Have you had a postcard from James?*
- *That was a delicious meal, wasn't it?*
- *'Where are you going?' asked Sue.*
- *'I turned down their offer.' 'Why?'*

2 You do not put a question mark at the end of an **indirect question**. You use a **full stop** instead:

- *Sue asked me where I was going.*
- *I explained why I had turned down their offer.*

You will learn more about indirect questions in Unit 71.

3 You sometimes use a **full stop** instead of a question mark at the end of a **request** that has the form of a question:

- *Could you close the window, please.*
- *May I offer my sincere condolences.*

The exclamation mark (!)

1 You put an **exclamation mark** at the **end** of an exclamatory sentence or an imperative sentence that shows **strong feeling**:

- *How astonishing!*
- *Go away and leave me alone!*

2 You also use an **exclamation mark** after single words or short phrases that are spoken loudly, such as cries or greetings:

- *'Help!' shouted the girl.*
- *'Good morning!' called the postman.*

3 People sometimes put an **exclamation mark** instead of a full stop at the end of a declarative sentence to show surprise, anger, etc:

- *Jane looked in the magician's hat. The rabbit had disappeared!*

 ISBN 978-81-8477-745-1

- *The man took the money and walked away. He didn't even thank me!*

You should not use exclamation marks like this too often in your written work.

The comma (,)

1. You use **commas** to separate items in **lists**:
   - *Uncle Tom has ten pets: four dogs, three cats, two rabbits and a parrot.*
   - *Patients under general anaesthetic cannot feel, hear or see anything.*
   - *It was a cold, wet, windy day.*

   A comma is not needed before ***and*** or ***or***. See Unit 20 for the rules about using commas between adjectives.

2. You often put a **comma** after a **sentence adverb**, a **linking adverb**, a **participial phrase**, an **adverbial phrase** or an **adverbial clause** that comes before the **main clause** of a sentence:
   - ***Unfortunately**, I have lost their phone number.*
   - ***However**, he did not have enough money.*
   - ***Deafened by the noise in the disco**, we went outside to talk.*
   - ***A hundred years ago**, this town was just a village.*
   - ***Before she left the house**, she checked that the key was in her pocket.*

   The comma represents the pause that you would make if you were saying these sentences aloud.

3. You put a **pair of commas** around a piece of extra information that is **not an essential part of the sentence**, such as a **noun phrase in apposition** (see Unit 7) or a **non-defining relative clause** (see Unit 64):
   - *Mr Brown, **our next-door neighbour**, offered to help.*
   - *These books, **which are very valuable**, belong to my grandfather.*

4. You put a **comma** before and/or after the name of a **person who is being addressed**:
   - *Is this your bag, **Mrs Lee**?*
   - *Thank you, **Tom**, for your help.*
   - ***Sally**, please give that old lady your seat.*

5. You put a **comma** before a **question tag**:
   - *Joe is a good dancer, **isn't he**?*
   - *This car doesn't go very fast, **does it**?*

6. You put a **comma** after ***yes*** or ***no*** in an answer:
   - *'Are you going to Peter's party?' '**Yes**, I am.'*
   - *'Are you going to Peter's party?' '**No**, I haven't been invited.'*

7. You put a **comma** before ***please*** in a polite request:
   - *Will you help me, **please**.*
   - *May I have another slice of cake, **please**.*

 ISBN 978-81-8477-745-1

As you learnt earlier, these requests do not require a question mark, even though they have the form of a question. Note also that you do not put a comma after ***please*** at the beginning of a sentence:

- ***Please*** *help me.*
- ***Please*** *may I have another slice of cake.*

8 You put a **comma** before a piece of **direct speech**, if the saying verb comes first:

- *Jack said, **'That's a good idea.'***
- *Sue asked, **'Which tool should I use?'***

If the saying verb comes after what is said, you put a **comma** before the **closing quotation mark** instead of a full stop:

- *'That's a good idea,' said Jack.*

However, if there is a **question mark** or **exclamation mark** before the **closing quotation mark**, you do not replace this with a comma:

- *'Which tool should I use?' asked Sue.*

9 You use **commas** to separate parts of an **address**:

- *Her address is 24 Empire Court, High Street, Newtown.*

You can also put a comma after the house or apartment number, but this is not essential.

The semi-colon (;)

1 A **semi-colon** is used between two main clauses that could stand as sentences on their own. You use a semi-colon to link them more closely, when a full stop and capital letter would be too big a break:

- *Alice loves animals; she has several pets.*
- *The larger bike is my brother's; the smaller one is mine.*

2 A **semi-colon** often does the same job as a **conjunction** (such as ***and***, ***but***, ***or***, ***so***, ***because***, ***while***). You can use one or the other, but **not both**:

- *I've lost my luggage **and** I don't know what to do.*
- *I've lost my luggage; I don't know what to do.*
- *We didn't go swimming **because** the water was too cold.*
- *We didn't go swimming; the water was too cold.*

However, you can sometimes put a **comma** before a **conjunction**:

- *I searched the room, **but** I couldn't find the missing book.*
- *Jane arrived early, **so** she had to wait.*

3 You can use a **semi-colon** to link sentences when the second sentence begins with another kind of **connector** (such as ***however***, ***consequently***, ***for example***, ***that is***). You usually put a **comma** after the connector:

- *I made several mistakes; **however**, nobody seemed to notice.*

 ISBN 978-81-8477-745-1

- *Mammals are warm-blooded; **that is**, their body temperature does not change in hot or cold weather.*

4 You sometimes use **semi-colons** instead of commas in a long, complicated list, especially if some of the items already contain commas:

- *Sally liked James. He had a pleasant, friendly manner; charm, tact and common sense; a stylish way of dressing; and, finally, plenty of money.*

Notice that, in this case, you may put a semi-colon before the last ***and***, to make the meaning clear.

The colon (:)

1 You use a **colon** to **introduce** items that **explain** or **add detail** to what has gone before:

- *Uncle Tom has ten pets: four dogs, three cats, two rabbits and a parrot.*
- *The first-aid kit contains the following items: bandages, plasters, antiseptic cream and disinfectant wipes.*
- *There are two reasons why doctors do not prescribe this drug: it has dangerous side-effects and it is very expensive.*

The colon follows a **main clause**. You do not use it in the middle of a clause. For example, you should not write *'The first-aid kit contains: bandages, plasters and antiseptic cream.'*

2 You can also use a **colon** to introduce something spoken, especially the **dialogue** of a play, a long **quotation** or an important **announcement**:

- *Mrs Brown: I may be late home from work today.*
  Mr Brown: That's OK. If I get back before you, I'll start cooking the dinner.
- *The presenter turned to face the camera and announced: 'My next guest is a young woman who has raised thousands of dollars for charity.'*

In the second example, you could replace the colon with a **comma**. However, you cannot use commas instead of colons in the first example.

Quotation marks (' ' or " ")

1 You use **quotation marks** in pairs around the **exact words** that someone says. This is called **direct speech**, and you will learn more about it in Unit 71. You can use **single quotation marks** (' ') or **double quotation marks** (" "):

- *'**Look out!**' cried the policeman.*
- *Jack said, '**There is no paper in the printer.**'*
- *I asked the man in the ticket office, "**When does the next train leave?**"*
- *"**I'm hungry**," said the little girl.*

Notice that the punctuation at the end of what is said comes **before** the closing quotation mark in direct speech. The following punctuation marks are possible: full stop, question mark, exclamation mark or comma. You should not put a semi-colon or colon at the end of a piece of direct speech.

 ISBN 978-81-8477-745-1

2. You can use **quotation marks** in pairs around the **title** of something, such as a story, poem or song:
   - *We have to write a story called '**A Trip to Outer Space**'.*
   - *The song '**Masquerade**' was written for the musical '**The Phantom of the Opera**'.*

3. You can also use **quotation marks** in pairs around a **particular word or phrase** in a sentence. You do this if you want to draw attention to the word or phrase for some reason:
   - *The abbreviation '**e.g.**' is short for a Latin phrase that means '**for example**'.*
   - *The president has several '**minders**', whose job is to protect him in public places.*

   Notice that other punctuation usually comes **after** the closing quotation mark unless it is part of the word or phrase itself.

4. If a piece of direct speech contains a word or phrase that needs quotation marks of its own, you have two choices. You can use **single quotation marks** for the direct speech and **double quotation marks** for the word or phrase. Or you can use **double quotation marks** for the direct speech and **single quotation marks** for the word or phrase:
   - *The teacher said, 'I want you to write a story called "A Trip to Outer Space".'*
   - *"What does the abbreviation 'e.g.' mean?" asked Mary.*

   Notice the position of the final full stop, between the two closing quotation marks, at the end of the first example.

The apostrophe (')

1. In a contraction, such as ***I'm***, ***he'll*** or ***haven't***, the apostrophe shows that one or more letters have been left out. You put the **apostrophe** in the place of the **missing letter(s)** and close up the space between the words:

I am	➔ *I'm*	*he has*	➔ *he's*	*we shall*	➔ *we'll*
they will	➔ *they'll*	*you would*	➔ *you'd*	*there is*	➔ *there's*
did not	➔ *didn't*	*let us*	➔ *let's*		

2. You also use an **apostrophe** to make **possessive forms** of nouns. If the **noun** does not end in **s**, you add **'s** to show possession:
   - *I was told to go to the **principal**'s office.*
   - *Miss Lee was standing beside **Andrew**'s desk.*
   - *The **children**'s parents have been informed.*

3. If the **noun** is **plural** and ends in **s**, you add the **apostrophe alone**:
   - *Mr Smith is marking the **students**' assignments.*
   - *The **dogs**' owners had to pay for the damage they caused.*

4. If the **noun** is **singular** and ends in **s**, you usually add **'s**:
   - *Who designed the **princess**'s wedding dress?*
   - ***James**'s bicycle has been stolen.*

 ISBN 978-81-8477-745-1

However, you can also use an **apostrophe alone** after names ending in *s*:

- *Many of Charles Dickens' novels are set in London.*

5 If the possessive form is made up of two names linked by *and*, you add *'s* (or *'*) to the second name only:

- *Are you going to Peter and Jenny's wedding?*
- *This is Mr Watson and Mr Collins' office.*

6 Remember that there is **no apostrophe** in the possessive determiner ***its*** and the possessive pronouns ***hers***, ***ours***, ***yours*** and ***theirs***:

- *The dog wagged **its** tail.*
- *These seats must be **ours**.*

Do no confuse the contraction ***it's***, short for ***it is*** or ***it has***, with the possessive determiner ***its***:

- *We can get some money from the bank if **it's** still open.*
- ***It's** been raining all day.*

And do no confuse ***whose*** with ***who's*** (short for ***who is*** or ***who has***), or ***their*** with ***they're*** (short for ***they are***):

- ***Whose** coat is this, and **who's** taken mine?*
- ***They're** eating **their** lunch.*

7 You sometimes shorten phrases such as ***the doctor's surgery*** and ***the baker's shop*** to ***the doctor's*** and ***the baker's***:

- *I have an appointment at the **doctor's** this afternoon.*
- *Joe went to the **greengrocer's** to buy some fruit.*

8 You can also use *'s* or *'* to make the possessive form of a period of time, when you want to say how long something lasts:

- *I think I'll take a week's holiday.*
- *He was sentenced to four years' imprisonment.*

9 You occasionally use *'s* to form the plural of single letters or short words that are not normally used as nouns:

- *Always dot your I's and cross your t's.*
- *Are the puppies he's or she's?* (an informal way of asking if they are male or female)

However, it is wrong to use an apostrophe in the plurals of other short or shortened words. You should not write '*one of my toe's*' or '*The school has three science lab's*.'

The hyphen (-)

1 You use a **hyphen** to form some **compound nouns** (nouns made up of two or more words), such as:

word-processor, self-confidence, make-up, passer-by, sister-in-law, forget-me-not

 ISBN 978-81-8477-745-1

Some compound nouns are written as one word (such as ***toothbrush***, ***classroom***, ***breakdown***) and some are written as two words (such as ***shopping mall***, ***washing machine***, ***fountain pen***). If you are not sure how to write a particular compound noun, look it up in a dictionary.

2 You also use a **hyphen** when you write out **numbers** from 21 to 99 and **fractions**:

twenty-one, thirty-seven, fifty-two, ninety-nine, two-thirds, three-quarters, one-fifth, seven-tenths

3 You sometimes need to join other words with a **hyphen** to show that they form a **single unit of meaning**, especially when they are used as **adjectives**:

- *J. K. Rowling is a **well-known** children's author.*
- *Reptiles are **cold-blooded**.*
- *She has a class of twenty **five-year-old** children.*
- *This fabric is very **hard-wearing**.*

The dash (–)

1 You use a **dash** to **introduce** a piece of text that **explains** what has gone before or **adds extra information**:

- *Jane isn't coming with us – she doesn't like long walks.*
- *The weather was awful yesterday – it's a bit better today.*

Using a dash in this way is similar to using a **colon** or **semi-colon** in more formal writing.

2 You can also use a **pair of dashes** to **enclose** a piece of additional information that is **not essential**:

- *I'll be spending my birthday – a Monday – at school, unfortunately.*
- *The main thing – and this is important – is to make sure that everyone knows what they have to do.*

Using a pair of dashes in this way is similar to using **brackets** or a pair of **commas** in more formal writing.

Brackets ( )

1 You use **brackets** in pairs to **enclose** a piece of additional information such as a **comment** or **explanation**:

- *The old lady now had no friends (**having quarrelled with the few she had**) and no close relatives.*
- *Jack is coming to the party with Sue (**his new girlfriend**) and her sister.*

2 If the information in **brackets** comes at the end of a sentence, you put the **full stop** after the **closing bracket**:

- *The old lady now had no friends (having quarrelled with the few she had)**.***
- *Jack is coming to the party with Sue (his new girlfriend)**.***

 ISBN 978-81-8477-745-1

However, if the information in **brackets** consists of a whole sentence, the **full stop** comes before the **closing bracket**:

- *I'll tell my parents the good news at the weekend. (They have no idea I went in for the competition.)*
- *You can click on the printer icon to print the document. (This is the quickest method.)*

Ellipsis points (...)

1 You can use a set of **three dots**, called **ellipsis points**, to show that you have **missed out** some words in the middle of a quotation:

- *Martin Luther King said, 'I have a dream that one day … the sons of former slaves and the sons of former slave owners will be able to sit down together at the table of brotherhood.'*
- *Winston Churchill said, 'We shall fight on the beaches … we shall fight in the fields … we shall never surrender.'*

2 You can also use **ellipsis points** to show that a sentence is **unfinished**, or to represent a **pause for thought**:

- *I don't usually sell my paintings, but when someone offers me a lot of money …*
- *It might just be possible … we would have to run all the way.*

Capital letters (A, B, C)

1 **Capital letters** are not punctuation marks, but it is important to know how and when to use them. The **first word of a sentence** always begins with a **capital letter**:

- *My mother is a doctor. She works at the local hospital.*
- *Where are our guests? They should be here by now.*
- *Stop making such a noise! You're giving me a headache.*

2 The first word of a piece of **direct speech** also has a **capital letter**, whether it comes at the beginning of the sentence or not:

- *'What time is it?' asked the boy.*
- *Alice said, 'This is my brother.'*

However, when the saying verb comes in the middle of a sentence of direct speech, you use a **lower-case letter** (such as *a*, *b*, *c*) to continue the direct speech after the verb:

- *'I haven't brought my swimming costume,' said Jane, 'so I can't go in the pool.'*

3 You also use **capital letters** for **proper nouns** (see Unit 4), such as names of people, places, days, months, festivals, nationalities and languages:

- *In April I am going to Beijing with Mum, Dad and my brother Jack.*
- *Miss Lee teaches English at Redwood High School.*
- *Uncle Tom and Aunt Sue live in Station Road.*

4 **Adjectives formed from the names of places** also begin with a **capital letter**:

- *The film is set in the Australian city of Melbourne and stars the Spanish actress Lola Montero.*

 ISBN 978-81-8477-745-1

- *'Is the Japanese alphabet the same as the one used in **C**hinese writing?' asked Sue.*

5 You always write the **personal pronoun *I*** as a **capital letter**:

- *May **I** have another cake?*
- ***I** will help you if **I** have time.*

6 The main words of a **title** usually have a **capital letter**:

- *Have you read '**H**arry **P**otter and the **D**eathly **H**allows'?*
- *We went to see '**T**he **G**olden **C**ompass' at the cinema yesterday.*

The articles (***a***, ***an*** and ***the***) and short prepositions and conjunctions (such as ***and***, ***but***, ***or***, ***of***, ***in***, ***at***, ***to*** and ***for***) do not have a capital letter unless they come at the beginning of the title.

7 You use **capital letters** when you **shorten** names or other words to their first letter:

- *The letter was addressed to Mrs **J. A.** Smith.*
- *The shop sells books, magazines, **CD**s and **DVD**s.*

You usually put full stops after the initials of a person's name, but you do not put full stops in abbreviations such as ***CD*** and ***DVD***. Notice also that the plural of ***CD*** and ***DVD*** has a lower-case ***s***.

8 You write ***Dear*** with a **capital *D*** at the **beginning of a letter**. You also use a **capital letter** to begin the word or phrase you put before your name at the **end of a letter**.

- ***D**ear Grandma … **L**ove from Billy.*
- ***D**ear Mr Jones … **Y**ours sincerely, Jane Smith.*

PRACTICE

Exercise 1

Each of the following sentences contains one punctuation mistake. Rewrite the sentences correctly.

1. The animals have'nt been fed yet.

____

2. 'What time is it,' asked Sue.

____

3. I didn't realize the man was unconscious, I thought he was just asleep.

____

4. Grandma is seventy two years old.

____

 ISBN 978-81-8477-745-1

5. 'There is no milk left', said Bill.

6. If you see Jane: tell her I want to speak to her.

7. Does this shop sell childrens' shoes?

8. I don't know what to wear for the party

9. Tom can speak three languages; English, Japanese and Malay.

10. You don't like cheese do you?

Exercise 2

Rewrite these sentences with ***capital letters*** *where they are needed.*

1. i am going to japan in august.

2. 'ask dad if he will lend you the money you need,' suggested paul.

3. we are moving to our new house in primrose lane on saturday.

4. carol's mum bought her a dvd of 'the golden compass' for her birthday.

5. 'those ornaments are very fragile,' said mr jones, 'so you must take care not to break them.'

6. sally's english teacher lent her a copy of john steinbeck's novel 'of mice and men'.

 ISBN 978-81-8477-745-1

7. mr lee and his wife are going to visit the great wall of china.

8. my friend alex lives in new mexico, a state in north america.

9. uncle jack said, 'i have been working for a british company since last september.'

10. most people in the uk have a holiday on christmas day.

Exercise 3

Rewrite the following passage, inserting all the missing ***punctuation marks.***

Jane was reading a letter from her father who was away on business He was in Birmingham a large industrial city in England His letter said that the hotel where he was staying was excellent the weather however was awful Jane laughed At that moment her brother entered the room What are you laughing at he asked Im reading Dads letter from England replied Jane Do you want to see it Not at the moment said her brother Im looking for one of my schoolbooks Its called Essential English Grammar You havent seen it anywhere have you Jane said that she hadnt My teacher will go mad if Ive lost it wailed her brother

 ISBN 978-81-8477-745-1

UNIT 71

DIRECT AND INDIRECT SPEECH

What do they look like?

'Can you lend me ten dollars, Mum?' asked Joe. His mother asked him why he needed the money. He said he wanted to buy some flowers for his teacher. 'She is leaving at the end of this week,' he explained. 'OK, I'll lend you the money,' said his mother, 'but you mustn't forget to pay me back.'

What are they?

1 **Direct speech** is **quoting** the **exact words** that someone says in **quotation marks**:

- *Tom said, **'I've lost my key.'***
- ***'Why haven't you done your homework?'** asked my teacher.*

2 **Indirect speech** is **reporting** what someone has said in a **noun clause**:

- *Tom said **that he had lost his key.***
- *My teacher asked me **why I had not done my homework.***

Indirect speech is sometimes called **reported speech**.

How do you use them?

Direct speech

1 You use **direct speech** in **narratives** and **recounts** to give the exact words that people say. You put the words in **quotation marks**. You put a saying verb (such as ***say***, ***ask***, ***reply***) before the opening quotation mark or after the closing quotation mark. The **subject** of the **saying verb** is the person who says the words:

- ***Joe asked**, 'Why are you crying, Sue?'*
- *'I've broken my camera,' **she replied**.*

You learnt about using **punctuation marks** with direct speech in Unit 70.

2 The person's spoken words may be an **incomplete sentence** or **more than one sentence**:

- *Jane said, **'Carol has invited me to her party. I don't want to go.'***
- ***'Why not?'** I asked.*

 ISBN 978-81-8477-745-1

3. The **saying verb** sometimes comes in the middle of the spoken words. When this happens, you **close** the quotation marks before the saying verb (and its subject) and **reopen** them after it:
   - *'If you don't know what the word means,'* ***he said***, *'look it up in the dictionary.'*
   - *'Why are you going to the doctor's?'* ***she asked***. *'You're not ill, are you?'*

   If the two parts of the spoken words make up **a single sentence**, you begin the second part with a **lower-case letter** and put a **comma** after the saying verb:
   - *'You have spelt my name wrong,' I said, '**b**ut it doesn't matter.'*

   If the spoken words are **two separate sentences**, you begin the second part with a **capital letter** and put a **full stop** after the saying verb:
   - *'You have spelt my name wrong,' I said**.** '**T**here should be an "e" at the end.'*

4. When you put the **saying verb** before the spoken words, its **subject** comes first, as in a normal declarative sentence:
   - ***The man asked***, *'Is this your bike?'*
   - ***Lucy said***, *'Come with me. I want to show you something.'*

   When you put the **saying verb** after the spoken words, or in the middle of them, its **subject** still comes first if it is a **pronoun**:
   - *'Is this your bike?'* ***he asked***.
   - *'Come with me,'* ***she said***. *'I want to show you something.'*

   However, if the **subject** is a **name** or a **noun phrase**, it can come before or after the **saying verb** when this follows some or all of the spoken words:
   - *'Is this your bike?'* ***asked the man***.
   - *'Is this your bike?'* ***the man asked***.
   - *'Come with me,'* ***said Lucy***. *'I want to show you something.'*
   - *'Come with me,'* ***Lucy said***. *'I want to show you something.'*

5. The verbs most commonly used with direct speech are ***say***, ***ask*** and ***reply***, but there are many others. Using a variety of different verbs makes your writing more interesting. Here are some other possible verbs of **speaking**:

   admit, agree, announce, answer, call, complain, confess, cry, declare, exclaim, explain, murmur, observe, retort, state, whisper

   - *'I forgot to post the letter,'* ***confessed*** *Jack.*
   - *'You have to turn the key twice to lock the door,' she* ***explained***.
   - *The principal* ***announced***, *'Miss Lee is leaving at the end of this term.'*
   - *'Come back!' I* ***cried***.

   You can give shape to a conversation by using verbs such as ***add***, ***continue*** and ***go on***:

   'I may be late home this afternoon, Mum,' said James. 'There's a meeting of the drama club.'
   'Thanks for warning me,' his mother replied.

 ISBN 978-81-8477-745-1

'I'm hoping to get a part in the next play,' he ***continued****.*
'That would be great,' said his mother.
'In fact,' he ***went on****, 'I might get the leading part this time.'*

You can also use **thinking** verbs with direct speech:

- *'That's strange,' she* ***thought****.*
- *'Why are dogs more friendly than cats?' I* ***wondered****.*

6 When two or more people have a **conversation** in a story, you usually start a **new paragraph** for each speaker:

'Where's my jacket?' asked Dad.
'In the bedroom,' answered Mum.
'I'm also looking for my car keys,' announced Dad. 'Has anyone seen them?'
'They're on the coffee table here in the lounge,' I called.

New paragraphs are usually **indented**. In other words, you leave a space at the left-hand side before starting the new line.

7 If the conversation only involves **two people**, you can sometimes **omit the saying verb** after the first two paragraphs:

'Do you like my new dress?' asked Mary.
'Yes, it's lovely,' replied Kate. 'Where did you buy it?'
'I got it at that new boutique in the high street.'
'Was it very expensive?'
'It would have been, but luckily they were having a half-price sale that day.'

Indirect speech

1 You use **indirect speech** to tell another person what someone has said. You do not use quotation marks in indirect speech, and you usually do not give the exact words that the person said:

- *Joe asked Sue why she was crying.*
- *Jane said that she did not want to go to the party.*

2 You always put the **saying verb** and its **subject** at the beginning of the sentence in **indirect speech**. It is usually followed by a **noun clause**, which you learnt about in Unit 65:

- ***The principal announced that Miss Lee was leaving.***
- ***Jane explained why she did not want to go to the party.***
- ***The man said that he was looking for his dog.***

Remember that you can often omit the word ***that*** at the beginning of the noun clause:

- ***The man said he was looking for his dog.***
- ***Mum told us we could stay up late.***
- ***I thought I had failed the exam.***

 ISBN 978-81-8477-745-1

3 Various changes have to be made to a sentence when you turn direct speech into indirect speech. You will learn about these in the following sections.

How do you change direct speech to indirect speech?

1 When you change direct speech to indirect speech, you remove the **quotation marks** and change the **capital letter** at the beginning of the spoken words to a **lower-case letter** (unless it is a proper noun):

- *The man said, 'It might rain.'* (direct speech)
- *The man said **it** might rain.* (indirect speech)

2 If the **saying verb** follows some or all of the spoken words, you have to move it to the beginning of the sentence in indirect speech, putting the **subject** before the **verb**:

- *'The rash could be an allergy,' **said the doctor**.* (direct speech)
- ***The doctor said** the rash could be an allergy.* (indirect speech)
- *'I must leave at once,' **I said**, 'because I must not be late.'* (direct speech)
- ***I said** that I must leave at once because I must not be late.* (indirect speech)

If the verb ***say*** is followed by a phrase mentioning **the person addressed**, you often change this to ***tell*** + **object** in indirect speech:

- *'I might need some help,' I **said** to **Alan**.* (direct speech)
- *I **told Alan** that I might need some help.* (indirect speech)

3 If the spoken words contain a **pronoun** or **determiner** in the **first** or **second person**, this often changes to a **different person** in indirect speech:

- *'**I** should have asked **my** parents to help **me**,' admitted Tom.* (direct speech)
- *Tom admitted that **he** should have asked **his** parents to help **him**.* (indirect speech)
- *Our teacher said, '**You** ought to pass **your** exams after working so hard.'* (direct speech)
- *Our teacher said **we** ought to pass **our** exams after working so hard.* (indirect speech)

4 You often have to change the **tense** of the verb in the spoken words. A verb in the **simple present** usually changes to the **simple past** in indirect speech:

- *'The milk **is** in the fridge,' said Alice.* (direct speech)
- *Alice said the milk **was** in the fridge.* (indirect speech)
- *The boy announced, 'I **want** a new bike.'* (direct speech)
- *The boy announced that he **wanted** a new bike.* (indirect speech)

If the spoken words contain a verb in the **simple past**, this usually changes to the **past perfect** in indirect speech:

- *She said, 'Peter **forgot** to lock the door.'* (direct speech)
- *She said Peter **had forgotten** to lock the door.* (indirect speech)
- *'I **saw** Mr Jones in the supermarket,' remarked Sam.* (direct speech)
- *Sam remarked that he **had seen** Mr Jones in the supermarket.* (indirect speech)

 ISBN 978-81-8477-745-1

Sometimes the tense does not change, for example when you are **stating a fact**:

- *'Penguins **cannot** fly,' he explained.* (direct speech)
- *He explained that penguins **cannot** fly.* (indirect speech)
- *Jane said, 'It **was** Paul's fault.'* (direct speech)
- *Jane said it **was** Paul's fault.* (indirect speech)

5 If the spoken words contain a **verb phrase**, its **auxiliary verb** changes as follows:

DIRECT SPEECH		INDIRECT SPEECH
am/is/are	➔	***was/were***
was/were	➔	***had been***
has/have	➔	***had***
will/shall	➔	***would***
can	➔	***could***
may	➔	***might***

- *I said, 'I **am going** to the shops.'* (direct speech)
- *I said I **was going** to the shops.* (indirect speech)
- *'We **were trying** to help,' said the children.'* (direct speech)
- *The children said they **had been trying** to help.* (indirect speech)
- *'The plane **has landed**,' said Dad.* (direct speech)
- *Dad said that the plane **had landed**.* (indirect speech)
- *Sue said, 'I **can speak** Japanese.'* (direct speech)
- *Sue said she **could speak** Japanese.* (indirect speech)

The auxiliary verbs ***had***, ***should***, ***would***, ***could***, ***might***, ***must*** and ***ought*** do not change:

- *'The police **could** not **prove** that the man **had been** murdered,' said Carol.* (direct speech)
- *Carol said the police **could** not **prove** that the man **had been** murdered.* (indirect speech)
- *Harry said, 'I **would like** to help.'* (direct speech)
- *Harry said that he **would like** to help.* (indirect speech)

In **negative statements**, you change ***does/do not*** to ***did not*** and you change ***did not*** + **base form** to ***had not*** + **past participle**:

- *Sue said, 'I **do not** want to go.'* (direct speech)
- *Sue said she **did not** want to go.* (indirect speech)
- *I said, 'The bell **did not ring**.'* (direct speech)
- *I said that the bell **had not rung**.* (indirect speech)

6 You sometimes have to change other words or phrases, such as those referring to **time** or **place**:

- *Joe said, 'I posted the letter two days **ago**.'* (direct speech)
- *Joe said he had posted the letter two days **earlier**.* (indirect speech)

 ISBN 978-81-8477-745-1

- *'I'll fix your bike* ***tomorrow****,' promised Dad.* (direct speech)
- *Dad promised he would fix my bike* ***the following day****.* (indirect speech)
- *'I have been waiting* ***here*** *for half an hour,' complained Sally.* (direct speech)
- *Sally complained that she had been waiting* ***there*** *for half an hour.* (indirect speech)
- *Mum said, '****These*** *cakes are for our guests.'* (direct speech)
- *Mum said* ***those*** *cakes were for our guests.* (indirect speech)

How do you change a direct question to an indirect question?

You have to make some **extra changes** when you turn a **direct question** into an **indirect question**.

1 You must change the **question mark** to a **full stop** and put the **subject** before the **verb**:

- *'Where* ***is*** ***the manager's office****?' asked the woman.* (direct question)
- *The woman asked where* ***the manager's office*** ***was.*** (indirect question)
- *Mr Jones asked us, 'What* ***have*** ***you*** *been doing all day?'* (direct question)
- *Mr Jones asked us what* ***we*** ***had*** *been doing all day.* (indirect question)

Remember that in some ***wh*****-questions** the *wh*-word (or the phrase it introduces) is the **subject** of the **verb**, so the order does not change in the indirect question:

- *'****Who*** ***owns*** *the land?' he asked.* (direct question)
- *He asked* ***who*** ***owned*** *the land.* (indirect question)
- *I asked the hotel manager, '****Which room*** ***has*** *the best view?'* (direct question)
- *I asked the hotel manager* ***which room*** ***had*** *the best view.* (indirect question)

2 You do not put ***that*** at the beginning of the noun clause in an indirect question. However, for ***yes/no*** **questions** and **alternative questions** you must put ***if*** or ***whether*** instead:

- *'Have the police caught the thief?' she asked me.* (direct question)
- *She asked me* ***if*** *the police had caught the thief.* (indirect question)
- *I asked the assistant, 'Is the jumper made of wool or cotton?'* (direct question)
- *I asked the assistant* ***whether*** *the jumper was made of wool or cotton.* (indirect question)

3 If the direct question contains the structure ***Does/Do*** + **subject** + **base form**, you usually change this to **subject** + **simple past** in the indirect question:

- *'****Does*** ***the torch*** ***need*** *a battery?' he asked.* (direct question)
- *He asked whether* ***the torch*** ***needed*** *a battery.* (indirect question)
- *Mum asked Jack, '****Do*** ***you*** ***want*** *cola or lemonade?'* (direct question)
- *Mum asked Jack if* ***he*** ***wanted*** *cola or lemonade.* (indirect question)

You change ***Did*** + **subject** + **base form** to **subject** + ***had*** + **past participle**:

- *Paul asked me, '****Did*** ***Kate*** ***pass*** *her driving test?'* (direct question)
- *Paul asked me if* ***Kate*** ***had passed*** *her driving test.* (indirect question)

 ISBN 978-81-8477-745-1

- *'**Did any of you see** the man's face?' asked the police officer.* (direct question)
- *The police officer asked whether **any of us had seen** the man's face.* (indirect question)

4 If the direct question contains the **name of the person addressed**, you make this the **object** of the verb ***ask*** in the indirect question:

- *'Would you like a cup of tea, **Uncle Jack**?' I asked.* (direct question)
- *I asked **Uncle Jack** if he would like a cup of tea.* (indirect question)
- *Paul asked, 'Did you pass your driving test, **Kate**?'* (direct question)
- *Paul asked **Kate** whether she had passed her driving test.* (indirect question)

How do you change a direct command to an indirect command?

You have to make some **other changes** when you turn a **direct command** into an **indirect command**.

1 You have to change the **imperative verb** of the direct command (which is the same as the **bare infinitive**) to a ***to*-infinitive** in the indirect command. You also often change the **saying verb** to ***tell***:

- *'**Listen** carefully,' **said** the teacher.* (direct command)
- *The teacher **told** the students **to listen** carefully.* (indirect command)

The verb ***tell*** needs an **object**, and this is sometimes given in the direct command:

- *Mary **said**, '**Be** quiet, **children**.'* (direct command)
- *Mary **told the children to be** quiet.* (indirect command)

2 For **negative** commands, you change the structure ***Do not*** (or ***Don't***) + **bare infinitive** to ***not*** **+** ***to*-infinitive**:

- *'**Do not press** the red button,' said our instructor.* (direct command)
- *Our instructor told us **not to press** the red button.* (indirect command)
- *The nurse said, '**Don't be** frightened, Billy.'* (direct command)
- *The nurse told Billy **not to be** frightened.* (indirect command)

3 If the direct command ends with an **exclamation mark**, you change this to a **full stop** in the indirect command:

- *'Go away**!**' said my brother.* (direct command)
- *My brother told me to go away**.*** (indirect command)
- *Jane said, 'Don't touch my model**!**'* (direct command)
- *Jane told everyone not to touch her model**.*** (indirect command)

4 You can use several other verbs in place of ***tell*** in the indirect command:

- *'Don't give up,' said Dad.* (direct command)
- *Dad **urged** me not to give up.* (indirect command)
- *'Do not press the red button,' said our instructor.* (direct command)
- *Our instructor **warned** us not to press the red button.* (indirect command)
- *Miss Brown said, 'Stop talking, everyone!'* (direct command)
- *Miss Brown **ordered** everyone to stop talking.* (indirect command)

 ISBN 978-81-8477-745-1

- *Peter said, 'Take an umbrella in case it rains.'* (direct command)
- *Peter **advised** me to take an umbrella in case it rained.* (indirect command)

5 If the direct command begins with ***Please***, you should omit this word from the indirect command but change the saying verb to ***ask***, ***beg*** or something similar:

- *Mum said, '**Please** leave your muddy boots outside.* (direct command)
- *Mum **asked** us to leave our muddy boots outside.* (indirect command)
- *'**Please** help me, John!' cried the girl.* (direct command)
- *The girl **begged** John to help her.* (indirect command)

PRACTICE

Exercise 1

*Change the following sentences from **direct speech** to **indirect speech**.*

1. 'Where are you going, Sue?' asked Tom.

    ____

2. 'My feet are sore,' I complained.

    ____

3. 'Put your books away, children,' said the teacher.

    ____

4. 'I have a piano lesson this evening,' explained Jane.

    ____

5. 'Please pass me the salt, Paul,' said Mum.

    ____

6. 'It will be quicker to go by train,' thought Jack.

    ____

7. 'Don't forget to phone me when you arrive,' she said to her husband.

    ____

8. 'You should have been here half an hour ago,' Mr Lee told us.

    ____

9. 'Do you need any help, David?' asked Kate.

    ____

10. 'Stand up straight!' said Miss Smith to Billy.

    ____

Exercise 2

*Change the following sentences from **indirect speech** to **direct speech**. Put the saying verb after the direct speech.*

1. Jane asked why the red light was flashing.

    ____

 ISBN 978-81-8477-745-1

2. The doctor told me not to worry.

3. Dad announced that he had been promoted.

4. She begged me to forgive her.

5. Jack explained that evergreen trees don't lose their leaves.

6. Mary told Peter that it was his turn to wash the dishes.

7. He said he had been playing football with his friends.

8. The lifeguard advised us not to go swimming that afternoon.

9. Sally asked her father where he was going the following day.

10. They said they had finished their work an hour earlier.

Exercise 3

Fill in the blanks in the following passage with the verbs in the box. Use each word only once.

added	advised	asked	enquired	explained
replied	said	suggested	told	warned

Tom ________ his teacher if he could sit nearer the front of the classroom. 'I can't see the board very well,' he ________. His teacher ________ him that he might need glasses. 'Perhaps you should visit the school doctor,' she ________. 'He can test your eyes, and he will be able to recommend a good optician.' Tom went to see the doctor at lunchtime. The doctor gave Tom an eye test and ________ whether he had been suffering from headaches. 'No,' ________ Tom. 'However,' he ________, 'my eyes are often very sore at the end of the day.' The doctor ________ him to go and see an optician, and gave him some names and addresses. 'You must take care of your eyes,' he ________ him. 'They have to last you a long time!' Tom thanked him and ________ that he would ask his mother to make an appointment with one of the opticians he had recommended.

 ISBN 978-81-8477-745-1

UNIT 72

SYNTHESIS AND TRANSFORMATION

What do they look like?

'Where's my jacket?' asked Dad. 'It's hanging in the hall,' answered Mum. Dad said he was also looking for his car keys. He asked if any of us had seen them, but nobody had. We all hunted for the keys, and Sally eventually found them. Mum sighed with relief as we left the house. 'Peace and quiet at last!' she said.

What are they?

Synthesis and transformation are two ways in which you can vary your sentences by joining some of them together (**synthesis**) or changing their structure (**transformation**). Your writing will be more interesting to read if you use a mixture of long and short sentences and a variety of different sentence structures.

1. **Synthesis** involves joining sentences together with **conjunctions** and other **connectors**, which you learnt about in Chapter 8:
   - *The fruit was ripe. It tasted delicious.*
   - *The fruit was ripe **and** tasted delicious.*
   - *The baby started crying. Mrs Jones picked the baby up.*
   - *Mrs Jones picked the baby up **when** it started crying.*
   - *Joe likes one of the girls. She has long black hair.*
   - *The girl **whom** Joe likes has long black hair.*

2. **Transformation** involves changing the structure of sentences. For example, you can change **direct speech** to **indirect speech** (see Unit 71):
   - *Mary said, 'It is raining.'*
   - *Mary said it was raining.*

   You can change the **voice** of **verbs** from **active** to **passive** (see Unit 34):
   - *Fire **had destroyed** the building.*
   - *The building **had been destroyed** by fire.*

   You can change the **indirect object** of a ditransitive verb to a **prepositional phrase** (see Unit 33):
   - *The teacher gave **each child** a piece of paper.*
   - *The teacher gave a piece of paper **to each child**.*

   You can substitute one **connector** for another (which may involve making other changes to the sentence as well):
   - *I don't wear a sunhat **if** the sun isn't shining.*
   - *I don't wear a sunhat **unless** the sun is shining.*

 ISBN 978-81-8477-745-1

How do you use them?

Synthesis

1 You can use **co-ordinating conjunctions** (such as ***and***, ***but***, ***or***) and similar connectors (see Unit 62) to join two or three **simple sentences** that have something in common, or which form a contrast. The resulting longer sentence is called a **compound sentence**, which you learnt about in Unit 67:

- *Joe is studying. Sue is practising the piano. Sarah is reading.*
- *Joe is studying, Sue is practising the piano **and** Sarah is reading.*

- *The day started wet. It improved later.*
- *The day started wet **but** improved later.*

- *I had not made the beds. I had not washed the dishes.*
- *I had not made the beds **or** washed the dishes.*

- *My mother likes reading. My father prefers watching television.*
- *My mother likes reading, **whereas** my father prefers watching television.*

Remember that you do not need to repeat the subject if it is the same in both (or all) clauses of the compound sentence.

2 You can use **subordinating conjunctions** and other connectors to change one simple sentence to an **adverbial clause** (see Unit 63) and link it to another simple sentence. The resulting longer sentence is called a **complex sentence**, which you also learnt about in Unit 67.

The sentences may be related by **time**:

- *The dog barked. The thief ran away.*
- ***When** the dog barked, the thief ran away.*

- *Jack cooked the meat. Anna prepared the salad.*
- *Jack cooked the meat **while** Anna prepared the salad.*

The sentences may be related by **reason**:

- *Alice never goes in a boat. She is afraid of drowning.*
- *Alice never goes in a boat **because** she is afraid of drowning.*

- *The weather was fine. We had lunch on the patio.*
- ***As** the weather was fine, we had lunch on the patio.*

The sentences may be related by **purpose**:

- *Jane carried the bowl carefully. She didn't want to spill the soup.*
- *Jane carried the bowl carefully **so that** she wouldn't spill the soup.*

- *The teacher opened the window. She wanted to let some fresh air into the room.*
- *The teacher opened the window **in order to** let some fresh air into the room.*

 ISBN 978-81-8477-745-1

The sentences may be related by **result**:

- *The woman spoke quietly. Her voice couldn't be heard above the noise of the machinery.*
- *The woman spoke **so** quietly **that** her voice couldn't be heard above the noise of the machinery.*
- *The doctor is a very kind man. All his patients like him.*
- *The doctor is **such** a kind man **that** all his patients like him.*

3 You can sometimes **change the order** of the original sentences when you create the complex sentence:

- *The dog barked. The thief ran away.*
- *The thief ran away **when** the dog barked.*
- *Jack cooked the meat. Anna prepared the salad.*
- ***While** Anna prepared the salad, Jack cooked the meat.*
- *Alice never goes in a boat. She is afraid of drowning.*
- ***Because** she is afraid of drowning, Alice never goes in a boat.*
- *The weather was fine. We had lunch on the patio.*
- *We had lunch on the patio **as** the weather was fine.*
- *The teacher opened the window. She wanted to let some fresh air into the room.*
- ***In order to** let some fresh air into the room, the teacher opened the window.*

4 You can use **relative pronouns** and other connectors to change one simple sentence to a **relative clause** (see Unit 64) and add it to another simple sentence. This forms a different type of **complex sentence**:

- *Bill wants a book. It is on the top shelf.*
- *Bill wants a book **that** is on the top shelf.*
- *This bracelet is made of gold. It was a birthday present from my aunt.*
- *This bracelet, **which** was a birthday present from my aunt, is made of gold.*
- *The woman dived into the lake to rescue the boy. The boy couldn't swim.*
- *The woman dived into the lake to rescue the boy, **who** couldn't swim.*

5 You sometimes **make other changes** to the original sentences when you create a complex sentence in this way:

- *Sam lent me a pen. I have lost it.*
- *I have lost the pen **that** Sam lent me.*
- *Alice is my best friend. She lives next door.*
- *Alice, **who** is my best friend, lives next door.*
- *The president was speaking to some people. They looked bored.*
- *The people **to whom** the president was speaking looked bored.*

6 You can also join sentences by changing one of them into a **participial phrase** (see Unit 40) or a **noun phrase in apposition** (see Unit 7):

- *Joe checked that all the doors were locked. Then he went upstairs to bed.*
- ***Having checked that all the doors were locked**, Joe went upstairs to bed.*
- *Mr Green is an old family friend. He made a speech at my sister's wedding.*
- *Mr Green, **an old family friend**, made a speech at my sister's wedding.*

 ISBN 978-81-8477-745-1

Transformation

1. A passage of dialogue in a **narrative** or **personal recount** can be made more interesting by using a mixture of **direct speech** and **indirect speech** (as in the piece of text at the beginning of this unit). In Unit 71, you learnt about the changes that must be made to **verbs**, **pronouns**, **determiners** and **other words** when you turn direct speech into indirect speech:
   - *'I finished my homework an hour ago,' said Tom.* (direct speech)
   - *Tom said he had finished his homework an hour earlier.* (indirect speech)
   - *'Have you read this book, Anna?' asked Sue.* (direct speech)
   - *Sue asked Anna if she had read that book.* (indirect speech)

2. An **information report** or a **factual recount** can be made more interesting by using a mixture of **active verbs** and **passive verbs**. Here is a passage containing equal numbers of each:

   *What **happens** to our household waste? Some of it **is recycled**. We **put** paper, cans and bottles into separate bins, which **are taken** to the recycling centre for processing. Kitchen rubbish **goes** into a special container in the garden. There it **decomposes** and **changes** into compost, which **can be spread** on the soil to fertilize it. Waste that **cannot be re-used** in either of these ways **is buried** in large holes in the ground at landfill sites.*

3. In Unit 34, you learnt how to change the active voice to the passive voice. The **object** of the active sentence becomes the **subject** of the passive sentence:
   - *The principal presented **the prizes**.* (active)
   - ***The prizes** were presented by the principal.* (passive)
   - *A large animal was following **me**.* (active)
   - ***I** was being followed by a large animal.* (passive)

   Some sentences are not suitable for transformation from active to passive. These include those with **intransitive** verbs, which do not have an object:
   - *A ship **appeared** on the horizon.*
   - *The dog **ran** away.*

4. You can also change passive sentences to active sentences. The **subject** of the passive verb becomes the **object** of the active verb:
   - ***The match** was won by the home team.* (passive)
   - *The home team won **the match**.* (active)
   - ***The library** is used by all the students.* (passive)
   - *All the students use **the library**.* (active)

   However, some sentences cannot be easily transformed in this way. In the following example, there is no way of knowing who built the museum, so you cannot rewrite the sentence with an active verb (which would need a subject):
   - *The museum **was built** in the nineteenth century.*

 ISBN 978-81-8477-745-1

5. In Unit 33, you learnt about **ditransitive verbs**, which have a **direct object** and an **indirect object**:
   - *The teacher gave **each child** **a piece of paper**.*
   - *Sam bought **his mother** **a box of chocolates**.*

   You can transform these sentences by moving the indirect object to the end of the sentence, where it becomes the **object** of a **preposition** (usually *to* or *for*):
   - *The teacher gave a piece of paper **to** **each child**.*
   - *Sam bought a box of chocolates **for** **his mother**.*

   You can sometimes make the same change in reverse:
   - *I showed my bruised toe **to** **the doctor**.* → *I showed **the doctor** **my bruised toe**.*
   - *Alice cooked an excellent meal **for** **her friends**.* → *Alice cooked **her friends** **an excellent meal**.*

6. Earlier in this unit, you learnt about linking sentences with conjunctions and other connectors, in the process called synthesis. You should try to vary the connectors you use. Here are some pairs of examples to show you how **one connector** can be replaced by **another**:
   - *Joe asked Miss Grant a question **but** she did not know the answer.*
   - *Joe asked Miss Grant a question; **however,** she did not know the answer.*

   - *Michael's team lost the contest **because** he made a silly mistake.*
   - *Michael's team lost the contest **as a result of** his silly mistake.*

   - *She didn't stop running **until** she reached the station.*
   - *She only stopped running **when** she reached the station.*

   - *My aunt and uncle moved to China ten years **ago**.*
   - *It is ten years **since** my aunt and uncle moved to China.*

   - *I had **not** made the beds **or** washed the dishes.*
   - *I had **neither** made the beds **nor** washed the dishes.*

   Notice that you often have to make other changes to the structure of the sentence when you replace the connector.

 ISBN 978-81-8477-745-1

PRACTICE

Exercise 1

Rewrite the following pairs of sentences as **one compound** *or* **complex sentence,** *using the connectors and other words provided.*

1. The man at the door asked to see my ticket. The man was wearing a uniform.
   who ____________________
2. It stopped raining. We went for a walk.
   ____________________ when ____________________
3. Peter has dark hair. His brother has fair hair.
   ____________________ but ____________________
4. Sally left the library. She had found the information she required.
   Having ____________________
5. I jumped into the water. Can you guess what happened next?
   ____________________ after ____________________
6. Mr Brown picked up the broom. He began to sweep the path.
   and ____________________
7. Jack took his grandparents' address on holiday with him. He wanted to send them a postcard.
   ____________________ so that ____________________
8. Carol must work harder. Otherwise she will fail her exams.
   If ____________________
9. The museum is open from Monday to Saturday. It is closed on Sunday.
   except ____________________
10. You must turn the key twice. This will lock the door securely.
    In order to ____________________

Exercise 2

Rewrite the following sentences using an appropriate method of **transformation.**

1. My brother painted all the pictures in this room.
   ____
2. 'Be a good boy!' said Mrs Smith to her son.
   ____
3. Lung disease can be caused by air pollution.
   ____

 ISBN 978-81-8477-745-1

4. I dropped the cup; however, it did not break.

5. Julie showed her ticket to the inspector.

6. Tom and Alan did not receive a prize.

7. Has anyone told you how to use the machine?

8. I last saw Michael in August 2008.

9. Emma asked if she could borrow my calculator.

10. We bought the new baby a teddy bear.

Exercise 3

Rewrite the following passage using ***synthesis*** *and* ***transformation*** *where necessary to make it more varied and interesting.*

Jack went into the kitchen. He wanted to make an omelette for his lunch. He opened the fridge. In the fridge he found some eggs and a packet of butter. He closed the fridge door. One of the eggs slipped out of his hand. The egg broke on the floor. Jack got down on his hands and knees. He began to clear up the mess. The phone rang. It was Carol. Carol was one of his college friends. She invited him to her house for lunch. Jack was delighted. He finished cleaning the floor. Then he set off for Carol's house. On the way he stopped at the florist's. He bought a bunch of flowers for Carol.

Exercise 4: grammar for writing

Write a short narrative or personal recount, about 100 words long, about mending something or solving a problem. Vary the way you write your sentences as much as you can.

 ISBN 978-81-8477-745-1

10 PARAGRAPHS & TEXTS

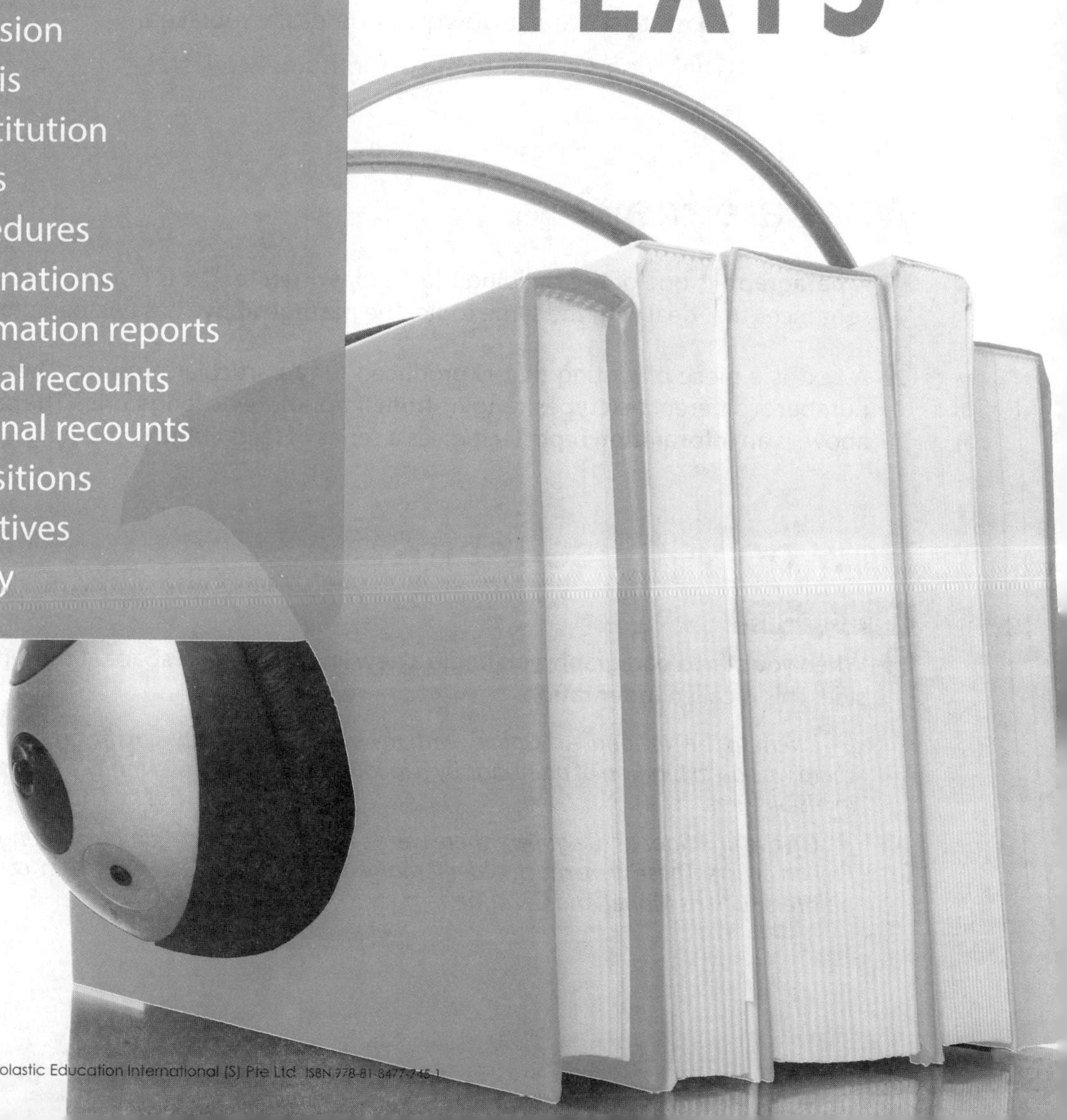

 ISBN 978-81-8477-745-1

UNIT 73

PARAGRAPHS AND TEXTS

What do they look like?

Coniferous trees are evergreen. This means that they do not lose their leaves in the winter. They have long narrow leaves called needles, and their fruit is a cone.

Many types of coniferous trees are grown commercially for timber. They grow quickly, so those that are cut down can be easily replaced. Their wood is used to make furniture.

What are they?

1. A **paragraph** is one of the building blocks of written text. It is made up of several sentences that deal with the same topic. The passage above has two paragraphs.

2. A **text** is a piece of writing that is produced for a particular purpose. There are a number of different **text types**, ranging from simple notes to long stories. The passage above is an **information report** – it gives a series of facts about something.

How do you use them?

Paragraphs

1. When you start a paragraph, you begin a new line and leave a space at the left-hand side. This is called **indentation**:

I went to the National Art Gallery with my parents yesterday. On the ground floor there was an exhibition of paintings by a local artist. I recognized many of the places in his pictures.

On the first floor of the gallery there were several rooms containing paintings by French artists. These were much older – many of them were by famous 19th-century painters such as Monet and Cézanne.

 ISBN 978-81-8477-745-1

2 Each paragraph should contain a sentence that tells the reader what the paragraph is about. This is called the **topic sentence**, and it usually comes at the beginning:

> ***On the first floor of the gallery, there were several rooms containing paintings by French artists.*** *Many of them were by famous 19th-century painters, such as Monet and Cézanne. The guide explained that these artists painted in a style called Impressionism.*
>
> ***There was a display of Japanese art on the second floor.*** *These were my mother's favourite pictures. She particularly liked the ones that featured birds and flowers.*

3 You can show how the sentences in a paragraph (or the paragraphs in a text) belong together by linking them with **connectors** and other devices. This gives the paragraph or text **cohesion**, which you will learn about in Units 74, 75 and 76:

> *There are many ways in which people can help to save the planet.* ***Firstly****, they can recycle more of their waste.* ***Secondly****, they can use their cars less.* ***For example****, they could go to work by bus or train instead of driving there.* ***Alternatively****, they could cycle or go on foot.*

Texts

There are many different text types, which can be grouped together as follows:

1 **Notes** are short messages that are usually written quickly for a **practical purpose**. They include emails, text messages on mobile phones, short letters, notices giving information to others and notes written as reminders for yourself. Notes often contain short forms of words or incomplete sentences:

- *See you on Wed at 6.30 – don't be late!*
- *No cycling on the promenade.*
- *Send cheque to Paul.*

You will learn more about **notes** in Unit 77.

2 **Procedures** are texts that tell you **how to do or make something**, such as a recipe or a set of instructions for operating a machine. They often take the form of a list of commands:

- *Break the eggs into a bowl. Add a little salt and pepper, and a few drops of water. Beat the eggs with a fork until they are thoroughly mixed.*
- *Switch on the computer. When the 'Welcome' screen appears, type in your name and password. Wait for the computer to load your personal desktop. Then click the icon for the software you want to use.*

You will learn more about **procedures** in Unit 78.

3 **Explanations** tell you **why something happens** or **how something works**. Writing of this kind is found in school textbooks, for example. It has the form of continuous text, often on a scientific subject:

- *Water has the chemical formula H_2O. It freezes at 0 degrees Celsius and turns into ice, which is a cold solid. It boils at 100 degrees Celsius and turns into steam, which is a fine mist.*

 ISBN 978-81-8477-745-1

- *Cars and other motor vehicles are powered by engines. They burn fuel, such as petrol or diesel. Moving parts connected to the engine make the wheels turn, driving the vehicle along.*

You will learn more about **explanations** in Unit 79.

4 **Information reports** provide **facts about something**, such as a country or a particular type of plant. They are found in encyclopedias, for example. The information is arranged in a systematic way:

- *London is the capital of England and the United Kingdom. It is a large city on the River Thames in the south-east of the country. There are many famous buildings and monuments, such as the Tower of London and the Houses of Parliament.*
- *Frogs are amphibians. This means that they can live on land or in the water. They spend the early part of their life swimming around as tadpoles, with a round body and a tail. Then they develop legs, which enable them to move around on land.*

You will learn more about **information reports** in Unit 80.

5 **Factual recounts** tell you what happened. They record or describe a **series of past events** in the order in which they occurred. News reports, for example, are factual recounts:

- *Heavy rain has caused severe flooding in many parts of the country. Rivers overflowed or burst their banks, and people living nearby had to leave their homes. Some older residents were rescued by boat. They have been given temporary accommodation in buildings on higher ground.*
- *Rail workers went on strike yesterday. There were no trains on any of the major routes, and many commuters were unable to get to work. A replacement bus service was laid on in some areas, but the journey was slow, due to all the extra traffic on the roads.*

You will learn more about **factual recounts** in Unit 81.

6 **Personal recounts** tell other people about **things you have done** or **things that have happened to you.** This type of text includes diary entries and autobiographies:

- *I was born in China and moved to Singapore with my family when I was five years old. After studying English and other languages at university, I became an international interpreter. My job takes me all around the world, and I meet many interesting people.*
- *I had a bit of an adventure on my way home from school yesterday. The bus broke down and I decided to walk the rest of the way. I took a short cut through the woods, where I found an old man lying on the path. At first I thought he was dead, but he was still breathing, so I used my mobile phone to call an ambulance.*

You will learn more about **personal recounts** in Unit 82.

7 **Expositions** are texts in which you give **your own opinion about something**. Examples of expositions include speeches, book or film reviews and readers' letters printed in newspapers or magazines. The aim of an exposition is often to persuade or convince other people:

 ISBN 978-81-8477-745-1

- *I believe that it is wrong to smack children. This is a form of physical violence, which should be made illegal. There are other ways of punishing children, or showing them that they have done something wrong. For example, they may be deprived of a treat or sent out of the room. This is often more effective, and is less likely to cause lasting harm.*
- *We are writing to complain about the plan to build a new airport near our village. This will destroy valuable agricultural land and wildlife habitats. The noise and traffic will also cause considerable discomfort and inconvenience to local residents.*

You will learn more about **expositions** in Unit 83.

8 **Narratives** are **stories** of all kinds, usually about **things that did not happen**. The main purpose of a narrative is to entertain people. However, some texts of this type, such as fables, are also intended to show people how they should behave:

- *Once upon a time, there was an old woman who lived all alone in a cottage. She had no relatives and very few friends because she was selfish and spiteful. Her only companion was a large black dog. It stayed with her faithfully, although she often treated it cruelly.*
- *Peter was a shepherd boy who looked after his father's sheep. He had to protect them from the wolves that lived in the forest. Sometimes, when he felt bored, he would cry 'Wolf!', even though nothing was wrong. The villagers came running to help him, and they were not at all pleased when Peter laughed at them. 'One of these days,' his father warned him, 'a wolf really will appear, and everyone will ignore your cries.'*

You will learn more about **narratives** in Unit 84.

9 **Poetry** has a distinctive form, being **written in lines** rather than as continuous text. These lines may or may not rhyme. The words used in poems are carefully chosen and arranged to create a particular effect:

- *Mary had a little lamb, its fleece was white as snow,*
And everywhere that Mary went, the lamb was sure to go.
- *The clock struck midnight;*
Twelve long, loud sounds rang through the air,
But no-one heard –
Everyone was dead.

You will learn more about **poetry** in Unit 85.

PRACTICE

Exercise 1

Read the following sentences and say which of the nine **text types** *listed above they come from. The first one has been done to help you.*

1. I sat by the lake and watched the children feeding the ducks. *personal recount*

2. The magician waved his wand and the prince turned into a frog. ________

3. The plant grows in hot, damp regions near the equator. ________

4. Hope to see you soon. ________

5. I do not think people should have to pay for emergency medical treatment. ________

6. Remove the old ink cartridge and dispose of it carefully. ________

7. A plane's wings are shaped in a way that gives it 'lift', which helps to keep it in the air. ________

8. There was a riot in the town centre yesterday afternoon. ________

Exercise 2

Write the ***topic sentences*** *for a five-paragraph essay about one of your grandparents or some other person of that generation, real or imaginary.*

____

____

____

Exercise 3

Rewrite the following passage in ***three*** *paragraphs. When you have finished, underline the* ***topic sentences****.*

The town of Rivermouth is on the south coast. Over the years, it has grown from a small fishing village to a large busy port. During that time, people have come to live here from all over the world. It is now one of the most multicultural places in the country. There is a wide variety of architecture, old and new, in different areas of the town. The oldest part is close to the place where the river meets the sea. There are many narrow streets full of interesting buildings, including some of the original fishermen's cottages. The northern part of the town was developed later, in the nineteenth and twentieth centuries. The town has a number of industries in addition to those centred on the port. There is a large car factory, and a new technology park has recently opened. It contains several small businesses producing electronic goods.

____

____

____

 ISBN 978-81-8477-745-1

UNIT 74

COHESION

What does it look like?

My sister and I were clearing out the attic. I found a pile of books, **some of which** were bound with leather. 'Could **these** be valuable?' I asked. My sister **said** that **she** didn't think **so**. **'However,' she added**, 'we should perhaps show **them** to an expert. The leather-bound **ones** look very old.'

What is it?

Cohesion makes a text easier and more interesting to read. You can give a text cohesion by using grammatical devices that link the words, phrases, sentences and paragraphs together. These **cohesive devices** may be words and phrases (such as **pronouns** and **connectors**) or techniques (such as **ellipsis** and **substitution**).

How do you give a text cohesion?

There are five different types of cohesion: **reference**, **conjunction**, **repetition**, **ellipsis** and **substitution**.

Reference

1. **Reference** chiefly involves the use of **pronouns** and other words or phrases to refer **back** to **someone or something previously mentioned**:
   - *Tom asked Alice if **she** would help **him** with **his** homework.*
   - ***The jeweller** examined **the rings**. **He** said that **none of them** were valuable.*
   - *Here are **the photos** I took at **summer camp**. **This one** is my favourite. **It** is a picture of all the new friends I made **there**.*
   - *As you learnt **earlier**, the word 'we' is a personal pronoun.*
   - *The use of drugs to treat cancer was mentioned in the **previous** chapter.*

2. It also occasionally involves referring **forward** to **someone or something about to be mentioned**:
   - *You may find **this** hard to believe, but **the pilot of the plane is afraid of heights**.*
   - *In the **next** chapter, we will discuss the effect of climate change on plants.*

 ISBN 978-81-8477-745-1

3 Using a **personal pronoun** in place of a previously used **noun** or **noun phrase** is a very common form of **reference**:

- *Sue and I can give James his birthday present when **we** see **him** tomorrow.*
- *Dad has lost his mobile phone again. **He** is always losing **it**.*

The personal pronoun ***it*** can also refer **back** or **forward** to a **situation** or **circumstance**:

- *Many people think they would like to learn how to fly a plane, until they find out how expensive **it** is.*
- ***It** isn't easy, feeding a family on a hundred dollars a week.*

4 You can also use **possessive** and **interrogative** pronouns and some **quantifiers** in this way:

- *This must be your prize, Jane – all the other winners have collected **theirs**.*
- *You have four hats to choose from. **Which** do you like best?*
- *I needed some sugar, but I couldn't find **any**.*

5 You use the **demonstrative pronouns *that*** and ***those*** to refer to **something just mentioned**:

- *Helen has lost her cat. **That** is why she looks upset.*
- *Bedrooms on the first floor have en suite bathrooms, but **those** on the second floor do not.*

6 You can use the **demonstrative pronouns *this*** and ***these*** to refer to **something just mentioned** or **something about to be mentioned**:

- *The battery may be flat. **This** is the most likely problem.*
- *You used a singular noun with a plural verb and you spelt one word wrong. **These** were your only mistakes.*
- *They haven't named the full team, but I can tell you **this** – Harry isn't in it.*
- ***These** are the main causes of obesity: eating too much and not taking enough exercise.*

7 You can use ***there*** to refer back to a **place** and ***then*** to refer back to a **time**:

- *Sam Brown lives in Penang. He moved **there** several years ago.*
- *I will try to finish the work at the weekend, as I have some free time **then**.*

Conjunction

1 **Conjunction** involves the use of **connectors** to link words, phrases, clauses or sentences:

- *You may bring your mobile phone to school with you; **however**, you must switch it off during lessons.*
- *We do not need a car. **Besides**, we have nowhere to keep one.*

 ISBN 978-81-8477-745-1

2. You learnt about using **connectors** in Chapter 8. Here are some longer examples, showing how connectors can give **cohesion** to a whole paragraph:
   - *There are many ways in which people can help to save the planet.* ***Firstly****, they can recycle more of their waste.* ***Secondly****, they can use their cars less.* ***For example****, they could go to work by bus or train instead of driving there.* ***Alternatively****, they could cycle or go on foot.*
   - *Doing voluntary work makes young people feel useful. It* ***also*** *gives them confidence,* ***and*** *helps to prepare them for adult life. Society as a whole benefits from this,* ***as well as*** *those directly helped by the youngsters.* ***Moreover****, because voluntary workers are unpaid, they do not put a strain on their country's economy.*

Repetition

1. **Repetition** involves **repeating words or structures**:
   - *It* ***rained*** *and* ***rained*** *all afternoon.*
   - ***Boys, boys, boys:*** *that's all she ever talks about.*
   - ***I looked in*** *my schoolbag,* ***I looked in*** *my desk drawer,* ***I looked in*** *my locker – I couldn't find my workbook anywhere.*

2. As well as giving a text cohesion, repetition can also **add emphasis**. The following example comes from a famous speech made by the British prime minister Winston Churchill during World War II:
   - ***We shall fight*** *on the beaches,* ***we shall fight*** *on the landing grounds,* ***we shall fight*** *in the fields and in the streets,* ***we shall fight*** *in the hills;* ***we shall*** *never surrender.*

3. You can also use repetition **for effect in poetry**, as in the following lines from the poem 'The Charge of the Light Brigade' by Lord Tennyson:
   - ***Cannon to right of them,***
Cannon to left of them,
Cannon in front of them
Volleyed and thundered.

Ellipsis

Ellipsis involves **omitting** unnecessary words to avoid repeating what has just been said:

- *John can run faster than I can (****run****).*
- *Is this your camera?' 'No, it isn't (****my camera****).'*

You will learn about **ellipsis** in Unit 75.

Substitution

Substitution involves **replacing** one word or set of words with another:

- *I haven't printed out my essay; I'll* ***do it*** (= print out my essay) *later.*
- *'Is it going to rain?' 'I hope* ***not*** (= I hope it won't rain).'

You will learn about **substitution** in Unit 76.

 ISBN 978-81-8477-745-1

PRACTICE

Exercise 1

Underline the word, phrase or clause that the word in bold print refers to.

1. If you see Sarah, tell **her** to phone me as soon as possible.
2. Tom offered the boy a drink, but he didn't want **one**.
3. I put the stapler back in the drawer, so it should still be **there**.
4. Jane shows her paintings to all her friends – she's very proud of **them**.
5. **It** might be a good idea to take an umbrella.
6. Visitors with tickets can go straight in. **Those** without must wait in the queue.
7. What concerns us is **this**: where will the money come from?
8. 'I need 100 grams of sultanas.' 'You'll find **some** in that cupboard, on the top shelf.'
9. She had hoped to catch an earlier train, but **that** was not possible.
10. You should visit England in August – the weather is warmer **then**.

Exercise 2

The bold words and phrases in the following passage are examples of cohesion. Say whether this is reference (Ref), conjunction (C), repetition (Rep), ellipsis (E) or substitution (S).

'Have you tidied your bedroom yet, Sally?' asked Mrs Smith. 'No, **I haven't** ( ),' replied Sally. 'I'll **do it** ( ) later.' Mrs Smith sighed. **It** ( ) wasn't easy, getting **her** ( ) children to look after **their** ( ) rooms. **However** ( ), Sally's room was not as untidy as **her brother's** ( ). He had a habit of dropping his clothes all over the place. There were **clothes on his desk, clothes on the bed, clothes on his chair and clothes on the floor** ( ) – anywhere but in the wardrobe! He always said he was too busy with his schoolwork and other activities to put things away, **but** ( ) **that** ( ) was just an excuse. In reality, he was simply a very lazy boy.

 ISBN 978-81-8477-745-1

Exercise 3

Fill in the blanks with the connectors in the box. You will need to use some of them more than once.

also	furthermore	but	otherwise	as well	despite
for example	in order to	first	however	if	and
in other words	in that case	or	finally	then	unless

You do not need exceptional talent to become a good musician; ____________, you should be prepared to do plenty of practice. ____________, you must choose an instrument. ____________ decide which is best for you, think about where you want to play: in an orchestra ____________ in a rock band. ____________, you have to consider your neighbours, ____________ you are going to practise at home. ____________, you should not choose the trumpet ____________ you live in a house with very thick walls!

It will help if you already know how to read music. ____________ you won't know what all the black dots and lines mean. You can teach yourself, ____________ it might be better to find a teacher. It is ____________ a good idea to hire your instrument rather than buying one straight away. ____________ you won't lose a lot of money ____________ you change your mind.

____________, remember that playing music is supposed to be fun. ____________, you should enjoy it. ____________, it ought to give pleasure to others ____________. You may find that, ____________ your best efforts, your music-making does neither of those things. ____________ it is probably time to give up ____________ find another hobby.

 ISBN 978-81-8477-745-1

UNIT 75

ELLIPSIS

What does it look like?

Kate: It's rather cold in here, isn't it?

Alice: Yes, it is. I would turn this heater on if I could, but I don't know how to.

Kate: Neither do I. We'll have to run around to keep warm.

Alice: You can if you want. I'll just sit here and shiver.

What is it?

Ellipsis is the **omission** of words that do not need to be repeated. The hearer or reader already knows – or can easily guess – what they are. This often happens in answers to questions and various other situations:

- *'Where are the paintbrushes?'* ***'In the cupboard.'*** (= The paintbrushes are in the cupboard.)
- *With your young eyes you can thread a needle more easily* ***than I can.*** (= than I can thread a needle)
- *Shall we go by bus* ***or train****?* (= or shall we go by train)
- *Harry was not at the meeting,* ***nor was Joe.*** (= nor was Joe at the meeting)
- *Come early* ***if possible.*** (= if it is possible to come early)

How do you use it?

1 As you learnt in Unit 69, the answer to a ***wh*-question** can often be reduced to the **piece of information** that the ***wh*-word** asks for:

- ***'Where*** *did you put my shirt?'* ***'In the wardrobe.'*** (= Your shirt is in the wardrobe.)
- ***'How*** *did you get here?'* ***'By bus.'*** (= I came by bus.)

2 You also learnt in Unit 69 that the answer to a ***yes/no* question** can simply be ***yes*** or ***no***. However, this is often followed by a **pronoun** and the **auxiliary verb** (or a form of ***be***) from the beginning of the question:

- *'Is she angry?'* ***'Yes.'*** (= Yes, she is angry.)
- *'Do you like sushi?'* ***'No.'*** (= No, I do not like sushi.)
- ***'Has*** *the dishwasher finished yet?'* ***'Yes, it has.'*** (= Yes, it has finished.)
- ***'Did*** *the man have a beard?'* ***'No, he didn't.'*** (= No, he did not have a beard.)

 ISBN 978-81-8477-745-1

Sometimes the word ***yes*** is omitted:

- *'**Were** the judges impressed?' '**They were**.'* (= Yes, they were impressed.)
- *'**Did** Sally forget your birthday again?' '**She did**.'* (= Yes, she forgot my birthday.)

Sometimes, the answer contains a **different auxiliary verb** from **the one in the question**:

- *'**Will** you tell your parents?' 'I already **have**.'* (= I have already told my parents.)
- *'**Is** Sam coming with us?' He **might**.'* (= He might come with us.)

3 You also use ellipsis in **question tags** and their **answers**:

- *'Miss Lee is in a good mood today, **isn't she**?' 'Yes, **she is**.'* (= Yes, she is in a good mood today.)
- *'You have never been to China, **have you**?' 'No, **I haven't**.'* (= No, I have never been to China.)

4 You often use ellipsis in **other responses**, such as **agreement** or **contradiction**:

- *'They have made a terrible mess of the garden.' '**They certainly have**.'* (= They have certainly made a terrible mess of the garden.)
- *'I think it is going to rain.' '**It may not**.'* (= It may not rain.)

A response may also be a ***wh*-word** or a short **question**:

- *'I'm going to England.' '**When?**'* (= When are you going to England?)
- *'You shouldn't go swimming straight after a large meal.' '**Why not?**'* (= Why shouldn't I go swimming straight after a large meal?)

5 You sometimes use ellipsis in the second part of a **compound or complex sentence**, after a **conjunction**:

- *We thought Dad would be angry, **but** he wasn't.* (= he was not angry)
- *I said I would finish my project today, **and** I have.* (= I have finished my project)
- *You have written far more **than** anyone else has.* (= than anyone else has written)
- *They can stay overnight **if** they want.* (= if they want to stay overnight)

There is often a **change in tense**, as well as the omission of the last part of the verb phrase:

- *Mum **hasn't noticed** the scratch on her car yet, but she soon **will**.*
- *I **didn't** understand, and I still **don't**.*

6 The words ***so***, ***neither***, ***nor***, ***either*** and ***too*** are often used in ellipsis to show that things (such as people's thoughts or feelings) are the same. You put the **subject** after the **verb** when you use ***so***, ***neither*** or ***nor*** in this way:

- *'I'm exhausted!' '**So am I**.'*
- *Tom did not feel very hungry, and **neither did Sue**.*
- *We weren't satisfied with our performance. **Nor was our director**.*

 ISBN 978-81-8477-745-1

You put *either* or *too* at the end, and you leave the **subject** in its usual place before the **verb**:

- *'I have never read any of her books.' '**I haven't** either.'*
- *The children were terrified, and **some of their parents** were too.*

You can use the structure **subject** + **negative verb** + *either* in place of *neither* + **positive verb** + **subject** or *nor* + **positive verb** + **subject**:

- *Tom did not feel very hungry, and neither **did Sue**.*
- *Tom did not feel very hungry, and **Sue didn't** either.*
- *'I have never read any of her books.' 'Nor **have I**.'*
- *'I have never read any of her books.' '**I haven't** either.'*

You can use the structure **subject** + **verb** + *too* in place of *so* + **verb** + **subject**:

- *'I'm exhausted!' 'So **am I**.'*
- *'I'm exhausted!' '**I am** too.'*
- *The children were terrified, and so **were some of their parents**.*
- *The children were terrified, and **some of their parents were** too.*

If the verb in the first part of the sentence or dialogue is in the **simple present** or the **simple past**, you use ***do*** in the second part.

- *'I **think** the girl is telling the truth.' 'So **do** I.'*
- *Tom **failed** the exam, and most of his classmates **did** too.*

7 Shortening a ***to*-infinitive** to ***to*** is another form of ellipsis:

- *'Who is going to provide the drinks?' 'Sally has offered **to**.'* (= to provide the drinks)
- *Bill finally accepted the medal, though he was initially reluctant **to**.* (= to accept the medal)
- *Please don't walk so fast. There's no need **to**.* (= to walk so fast)
- *I think you can change the size of the picture, but I don't know how **to**.* (= to change the size of the picture)
- *'Don't drop the tray.' 'I'll try not **to**.'* (= to drop the tray)

8 You can sometimes omit the subject and verb from an **adverbial clause**:

- *You can write on both sides of the paper **if necessary**.* (= if it is necessary)
- ***While in China**, I shall visit my grandparents.* (= While I am in China)

9 You use ellipsis to shorten a **relative clause** to a **participial phrase** or a **prepositional phrase**:

- *The girls looked at the pictures **hanging on the walls**.* (= that were hanging on the walls)
- *None of the people **in the theatre** noticed anything unusual.* (= who were in the theatre)

10 You often do not need to repeat a noun after **numbers**, **possessive nouns** and **superlatives**:

- *I have one sister. My friend Sarah has **three**.*
- *Alan's suitcase was on the carousel but **Tom's** was missing.*
- *There were many suggestions, and **the most useful** were passed on to the president.*

 ISBN 978-81-8477-745-1

PRACTICE

Exercise 1

Complete the answers to the following questions with a **pronoun** *and a positive or negative* **verb**. *The first one has been done to help you.*

1. 'Has Jane found her watch yet?' 'No, *she hasn't*.'
2. 'Can you hear a ticking noise?' 'No, ________.'
3. 'Are these your boots?' 'Yes, ________.'
4. 'Was the bed comfortable?' 'Yes, ________.'
5. 'Will your brother help us?' 'No, ________.'
6. 'Has it stopped raining yet?' 'Yes, ________.'
7. 'Did the critics like the film?' 'No, ________.'
8. 'Must I wear a safety helmet?' 'Yes, ________.'
9. 'Does this box have a lid?' 'No, ________.'
10. 'Shouldn't the drinks be in the fridge?' 'Yes, ________.'

Exercise 2

Rewrite the following sentences using **neither** *of instead* **either**, *and* **so** *instead of* **too**. *The first one has been done to help you.*

1. Sam is frightened of spiders, and his sister is too.

   Sam is frightened of spiders, and so is his sister.

2. None of my classmates noticed my mistake, and the teacher didn't either.

   ____

3. Sally hasn't finished her assignment, and I haven't either.

   ____

4. The door was locked, and the windows were too.

   ____

5. I can't open this jar, and Dad can't either.

   ____

 ISBN 978-81-8477-745-1

6. Sue has apologized, and you should too.

7. That pen won't write, and this one won't either.

8. Joe is going to the wedding, and his parents are too.

9. The farmhouse has been demolished, and some of the outbuildings have too.

10. Joe doesn't wear glasses, and none of his friends do either.

Exercise 3

In the following passage, cross out all the words that could be omitted using ***ellipsis****.*

Joe wanted to photocopy some documents. 'Is there a photocopier at the library?' he asked his wife. 'Yes, there is a photocopier at the library,' she replied. Joe put the documents into his briefcase and he set off for the library. When he got there, he asked the woman who was standing behind the information desk where the photocopier was. 'We have three photocopiers,' she replied. 'One photocopier is over there in the reference department and there are two more photocopiers upstairs.' 'Which machine is the easiest one to operate?' asked Joe. 'I haven't used a photocopier for some time. I may have forgotten how to use one.' The woman asked Joe if his documents were in colour or if they were in black-and-white. 'They are in black-and-white,' replied Joe. 'In that case,' said the woman, 'I recommend that you use the machine in the reference department. It is very simple to operate, but if you have any difficulty, the librarian there will show you what to do.'

 ISBN 978-81-8477-745-1

UNIT 76

SUBSTITUTION

What does it look like?

David:	Is this the **right** train?
Peter:	I think **so**.
David:	We need to be sure. We don't want to get on the **wrong one**. I **did that** last week and ended up a long way from where I wanted to go.
Peter:	That must have been very **annoying**.
David:	Yes, it was **infuriating**.

What is it?

1. **Substitution** is the use of words such as ***so***, ***not***, ***do*** and ***one*** to replace a **more specific expression** that has just been used:
   - *'Have you got everything you need?' 'I think **so**.'* (= I think I have everything I need)
   - *Which bag do you prefer – the brown **one** or the black **one**?* (= the brown bag or the black bag)

2. Another form of substitution, called **lexical substitution**, involves the use of **synonyms** (words with similar meanings), **antonyms** (words with opposite meanings) and other sets of related words:
   - *A **huge** monster appeared, with an **enormous** head, a **large** round body, **long** legs and **big** flat feet.*
   - *I've **won** every match I've played so far, and I do not intend to **lose** this one!*

How do you use it?

Using *so* and *not*

1. You can use **so** in place of a **noun clause** after verbs such as ***hope***, ***think***, ***believe***, ***expect***, ***suppose***, ***say*** or ***seem***:
   - *'Is the bridge safe?' 'I think **so**.'* (= I think **the bridge is safe**.)
   - *'Has everyone heard the news?' 'I expect **so**.'* (= I expect **that everyone has heard the news**.)
   - *'You have to fill in this form.' 'Who says **so**?'* (= Who says **I have to fill in the form**?)
   - *'Has the concert been cancelled.' 'It seems **so**.'* (= It seems **that the concert has been cancelled**.)

 ISBN 978-81-8477-745-1

2 You sometimes use ***not*** when the noun clause is negative:

- *'Will the plant die?' 'I hope **not**.'* (= I hope **that the plant will not die**.)
- *'Was anything broken?' 'It appears **not**.'* (= It appears **that nothing was broken**.)

However, you often use a **negative verb** with ***so*** instead:

- *'Will Sally mind if I borrow her calculator?' 'I **don't suppose so**.'* (= I suppose **Sally will not mind if you borrow her calculator**.)
- *'Are there any biscuits left?' 'I **don't think so**.'* (= I think **there are no biscuits left**.)

Using *do*

1 You can use ***do*** with ***so*** to refer back to **an action or activity** already mentioned:

- *Anna hated **hurting people**, and never **did so** deliberately.*
- *If you haven't **paid your subscription** yet, please **do so** as soon as possible.*

2 You sometimes use ***do*** with ***it*** or ***that*** in a similar way:

- *Jane said she would **make the cake**, but you could **do it** instead if you like.*
- *'Have you **phoned Michael** yet?' 'No, Iíll **do that** now.'*

Using *one* or *ones*

1 You can use ***one*** as a substitute for a **singular countable noun**:

- *I enjoy my **job**, but I'd prefer **one** with less stress.*
- *May we sit at a different **table**? This **one** is in a draught.*
- *It was Joe's **idea**, and nobody else could think of a better **one**.*
- *Give me your **email address** if you have **one**.*

2 You use the plural form ***ones*** as a substitute for a **plural countable noun**:

- *These **trousers** are a bit tight; the other **ones** fit me better.*
- *The **photos** I took on holiday this year are not as good as the **ones** I took last year.*

3 You cannot use ***one*** or ***ones*** as a substitute for an **uncountable noun**. You must use ***some*** or ***any*** instead:

- *'Can I have **ice cream** for dessert?' 'No, there isn't **any** left.'*
- *The plants looked as if they needed **water**, so I gave them **some**.*

Lexical substitution

1 Using **synonyms** can make your writing more interesting, as well as binding the text together:

- *I saw a **lovely** jumper on a dummy in the shop window. It was a **beautiful** shade of blue. I thought it would look **nice** with the trousers I was wearing, so I went inside to try it on. However, it did not look as **attractive** on me as it did on the dummy.*
- *Bill **ran** out of the house and **sprinted** to the bus stop, only to see the bus pulling away from the stop. He would have to go on foot instead, so he **sped** off down the road. Arriving at the building where he worked, he **dashed** up the stairs and **raced** along the corridor to his office.*

 ISBN 978-81-8477-745-1

2. Using **antonyms** helps to link and contrast different parts of a sentence or paragraph:
   - *Jack sold his **old** bike and bought a **new** one.*
   - *Carol **arrived** at the interview feeling full of confidence, but it did not go well. She **departed** with a very glum face.*

3. You can also use other sets of words and phrases that are related in meaning. In the following example, all the highlighted words have something to do with having fun and socializing:
   - *Everyone **enjoyed themselves** at the **party**. The younger children **played games**, the older ones **danced** to pop music, and the adults **chatted** to each other, **making new friends** and generally **having a good time**.*

PRACTICE

Exercise 1

Write down the word, phrase or clause that the words in bold print have replaced. The first one has been done to help you.

1. I'm going to make myself a cup of tea. Would you like **one**? (= *a cup of tea*)
2. Sue promised to phone me but she hasn't **done so** yet. (= ________)
3. 'Have all the tickets been sold?' 'I hope **not**.' (= ________)
4. The printer may have run out of paper – you'll find **some** on the shelf below it. (= ________)
5. These shoes have white laces and those have black **ones**. (= ________)
6. Tom couldn't thread the needle, so I offered to **do it** for him. (= ________)
7. 'Do we need a visa?' 'I believe **so**.' (= ________)
8. Be careful with the paint. If you spill **any**, wipe it up immediately. (= ________)
9. 'Have the police caught the thief?' 'It appears **not**.' (= ________)
10. I haven't finished my essay yet. I'll **do that** this evening. (= ________)

Exercise 2

Fill in the blanks with an appropriate synonym or antonym of the word in bold print.

1. Dad managed to **mend** the puncture but he couldn't ________ the damaged wheel.

 ISBN 978-81-8477-745-1

2. The shops open **early** and close ______________, which makes a very long working day for the staff.
3. I **tossed** the empty can to Sally, who ______________ it into the bin.
4. Billy was **asleep**, but his brother was ______________.
5. She **gave** her ticket to the inspector. He punched it and ______________ it back to her.
6. James **spotted** two errors and his teacher ______________ three more.
7. The dog has very **long** ears but a very ______________ tail.
8. He is a **talented** artist and a ______________ writer.
9. I **hate** classical music, whereas my friend Sally ______________ it.
10. It was a very **warm** day, but the water was refreshingly ______________.

Exercise 3

*Rewrite the following passage using **substitution** to give it more cohesion.*

Jane tripped and fell down the stairs. Her brother heard the noise and ran to see what was wrong. 'Have you hurt yourself?' he asked. 'I don't think I have hurt myself,' she replied. However, her back was painful and her elbows were painful. She stood up, but as she stood up, she felt a sharp pain in her foot. She sat down again on the bottom stair and looked at her ankles. The right ankle was badly swollen. 'I think you should go to the hospital,' said her brother. 'It looks as if you have broken your ankle.' 'I hope I haven't broken it,' said Jane. 'I'm supposed to be playing in a hockey match tomorrow.'

____

____

____

____

____

____

____

 ISBN 978-81-8477-745-1

UNIT 77

NOTES

What do they look like?

Dear Kate,

Thanks for sending the photo of your new nephew. He looks adorable! What does it feel like to be an aunt? And how are your brother and sister-in-law coping with parenthood? I guess they won't be doing so much travelling around now!

Hope you have a great time in Tokyo – call me when you get back.

love

Sally

What are they?

A **note** is a text that sends a message, gives a reminder or provides information as briefly as possible. It often contains only the most important words, and sometimes even these are shortened. The following types of texts may be notes:

- **emails**
- **short informal letters**
- **shopping lists**
- **text messages**
- **signs and notices**
- **lesson notes**
- **postcards**
- **advertisements**
- **essay plans**

What are their main language features?

1. Some types of notes contain **imperative verbs**. These include notices in public places and reminders you write to yourself:
   - *Please **use** the footpath.*
   - ***Pay** electricity bill.*

   Some signs and notices have **gerunds** instead:
   - *No **cycling** or **skateboarding**.*

2. Some types of notes use indicative verbs but **omit the subject pronoun** and/or **part of the verb phrase**. These include short emails and postcards:
   - *See you tomorrow at 6.30.* (= ***I will** see you …*)
   - *Having a great time here in Thailand.* (= ***We are** having a great time …*)

 ISBN 978-81-8477-745-1

3. Other words may be omitted, such as **articles** or the verb ***be***, especially from an advertisements or at the beginning of an informal letter:
   - *All items in very good condition, some brand new.* (= *All **the** items **are** in very good condition, **and** some **are** brand new.*)
   - *Just a quick note to say thank you for the lovely flowers you sent me.* (= ***This is** just a quick note …*).

4. Most types of notes use **contractions**:
   - ***We're** having a party – can you come?*
   - ***I'll** send you a photo.*

5. Many use other **shortened forms** of words:
   - *Hope to finish the work **Fri pm, v.** sorry for the delay.* (= … ***Friday afternoon, very** sorry …*)
   - *Let me know **asap** if you can't come.* (= … ***as soon as possible** …*)

   Text messages sometimes replace a whole word with a single letter that sounds the same:
   - ***C U** at 6.* (= *I'll **see you** at 6.*)

6. Notes often contain **prepositional phrases**:
   - *Do not park **outside these gates.***
   - *I'll meet you **by the bridge at 9.30.***

How do you write them?

1. When you write a **short informal letter**, you put ***Dear*** before the name of the person you are writing to, as you would in any other kind of letter. You normally write in complete sentences, though the first and last sentence may be shortened:

> *Dear Uncle Jack,*
>
> *Sorry to hear you're not well. I was going to come and see you at the weekend, but Mum said you probably won't want any visitors. Many thanks for my birthday card – I'm sending you a photo of my birthday party, to cheer you up a bit!*
>
> *Hope you feel better soon.*
>
> *love*
>
> *Tom*

 ISBN 978-81-8477-745-1

2 When you write an **email**, you can put ***Hi*** or ***Hello*** in front of the person's name instead of ***Dear***, or you can just type the name. Your message does not have to be in complete sentences, and you can use any short forms that the other person will understand:

> *Hi Sue*
>
> *Hope all is well with you. Any news about Bill's job yet? We're all keeping our fingers crossed for him! See you on Fri – don't be late!*
>
> *love*
>
> *Carol*

3 When you write a **postcard**, you usually just write the message, using shortened sentences and other short forms, and put your name at the end:

- *Having a great time here in Japan. Hotel is v. comfortable, and the food is superb! Visited a beautiful garden today, tomorrow we're off to Tokyo. Weather mostly good, tho' it's raining at the moment. See you soon. love Bob and Mary*

4 When you write an **advertisement**, you give only the relevant information, in phrases or incomplete sentences:

- *FOR SALE: Assorted children's clothing, various sizes, for boys and girls aged 5–10. Each time individually priced.*
- *LOST: Black cat with white paws, wearing red collar with name tag 'Snowball'.*

5 When you write **notes** during a lesson (or while doing research on the Internet, for example), your aim is to put down key words that will remind you what the teacher said (or what you have read). You can use any short forms that you will understand when you read the notes later:

> *sources of electricity, pros and cons:*
> *solar – from sun, renewable energy, but solar panels expensive*
> *wind turbines – no pollution, but not v. efficient, spoil landscape*
> *nuclear power stations – danger if sth goes wrong, problem of waste disposal*
> *coal-fired power stations – pollution, using up fossil fuels*

6 When you write an **essay plan**, you decide what information you are going to give in each paragraph and put down the important facts, in incomplete sentences:

> *Coniferous trees: evergreen. Do not lose leaves in winter – long narrow leaves called needles – fruit is a cone.*
> *Types include pine, fir, spruce, cedar. Grow in cold places, on high ground.*
> *Many types grown for timber. Grow quickly, can be easily replaced. Wood used for furniture.*

 ISBN 978-81-8477-745-1

PRACTICE

Exercise 1

Read the following passage, then write an appropriate **advertisement** *at the end.*

Bill bought a new digital camera and decided to sell his old one, which his parents had given him two years earlier. He had always used it carefully, and kept it in its matching case, so it was not damaged. The old camera was a Panji Funpix with 10 megapixels and a 3X optical zoom. It still worked perfectly well, but the new camera had a better zoom and some other useful features. It was also larger and used different batteries, so Bill planned to sell the old case and some spare batteries with the camera. He thought the whole package was worth about 100 dollars. Here is the advertisement he wrote:

____

____

____

____

____

____

____

Exercise 2

Here is Jane's diary for her holiday in London. On Friday morning, she sent her parents a postcard with a picture of the London Eye (a big wheel that carries you slowly up for a bird's-eye view of the city) on the front. **Write the postcard** *in about 75 words.*

Sunday: flew to London.

Monday: v. tired, read book at hotel in morning, walked in Hyde Park pm.

Tuesday: visited Tower of London, went on London Eye – fantastic views all round

Wednesday: rain, went round V & A Museum

Thursday: sunshine, river trip to Greenwich, visited observatory – v. impressive

 ISBN 978-81-8477-745-1

Friday:	guided tour on open-topped bus – Trafalgar Square, Houses of Parliament, etc.
Saturday:	visited Buckingham Palace – crowds of people outside. Went shopping, then back to airport
Sunday:	arrived home

Exercise 3

Write the plan for an essay entitled 'Looking after your health' in note form.

 ISBN 978-81-8477-745-1

UNIT 78

PROCEDURES

What do they look like?

If the fire alarm rings, leave the building immediately. Do not stop to pick up your belongings. Go to the assembly point at the end of the car park and give your name to the hotel manager, who will be waiting there. Do not re-enter the building until you have been told that it is safe to do so.

What are they?

A **procedure** is a text that tells you **how to do or make something,** listing the steps in the order in which they must be performed. The following types of texts are usually procedures:

- **recipes**
- **science experiments**
- **instructions for assembling models, operating machines, etc.**
- **what to do in an emergency**
- **directions to a place**
- **the rules of a game**

What are their main language features?

1. A procedure usually contains **imperative verbs** that tell you what to do:
   - ***Turn*** *left at the crossroads.*
   - ***Screw*** *the handle to the front of the drawer.*

2. Other verbs are often in the **present** or **future** tense:
   - *Each player* ***takes*** *seven letter tiles from the bag.*
   - *The machine* ***will make*** *a beeping sound when the bread is cooked.*

3. **Connectors,** such as ***first***, ***next***, ***then*** and ***finally,*** are sometimes used to link the steps of a procedure:
   - *Plug the red wire into the socket at the side of the main unit.* ***Then*** *switch the machine on.*
   - ***First****, put the oil and vinegar into a bowl.* ***Next****, add some salt, pepper and mustard powder.*

 ISBN 978-81-8477-745-1

4 **Adjectives** of size, shape, colour and material are used to describe the things you will need:

- *Take a sheet of paper and cut it into* ***long, narrow*** *strips.*
- *The kit contains the following items: a piece of* ***white plastic*** *tubing, a* ***small metal*** *bowl, ...*

5 Many procedures contain **quantifiers**, especially numbers and units of measurement:

- *Cut the wire into* ***five*** *pieces, each* ***10 cm*** *long.*
- *Add* ***a little*** *water to the mixture.*

6 The **steps** of a procedure, or the **things required**, are often given in the form of a **list**, with appropriate **punctuation** (colon, commas) or numbered items:

- *You will need the following tools: a hammer, a screwdriver, a saw and a pair of pliers.*
- ***1.*** *Click on the word 'File' at the top of the screen.*
  2. *Select 'Print' from the drop-down menu.*
  3. *Type the number(s) of the page(s) you want to print.*
  4. *Click 'OK'.*

7 Explanatory information (such as the meaning of a technical term) may be provided in the form of **noun phrases** or **relative clauses**:

- *Attach the halyard* ***(the rope that hoists the sail)*** *to the upper corner of the mainsail.*
- *Press the 'Start' button,* ***which you will find at the left of the control panel.***

How do you write them?

1 First, you should state the **aim** of the procedure. This may be in the form of a **heading**, or it may be an introductory sentence:

- *HOW TO OPERATE THE DISHWASHER.*
- *Here is a recipe for a delicious chocolate cake.*
- *The aim of the experiment is to prove that water contains oxygen.*

2 Next, you may need to provide a list of any **ingredients**, **materials**, **tools** or other **equipment** required:

- *The box contains the following items:*

  a playing board — *two dice*
  six red counters — *six blue counters*

- *You will need the following ingredients:*

  200g flour — *200g butter*
  200g sugar — *3 large eggs*

 ISBN 978-81-8477-745-1

3 Then, you give the **instructions**, breaking them down into simple steps. It is important to arrange these in the order in which they must be performed. You can write them as **continuous text** (with or without **connectors**) or as a **list**, with each item on a new line:

- *Click on the word 'File' at the top of the screen. Select 'Print' from the drop-down menu. Type the number(s) of the page(s) you want to print. Click 'OK'.*
- ***First**, click on the word 'File' at the top of the screen. **Next**, select 'Print' from the drop-down menu. **Then**, type the number(s) of the page(s) you want to print. **Finally**, click 'OK'.*
- *Click on the word 'File' at the top of the screen.*
Select 'Print' from the drop-down menu.
Type the number(s) of the page(s) you want to print.
Click 'OK'.
- ***1.** Click on the word 'File' at the top of the screen.*
***2.** Select 'Print' from the drop-down menu.*
***3.** Type the number(s) of the page(s) you want to print.*
***4.** Click 'OK'.*

It may be useful to break up a long procedure into sections with subheadings. For example, a recipe might have the subheadings ***Ingredients***, ***Preparation***, ***Cooking*** and ***Serving***.

4 Some procedures have a final sentence that states the **result**:

- *The dishwasher is now ready to use.*
- *The experiment proved that water contains two elements: hydrogen and oxygen.*

PRACTICE

Exercise 1

*Read the following sentences and say which type of procedure they come from. Write **recipe**, **experiment**, **instructions**, **emergency**, **directions** or **rules**.*

1. Give seven cards to each player. ____________
2. Pour the mixture into an ovenproof dish. ____________
3. Do not attempt to move the injured person. ____________
4. Gently heat the liquid in the test tube. ____________
5. Take the next turning on the left. ____________
6. Press the 'Eject' button and remove the disc. ____________
7. Peel and slice the apples. ____________

 ISBN 978-81-8477-745-1

8. Measure the height of the plants each day. ______________

9. Remove the battery from the charging unit. ______________

10. Go straight on at the traffic lights. ______________

Exercise 2

*Read the following passage about cooking stir-fried chicken. Then, write down the **recipe** that Tom might have used. (You do not need to list the ingredients at the beginning.)*

Tom cut two chicken breasts into thin slices. Then he put some oil, soy sauce, sugar and chilli powder into a bowl and mixed them together. He added the sliced chicken to the mixture and put the bowl in the fridge. Next he prepared the vegetables by removing the seeds from a pepper, peeling a carrot and an onion, cleaning some mushrooms and chopping them all into small pieces. He took his wok from the cupboard, put a little oil in it and placed it on the hob, which he turned up to its highest heat. When the oil was very hot he took the chicken from the fridge, put it into the wok and stir-fried it for a few minutes. Then he added the chopped vegetables and stir-fried the whole mixture for ten minutes more.

Exercise 3

*Write a **procedure**, 150–200 words long, for using a piece of equipment that you are familiar with, such as a digital camera, a mobile phone or a DVD recorder.*

 ISBN 978-81-8477-745-1

UNIT 79

EXPLANATIONS

What do they look like?

Electricity usually comes from a power station, where coal or oil is burnt to create heat. This turns water into steam, which drives the machines that produce the electricity. Other sources of energy may be used for the same purpose, such as solar power (from the sun), hydroelectric power (from the force of falling water), or nuclear power.

What are they?

An **explanation** is a text that helps you to understand something. It may explain **why something happens**, such as an earthquake or a thunderstorm. It may explain **how something works**, such as a car or the human heart. It may also explain **something in the past**, such as how life on earth began. The following types of texts may be **explanations**:

- **encyclopedia entries about science and technology**
- **technical articles in magazines**
- **textbooks**

What are their main language features?

1. An explanation usually contains a mixture of **active** and **passive** verbs in the **present** tense:
   - *Blood **is pumped** around your body by your heart. It **passes** through your veins and arteries.*
   - *The alarm **is triggered** by a sensor that **detects** movement.*

2. **Connectors** are used to show **sequence**, **purpose**, **cause**, and **effect**:
   - *The pupil contracts in bright sunlight **so that** less light enters the eye.*
   - *The molecules move further apart; **consequently**, the substance expands.*

3. Technical terms may be explained with **noun phrases**:
   - *The pupil **(the black spot in the middle of the eye)** contracts in bright sunlight.*
   - ***Hot molten rock** called magma rises to the top of the volcano.*

 ISBN 978-81-8477-745-1

How do you write them?

1. First, you should say **what you are going to explain**. You usually do this in the form of a **title**:
   - *HOW A COMPUTER WORKS*
   - *THE ORIGINS OF LIFE ON EARTH*

   Alternatively, you could begin the text with a question:
   - *Have you ever wondered how a computer works?*
   - *Where does electricity come from?*

2. Then, you provide the explanation, in the form of **continuous text**, divided into **paragraphs**:

   > *Electricity usually comes from a power station, where a fuel such as coal or oil is burnt to create heat. This turns water into steam, which drives the machines that produce the electricity.*
   >
   > *The electricity comes to your home through wires. Other wires inside the building then take the electricity to sockets on the walls. When you put a plug into one of these, the electric current is carried to your toaster, hair-dryer, television or computer.*
   >
   > *Some pieces of electrical equipment use batteries instead of wires and plugs. These are usually small devices that you can carry around, such as mobile phones. Some batteries are rechargeable. They can be refilled with electricity, so you do not have to buy a new one when the old one stops working.*

3. You usually end the explanation with a **closing remark** about **what you have explained**:
   - *Electricity is such an important part of modern life that it is hard to imagine how people ever managed without it.*
   - *This is why cars need to be serviced regularly to keep them in good working order.*

 ISBN 978-81-8477-745-1

PRACTICE

Exercise 1

*Rewrite the following sentences in a way that **explains the technical terms** in bold print. You may need to use a dictionary to find the meaning of the words. The first two have been done to help you.*

1. The **pupil** contracts in bright sunlight.

   *The **pupil (the black spot in the middle of the eye)** contracts in bright sunlight.*

2. **Magma** rises to the top of the volcano.

   ***Hot molten rock called magma** rises to the top of the volcano.*

3. The electricity crosses the land in wires held up by **pylons**.

   ____

4. The **retina** receives the image and sends it to your brain.

   ____

5. The water **evaporates** and rises into the air.

   ____

6. **Tartar** can form on your teeth if you do not clean them properly.

   ____

7. The insects carry **pollen** from one flower to another.

   ____

8. Nuclear energy can be produced by **fission**.

   ____

Exercise 2

*Write an **explanation**, 150–200 words long, called 'What Happens When a Volcano Erupts'. You may find the information you require in reference books or on the Internet, but you must put it into your own words.*

____

____

____

____

 ISBN 978-81-8477-745-1

UNIT 80

INFORMATION REPORTS

What do they look like?

Influenza (often called 'flu') is a disease that is caused by a virus. There are many different influenza viruses, which is why the disease is so difficult to control. The virus can easily be spread from one person to another by coughing or sneezing. Vaccination can provide protection against some forms of the disease.

What are they?

An **information report** is a text that presents a series of **facts** about something, such as an animal, a plant, a country or a disease, in a systematic way. The following types of texts may be information reports:

- **encyclopedia entries about places or the natural world**
- **fact sheets**
- **information pamphlets**
- **tourist guides**
- **brochures and other publicity materials**

What are their main language features?

1. An information report usually contains a mixture of **active** and **passive** verbs. They are mainly in the **present** tense, but **past** tenses are also used (for example, to talk about an extinct animal or about the history of a place):
   - *Penguins **have** flippers instead of wings. They **are found** in cold regions of the southern hemisphere.*
   - *The palace **stands** on a hill in the northern part of the city. It **was built** in the tenth century.*

2. **Pronouns** and **determiners** are usually in the **third person**:
   - *Owls are nocturnal. **They** hunt **their** prey at night.*
   - *The tree is deciduous. This means that **it** sheds **its** leaves in the winter.*

 ISBN 978-81-8477-745-1

3 **Adjectives** of size, shape, colour, quality and type are used to describe things:

- *The fruit has **thick orange** skin and **soft sweet** flesh.*
- *A telescope is a **long cylindrical optical** instrument.*

4 **Comparatives** and **superlatives** are used to compare and contrast:

- *The female bird is **smaller** and has **less colourful** plumage than the male.*
- *Mount Everest is the **highest** mountain in the world*

5 **Relative clauses** are often used to add information:

- *The chameleon has a long tongue, **which it uses to catch insects.***
- *A lever is a tool **that is used to lift heavy objects.***

How do you write them?

1 An information report often begins with a short **definition** containing the verb ***be***. It states **what the animal, plant, place or thing is:**

- *Tahiti **is** an island in the Pacific Ocean.*
- *Measles **is** an infectious disease.*

2 Next, you give the **facts**, usually in the form of **continuous text**, divided into **paragraphs**. For an information report about a country, you might give the name of its capital, its main geographical features (such as mountains and rivers), its climate and its chief industries. For an information report about an animal, you might say what it looks like, where it lives and what it eats. Here are the first two paragraphs of an information report about elephants:

> *Elephants are large mammals with grey skin. Instead of a nose they have a long trunk, which they can use to pick up and carry things. At each side of their mouth there is a long curved tooth called a tusk.*
>
> *Elephants are found in Africa and India. The main difference between African elephants and Indian elephants is the size of their ears: African elephants have larger ears and Indian elephants have smaller ears. Elephants are also found in other countries of Asia, and can be seen in zoos and wildlife parks all round the world.*

It may be useful to break up a long information report into sections with subheadings. For example, a fact sheet about a disease might have the subheadings ***Cause***, ***Symptoms***, ***Treatment*** and ***Complications***.

3 You often end an information report with a **closing remark** about the **subject**:

- *Sadly, this attractive and unusual bird is now an endangered species.*
- *A cure for the disease has yet to be found.*

 ISBN 978-81-8477-745-1

PRACTICE

Exercise 1

*Expand the short passage at the beginning of this unit into a **fact sheet** about influenza, using the headings provided. You should write 20–40 words in each section.*

INFLUENZA

Cause

Influenza is a disease that is caused by a virus. There are many different influenza viruses, which is why the disease is so difficult to control. The virus can easily be spread from one person to another by coughing or sneezing. Vaccination can provide protection against some forms of the disease.

Symptoms

____

____

____

Treatment

____

____

____

Complications

____

____

____

Exercise 2

*Write an **information report** about Thailand, about 150 words long, in the style of an encyclopedia entry. You may find the information you require in reference books or on the Internet, but you must put it into your own words.*

____

____

____

____

____

____

 ISBN 978-81-8477-745-1

UNIT 81

FACTUAL RECOUNTS

What do they look like?

Charles Dickens was an English writer. Born in Portsmouth in 1812, he later moved to London with his family. They were very poor, so Charles had to leave school at the age of 15 to take an office job. He subsequently became a journalist and began writing fiction. His best-known novels include *Oliver Twist* and *Great Expectations*. Dickens died in 1870.

What are they?

A **factual recount** is a text that describes a **series of past events** in the order in which they occurred. Unlike a **personal recount**, which you will learn about in Unit 82, a **factual recount** can be written by anybody. The writer may have witnessed the events they describe, or they may have simply heard or read about them. The following types of texts may be factual recounts:

- **newspaper articles**
- **encyclopedia entries about historical events or famous people**
- **biographies**
- **sports commentaries**

What are their main language features?

1. A factual recount usually contains a mixture of **active** and **passive** verbs, mainly in the **simple past** and the **past continuous**:
   - *A jeweller's shop in the town centre **was robbed** yesterday afternoon. A masked man **entered** the shop and **threatened** the owner with a gun.*
   - *The train **was travelling** at a speed of 180 kilometres per hour when the accident **occurred**.*

   The **present tense** is sometimes used instead, especially in sports commentaries:
   - *Jones **kicks** the ball to Thomas, who **takes** a shot at the goal. The goalkeeper **dives** in the wrong direction and the ball **goes** straight to the back of the net.*

 ISBN 978-81-8477-745-1

2. **Pronouns** and **determiners** are in the **third person**:
   - ***She*** *spent the early part of* ***her*** *career playing small roles in television dramas.*
   - *The truck overturned, shedding* ***its*** *load on the expressway.*

3. **Connectors** such as ***then***, ***next***, ***when*** and ***after*** are used to show the sequence of events:
   - *The fire began in the barn,* ***then*** *spread to other outbuildings.*
   - ***After*** *leaving university, he travelled around the world.*

4. **Adjectives** of various kinds are used to provide vivid descriptions:
   - *The man had been killed with a* ***violent*** *blow to the head from a* ***blunt*** *instrument, possibly a hammer.*
   - *The president's wife was wearing a* ***red silk*** *dress, with a* ***diamond*** *necklace and* ***black high-heeled*** *shoes.*

5. **Prepositional phrases** indicate the place and time of events:
   - *She left Singapore* ***in 1990*** *and moved* ***to Tokyo****.*
   - *The truck skidded* ***on a slippery patch of road*** *and collided* ***with a car in the outside lane****. The vehicles* ***behind them*** *were unable to stop and crashed* ***into each other****.*

How do you write them?

1. You can begin a factual recount with a statement of **what happened** and when or where it happened. If the recount is a **biography** (the story of someone's life), you might begin by saying **what the person is famous for**:
   - *World War II began in 1939 after Germany invaded Poland.*
   - *Sir Edmund Hillary was the first person to reach the summit of Mount Everest.*

2. Next, you describe the **events** in the order in which they happened. You should do this in **continuous text**, divided into **paragraphs**, using words or structures that make the text interesting to read:

   > *A jeweller's shop in the town centre was robbed yesterday afternoon. A masked man entered the shop and threatened the owner, Janet Collins, with a gun. He demanded the key to the display cabinet where the most expensive rings were kept.*
   >
   > *Miss Collins handed over the key. While the robber emptied the contents of the cabinet into the bag he was carrying, she reached for the alarm button below the counter and pressed it.*

3. You usually end the recount with the **final event**, or the **result** of what happened:
   - *The robbery lasted less than five minutes, and the robber had already left when the police arrived.*
   - *The cost of the damage caused by the fire is estimated to be about a million dollars.*

 ISBN 978-81-8477-745-1

PRACTICE

Exercise 1

Write a factual recount of an event, such as a festival, a political demonstration, a road accident or Sports Day at your school. Your recount should be about 200 words long in the style of a newspaper article.

Exercise 2

Write a factual recount, about 150 words long, in the form of a short biography of a famous person.

 ISBN 978-81-8477-745-1

UNIT 82

PERSONAL RECOUNTS

What do they look like?

I set off in my yacht after lunch. At first, the sea was calm, and it was all very pleasant. Then, suddenly, everything went wrong at the same time. The wind picked up, and one of the ropes controlling the sails got tangled up. As I went to sort it out, I tripped and fell.

What are they?

A **personal recount** is a text that records or tells other people about **things you have done** or **things that have happened to you.** The following types of texts may be personal recounts:

- **letters to friends or relatives**
- **autobiographies**
- **conversations**
- **interviews**
- **diary entries**

What are their main language features?

1. A personal recount usually contains a mixture of **active** and **passive** verbs, mainly in the **simple past** and the **past continuous**:

   - *I **was watching** television in the lounge when I **heard** a loud bang, like an explosion.*
   - *To my horror, I **realized** that I **was being followed**.*

   You occasionally use the **present tense**, for example, to add information about yourself:

   - *I **am** not normally afraid of spiders, but this one was huge!*

2. **Pronouns** and **determiners** are mainly in the **first person**:

   - ***I** took out **my** mobile phone and called the police.*
   - *The man asked **us** the way to the station.*

   However, the **third person** is used to refer to people and things around you:

   - ***It** was a sunny day, so I went for a walk in the park.*
   - *I called **her** name, but **she** did not hear me.*

   You also sometimes use the **second person** in letters and conversations:

   - ***You**'ll never guess who I saw in the shopping mall yesterday!*

 ISBN 978-81-8477-745-1

3. **Connectors** such as ***then***, ***later***, ***while*** and ***as,*** are used to show how events are related in time:
   - *I read a magazine* ***while*** *I waited for the train to arrive.*
   - *I got washed and dressed,* ***then*** *went downstairs for breakfast.*

4. **Adjectives** and **adjectival phrases** are used to provide vivid descriptions and express strong feelings:
   - *A* ***scruffily dressed young*** *man asked me if I could spare him a few dollars.*
   - *We were* ***absolutely terrified****!*

5. Unlike many other text types, a personal recount can contain **adjectives of opinion**, stating your own thoughts and feelings about something:
   - *I thought the bride looked* ***beautiful****.*

6. You can use a variety of **adverbials**, especially **prepositional phrases**, to add information about actions:
   - *I dived* ***into the water*** *and swam* ***across the lake****.*
   - *We ran away* ***as fast as we could****.*

7. A personal recount may contain **direct and indirect speech**:
   - ***'I've lost my ticket,'*** *I said to the inspector. He told me* ***that I would have to buy another one****.*
   - *Mum asked me* ***where I was going. 'To the shops,'*** *I replied.*

8. An informal personal recount, such as a letter to a friend, may contain **contractions**:
   - *Unfortunately, we* ***couldn't*** *see the view because it was rather foggy that day.*
   - *I* ***didn't*** *read the recipe properly, so the cake was a disaster!*

How do you write them?

1. You usually begin a personal recount with a **statement that sets the scene**, sometimes containing a verb in the **past continuous:**
   - *Last week, I went to the National Science Museum with my friend Sue and her parents.*
   - *I* ***was standing*** *at the bus stop when I heard someone call my name.*

 ISBN 978-81-8477-745-1

2. Next, you describe the **events** in the order in which they happened. You should do this in **continuous text**, divided into **paragraphs**, varying your words and sentence structures to make the text interesting to read:

> *While I was walking home from school yesterday I noticed a bundle of banknotes lying on the pavement. I looked around to see who might have dropped them, but there was nobody nearby. However, as I bent down to pick them up, I heard a voice behind me.*
>
> *'That money belongs to me,' said a man who had just come out of one of the shops. I looked at him closely. He did not look like a wealthy person, so I didn't believe him.*
>
> *Fortunately, there was a police station on the opposite side of the road. I told the man that I was going to take the money over there and hand it in. He could come with me and claim it if it was really his.*

Above all, you should try to avoid starting several consecutive sentences (that is, sentences that come one after another) with the personal pronoun ***I***.

3. You usually end the recount with the **final event**, or a **personal comment** on what happened or what you did:
    - *Needless to say, the man quickly disappeared.*
    - *The museum is one of the most interesting places I have ever visited.*

PRACTICE

Exercise 1

Here is Jane's diary from her holiday in London again. In Unit 77, you used it to write a postcard. This time, convert the events of the diary into a letter from Jane to her grandfather, written just after her return home.

Sunday: flew to London.

Monday: v. tired, read book at hotel in morning, walked in Hyde Park pm.

Tuesday: visited Tower of London, went on London Eye – fantastic views all round

Wednesday: rain, went round V & A Museum

Thursday: sunshine, river trip to Greenwich, visited observatory – v. impressive

Friday: guided tour on open-topped bus – Trafalgar Square, Houses of Parliament, etc.

Saturday: visited Buckingham Palace – crowds of people outside. Went shopping, then back to airport

Sunday: arrived home

 ISBN 978-81-8477-745-1

Exercise 2

Write a personal recount, about 150 words long, about an exciting or amusing experience.

 ISBN 978-81-8477-745-1

UNIT 83

EXPOSITIONS

What do they look like?

> I would like to protest about the amount of litter in our town. Although there are local laws about dropping litter, nobody seems to enforce them. Not only do all these discarded cans and wrappers make our lovely town look ugly and untidy, but they can also be a hazard to health and safety.

What are they?

An **exposition** is a text that gives a personal opinion about something. It often has the aim of persuading or convincing other people. The following types of texts are usually expositions:

- **book and film reviews**
- **letters to newspapers or magazines**
- **speeches**
- **debates**

What are their main language features?

1. The personal opinions expressed in an exposition are usually introduced by a **thinking verb** (such as ***think***, ***believe***, ***consider***, ***feel***) in the first person, **present** tense and **active** voice:
   - *I **believe** that young offenders should not be sent to jail.*
   - *I **think** this is a very well-written book.*

   Other verbs are often in the third person and **passive** voice:
   - *I believe that they **should be helped**, not imprisoned.*
   - *The airport will cause traffic congestion if it **is built** too close to the town.*

2. You use **modal auxiliary verbs** (such as ***should***, ***must***, ***could***, ***will***) to say what is right, sensible, necessary or possible:
   - *Something **must** be done about this problem.*
   - *The airport **will** cause traffic congestion.*

 ISBN 978-81-8477-745-1

3 Expositions can contain a variety of different **connectors**. You use connectors, such as ***firstly***, ***secondly*** and ***in conclusion,*** to put your arguments in **sequence** and to **sum up** at the end:

> *I believe that school uniform is a good thing.* ***In the first place****, students who wear uniform do not have to worry if they cannot afford to buy fashionable clothes.* ***Secondly****, they do not have to think about what they are going to wear each morning when they get dressed for school.*
>
> ***In conclusion****, I feel that the arguments for school uniform outweigh those against it.*

You use connectors, such as ***therefore***, ***if*** and ***consequently,*** to link **cause** and **effect**, or to show the **reason** for your opinion:

- *I believe these devices are dangerous;* ***therefore****, they should be banned.*
- *The plot of the story is very complicated.* ***Consequently****, it is rather hard to follow.*

You use connectors, such as ***also***, ***in addition*** and ***besides,*** to **add extra information** that reinforces the point you are making:

- *Germs can multiply on food wrappers discarded as litter.* ***In addition,*** *the glass from broken bottles can cause injury to people and animals.*
- *The new leisure centre will be very expensive to build;* ***besides****, it is not really needed.*

You can use connectors, such as ***however***, ***but*** and ***on the other hand,*** to introduce a **contrasting** idea, such as an **opposite** viewpoint:

- *There are dangers for children in using the Internet.* ***On the other hand****, it can be very useful for their schoolwork.*
- *Some of the special effects were not very good;* ***however****, this did not spoil my enjoyment of the film.*

4 Expositions often contain **adjectives of opinion**:

- *This* ***ugly*** *new building has ruined the village.*
- *The special effects were particularly* ***impressive****.*

5 People sometimes use **rhetorical questions** to make their readers or listeners feel involved in what they saying:

- ***What is the point of building a new leisure centre?*** *The existing one is hardly ever used.*
- *This sounds like a good idea, but* ***who is going to pay for it?***

6 You can also use **repetition** to emphasize a point:

- *We cannot let this happen and we must not let it happen.*
- *Children need discipline; they need guidance; they need help; they need love.*

 ISBN 978-81-8477-745-1

How do you write them?

1. You begin an exposition with a **statement of your opinion** on the subject you are going to talk or write about:
   - *'The Unknown Soldier' is the most exciting book I have ever read.*
   - *I am writing to protest about the plan to build a supermarket on the edge of the village.*

2. Next, you give the arguments that support your opinion, in the form of **continuous text** divided into **paragraphs**. You may also need to state the opposite viewpoint, and give reasons why you think this is wrong:

   The site of the new supermarket is an important wildlife habitat. If it is destroyed, many rare species will disappear from the area.

   The supermarket will also have a disastrous effect on the existing shops. They are bound to lose a lot of business to their new rival, and some may have to close as a result.

   It has been argued that the new supermarket will give the villagers a lot more products to choose from when they go shopping. But will all the villagers be able to take advantage of this? Those without cars may find it hard to get there, or to carry their purchases home.

3. You usually end the exposition with a statement that **sums up** what you have said. In some cases, you may also wish to state what action needs to be taken:
   - *In short, I think that the supermarket should not be built.*
   - *I urge you to take immediate action to remedy the problem, such as putting more litter bins in public places.*

PRACTICE

Exercise 1

Fill in each blank with a different ***modal auxiliary verb****.*

1. I think parents ________________ be held responsible for crimes committed by their children.

2. The council ________________ take immediate action to prevent a serious accident occurring at this dangerous junction.

 ISBN 978-81-8477-745-1

3. The money they are planning to spend on the new leisure centre ______________ be used for a wide range of more deserving projects.

4. I ______________ like to complain about the service I received at your restaurant yesterday evening.

5. This change in the law ______________ discourage many people from doing voluntary work.

6. I believe that global warming ______________ be halted if all nations play their part.

Exercise 2

*In about 150 words, write a **review** of a book you have read or a film you have seen.*

 ISBN 978-81-8477-745-1

UNIT
84

NARRATIVES

What do they look like?

It was Sally's first day at work. She had taken a holiday job at her local supermarket, to earn some money before going to university. Her main task was to load the shelves with goods, and she expected this to be quite easy. However, things began to go wrong from the moment she set foot inside the store.

What are they?

A **narrative** is a text that tells a **story**, usually about **things that did not happen**. Its main aim is to **entertain** those who read or hear it. Some narratives, such as **fables**, are also intended to **make people think** about the issues raised in the story, and perhaps to **learn a lesson** from what happens at the end. The following types of texts are usually narratives:

- **short stories**
- **novels**
- **myths and legends**
- **fables**
- **jokes**

What are their main language features?

1. The main action of a narrative is usually in the **simple past** and the **active voice**:
   - *The girl **opened** the box and **looked** inside.*
   - *James **lived** with his parents in a large house at the top of a hill.*

   However, the **past continuous** and the **past perfect** are often used to set the scene or to add background information:
   - *The sun **was shining** and the birds **were singing** in the trees.*
   - *Sam **had** never **been** in a helicopter before.*

2. A wide range of **adjectives** and **adverbs** are used to provide vivid descriptions of people, things, places and events:
   - *The sun was shining **brightly** in a **clear blue** sky.*
   - *A **slimy black** slug crawled **lazily** across the path.*

3. **Prepositional phrases** add information about actions:
   - *He picked up the bag and threw it **into the river**.*
   - *Howling **with pain**, the dog ran **out of the house** and **across the garden**.*

 ISBN 978-81-8477-745-1

4. **Pronouns** and **determiners** are mainly in the **third person**:
   - ***She** grabbed **her** jacket and ran to the bus stop.*
   - ***They** stopped for a while to rest **their** weary feet.*

   However, some narratives are written in the **first person**, even though the events they describe are not true. Writers sometimes do this to make the story seem more believable:
   - ***My** parents died when **I** was a little boy. **I** was brought up by **my** aunt, who had no children of her own. She treated **me** badly, and at the age of twelve **I** ran away to sea.*

5. **Connectors** such as ***then***, ***before***, ***while*** and ***when*** are used to show how events are related in time:
   - *One day, **while** sweeping the path, she noticed a small shiny object on the ground.*
   - *The man looked around to check that no-one was looking, **then** he slipped the key into his pocket.*

6. Most narratives contain **direct and indirect speech**:
   - ***'Is this your dog?'** asked the policeman. Jane shook her head. She explained **that the dog had been following her around all day**.*
   - *The farmer told Bill **he would have to pay for the damage**. **'I don't have any money,'** protested Bill.*

7. Sentences containing **existential *there*** (see Unit 66) are sometimes used to set the scene:
   - ***There** once **was** an old sailor called Tom Hawkins.*
   - *At the top of the hill **there stood** a large house, which had been empty for many years.*

8. **Inversion** (see Unit 50) is sometimes used at the beginning of a sentence or clause. In other words, the sentence or clause begins with an **adverb**, and the **subject** follows the **verb**:
   - ***Down came the rain**, and everyone ran for shelter.*
   - *He pressed the switch, and **out went all the lights**.*

How do you write them?

1. You usually begin a narrative with an **introductory section** that **sets the scene**, often **describing the main character(s)** or stating the **time and place of the action**. This may be a single sentence or a whole paragraph:
   - *Princess Vanita was a beautiful young woman who lived in a fine palace surrounded by attractive things.*
   - *It was a warm afternoon in early spring. The sun was shining brightly in a clear blue sky and a light breeze rustled the leaves of the trees. Bees were humming as they flew from flower to flower. There was no other sound in the garden.*

 ISBN 978-81-8477-745-1

2 Then, you say **what happened.** Unlike a recount, a narrative does not always give the events in the order in which they occurred:

> *Joe lived in an apartment in the city centre. He had moved there with his parents when he was ten years old. Before that, the family had lived on a farm. Joe had been happy living in the countryside. He did not like city life, and decided to run away from home.*

You should make the middle part of your narrative as interesting as possible. You can do this by using such techniques as **synthesis** and **transformation** (see Unit 72) and **lexical substitution** (see Unit 76). You can also break up the action with **descriptive passages** and **direct speech**:

> *One day, while walking in her garden, the princess noticed a hairy brown caterpillar crawling up the stem of one of her favourite plants.*
>
> *'Go away!' she cried. 'You are an ugly creature, and I will not have you on my land.'*
>
> *The caterpillar took refuge in a field nearby. There it lived happily for a while, eating the leaves of the crops (much to the annoyance of the farmer).*
>
> *Some time later, the caterpillar turned into a butterfly, emerging from its chrysalis in a form beyond all recognition. Its large, brightly coloured wings were patterned with spots and other markings.*
>
> *The butterfly flew straight to the princess's garden, where it settled on a flower near her window. She rushed outside to welcome this beautiful new creature, but it immediately fluttered away.*

3 You usually close the narrative by saying **what happened in the end**. Like the introductory section, this can be a single sentence or a whole paragraph:

- *'You banished me once,' called the butterfly as it departed, 'and now I will never return.'*
- *Joe looked around at all the familiar objects in the apartment. He had only been away for a week, but it felt more like a year. He vowed never to run away again. It was good to be home.*

If the narrative is a **fable**, it usually ends with the **moral** of the story (that is, the lesson to be learnt):

- *People should be content with what they have, not greedy for more.*

 ISBN 978-81-8477-745-1

PRACTICE

Exercise 1

In about 120 words, retell the story of a folk tale, myth or legend that you are familiar with.

Exercise 2

Write a story called 'Man's Best Friend', about a dog and its master, in 200–250 words. Use your imagination to create your own narrative; do not simply recount the plot of a book you have read or a film you have seen.

 ISBN 978-81-8477-745-1

UNIT 85

POETRY

What does it look like?

I am a thousand winds that blow,
I am the diamond glints on snow,
I am the sunlight on ripened grain,
I am the gentle autumn's rain.
When you awaken in the morning's hush,
I am the swift uplifting rush
Of quiet birds in circled flight.
I am the soft stars that shine at night.

What is it?

Poetry is written in **lines**, rather than as continuous text. The main aims of poetry are to **entertain people**, to **arouse their emotions** or to **make them think**. The following types of texts are usually poetry:

- **poems**
- **songs**
- **verses on greetings cards**
- **advertising jingles**

What are its main features?

1 Many poems and songs have lines that form a **rhythmic pattern**, based on the number of syllables. In the following nursery rhyme, all the lines contain seven syllables:

Twinkle, twinkle, little star,
How I wonder what you are!
Up above the world so high,
Like a diamond in the sky!

If you say these lines aloud, you will notice that there is also a rhythm in the way the words are **stressed**. In each line, the main stress falls on the first, third, fifth and seventh syllables.

 ISBN 978-81-8477-745-1

2 The lines of traditional poetry often **rhyme**. That is, pairs of lines end with the same sound. Sometimes, one line rhymes with the next, as in the nursery rhyme above. Sometimes, alternate lines rhyme, as in the following example from a poem by William Wordsworth:

I wandered lonely as a ***cloud***
That floats on high o'er vales and ***hills****,*
When all at once I saw a ***crowd****,*
*A host, of golden daffo****dils****.*

Notice also that each line begins with a **capital letter**, whether it starts a new sentence or not.

3 In a type of modern poetry called **free verse**, the lines can be of any length. They usually do not rhyme and they sometimes do not begin with a capital letter (unless they start a new sentence):

Do not ask me to stand still and remember,
at the eleventh hour of the eleventh day of the eleventh month.
I was born in peacetime:
I have no recollection
of either of your wars.

4 The **sounds of words** are important in all kinds of poetry. Words may be chosen because they begin with the same letter or contain the same vowel sound:

- *the **d**ull, **d**ark, **d**reary **d**ays of **D**ecember*
- *The **s**nake **s**lithered **s**ilently across the **s**and.*
- *Her sh**y** sm**i**le l**igh**ts up her face.*
- *The man r**o**de sl**o**wly h**o**me al**o**ne.*

5 **Adjectives** and **noun phrases** are used to give vivid descriptions or to say what something is like:

- *in the **cool, dappled** shade of the **swaying leafy** branches*
- *The surface of the water was as smooth as **a freshly ironed sheet**.*
- *The monster reared up before him like **a mountain of death**.*

6 **Repetition** can add to the rhythmic effect, as in the following example from a poem by John Keats:

And she forgot *the stars, the moon, and sun,*
And she forgot *the blue above the trees,*
And she forgot *the dells where waters run,*
And she forgot *the chilly autumn breeze.*

7 **Inversion** (see Unit 50) can also add rhythm to a line. In other words, the line begins with an **adverb** or **preposition**, and the subject follows the **verb**:

- ***Over*** *the fence **jumped the little gypsy boy**.*
- ***Up*** *and up **flew the eagle**, soaring above the trees.*

 ISBN 978-81-8477-745-1

How do you write it?

1 First, you must decide whether you are going to write traditional poetry or free verse. If you are writing a comic poem, or the words for a song, it is often better to use rhyming lines with a rhythmic pattern:

If all the world were paper,
And all the sea were ink;
If all the trees were bread and cheese,
What would we do for drink?

If you want to set down your feelings about something, or to create a vivid description, it might be better to choose free verse:

I have passed through the valley of the Somme,
where the shadow of death lies across the fields
dotted with military cemeteries.
Among the neat rows of gravestones,
clean and white like bleached bones,
I have stood still and remembered.

2 Then, you can begin writing your poem. As you choose your words and phrases, bear in mind all the features listed above, especially those relating to rhythm and the sounds of words. If you are writing free verse, try not to make the lines too long. Short lines are often more effective:

- *Hate harms the heart.*
  Like a worm in fruit,
  it eats away
  unseen, until
  nothing remains
  but an empty shell.

3 Poems do not have paragraphs, but they can be divided into verses in a similar way. In traditional poetry, the verses usually have the same number of lines:

Terry was a tortoise,
Terry loved to roam,
And he hated children,
So he left his home.

But he walked so slowly,
He couldn't get away.
The children saw him leaving
And told him he must stay.

 ISBN 978-81-8477-745-1

PRACTICE

Exercise 1

Write a rhyming line with the same rhythmic pattern as the given line.

1. I strolled along the country lane,

   ____

2. The thunder roared, the lightning flashed,

   ____

3. She watched the spider cross the floor

   ____

4. They ran and ran and did not stop until

   ____

5. He wore a velvet cloak of midnight blue

   ____

6. The waves broke gently on the silver sand

   ____

7. The setting sun glowed red

   ____

8. Nobody said a word;

   ____

Exercise 2

Write a poem in free verse called 'The Old Man'. Your poem should be at least 15 lines long.

____

____

____

____

____

____

 ISBN 978-81-8477-745-1